The Story of
WINCHESTER
in
Virginia

The Oldest Town in the Shenandoah Valley

Frederic Morton

HERITAGE BOOKS
2007

HERITAGE BOOKS
AN IMPRINT OF HERITAGE BOOKS, INC.

Books, CDs, and more—Worldwide

For our listing of thousands of titles see our website at
www.HeritageBooks.com

A Facsimile Reprint
Published 2007 by
HERITAGE BOOKS, INC.
Publishing Division
65 East Main Street
Westminster, Maryland 21157-5026

Copyright © 1925 Frederic Morton

— Publisher's Notice —
In reprints such as this, it is often not possible to remove blemishes from the original. We feel the contents of this book warrant its reissue despite these blemishes and hope you will agree and read it with pleasure.

International Standard Book Number: 978-0-7884-1770-2

APPEAL OF THE PEOPLE OF WINCHESTER TO WASHINGTON FOR PROTECTION
(PAINTING BY FELIX O. C. DARLEY)
(Used by Permission of Jones Brothers Publishing Company, Cincinnati, Ohio)

DEDICATED

TO THE

KIWANIS CLUB

OF WINCHESTER

WHICH PROPOSED AND MADE POSSIBLE THE PUBLICATION
OF THIS HISTORY SO THAT THE PAST OF WINCHESTER
MIGHT BE PRESERVED AS AN INSPIRATION
FOR THE DAYS YET TO COME

In three centuries Winchester has sent her sons forth to battle under three different flags in seven wars. Only sixty years have passed since her streets were the battle-ground of contending armies. But from the staunchness of her Scotch-Irish, the solidity of her English, the thrift of her Valley-Dutch, and the courage of all, has been builded a town with a worthy past, a prosperous present, and a hopeful future.

ROSTER OF KIWANIS CLUB

Bailey, F. W.
Barton, R. T.
Beck, Paul
Bell, Andrew
Bosserman, W. H.
Brooks, S. C.
Browne, H. C.
Brown, R. B.
Brumback, C. I.
Bushnell, George B.
Canter, J. Harvey
Cather, T. Russell
Cather, J. Howard
Clowe, M. B.
Cooper, E. B.
Cox, Walter
Davidson, H. R.
Davis, C. A.
DeWitt, R. C.
DuShane, J. R.
Good, I. N.
Gearing, Frank
Glass, Robert McC.
Goode, Wendell B.
Gray, Foster
Green, R. C.
Hunt, M. M.
Hamburger, Myer
Hansbrough, G. M.
Hardy, W. G.
Harloe, C. B.
Hawthorne, D. E.
Hockman, L. L.
Hollis, L. C.
Hoshour, S. C.

Jamison, O. L.
Jarman, A. M.
Keeler, C. R.
Lovett, Frank
McCormick, L. W.
Oakes, Jesse C.
Orndoff, J. M.
Parsons, Graham
Phillips, John W.
Pierce, Noble C.
Pifer, H. I.
Pifer, W. R.
Ramsey, W. L.
Richard, J. A.
Richards, Nelson
Richards, Boyd
Rittenour, D. W.
Ritter, Carl
Robinson, C. A.
Rosenberger, R. R.
Sartelle, H. M.
Schmidt, H. A.
Shaffer, R. A.
Sheetz, H. C.
Smith, C. F.
Smith, C. M.
Snapp, E. J.
Snarr, G. G.
Solenberger, H. M.
Swimley, A. C.
Switzer, B. V.
Trier, T. J.
Williams, Philip
Yost, E. C.

CONTENTS

I	The Historical Background	13
II	The Local Geography	22
III	Lord Fairfax and the Northern Neck	28
IV	The Beginnings of Winchester	34
V	Winchester as a Frontier Town	43
VI	War with the French and Indians	61
VII	Later Colonial Period	84
VIII	The Middle Period	96
IX	An Annalistic Chapter	115
X	Winchester's Railroads	128
XI	The Public Square	134
XII	War and its Forerunners	143
XIII	Military Events of 1864-65	159
XIV	Behind the Southern Lines	179
XV	Bench, Bar, and Legislative	196
XVI	The Churches and the Fraternities	205
XVII	Journalism and Literature	221
XVIII	The Educational Record	231
XIX	The Cemeteries	246
XX	The Recent Period	252

APPENDICES

A	Inhabitants of 1788	266
B	Lot-Owners, 1782	272
C	Civil Officers	273
D	French and Indian War	276
E	Revolutionary War	280
F	Soldiers of 1812	283
G	Civil War	284
H	Soldiers of the World War	301
	General Index	315
	Index of Names	322

FOREWORD

The Winchester of Virginia is nearly or quite two centuries old. It is even older than several of the well-known cities lying on or near the Atlantic shore. It is the first namesake of the capital city of Alfred the Great. As a focus of striking incidents in American history it holds a prominent place. For almost forty years it may be said to have been the capital of the Northern Neck of Virginia, a proprietary domain in the colonial era that was not essentially unlike Pennsylvania, Maryland, or Delaware, save in the absence of political autonomy. It was the headquarters of George Washington during the trying years of the military apprenticeship that enabled him to carry the War for Independence to a victorious conclusion.

Not only is Winchester the earliest county seat within the great Appalachian region, but as a center of trade in the pre-railroad era, it was of an importance much greater than its actual size would seem to warrant. As the gateway to the Shenandoah Valley its possession was fiercely contested during much the greater part of the War of 1861.

Through a chain of unfortunate economic incidents, the city failed to develop into a large commercial and manufacturing point on a direct line of railway linking the Atlantic coast with the basin of the Mississippi. Yet by reason of the phenomenal good fortune of Winchester in becoming the beneficiary of large philanthropies, and also by reason of the recent revolutionizing of travel by the macadamized road and the motor vehicle, it would seem as though the latter days of the metropolis of the Lower Shenandoah will be her best days.

Two books are devoted specially to the area once comprised in the county of Frederick, and other volumes deal more or less broadly with special phases of local history. But until now there has been no attempt to set forth in a somewhat exhaustive manner the story of Winchester as a political and economic unit.

In his attempt to present this story, the author has had the advantage of a wealth of source material.

There were first the public records of Frederick county, and these are fairly intact. There were papers of much interest in the archives of Virginia at Richmond, and in the libraries of both Washington and Richmond were volumes, not to be found in Winchester, which threw much light on various special topics. The aid given the files of the local newspapers is inestimable. For 1787-1791, the "Gazette" furnishes more than a mere glimpse into the prosperous period that closely followed the Revolution. For 1811-1814, a period that almost coincides with the second war with England, there was the valuable assistance of the "Constellation." And although the newspaper record does not become nearly continuous until 1841, the help afforded by stray copies of various papers was by no means insignificant.

Chapter V is based almost wholly on "The Life and Times of Washington", by Schroeder and Lossing. The particular merit of this work lies in its copious extracts from the letters of Washington and others. The data for Chapter IX are exclusively from the files of the earlier local journals. The first of the two chapters on the military events of the War of 1861 rests mainly on "Stonewall Jackson and the American Civil War," by G. F. R. Henderson. The second is based on a manuscript history of the Valley Campaign of 1864, written by the late Andrew N. Campbell of Union, West Virginia. Judge Campbell was a soldier in that campaign, and though he writes as an eye-witness, his statements are buttressed upon official reports and other authoritative sources. His monograph, which was very kindly loaned by his daughter, Miss Nannie E. Campbell, is lucid, comprehensive, and fair-minded. In preparing the two chapters, other works, from both the Federal and Confederate viewpoints, were freely consulted. Among them were "The Story of the Civil War," by John C. Ropes, "Abraham Lincoln: A History," by Nicolay and Hay, "A Sketch of the Battle of Winchester," by M. L. Brooking, "The Shenandoah Valley in 1864," by G. E. Pond, the "Personal Memoirs of U. S. Grant," the "Personal Memoirs of P. H. Sheridan," "Johnston's Narrative," by J. E. Johnston, the "Autobiography of J. A. Early," and an able summary of the Valley Campaign of 1864 by Captain L. W. V. Kennon and published in the New York Sun in 1897. For the material used in the chapter on "Behind the Southern Lines," the author is mainly indebted to "The Valley Campaigns," by Thomas A. Ashby, "Reminiscences of the Confederate War," by Mrs. E. C. R. Macon, and the series of letters by Miss Kate McVicar, which were published in the "Evening Star" of Winchester.

For the chapter on church history, mention is due to "The Planting of the Presbyterian Church in Northern Virginia," by Dr. J. R. Graham, and to "Methodism and Early Days in Stephens City."

Among the source-books of a more general nature must be named, "A History of the Valley of Virginia," by Samuel Kercheval, "Shenandoah Valley Pioneers and Their Descendants," by T.

K. Cartmell, "A History of the Lower Shenandoah Valley," by J. E. Norris, "Chronicles of Border Warfare," by Samuel Withers, the "Life of John Marshall," by A. J. Beveridge, "Travels Through North America," by A. Burnaby, "What I Know about Winchester," by W. G. Russell, the "Early History of Winchester," by D. H. Conrad, and "Winchester and Its Beginnings," by W. W. Glass. The three last named were published only in the newspapers of Winchester, and are available only in their files or in scrap-book collections.

Last, but by no means least are the papers left by Colonel James Wood, the founder of Winchester. These gave invaluable assistance in several places. Useful suggestions came from Boutwell Dunlap of San Francisco.

The material was ample for a much larger book. But since only a volume of a specified size was practicable, conciseness of statement became very necessary while endeavoring to follow the spirit of the following lines by the late Miss Kate McVicar:

> "Let us gather up the legends of our city's olden time;
> Embalm them in our stories and weave them in our rhyme;
> Brush off the dust of ages that time has o'er them cast,
> Lest a newer age efface all the memories of the Past."

The contact of the author with the citizens of Winchester who projected this work and made its publication possible has been invariably pleasant and the same is true of all other persons who have rendered assistance.

The author's first visits to Winchester were in 1886 and 1891. Since September, 1921, this town has been his domiciliary home.

FREDERIC MORTON.

Winchester, Virginia,

February 2, 1925.

I

THE HISTORICAL BACKGROUND

Colonial Virginia — The Other Colonies — The Europe of 1724

> Much the greater part of the country between the Little North Mountains and the Shenandoah River, at the first settlement of the Valley, was one vast prairie, and like the rich prairies of the West, offered the finest possible pasturage for wild animals. — Samuel Kercheval.

"Two Centuries of Winchester" would be a very proper title to this book. As is pointed out in a later chapter, the beginning of white settlement at this point goes back quite two hundred years, and there had already been an Indian village at least thirty years.

To understand clearly the conditions and the circumstances under which this town came into existence, it will be of interest to examine the background; to see what Virginia and America were in 1724, and then to glance at those countries of Europe from which the settlers of Winchester came as direct immigrants. The comparison between the then and the now will afford a succession of surprises. It will bring out a greater number of striking contrasts than we have the space to explain.

Westward to a line drawn from Alexandria to Petersburg, and thence due south to the boundary of North Carolina, Virginia was fairly well occupied in 1724. Farther inland, but scarcely touching the Blue Ridge at any point, was a very light sprinkling of people. The entire population was scarcely 150,000. The negro slaves were perhaps 40,000. Probably more numerous were the indentured white servants. There were also a few Indians, nearly all of them east of the Blue Ridge.

The ruling voice in Virginia did not approve of towns and would not encourage them. There were consequently no cities. The largest settlement was Norfolk, but it was not yet an incorporated borough, and it is very doubtful if it had a thousand inhabitants. The only other actual seaports were Hampton and Yorktown. Alexandria and Fredericksburg had only just begun to exist. Petersburg, named for Peter Jones, was not founded until 1733, and Richmond was not laid out until 1737, although four years earlier William Byrd had decided to found a town at this point.

The 100,000 whites—only one-third more than the present number of people in the counties of Frederick, Warren, Clarke, Jefferson, and Berkeley—were nearly all of English birth or descent. There was a small minority of Scotch, Welch, and Irish. Those others whose homelands were on the continent of Europe were exceedingly few. They were limited to Huguenots from France, some newcomers from the valley of the Rhine, and a very few Hollanders from New York.

As in England, the structure of society was aristocratic, although a titled nobility never gained a real foothold on the American shore. The planters were the dominant class, and they were of much the same type as the country squires of England. They were wealthy in land and in the control of labor, and because of this fact they were the governing element. Far more numerous were the yeomen, who were generally poor. Between the planters and the yeomen were the "pretenders," who were on a level with the former in birth and culture, but much inferior in means and influence. They had energy and enterprise, and by sheer ability they often rose into the planter class. A fourth and very numerous group were the indentured white servants, sometimes criminals. Morally and intellectually, they were oftentimes very indifferent. During their years of servitude their status was a thinly veiled slavery, and the planters were their masters. When they became free they were yeomen, and if they had character and energy they prospered. If they did not, they lived on the line of least resistance and were a worthless and undesirable element. The lowest class in the social system were the negroes, nearly all of whom were slaves. The yeoman occasionally owned a single slave, or a very few. A relatively larger number were owned by the pretenders, but the planter was always an owner of servants or slaves, or both.

Because society was organized on an aristocratic basis, class terms were in constant use, even in deeds of conveyance. The planters, and in some degree the pretenders, were styled "gentlemen," this term being used as a mark of social rank. In theory, at least, the ancestors of the gentleman had always been free. He had a coat of arms and had the privilege of wearing a sword. In an increasing degree the use of the title became elastic, especially west of the Blue Ridge, where the justice, regardless of his social origin, was a gentleman ex officio. In court proceedings, the gentleman, yeoman, servant, freedman, or slave, is mentioned according to his class.

The planter built his "great house" well back from the public road and as far from his neighbors as possible. He held that the colony was in his own keeping, and he made and administered the laws. Being a man of power and not backward in its use, he was dictatorial, yet he was also generous, courteous, and high-minded. Through force of custom he was looked up to by all the other social groups.

The pretenders were professional and business men. The yeomen constituted a middle class, although some of them did not own the farms they tilled. Many of the white freedmen were ignorant and uncouth, disorderly and troublesome. They lived in untidy cabins and subsisted mainly on corn bread and the flesh of razor-backed hogs.

The almost entire absence of towns and villages was due to geography as well as to the customs of the people. Streams like the Potomac, the York, and James are drowned rivers, and may be ascended by sailing vessels more than a hundred miles. No planter was very far from the wharf to which his tobacco hogsheads were rolled by horsepower, and on which were unloaded the supplies ordered from England. The planter's wharf was consequently his seaport. All roads were very poor, travel was by horseback, and streams were crossed by fording or by boats.

Agriculture, usually on a large scale, was almost the sole industry of colonial Virginia. As an export staple, tobacco was far in the lead, although some flour was shipped to the West Indies. This one-crop system did not make for a healthy prosperity, except to the merchants. Money was scarce, and the planter was very often in debt.

As the king's proxy, the royal governor was no mere figurehead, and he lived in style. If so inclined, he would dodge the instructions of the king, and through his use of patronage he could often bend the House of Burgesses to his will. Though appointed from Britain, and returning to Britain when superseded, his salary and perquisites, amounting yearly to $10,000, came out of the colonial treasury. He came, not because Virginia needed or really wished an alien governor, but because a court favorite wanted a salary. In fact, the executive who came across the Atlantic was sometimes only a proxy, the recipient of the honor remaining in England.

The Governor's Council was in effect an upper house to the colonial legislature, and it was also a supreme court. Its members held office by appointment. The members of the House of Burgesses—two from each and every county—were chosen by popular vote, but the suffrage was very much restricted.

When a new county was to be organized, the governor appointed from the list of nominees by the court of the parent county a number of men to serve as "worshipful justices." Vacancies were filled in the same way. The county court was therefore self-perpetuating, and so it remained until 1852. Quite as a matter of course it was composed of members of the more influential families. It appointed the clerk, the jailer, the road overseers, and the constables, and it nominated and confirmed the officers of the militia. Its powers were more extensive than those of the present board of supervisors, and in the case of a slave it could decree the death penalty.

The sheriff was a senior justice, nominated by the court, and commissioned by the governor. The term was very short, but as the justices served without pay in any other manner, this political plum was passed around as often as possible. The sheriff enjoyed the honor and a fat share of the perquisites, and his deputies performed the actual work.

The county lieutenant was in some degree a deputy governor. He was military commandant, and if he took the field he held the honorary rank of colonel. The coroner was a conservator of the peace and his office was much more important than it is now.

Each county was a parish, and if large it contained two or three parishes. In England the parish is the smallest administrative unit, and its functions are similar to those of the New England township. In Virginia it was less fully developed, but it may be said of the county that it attended to matters too large for the parish and too small for the colonial government. In each parish was a vestry of twelve men, and like the county court it was a closed corporation, the board filling its own vacancies. It was presided over by the parish rector, and its executive officers were the two church-wardens. The functions of the vestry were partly civil and partly ecclesiastical. Every parish was supposed to have one rector of the established church, and the vestry provided him with a church building and a glebe farm. The cost of these, and also his yearly salary of 16,000 pounds of tobacco were met by public taxation, the vestry laying levies for these purposes and collecting them through its churchwardens. The same officers also looked after the behavior of the community. In case of misconduct they made complaint to the grand jury, which could then issue a presentment. They also bound out orphans and bastard children.

The county levy was fixed by the county court. The public levy, looked after by the Governor's Council, consisted of a quitrent of one shilling a year on each fifty acres, and sundry duties on export tobacco and on imports.

All crimes and chancery causes, unless of a grave nature, were tried before the county court, and those of first concern before the Governor and Council.

In 1692 Virginia authorized one postoffice in each of its counties but until after 1738 there was only one weekly mail to Pennsylvania, and until 1752 there was no regular postal service with the British Isles.

The Church of England was the established church in Virginia as well as in the mother country. A limited toleration to other sects began in 1748, but all restrictions were not swept away until during the American Revolution. To a prescribed extent all adults were supposed to attend the services of the establishment, and might be prosecuted if they did not. Until the fall of 1781, the marriage ceremony could not legally be performed by ministers of other denominations.

Education was viewed as a private interest, and there was very much illiteracy. Tuition had to be paid for, except in the case of the very few charity schools, which were maintained by private benevolence, and were known as free schools. The well-to-do families employed private tutors, and sometimes these were Episcopal clergymen.

The soil of the Tidewater is not naturally fertile. When the stumps were gone, a field was thrown out of cultivation and another was cleared. In the middle of the eighteenth century Washington was telling the Virginians that if this shortsighted pillaging of the soil were continued it would drive the people of the lowlands into the mountains.

The colonial civilization of Tidewater Virginia was picturesque, and it contained elements of strength and value. It developed strong leadership, and it bred statesmen for the exacting times of the American Revolution. But in an economic sense it was weak. In a new country people are not content to work as tenants or for wages. To work their lands the planters resorted first to servitude and then to slavery, yet even these forms of controlled labor could not make headway against the impoverishment of the soil. The Tidewater was already on the decline when the war for American independence broke out.

We have described at some length the colonial Virginia east of the Blue Ridge, because it was this older Virginia which opened to settlement the country beyond the Blue Ridge. It was this Virginia which framed the laws under which the new settlers were to live, and it gave an impress to their political thought and to their customs, both social and economic.

Let us now for a few moments turn our attention to the colonies considered as a group.

They were not yet thirteen in number. Georgia did not come into existence until the year after it is definitely known that there were white settlers within the corporate limits of Winchester. Settlement did not extend beyond the Kennebec River in the north and the Savannah River in the south. On an average this belt was scarcely eighty miles broad. The west end of the little colony of Massachusetts was as yet unoccupied. Much more than one-half of New York was held by the Iroquois League. The uplands of both the Carolinas were a solitude except for the presence of the Cherokees and the Catawbas.

Over an area comparable in size with Virginia, as the state limits existed in 1860, was a population of not quite a half million. It was smaller by one-fifth than the inhabitants in 1920 of the thirty-one counties west of the Blue Ridge. The four-fifths who were white were overwhelmingly of British descent, and a large majority of those whose homeland was the British kingdom were of English birth or origin. There were some Hollanders, Germans, Huguenots, and Swedes, but thus far, and in fact much longer, the land knew nothing as to citizens from the south, middle, and east of Europe.

All the half-dozen cities and nearly all the towns lay on navigable waters. Boston was at this time the metropolis, but it was passed by Philadelphia about 1750. The houses of the more prosperous people were strongly built and quite roomy, yet less elegantly furnished than the better class of homes in any American town of the present century. Away from the coast the houses were of logs, or were crudely constructed of stone.

Farming was carried on in a primitive, laborious, and wasteful manner. The surplus for export was contributed almost wholly by the Middle and Southern colonies, and no ship might visit an American port unless it flew the British flag. By reason of its climate and soil the New England section had turned its chief attention to commerce and the fisheries, and a three-sided system of exchange caused it to prosper. The home-built ships of New England carried colonial produce to the West Indies, and there exchanged it for sugar and other staples. This cargo was taken to England and turned into British manufactured goods for the return voyage.

The only colleges were Harvard, Yale, and William and Mary. Outside of New England there were no public schools, and yet there was less illiteracy than in Europe. In every colony there was no inconsiderable number of persons who were well grounded in the higher education of that day. The only newspapers were the two printed in Boston, although others were soon to appear in several of the colonies. A regular mail service, either within the commonwealths, or with the British Isles, was still in the future.

Except in Rhode Island and Pennsylvania, a state church was supported from the public treasury, and all adults were expected to attend its houses of worship a certain number of times each year.

It was a dark age with respect to medical knowledge. Hygiene was little understood or observed, physicians were not held in high esteem, and quacks and quack remedies were legion.

In no colony was society more than nominally democratic, and even in 1789, when the Federal government went into operation, only one person in twenty-five was a qualified voter.

Taverns were rather frequent and often they were poor. They always kept liquors and wines in variety, and the use of these was very general. In the South any traveler was sure of free entertainment in the plantation houses.

The roads were exceedingly bad and the larger streams were never bridged. No person undertook a journey except in case of necessity, and he did not go by land if he could reach his destination by water. A will was considered a very proper document to have ready, before a start was made on any tour of importance.

Because of the slowness and difficulty of travel, the slight amount of correspondence, and the almost complete absence of the newspaper, each colony was in a very practical sense a foreign land to every other. And as a matter of course, the lack of mutual acquaintance made for prejudice. In each colony there was a fondness for casting slurs at the others. There were, however, differences between the colonies. These differences were due in part to diversity in denominational opinion, and in part to social and economic conditions. As a matter of sentiment and convenience, each colony was content to remain a component part of the British realm, but it insisted on managing its internal affairs very much as it pleased.

The outside world was very imperfectly understood. The traveler was commonly suspected of being a retailer of lies, and this was often the case. But in his defense it must be stated that there was no intercourse with Latin America, excepting the West Indies. Africa was known only on its coast. China and Japan were hermit nations and had no use for the white man. Australia was less known than is the Antarctic Continent today. The areas east of Russia or beyond our own Mississippi, were blank spaces on the map, and their outlines were guessed at. The great Pacific was less visited by the white navigator than is the Arctic in our century. Every sea was infested with pirate ships, and the pirates were of every color known to the human race.

Our picture is not complete without a glance at the Europe of two centuries ago. That continent is one-third larger than the continental United States, and in 1724 was only one-half more populous. Whatever may be said of it now, it was certainly not crowded then.

With twice the area of the Virginias, the Britian of two centuries ago had only twice their present population. London, then as now the largest city of the continent, was no larger than the Baltimore of the present day. The British Isles fed themselves, and their own forests supplied the timber for their numerous ships. Large districts were thinly peopled, and in the north of Ireland, whence the Scotch-Irish were about to emigrate on a large scale, wolves were as great a nuisance as in the Valley of Virginia. People did not leave Britain for America because there was too little room at home. They emigrated because of political, economic, or religious annoyances, which did not exist in the same degree on this side of the Atlantic.

On the continent of Europe, France was the country most populous and influential and likewise the richest. Its king, the celebrated Louis XIV, had recently dealt his native land a most grievous injury. He ordered his Protestant subjects to give up their faith, and forbade their leaving his kingdom unless they did. But to the number of 400,000 they did get away, and they were filled with resentment at this display of religious bigotry. They were welcomed in England, Holland, and Germany, and in those counties they became an element of great strength and usefulness. Many of them reached America, but unlike the French Canadians of today, they gave up the use of the French tongue and did not seek to settle by themselves. On the other hand, they diffused themselves among the colonists already here.

Holland had recently been the foremost commercial country of Europe, but had been worsted in her competition with England. Her one American colony of New Amsterdam was founded primarily for trading purposes. True to their commercial instincts, the men who settled New York traded extensively with the Indians. The Hollanders knew a good thing when they saw it, and after John Vanmeter had visited the Shenandoah and the South Branch, he counseled his sons to secure large landed possessions in this quarter. They acted on his advice.

Germany was not then a united nation, and it had not recovered from the frightful devastation of the Thirty Years War. The Palatinate, a province on the Rhine, had been very lately ravaged by the armies of Louis XIV with something of the thoroughness displayed by the Germans themselves in the World War. William Penn, who was able to converse in German, invited the refugees to Pennsylvania. Thus began an exodus which during the next half-century equaled in volume the movement from the north of Ireland to which we have referred. These Palatines were joined by many people from Switzerland, Alsace, and Baden. Thus the German emigration of the eighteenth century was almost exclusively from the upper Rhine. It was German in speech, but in blood it was not typically German.

It is not worth while to extend our survey of Europe, because there was no emigration to America from the countries in the south and east. Russia in particular was backward and barbarous. It was only twenty years prior to the settling of Winchester that Peter the Great had founded Petersburg (Leningrad) in a swamp that was frostbound half the year. As for Berlin, now the third city in Europe, it was not quite so large as the Hagerstown of 1924.

II

THE LOCAL GEOGRAPHY

The Lower Shenandoah — The Horizon — Soil — Streams — Climate — Health — Place Names — Scenic Attractions — Historic Associations

> Winchester, or Frederickstown, a post town of Virginia and the Capital of Frederick County. It is a handsome and flourishing town, standing on low and broken ground. It is a corporation and contains 1780 free inhabitants and 348 slaves. It was formerly fortified but the works are now in ruins. — Morse's American Gazetteer for 1810.

The business quarter of Winchester lies in the basin of the little stream known as Town Run. It is therefore depressed, but the gradual improvement of the streets and lots has made it almost level throughout. In every direction is slightly rising ground; Fort Hill in the north, Church Hill in the east, Potato Hill in the south, and Academy Hill and Powell's Ridge in the west. But these elevations are gentle in ascent, and are broadtopped belts of tableland rather than true hills. Even the tower of the Handley school does not rise high enough to permit a quite satisfactory examination of the field of view. Yet the general features of the same may easily be studied.

Running twenty miles southward, a little more than twenty miles northward, and a similar distance east and west, lies the Lower Shenandoah Valley, as distinguished from the Middle Valley between Strasburg and Harrisonburg, and the Upper Valley above Harrisonburg. To speak accurately, it is not a true valley, but a long and relatively narrow plain, separated by the narrow rampart of the Blue Ridge from the plain of Piedmont Virginia. The watercourses around Winchester are not tributaries of the Shenandoah, but turn directly to the Potomac.

The altitude of Winchester is about seven hundred feet above the sea level, and rather more than four hundred feet above the Potomac at Harper's Ferry. Eastward, over a moderately rolling country, it is fifteen miles to the Shenandoah, this river closely hugging the western foot of the Blue Ridge. The altitude of the mountain wall being here only 1400 feet above the tide, the distance to the summit is only two miles, and it is only one mile farther to the town of Bluemont at the eastern base. The shallow pass used by the Berryville Pike was once known as Williams' Gap, but has long been called Snicker's Gap, apparently from Moses Snicker, who was keeping a tavern at the river-ford in 1758. Two years earlier, the county court of Frederick ordered some rocks blasted out which were obstructing the highway. Northward, the Blue Ridge maintains a nearly uniform height to the canyon at Harper's Ferry, through which the Potomac emerges from the Valley into the coast plain. This cleft, distant twenty-five miles from Winchester in an airline, may be discerned only from some commanding point.

Eight miles south of Snicker's Gap is the much deeper rift known as Ashby's Gap. It is conspicuous in the eastern sky-line. About the same distance farther south is Manassas Gap, formerly Manasseh's Gap. A few miles still further south is Chester Gap, commemorating the name of Thomas Chester, a pioneer settler. Between these two passes is the high prominence of Mount Marshall.

A very little south of Chester Gap the Blue Ridge is eclipsed by a rugged uplift which seems to run across the Shenandoah Valley for six miles. To the eye this distance is nearly enough to terminate the Valley in that quarter. But in reality, the observer is viewing the triple ends of Three-Top, or Massanutten Mountain. Four miles to the west of Winchester is the inconspicuous Little North Mountain, rising four hundred feet above the town. It is the foothill ridge to Great North Mountain, the western limit to the Shenandoah Valley and the beginning of the Alleghany System proper. Beyond Great North Mountain there is no plain until the Ohio River is approached. Uplift succeeds uplift in rapid succession for a breadth of more than one hundred miles.

The north, or rather the northeast, is the only quarter in which no mountain appears. The course of the Potomac from Hedgesville to Harper's Ferry—more than thirty miles—is the only mark of separation between the Shenandoah Valley and its continuation, the Cumberland Valley of Maryland and Pennsylvania.

We have been using the terms north, east, south, and west in a general sense, the actual direction of the Shenandoah Valley being nearly northeast and southwest.

The twenty-mile breadth of the Lower Valley is an alternation of soil belts. The "fat lands" of the limestone areas, though somewhat difficult of tillage, have long been renowned for their yields of corn, grain, and hay. The slate lands are less fertile and are encumbered with thin, loose rocks, yet they produce wheat of excellent quality. To a great extent, the soils of the Winchester region are so unusually well adapted to tree fruits that the growing of apples and peaches has become the leading farm interest. Thus the district tributary to Winchester is of high agricultural value and has always been the leading factor in the life of the town.

Limestone belts are noted for their deep, strong springs, several of which occur within the corporate limits of Winchester. Rising from a considerable depth, these waters are exceedingly pure. They are very strong and very constant, the Hollingsworth spring alone having a flow of 250 gallons a minute.

Winchester is not close to any considerable stream. Opequon Creek rises in Little North Mountain, and coursing first to the south, then to the east, and finally to the northeast, makes a curve around the city, but nowhere comes nearer than about five miles. Abraham's Run is a tributary a very little south of the town. A little to the north are the sources of Red Bud Creek, another affluent.

The Opequon is the subject of these lines by a local poet:

> Streamlet, flashing through the meadow,
> Now in sunshine, now in shadow,
> Curving with a fairy billow,
> Now 'round rock and now 'round willow,
> Singing through the breezy wildwoods,
> Songs as gay and glad as childhood's,
> Oft to hear these do I linger,
> Ne'er knew I so sweet a singer.

In climate Winchester is very highly favored. The latitude —39 degrees, 11 minutes—is the same as that of Cincinnati, and it is also the parallel of the center of population for the United States. The hundred-mile breadth of the Alleghanies breaks the force of the great air-currents that use as a playground the immense breadth of the Mississippi basin. The distance of nearly two hundred miles to the Atlantic prevents, with the help of the prevailing winds, a climate of an oceanic type. The prolonged, drizzling rains of the seashore scarcely ever occur here. And not only is the humidity less than on the coast, but it is less than is found on the western slope of the Appalachians. The mean temperature—about 53.5 degrees—is that of Philadelphia, the altitude being enough to offset a difference of three-fourths of a degree in latitude. Hot waves are not so oppressive as at Washington or Baltimore, or at such inland points as Cincinnati or St. Louis. The average winter is not at all severe, and because of the low humidity the winter wind is less keenly felt than on the Atlantic shore. Thanks to good air-drainage and the absence of any low-banked river, a fog is rarely seen.

There are indeed variations in the seasons of different years. January 13, 1912, the mercury registered twelve degrees below zero. July 12, 1914, it stood at ninety-eight degrees above. In the winter of 1839-40, there was intense cold for ten days, the snow lying two feet deep on a level and five feet in drifts. But such extremes are infrequent. Save to a very small extent, the summer heats do not interfere with active exertion, either physical or mental. So light is the snowfall of the average winter that there are few opportunities to use a sleigh. In some winters there are no opportunities at all. The percentage of bright sunshine is comparable to that of the country west of the Mississippi. An all-day rain may be followed by a cloudless day. The rainfall is ample and well-distributed. Even the severe drouth of 1881 did not interrupt the streams which are classed as perennial.

Though it is shielded from the atmospheric disturbances of the West, the great length of the Shenandoah Valley does not render Winchester quite exempt from high winds and electrical storms. In 1876 occurred a storm never exceeded in thirty-two years for its display of thunder and lightning. Houses were struck in all parts of the city and one was partially burned. What is regarded as the fiercest gale in the history of the city took place in the cold night of March 1-2, 1914. It reached a velocity of seventy-five miles an hour, and pedestrians were swept off their feet. Signs and shutters were wrenched loose, chimneys were wrecked, and trees were uprooted, particularly in the cemeteries. Several dwelling houses and the hall of the colored Odd Fellows were partially demolished, and the aggregate damage was between $60,000 and $100,000. But there was little damage to the orchards.

The rotary storm is exceedingly rare, and because of the narrowness of the Lower Valley it cannot develop to the dimensions known in the prairie states. A wind of this sort coming May 12, 1886, broke window glass on western exposures to the extent of $1500, ruined gardens and flower-beds, and broke down several old trees.

Since Winchester does not lie on any large watercourse, it is not subject to destructive floods. But Town Run occasionally throws such a deluge into the city as to cause a depth of two or three feet on Water Street.

The healthfulness of this locality is well known, and is greatly due to the pureness of the springs from which comes the water supply. When an epidemic does come it is of a mild type. Winchester was unharmed by the cholera scourge of October, 1832, although a visitor died here of the disease. In the visitation of influenza in 1918, there were almost no fatalities among the townspeople.

The general salubrity of the climate is reflected in the good physiques and clear complexions which may often be seen, and in the number of aged people. The most conspicuous instance of longevity is that of Frances Ellen Davenport, who was born in this city, February 11, 1811, and died December 20, 1915. She married Joseph Hare in 1827, and was the mother of eight children. A near-centenarian was Miss Margaret A. Williams, who was born in Frederick county February 22, 1814 and died in Winchester December 9, 1912.

Unlike his brethren of the seaboard, the settler of the middle Appalachians was very chary in his adoption of Indian place-names. In this region the most conspicuous exception is the word Shenandoah, which, throughout the eighteenth century, was spelled in almost as many different ways as possible. Current opinion has long insisted that it has the poetical meaning, "Daughter of the Stars." The word Opequon has been observed in twenty-four orthographic forms. According to Foote, an excellent authority, the correct spelling is "Opecquon." This was for a while the name of the local settlement, and it would be the name of the city today, if the early inhabitants had remained content with the aboriginal term. The meaning seems to be forgotten.

The mountain background at Winchester is low and distant, and relieves the town from having the cramped appearance of a place in a deep valley between lofty ridges. Henderson, the biographer of Stonewall Jackson, says that, "the country around Winchester,—the gently rolling ridges, surmounted by groves of forest trees, the great North Mountains to the westward, rising sharply from the Valley, the cosy villages and the comfortable farms, and, in the clear, blue distance to the south, the towering peaks of the Massanuttens—is a picture not easily forgotten. And the little town, quiet and old-fashioned, with its ample gardens and red brick pavements, is not unworthy of its surroundings."

As will be more fully shown in later chapters, the historic associations of Winchester are highly interesting. The four passes visible in the Blue Ridge repeatedly resounded to the tramp of armies in the war of 1861. Up the Cumberland and Shenandoah valleys ran an aboriginal road, used by Northern and Southern Indians in their intertribal wars, and later by Scotch-Irish and German immigrants on their way to people the Upper Shenandoah and the uplands of the Carolinas. It was here that Washington gained the apprenticeship that enabled him to win the Revolution. A half-day's walk to the southeast was Greenway Court, the home of his friend and patron, Lord Fairfax. And in 1861-64, as registered by the number of engagements, the Lower Valley was the most fiercely contested area in the whole theater of war. It then earned the name of the "Flanders of America."

III

LORD FAIRFAX AND THE NORTHERN NECK

> November 17, 1749. The Right Honorable Thomas Lord Fairfax, Baron of Cameron in that part of Great Britain called Scotland, and proprietor of the Northern Neck, produced a special commission to be one of his Majesty's Justices of the Peace — Minutes of County Court of Frederick County, Virginia.

During the era of exploration in North America, the British government granted generous slices of this continent to chartered companies and court favorites. And following the idea that it is not well to do things by halves, the grants ran inland far toward the setting sun.

With his propensity for giving away land that did not belong to him, that libertine and spendthrift, Charles II of England, gave to certain of his satellites a portion of the chartered territory of Virginia. The date of the transaction is 1664, and the grantees were Lord Hopton, Lord Culpeper, Lord Berkeley, the Earl of Saint Albans, Sir William Morton, Sir Dudley Wyatt, and Thomas Culpeper. The grant was given the name of the Northern Neck of Virginia, and it was defined as lying between the Potomac and the Rappahannock. Virginia was still an infant colony, and settlement had scarcely ventured above the Fall Line, which marks the head of navigation in the rivers of Virginia. The existence of the Blue Ridge was known, but the country beyond had not yet been explored by the English. It was assumed that the Potomac rises in the Blue Ridge, which, as a matter of course, was understood to be the western line of the Northern Neck.

The grant to Culpeper and his associates was of the same nature as the grants to William Penn and Lord Baltimore. The one notable difference was that it did not create a new colony. Yet until the Revolution, the Northern Neck was a domain within a domain, being regarded as distinct from the rest of Virginia. As a grantee, the proprietor had no political power, but he gave deeds to all lands not previously devised. He therefore held the title to the soil. The headright law, a beneficent measure similar to the homestead law of our national government, was not permitted a foothold north of the Rappahannock. And in the tidewater end of the Northern Neck, society was more aristocratic than elsewhere in Virginia.

THOMAS, LORD FAIRFAX

By deeds of conveyance, Alexander Lord Culpeper acquired in 1681 the sole ownership of a territory, which, as then understood, comprised fourteen of the present counties of the Old Dominion. His sole heir was his daughter Catharine, who married the fifth Lord Fairfax, a descendant of the commander-in-chief of the Parliamentary army in the English civil war. Her son Thomas was born in 1692, and title to the Northern Neck passed to him by entail when he was eighteen years old. While he was a student in the University of Oxford, his mother and his maternal grandmother exerted pressure upon him to cut off the entail of the Fairfax estates in England, in order to save the heavily mortgaged Culpeper estates. In return he was promised the Northern Neck. The young man gave the consent which he could not well avoid, but the transaction embittered him against both mother and grandmother. And being jilted by the woman to whom he was engaged, he remained to the end of his life a bachelor with an unyielding aversion to the other sex.

Fairfax made a visit to Virginia in 1736. He now learned that the Potomac rises west of the Blue Ridge, the source of the North Fork of that stream having been found in the same year. In 1737 he sailed to England to secure a definition for his boundaries, and the points at issue between himself and the Crown were settled in 1745. In 1742 he returned permanently to Virginia, after selling his estates in England, and for a while he lived with his cousin William Fairfax on the plantation of Belvoir, twelve miles below Mount Vernon. At his request, William Fairfax had moved here from Massachusetts to become the general business manager for the Northern Neck, and in 1742 a land office was opened.

In 1746 a line was surveyed from the Fairfax Stone, at the source of the North Branch of the Potomac, to the source of the Rapid Ann in the Blue Ridge. As first laid down, this boundary crossed the North Fork of the Shenandoah at Narrow Passage Creek. In 1755 it was moved southward. The northern limit of Rockingham county, so far as it lies within the valley of the North Fork, is a part of this line, and it is the only part that remains a political boundary.

In 1748 Lord Fairfax settled on a "manor" of 10,000 acres which he reserved for himself. He thought of building a castle, but contented himself with the erection of Greenway Court, a one-story house about eleven miles southeast of Winchester. A verandah, facing the Blue Ridge, ran the whole length of the building.

Rising above the roof with its dormer windows were two wooden belfries, in which were alarm bells. There were also a clock and a sundial. In addition to the windows, the roof was ornamented with nesting houses for the swallows and martins. The proprietor did not sleep in the mansion, but always in an outside building only twelve feet square. All around were the cabins of his negro slaves. Beyond were woods. There was no attempt at cultivation, Fairfax using the manor as a hunting preserve and living on the quitrents he exacted from the settlers. Greenway Court stood more than a century, and was torn down a little before 1859.

The proprietor was fond of the chase, but he was also fond of books, and possessed literary ability, although he did not make use of this talent. In his home he was hospitable and sociable, sometimes entertaining twenty persons on the same day. But his latchstring was on the outside only to male acquaintances. In his time only one white woman saw the interior of Greenway Court, and though she gained entrance by stratagem and out of mere curiosity, Fairfax saw to it that her call was very brief.

The man who had for once and all turned his back on the aristocratic society of England lived at Greenway Court the rest of his life, attaining the age of ninety-one. During the American Revolution he was a Tory, like all the other Fairfaxes, but his attitude seems to have been entirely passive. He was never molested, and when the news came of the surrender of Cornwallis to his friend Washington, he told his body servant that the time had come that he be put to bed. He died soon afterward and was buried in the Episcopal church at Winchester. When the building passed out of use his remains were removed to the chancel of the church at the corner of Water and Washington streets, where his memorial tablet may be seen.

In spite of coming to the backwoods of America, Fairfax was none the less an aristocrat. He was particular as to his wearing apparel. He had a velvet suit and other suits in brown, blue, and drab, scarlet and green silk coats, scarlet-laced, green damask-laced, and gold tissue waistcoats, and scarlet plush and black velvet breeches.

With the coming of Fairfax to Greenway Court began a long period of persistent annoyance to the settlers in the Shenandoah. Isaac and John Vanmeter had already secured grants of 80,000 acres from the Crown. These tracts were purchased by Yost Hite*

---

* In the court records of the time, Hite's forename is inaccurately spelled "Joist." The author prefers the form "Yost," because it indicates the actual pronunciation, and also because it was often used in the eighteenth century.

and his partners, and the lands were advertised for sale at the rate of three pounds ($10) for one hundred acres. The advertising secured a wide publicity for the Lower Shenandoah, and many settlers purchased from Hite. Such tracts were called "minor grants." By the terms of the compromise between Fairfax and the Crown, these transfers were to be respected, as were also all transfers by Fairfax found to lie south of the Fairfax Line, the position of which has already been given. But after his arrival, Fairfax took in the situation with an ill grace. He held that all persons living on the minor grants were squatters, and he demanded that quitrents should be due from 1745. A Crown grant was given in perpetuity, though subject to an annual quitrent of one shilling for each fifty acres. But Fairfax sold only leaseholds running ninety-nine years, and demanded the payment of what he styled "composition money" at the time of making the transfer. An arrearage of two years in the quitrent worked a forfeiture of the title. The indignant Hite promptly brought suit, but Fairfax was very hard on all who opposed his pretensions, and since he was a member of the privileged class he had great influence in the seats of authority. While he lived, he was able to prevent a decision. Although the suit was brought in 1749, it was not decided until 1786, and by this time neither litigant was living. About five hundred holdings were affected by the decision, which was in favor of Hite's contention. It seems to have caused a feeling that the shoe was now adjusted to the other foot, since a petition of December 7, 1786 complained that, "people were promised that whichever way the matter should go, they would be secure. Now they are on the brink of losing all, since only those who took title under grantee from the Crown can hold land."

The farmer settling on Fairfax land was compelled to pay for each fifty acres ten shillings in "composition money" and a yearly quitrent of two shillings. And since this was in sterling and not Virginia currency, the respective sums were $2.50 and 50 cents. These sums appear small, yet the purchasing power of the dollar was far greater then than now. The quitrent, whether to the Crown or to a proprietor, was paid very reluctantly, since it was regarded as a cloud on the title.

Fairfax was in no true sense a founder of Winchester. James Wood created an opportunity, and Fairfax took advantage of it to exact additional revenue. Not even the lots on which the dissenting churches were built were granted gratuitously. His attitude is in marked contrast to that of William Byrd, the founder of

Richmond. To any person who would build a house not smaller than of a prescribed size, Colonel Byrd gave a lot without charge. To the settlers of Winchester the quitrents on the town lots were in effect extortionate, and were paid under protest.

One of the effects of the Revolution was to do away with the quitrent system.

Lord Fairfax willed his interests in the Northern Neck to Denny Fairfax, a nephew living in England. A petition of 1793 raised the question whether the devisee, being an alien, was competent to hold the estate. Denny Fairfax, likewise a bachelor, left the property to his relative, General Philip Martin, also unmarried. By him the Fairfax interests were sold to John and James Marshall, and Raleigh Colston. Through an act of confiscation the estate of Virginia had come into control of the Northern Neck. But by a compromise between the Marshalls and the State, the act was overthrown on the ground that although Fairfax was a Tory, he was not a public enemy.

Viewed in a broad light, Lord Fairfax was honorable and public-spirited. He even won some degree of popularity. He was a member of the county court, a county lieutenant, and an overseer of roads. He advanced money to settlers for the improvement of their holdings, and he gave his excess revenues to the poor. In the French and Indian war he exerted himself greatly for the defense of the frontier, and he refused to abandon Greenway Court, though warned of his danger from Indian attack.

The eighteenth century was an age of special privilege, and the viewpoint of Fairfax was that of royalty. He had no sympathy with the growing democratic spirit of America, especially as witnessed on the frontier. It is a matter of doubt whether he even comprehended this spirit. He styled the settlers his "retainers," a term that could not fail to be offensive to many of them.

Lord Fairfax was therefore a product of a system, and for this system he was in no way responsible. The system was English, and in his eyes it was eminently right and proper. It had the sanction of centuries of usage, and in that country was acquiesced in by all classes of society. But it would not work when transplanted to American soil. It was increasingly out of harmony with American thought, and it collapsed in the upheaval of the Revolution.

In "New Virginia" it was felt to be a gross injustice that a man should have title to five millions of acres of the public domain, on no other ground than that of aristocratic privilege, and be supported by what was, in principle, a tax upon the public. Fairfax would have been wise in showing a conciliatory spirit, and in freely recognizing the validity of the minor grants. There was plenty of land in this naked country, and yet he was unceasing in his efforts to eject the settlers he found here upon his arrival.

Yet Fairfax remains a picturesque character in American history. Here in the wilderness, attempting to live a baronial life, was a member of the British nobility, who had been trifled with by the woman he would have married, and who had expatriated himself from his native land. He came when well advanced in middle age, and this circumstance may go far to explain why he failed to put himself more in harmony with the new environment. His lack of pliability—a very English characteristic—caused him to be a misfit, but he is to be judged by his own age and not by ours. America can afford to be lenient to his memory.

IV

THE BEGINNINGS OF WINCHESTER

Primeval Appearance of Site — Shawnee Village — "New Virginia"— County Organizations — Exploration —"Potomoke" — Early Comers — Reasons for the Town — Winchester, England.

> Old Mrs. Sperry, who lived on the corner of Piccadilly and Braddock streets, remembers when she first saw the site of Winchester, in 1738, when there were but two cabins built on the town run. — David Holmes Conrad on Early History of Winchester.

It is now in order to determine how the Lower Shenandoah looked while it was still a wilderness.

Except to a comparatively insignificant degree, the contour of the country was the same as it is now, and the smaller streams were probably more constant in their flow. The mountains were forested, but despite a common opinion to the contrary, the valley lands were for the most part a prairie. These prairies were artificially produced, since everywhere in Appalachian America the surface tends to cover itself with wood. The Shenandoah was a hunting preserve of the red men, and at the close of each hunting season it was their custom to fire the grass. This was done to attract the buffalo, an animal which has no use for the forest. By opening new pastures, the range of the buffalo herds was extended eastward, and a new food supply was secured. But the pastures were used freely by the elk and the deer as well as the buffalo.

The wooded tracts were so nearly free of undergrowth that they could be traversed by a wagon with little difficulty. Groves occurred here and there, and one of them occupied the knoll on which the courthouse at Winchester was built. We are assured by Kercheval that the wild grass was five feet high and was intermixed with much peavine, a legume fattening to the domestic animals of the white settlers. By 1745, the Valley of Virginia was occupied by immigrants for a distance of two hundred miles from the Potomac, and the grass-firing by the Indians came to an end. Tracts not in tillage, meadow, or pasture began to revert to a forest growth, and thus came an increase in the extent of woodland.

That there was a resident population in the Valley, prior to the coming of the whites, admits of no reasonable doubt. But in 1671-1674, the scanty remnant of the red people was driven out or exterminated by the Iroquois from the country south of Lake Ontario. Peyton mentions the Senedos as a tribe on the North Fork of the Shenandoah, and says that they were crushed by these "Romans of the New World." But this statement is no longer regarded as resting on good authority. It is significant that the treaty of Albany in 1722 says nothing of the Senedos. There would necessarily have been mention, had the tribe recently dwelt here.

The Shawnees have fitly been designated as the "Bedouins of America". No other Indian tribe has been so restless. The migrations of the Shawnees have been traced from near the Atlantic shore far toward the Mississippi, and from the middle districts of Pennsylvania and Ohio southward nearly to the Gulf of Mexico. About 1690, a party of these nomads, moving northward from the Carolinas, established a village at what has ever since been known as the Shawnee Spring. It remained until the spring of 1754, when the clan suddenly went to join its kinspeople on the Scioto. The latter had warned their brethren in the Valley that war was brewing between the English and the French, and that the tribe should side with the latter.

The Shawnee village at Winchester was small, and it is very doubtful if it included so many as one hundred persons. There was another little village of the Shawnees at Old Fields on the South Branch, in what is now the county of Hardy. The name Tuscarora in Berkeley commemorates a sojourn of that tribe during its migration from North Carolina to New York. But within the historic period there have been no other permanent settlements of the red men in the whole length of the Valley.

In 1724 the section of Virginia west of the Blue Ridge bore about the same relation to the Virginia east of it that the Louisiana Purchase bore to the United States of 1803. This hinterland was claimed as a possession of the colony under the terms of its charter, but John Marshall states that even so late as 1758 the Blue Ridge was regarded as the proper inland boundary of Virginia. When settlers began to flock in, it was styled "New Virginia," and a Winchester paper of 1813 speaks of this town as the "metropolis of New Virginia." It is significant that no county boundary runs across the Blue Ridge. Until 1861, the counties east were called the Eastern District, and the counties west were called the Western

District. This distinction was carried into census reports and into the statistical returns published by the state government. But for the war of 1861, there can be little doubt that the entire Western District would have achieved statehood for itself, just as Kentucky had already parted company with the remainder of the commonwealth.

The laws of the colony were supposed to have the same force in New Virginia as in the older territory east of the Blue Ridge. But while in theory local government was the same in the former region as in the latter, such was not the case in practice. This was solely because of the difference in the character of the inhabitants. The ruling class of the Eastern District was intolerant, both in politics and religion. In that section government, church, education, and the aristocracy were all closely allied. But west of the Blue Ridge the vast majority of the people were dissenters, either from the north of Ireland or from Germany, and their point of view was not that of the "Tuckahoe."

Until 1720, what was later to be called the Western District was a No Man's Land with respect to county organization. Spottsylvania was then created, and it was the first county in Virginia to have its limits defined with something like scientific precision. The western line followed the South Branch of the Shenandoah from a point a few miles south of Front Royal to a point near Port Republic. The new county therefore took in a quite insignificant part of the Shenandoah region. In 1734, Orange was set off from Spottsylvania, and it was defined as extending to the "westernmost limits" claimed by Virginia. This was because of the immigrants now flocking into the Valley. In 1738, Orange was cut down to the portion east of the mountain wall, and the portion west was made into Frederick and Augusta. The line between the new counties ran from the source of the North Branch of the Potomac to the source of the Rapid Ann in the north angle of what is now the county of Greene. But neither county was to be organized until there was a larger population in the Valley. This is why Frederick was not organized until November, 1743, and Augusta not until December, 1745. Meanwhile, the two divisions were called districts, and they remained under the jurisdiction of Orange.

When Hite and his companions settled just above Winchester in the fall of 1731, they were outside the domain of any authorized county. But Hite was not a typical frontiersman, and the Lower Valley had been prospected long before his arrival. He was a man of means, and he brought civilization with him. The actual date of white settlement at and around Winchester thus becomes a question of interest. The date of the earliest survey or patent is not conclusive. All along the American frontier the land-purchasing settler has been preceded by the squatter. This personage often made marks on trees, but he wrote his dates in the sand if he wrote them at all.

In the fall of 1671, Abraham Wood was in charge of Fort Henry, where is now the city of Petersburg. He sent out a party that found New River and followed it to the falls below Hinton. Even this early, trees were found with "scrabblements" upon them. About the same time John Lederer claims to have crossed the Blue Ridge much farther to the north. But his narrative is foggy, and its trustworthiness is in dispute.

At the head of a large party from the Tidewater, Governor Spotswood crossed at Swift Run Gap * in 1716, but went no farther than the south bank of South River. He was not visiting what had until now been a terra incognita. But the world was not willing to take very seriously the accounts given by trappers and traders. So it could now be said that the Valley was officially discovered. Yet it is rather singular that the expedition should stop short when it was only at the threshold of the transmontane region.

Bona-fide settlers had preceded Spotswood. His letters show that there were people west of the mountains in 1712. In 1707, Louis Michel of Switzerland drew a good map of the Lower Valley in the interest of its colonization by his own countrymen. The British government was at this time wishing to keep its people at home, so that they might fight its frequent wars with the French. It was willing to see the Shenandoah occupied by Protestants from Continental Europe. It is probable that Hite came as a result of the visit by Michel, although he was a native of Alsace and not of Switzerland. But even as early as 1632, the French had mapped the Shenandoah as far south as Port Republic. Their trappers were venturesome, and their Jesuit missionaries with Iroquois guides were indefatigable in exploration.

Concerning the settlement of "Potomoke," Dr. James R. Graham made a painstaking inquiry, and his conclusions seem worthy of full credence. In 1719 the Synod of Philadelphia sent

---

* He attempted to get through Swift Run Gap, but actually crossed at Milam's Gap, farther to the north, and reached South River at the town of Shenandoah, or in its near vicinity.

Daniel McGill to a settlement called Potomoke to "put the people into church order." This was done in response to a letter from the settlement. These people were unquestionably on the Potomac River, and Dr. Graham argues very conclusively that they were living at and around Shepherdstown. He might have added that they could not have been east of the Blue Ridge, for as far down as the early decades of the eighteenth century the government of Virginia was making life miserable for any and all groups of dissenters. The difference in spelling between Potomac and Potomoke is of no importance. People then spelled by sound, and they often took twenty shots at a geographical word without once hitting the bull's eye. In support of Dr. Graham's contention is an entry of 1748, in the account-book of James Wood, mentioning the cost of a trip to Potomoke.

In Maryland the Blue Ridge is vastly nearer to the Chesapeake than is the case in Virginia, and the inland march of settlement was relatively more rapid. People were settled at Frederick in 1712. Settlers so near as that would not let the grass grow under their feet before pushing onward to the inviting limestone lands of Jefferson county. In fact, Mr. Charles E. Kemper has found that which goes to prove that people had come to the south bank of the Potomac as early as 1717. This may be taken as the approximate beginning of white occupancy of the Shenandoah Valley.

But when Dr. Graham speaks of a gravestone in an old Presbyterian burial ground five miles south of Shepherdstown, the German inscription on the slab being read as "Kathrina Beierlin died 1707," he falls into a very unintentional error. It is quite impossible that the date could be so early as 1707. It was tedious to the pioneers to cut letters and figures in hard ironstone. A shallow and imperfectly inscribed "2" has been read as an "0". In his own inspection of old gravestones, the writer has found instances where such a mistake could easily occur.

Mr. Kemper finds also that traders and prospectors were visiting the South Branch by 1717. It is known that about 1725 John Vanmeter accompanied a party of Delawares to their defeat near Franklin by the Catawbas. This is not saying that the trip was his first, or that he was the only trader of that early period to visit the South Branch.

John Howard and his son, if the story concerning them be correct, were more venturesome than Vanmeter. They traveled as far as the Mississippi, where they were captured by the French and taken to Europe. After their release they gave to Lord Fairfax a glowing account of their travels, and his interest in the western limit of his grant was greatly stimulated.

After this long but rather necessary discussion, we come to Winchester itself.

To the prospectors of the first quarter of the eighteenth century, the Shenandoah was an inviting country, and there were no resident Indians except the little band at the Shawnee Spring. Moreover, the red men were quite willing that the whites come in. They noticed that the palefaced immigrants were from Pennsylvania, and they assumed that the relations between the races would be the same as within the Quaker colony. William Penn's successful and commonsense handling of the race question was fresh in their minds. The Scotch-Irish, who had an inveterate propensity for stirring up trouble with the redskins, were not yet in political control of Pennsylvania. When that time arrived, the Indian found the Pennsylvanian no better than the detested "Long Knife," as he learned to call the Virginian in the French and Indian war.

There was strong reason for white people to come to the Lower Valley, and they came. The members of the advance guard did not trouble themselves with legal formalities when it came to choosing a plot of ground. They settled where they pleased. And why not? The Valley was practically a vacant land, the Indians did not object, and no private individual had asserted ownership. If the newcomer were called upon to defend possession, that was a question for the future. Suficient for the present was the good thereof.

And yet the settlers were not swift in pushing southward from the Potomac. For a while, the incoming wave was a very thin stream, and near the river the lands seemed more attractive than high up on the Opequon.

The early comers were not exclusively Scotch-Irish and Germans from Pennsylvania. There was also an English element from the east of Virginia, but it was less conspicuous in the present Frederick area than in the adjoining county of Clarke.

According to Mr. Kemper, the first attempt to acquire land in the Shenandoah, by way of legal procedure, was by William Russell and Larkin Chew, the date of their claim being October 18, 1728. On a tree near Winchester William Beverley found the legend, "R C 1729," the letters being the initials of Robert Carter, a land prospector. Immediately south of the Shawnee village was Abraham Hollingsworth's survey of 583 acres, dated November 23,

1732. But by a tradition in the family, he had already been living here several years as a squatter. Yost Hite located at Bartonville in the fall of 1731, and according to Foote, his was the first regular settlement in the neighborhood. But according to Hawkes, the first cabin in the valley of the Opequon was built near Bunker Hill in 1726 by Morgan ap Morgan.

By tradition the first white men's houses within the corporate limits of Winchester were built in 1732. According to a Mrs. Sperry, said to have been born in 1716, there were in 1738 two cabins occupied by Germans. It has been ascertained that they were on opposite sides of Town Run and near the line of Main Street, the one to the southwest standing in the rear of the residence of George W. Kurtz. But old people often have a weak grasp on dates. There is at least an even chance that what is placed at 1738 properly belongs to a date earlier by several years. The very fact that there had been an Indian village at Shawnee Spring since about 1690 almost proves the presence before 1732, and probably before the arrival of Hollingsworth, of at least one or two white traders.

In 1729, Governor Gooch reports that Virginians are eager to take up land "among the Great Western Mountains." By 1734, families to the number of fifty-four had located in this vicinity. The Act of Assembly creating Frederick county in 1738 relates that, "great numbers of people have settled themselves of late on the northwest side of the Blue Ridge." Not all this influx could have been subsequent to 1732, or even 1729. The amount of time is insufficient. All in all, the presumption is strong that by 1724 there were one or more white people within the present limits of Winchester. It is improbable that no one came earlier than 1732.

Why should a town grow up so near the western edge of the Lower Valley, rather than near the center? To this question there are three interrelated answers; the Indian village, the Indian road, and the several copious springs. As to the Shawnee Spring, near which the Indian village lay, it is a local proverb that "one who drinks of the water will be seen to return." The natives showed good judgment in selecting sites for their villages. It has often been remarked that where the Mound Builders of the Mississippi Valley had a village, there is now in most instances a city or town of the white people.

Crossing the Potomac at Williams Ferry—now Williamsport —and pursuing as far as Harrisonburg a route almost identical with the Valley Turnpike, was a war trail of the red men. It was a through line of travel between North and South. An aboriginal path of this kind was broad enough for a wagon, and therefore answered every purpose of the white settler. Very naturally he never thought of making a road when there was already one in existence, and that served his purpose sufficiently well. So in the spring of 1745 what was called the "Indian Road" was accepted as a public highway by county court authority. Just south of the Shawnee village was a fork, the left-hand branch leading to the Luray valley, and giving an additional reason why the white man should build a town here. A further reason attaches itself to the strong and never-failing springs. To the pathfinder, these suggested camping spots and mill-sites. To the town builder, they suggested a dependable supply of water for all purposes.

In a state of nature, the town-site was less attractive than now, and is unfavorably commented upon by early visitors. Town Run was bordered by swampy ground and was called a marsh. And since the business quarter lies in a basin, the streets used to be continuous mudholes in wet weather. The progressive levelling of the basin and the installation of drainage courses have quite effectually remedied the early disadvantage.

For several years the immediate locality and the surrounding district bore the name Opequon. After the building of the courthouse, the village around it was commonly called Frederick's Town. But as a loyal son of his native city, James Wood selected the name Winchester. It is used in the Act of Assembly designating the town, and it speedily won general acceptance.

Winchester is one of the oldest and most historic cities of England. It dates back to the period of the Roman occupation, as would otherwise be evident from the early form of its name—Winton-ceaster—meaning "Winton Camp." "Chester" and "cester" are forms of the Latin word "castra," the Roman word for camp. Like its namesake, it lies in a basin, and the chalk hills by which it is engirdled take the place of the limestone heights around the Virginian Winchester. A farther correspondence appears in the six radiating highways. The city is famous as an educational center, and it has a public library. It is also noted for its magnificent cathedral of Norman architecture, 556 feet long, and the longest building of its kind in England.

The English Winchester is 66 miles from London and 12 from Southampton, the nearest seaport. The area is three square miles, and the present population is a little more than 20,000. But when the Virginian Winchester became a town, there were in all England only five cities of more than 6000 inhabitants. It is altogether probable, therefore, that in the days of the Saxon kings it was much smaller than is now its first namesake in North America.

Winchester is of particular interest as the capital of Alfred the Great, by common consent the wisest and best of the long line of English kings. Under Norman rule it was a place of great commercial importance, and for many years was the seat of a large woolen industry. The nearness of London, which supplanted it as the capital of England, has stood in the way of its becoming a large city.

In 1889, upon the dedication of a statue of Alfred the Great at Winchester, England, the mayor and aldermen of the Virginian Winchester were invited to be present. The oration of the day was by Lord Roseberry. And after the World War the English Winchester presented its first American namesake with the flag which is to be seen in the rotunda of the Handley Library.

V

WINCHESTER AS A FRONTIER TOWN

A Site in the Forest — Early Comers — The Founder and His Difficulties — Act of 1752 — James Wood — Fairs — Taverns — Houses — People — Appearance of Town — Pioneer Annals — Money and Values

> And whereas it is now judged necessary that a fort should be immediately erected in the town of Winchester, in the county of Frederick, for the protection of the adjacent inhabitants from the barbarities daily committed by the French and their Indian allies. — Act of General Assembly of Virginia of March, 1756.

Although the white pathfinder generally found a prairie in the lowlands of the Shenandoah, we have good evidence that Winchester was built in a forest, the marshy ground along the course of Town Run being probably an exception. Not even the Shawnee Spring could have induced a clan of Indians to place a village near it, had the country around been deforested. Where there was no wood, the red man had no fuel. He built a new village on another site, as soon as it became impossible to collect a sufficient supply of fallen limbs and other down timber from within a convenient radius. One of the other proofs is the court order to "cut a roadway through the dense forests to the grass land both to the north and the south."

The treaty negotiated by Spotswood with the natives did not exclude the latter from the Shenandoah, although it forbade their going east of the Blue Ridge. On the other hand it did not forbid the whites from settling west of the same mountains.

When Yost Hite settled above Winchester in the fall of 1731, he came with sixteen families. Within four years arose the Opequon settlement of Presbyterian families, their church at Kernstown being the nucleus. Quite as early, if not earlier, appeared a large immigration of Friends, whose center was the Hopewell church, five miles north of Winchester. When John Ross was married to Lydia Hollingsworth, October 1, 1735, there were 47 witnesses. We are told that by this time 54 families had located within a few miles of the Shawnee Spring. After it had once fairly begun, the settlement of the Lower Valley was rapid. In

1744 there were 1283 tithables in Frederick, indicating a population of rather more than 5000. Yet it must be remembered that the county then ran about 70 miles up the Valley from the Potomac, and that for ten years people had been settling on the South Branch.

As we have already pointed out, the first white man's house within the corporate lines of Winchester was built at some unascertainable date prior to 1732. Six years later the county of Frederick was defined, although its organization was to await the appearance of a larger population. In the Tidewater, which was dominated by the plantation interest, a county seat seldom meant anything more than a courthouse, a jail, a tavern, and one or two private homes. As late as 1759, the English traveler Burnaby remarks that half of the towns authorized by the legislature had only four or five houses each.

But the Piedmont belt of Virginia and the country west of the Blue Ridge were from the first a domain of small or relatively small farms. Throughout this section, a county seat has always meant a town. And when James Wood placed his homestead so near the Shawnee Spring, we may assume that it was because he saw that the locality offered more promise than any other of becoming the county seat. The reasons therefor are stated in the preceding chapter.

In laying off lots and thus starting a town, Wood came at once against the Fairfax monopoly and had to move with care. Lord Fairfax had not yet returned permanently to America, but the nature of his pretensions was understood. So when Wood asked the permission of the court to set aside a portion of his land for the use of the new county, March 9, 1744, he said his title was not complete. In accordance with a legal practice of the time, the county court required Wood to execute a bond of 1000 pounds, the bond making specific mention of the Fairfax claim.

It is not necessary to quote the preamble to the bond, which contains the names of the justices of Frederick; namely, Morgan Morgan, Thomas Chester, David Vance, Andrew Campbell, Marquis Calmes, Thomas Rutherford, Lewis Neill, William McMachen, Meredith Helms, George Hoge, and John White. The essential portion of the instrument reads thus:

"The condition of the above obligation is such that whereas the above bound James Wood, having laid off from the tract of land on which he now dwells at Opequon, in the county aforesaid, 26 lots of land containing one-half an acre each, together with two streets running through the said lots, each of the breadth of 33 feet, as will more plainly appear by a plan thereof now in the possession of the said Morgan Morgan, Marquis Calmes, and William McMachen. And whereas the said James Wood, for divers good causes and considerations him thereunto moving, but more especially for and in consideration of the sum of five shillings to him in hand paid, the receipt whereof he doth here acknowledge, hath bargained and sold, on the conditions hereafter mentioned, all his right, title, interest, property, and claim, to 22 of the said lots to the aforesaid Morgan Morgan, &c, his Majestie's Justices of the said county for the time being, and their successors, to be disposed of by them for the use of the said county as they shall judge most proper, the said lots being numbered in the beforementioned plan as follows, viz: Nos. 1, 2, 3, 6, 7, 8, 9, 10, 11, 12, 14, 15, 16, 17, 19, 20, 21, 22, 23, 24, 25, and 26, on the following conditions, viz: that they, the said Justices, or their assigns, shall, within two years from the day of the sale of the said lots, build or cause to be built on each lot, one house, either framed work or squared logs, dovetailed, at least of the dimensions of 20 feet by 16, and in case any person in possession of a lot or lots fail to build, within the time limited, the property of the said lot or lots to return to the said James Wood, his heirs or assigns. And whereas the said James Wood, not having yet obtained a patent for the said land, can only give bond to warrant and defend the property of the said lots to the said Justices, their successors or assigns. Now if the said James Wood, his heirs, executors, and administrators, shall from time to time, at all times hereafter, maintain, protect, and defend the said Justices, their successors or assigns, in the peaceable and quiet possession of the beforementioned lots of land from all persons whatsoever, Thomas Lord Fairfax, his heirs, or any other person claiming under him or them only excepted. And further, if the said James Wood, his heirs, etc., shall hereafter obtain either from His Majesty by patent, or from the said Thomas Lord Fairfax or his heirs, a better title to the land of the said James Wood, his heirs, etc., shall within one year, if required, make such other title for the said lots to the said Justices or their successors as their counsel learned in the law shall advise, so far forth as his own title shall extend. Now if the said James Wood, his heirs, executors, and administrators, shall well and truly perform all and singular the above conditions, then this obligation to be void, otherwise to be and remain in full force and virtue.

J. Wood.

Sealed and delivered in the presence of
Wm Jolliffe
Jno. Newport
Thos. Postgate

Recorded March 10, 1743."

By the New Style calendar, the above date is March 21, 1744.

In his attitude toward the exactions of the proprietor of the Northern Neck, Wood did not take the same view as Hite. The latter gave rein to his indignation and brought suit. The former preferred to bend, rather than run the possibility of being broken, and he chose to pay the quitrent demanded by Fairfax. It is clear that the men who purchased from him accepted the encumbrance under protest. Several put on record their resentment at coming under what they styled a "yoke." But Wood carried his point. Litigation, with its risk of dispossession, was avoided, although there was a flow of coin to the purse of the lord of Greenway Court.

It was the common practice in colonial Virginia, and it even survived the Revolution, for the man who laid out a town to require the payment every year of a quitrent on the lots sold by him. The settlers at Winchester undoubtedly expected to have to pay a quitrent. Their grievance was not the quitrent in itself, but that Fairfax controlled the situation and required an annual payment which they felt to be unreasonably high. There was, nevertheless, great restiveness under the quitrent system. The quitrent was not only regarded as a cloud on the title, but it was in the nature of a tax, and taxes are never popular. After the colonies became independent, the pressure was such that in Virginia the necessity of paying quitrent was abolished in 1785 by a statute law. Even a dissenting congregation at Winchester might be dispossessed of its church-lot if the quitrent were more than thirty days in arrears. At very nearly the same time, Colonel William Byrd, the founder of Richmond, was giving away a lot to any comer who would build on it a house at least sixteen feet by twenty-four. This liberality was not likely to cause him loss, because the unsold lots would rise in value.

According to tradition, Fairfax wished the county seat at Stephensburg, now Stephens City, probably because it would be nearer to Greenway Court and more convenient to reach. The tradition goes on to point out that Wood was equal to the occasion. He needed one more vote among the justices, in order to secure the seat of local government for Winchester. He knew who might be won over, and with the instincts of the successful politician and business man, he approached the balance of power with a flowing bowl. Under the inspiration of the toddy, the magistrate saw a great light and followed whither it led. But the lord of Greenway Court was so chagrined that he would not speak to this man afterward.

Wood first laid off 26 half-acre lots, with two streets, 33 feet wide, running through them. He conveyed these lots to the county, and after a usage of the time, the county sold the lots to individual purchasers. But because of the delay in getting a complete title, the town was not chartered until 1752. When this time came, Fairfax had added 54 lots of his own, making a total of 80. This fact explains the wording of the charter, wherein it defers to the approval of Fairfax in the matter of lots and streets. The Act reads as follows:

1. Whereas it has been represented to this General Assembly that James Wood, gentleman, did survey and lay out a parcel of land, at the Court House in Frederick County, in twenty-six lots of half an acre each, with streets for a town, by the name of Winchester, and made sale of the said lots to divers persons, who have since settled and built, and continue building and settling thereon; but because the same was not laid off, and erected into a town, by Act of Assembly, the freeholders and inhabitants thereof will not be entitled to the like privileges, enjoyed by the freeholders and inhabitants of other towns in this Colony:

2. Be it enacted by the Lieutenant Governor, Council, and Burgesses, of this present General Assembly, and it is hereby enacted, by the authority of the same, That the parcel of land lately claimed by the said James Wood, lying and being in the county of Frederick aforesaid, together with fifty-four other lots of half an acre each, twenty-four thereof to be laid off in one or two streets on the East side of the former lots, the street or streets to run parallel with the street already laid off, and the remaining thirty lots to be laid off at the North end of the aforesaid twenty-six, with a commodious street or streets, in such manner as the proprietor thereof, the Right Honorable Thomas Lord Fairfax shall think fit be, And is hereby constituted, appointed, erected, and established, a town, in the manner already laid out, to be called and retain the name of Winchester, and that the freeholders of the said town, shall, for ever hereafter, enjoy the same privileges, which the freeholders of other towns, erected by Act of Assembly, enjoy.

3. And whereas allowing fairs to be kept, in the said town of Winchester, will be of great benefit to the inhabitants of the said parts, and greatly increase the trade of that town; Be it therefore

enacted, by the Authority aforesaid, That for the future two fairs shall and may be annually kept and held in said town of Winchester on the third Wednesday in June, and the third Wednesday in October in every year, and to continue for the space of two days, for the sale and vending all manner of cattle, victuals, provisions, goods, wares, and merchandizes, whatsoever; on which fair days, and two days next before, and two days next after, the said fairs, all persons coming to, being at, or going from same, together with their cattle, goods, wares, and merchandizes, shall be exempted, and privileged, from all arrests, attachments, and executions, whatsoever, except for capital offences, breaches of the peace, or for any controversies, suits, or quarrels, that may arise and happen during the said time, in which process may be immediately issued, and proceedings had, in the same manner as if this act had never been made, any thing hereinbefore contained, or any law, custom, or usage, to the contrary thereof, in any wise, notwithstanding.

4. Provided always, That nothing herein contained, shall be construed, deemed or taken, to derogate from, alter, or infringe, the royal power and prerogative of his Majesty, his heirs and successors, of granting to any person or persons, body politic and corporate, the privileges of holding fairs, or markets, in any such manner as he or they, by his or their royal letters patent, or by his or their instructions, to the Governor, or Commander-in-Chief of this domain, for the time being, shall think fit.

In the original Winchester were therefore 80 lots. In the survey for Fairfax made December 10, 1753, there appear these streets and lanes: Fairfax Road, Cumberland Road, Potomack Road, Mount (Mountain?) Road, Wappacomo Road, Bow Lane, Common Lane, and Woodstock Lane. The lanes were 20 feet wide. With the exception of Fairfax Road—30 feet across—the "roads" were 33 feet wide. This was perhaps to make them conform to the streets already laid off by Wood.

Attached to each in-lot (house-lot) was an out-lot of three to five acres for gardening and pasturage purposes. As fast as the out-lots passed into private ownership, they were fenced. The ones unsold were commons, and the boys had unlimited use of them for their sports. Fort Loudoun was built on one of these commons. Another, in the south of town, was long uninclosed and was called Sheep Hill. It was ten acres in extent, and was used for 120 years as a muster ground and place for public executions.

Every in-lot was sold under the condition that the buyer should erect within two years a house of squared, dovetailed logs, at least sixteen by twenty feet on the ground. That this stipulation was rapidly complied with appears in the number of houses found here by the Moravian missionaries of 1753, and in the court mention in 1748 of houses recently built at the south end of Main street. But since no out-lot might be built upon, the natural effect of this restriction was to limit the growth of the town.

The first enlargement of Winchester was in September, 1758, when Wood received legislative permission to add 106 acres on the west side. This annex has always been known as "Wood's Addition." Fairfax's Addition followed only five months later. The master of Greenway Court was then permitted by the Assembly to add 173 lots on the east. In October, 1782, an out-lot belonging to Thomas Edmondson was included in the town and laid off into half-acre lots. There seems to have been no further enlargement of Winchester until 1905. In 1921 the corporate limits were further extended, and now include an area of about 2240 acres.

The early lot-owners, so far as their names have been recovered from the faded list in the archives of Virginia, are these, the town-lot number following the name:

Bostin, Martin	71	Lemon, ———	2
Bratten, Jesse	69	Lemon, James	39
Brinker, Henry	7	McCloun, Thomas	67
Bruce, George	23	McDonald, Alexander	3
Bush, ———	66	McGuire, Edward	61
Caldwell, ———	22	Martin, Thomas Bryan	18, 26
Calmes, Marquis	16	Mercer, George	43
Carlyle, John	74	Neill, Lewis	17
Castleman, Ludovick	49	Otto, Tobias	58
Cochran, William	14, 57	Palb, Merder	41
Cocks, William	8	Parkins, ———	13
Craigen, Robert	68	Perkins, Isaac	15
Earle, Samuel	33	Pilcher, James	20
Feif, James	54	Sperry, Peter	80
Fritley, Andrew	47	Stephens, Daniel	46
Greenfield, John	60, 76	Stephens, Lewis	51, 52, 53
Hambert, Godfrey	70	Steward, John	48, 72
Harrow, John	75	Washington, George	77
Hite, John	30, 31	Weitreit, ———	6
Hope, ———	10	Wetsell, Christopher	79
Howard, John	25	Wood, ———	4, 5
Jones, John	21, 24	Woods, Thomas	9

Not all these persons were residents of Winchester, and perhaps several were not residents of Frederick. Several of the names are German, but if the earliest comers were of that nationality, as has been affirmed, they were soon outnumbered by immigrants from the British Isles. One wonders whether the John Howard were identical with the man of that name whose story of adventure had such an appeal to Fairfax. And one looks in vain for the two Germans, Thomas Mehrlin and John Salling, who are said by Klauprecht to have left their homes in Winchester in 1740 to prospect lands to the southward. Salling, who relocated at the head of Balcony Falls in Rockbridge county, had an interesting captivity among the Indians, who took him as far as the lower Mississippi. John Marlin, who may have had a middle name Thomas, as Salling had a middle name Peter, appears again as a trapper and trader in Augusta county. But there is some ground for doubting whether Salling ever lived in this town.

The act incorporating Winchester authorized the holding of fairs in the months of June and October. The fair opened on the third Wednesday in these months and continued two days. So important was the event that any person in attendance was exempt from arrest or attachment; not only during the fair itself, but for two days before and two days after, so that the exemption might cover the time spent in coming and going. For many years these fairs were a regular feature in the life of Winchester and went very far to make this town a commercial center.

But the modern fair was as unknown to the pioneers of two hundred years ago as their fair is unknown to us. A vestige of it lingers in the "no profit" or "special bargain" day that is occasionally advertised by the business houses. The fair of the eighteenth century was above all else a time for buying and selling and for transacting other business. Merchants and pedlers came from the distant seaports stocked with wares to sell to the country people who were sure to flock to town, either to make purchases or to see and be seen. For centuries the fair was a very necessary institution in the European countries, and it has been banished—unless in Russia—only by the coming of easy and rapid transportation. When considered apart from its business features, the fair of colonial America was much like Independence or Decoration Day, or the day that brings a circus to town. A custom of the time was the "fairing," by which was meant the present of finery which the young man was privileged, by general consent, to give to the girl who interested him, even though she might never have seen him before.

In the eighteenth century the tavern was called an "ordinary," and if we could see for ourselves the tavern of colonial Virginia, we would probably consider it very ordinary. There is some uncertainty as to who was the first tavern-keeper in Winchester. Duncan O'Gullion, who seems to have lived in the town, was granted license by the court of Frederick June 8, 1744. Since William Hoge, Jr. was granted the first ordinary license in Frederick, Mr. Cartmell in his history undoubtedly means that the hostelry of O'Gullion was the first in Winchester. It will be noticed that this pioneer innkeeper had a Scotch forename and an Irish surname. In refusing to take the oath of allegiance to the Hanoverian kings of England, he shared a feeling that prevailed among the Catholic Irish and the Protestant Highlanders. O'Gullion constructed for 80 pounds ($267) the first jail in Frederick, and it is an irony on the performance that he was imprisoned in it for debt.

Henry Heath, John Stuart, and Peter Wilt were given license December 2, 1755 to keep taverns in Winchester, and in 1757 permits were issued to Andrew Mealey and Jacob Sower. Thus is confirmed the statement that after the French and Indian war had begun there were five or six taverns here. But it is not to be taken for granted that until 1755 there was only one. The earliest entries in the order-book do not tell us where the applicant lived. Heath's inn was on Braddock Street, on the lot now occupied by the Methodist Episcopal Church, South, and it was patronized by Washington while stationed in Winchester on military duty. Across the street were the camp and drill grounds of the regiment quartered in the town, and we need seek no other reason for Washington's choice of this tavern.

With respect to the accommodations in the country homes, the following quotation from Washington's journal of 1748 is of interest:

"I have not slept above three or four nights in a bed; but after walking a good deal all day, I have lain down before the fire upon a little hay, straw, fodder, or a bear's-skin, whichever was to be had, with man, wife, and children, like dogs and cats, and happy is he who gets the berth nearest the fire. Nothing would make it pass off tolerably but a good reward. A doubloon is my constant gain every day that the weather will permit my going out, and sometimes six pistoles. The coldness of the weather will not allow of my making a long stay, as the lodging is rather cold for the time of year. I have never had my clothes off, but have lain and slept in them, except the few nights I have been in Fredericktown (Winchester)."

Until after 1800, the rates which the innkeeper might charge for meals, lodging, stablage, and liquors were minutely regulated by the county court, and had to be posted on the wall of the public room. Thus the charge in 1744 for a warm meal was sixpence (8 cents), for a cold meal fourpence (5 cents), and lodging threepence (4 cents). The charge for stablage, fodder, or pasturage over night, or a gallon of corn or oats was fourpence. The meal was called a "diet," and a distinction in price was made between dinner and other meals, especially breakfast; also between warm and cold meals. The "servant's diet" was at a lower charge than the master's. In the matter of lodging the court stipulated that the sheets should be clean, and it sometimes authorized the innkeeper to charge more for sleeping on a feather bed than on a straw tick. If two guests were put into the same bed, the price to each was reduced, and if three occupied the bed, it was sometimes if not always the case that the landlord might not charge anything at all.

Every tavern kept rum, brandy, whisky, wine, beer, and cider, and the use of these was almost universal. At the present day it is repeatedly alleged that although there was much drinking in the "good old times," there was little drunkenness. This delusion is utterly overthrown by the facts. There is overwhelming evidence that gross intoxication was exceedingly prevalent. The drinking places in Winchester were a constant annoyance to Washington, but his complaints that they ignored his orders in serving liquors to his men were summarily dismissed by a court that itself ignored his military title and speaks of him as "George Washington, Esq."

Log was the building material almost universally used on the frontier, but the abundance of limestone easily induced the building of many stone houses, since, in their homelands, the immigrants had been accustomed to living in stone cottages. These stone houses were somewhat rudely built, but as a rule, all the homes were comfortable in size. It is further to be noted that although Winchester was at this time a pioneer town, it never possessed the pioneer characteristics in full measure and was not long in discarding them. This was because the nearest seaport is only seventy miles away. So long as they were within convenient distance of navigable water, the more substantial settlers of America never accepted the log cabin as more than a passing phase of life in a new country.

During the short period covered by the present chapter, the only attempt at a description of Winchester, of which we have any knowledge, is the brief entry in a journal by two Moravian missionaries. On the night of October 17, 1753 (O. S.) their lodging place was 12 miles north on the road from Pennsylvania. Traveling afoot, they arrived in "Frederickstown" at noon after having found no water for seven miles. The journal mentions the town as containing about 60 houses, rather poorly built. Probably the two stores that were here in 1756 were already in existence. At the Hollingsworth mill the missionaries bought some bread and corn.

Since this book does not assume to be a history of Frederick county, it is foreign to its purpose to give general mention to the facts of county organization or county annals. Winchester, the oldest county seat in the Appalachians, was merely a point where population had thickened up in a small degree. Of the thirteen members of the first county court, not one, so far as we can tell, lived in the town. James Wood, the county clerk, was the only resident official excepting the jailor. It is a fair guess that Thomas Rutherford, the first sheriff, was his brother-in-law. For a while, Gabriel Jones was king's (prosecuting) attorney, but he served Augusta in the same capacity, and his home was near Port Republic.

However, a few extracts from the court proceedings of 1743-1756 are pertinent to the scope of this book and will rather forcibly illustrate the character of the times.

In 1754 the tithables of Winchester and its vicinity were ordered to keep up the road to Greenway Court.

Edward Doyle was ordered to Williamsburg to stand trial for biting off a part of the nose of Joseph King, and James Knapp was sent to the same tribunal to be tried for counterfeiting.

For taking a prisoner to Williamsburg, the capital, about 1757, James Keith was allowed 25 shillings ($4.17).

For abusing his wife, Michael Kelly was to be given fifteen lashes.

That Washington's soldiers were rougher than those of 1861 would appear from the statement that Mary Crossley was "wounded and evilly treated by a soldier of the Virginia Regiment and in fear of her life."

In the May court of 1758, John Stewart, one of the tavern-keepers of Winchester, was presented for card playing. There were nine presentments for swearing and four for lewdness. The illegal selling of liquor sometimes brought men before the same tribunal.

In 1758 bounty was paid on 180 old wolves and 50 cubs, at the rate of 100 pounds of tobacco for the former and 50 for the latter.

When the orphan children, Henry and Mary Waughdy, were bound out, the former was to learn shoemaking and to be taught to "read, write, and cast accounts." The latter was to be taught to read, knit, sew, and spin. When Mary Roberts was bound out to William Chapline, he was to teach her to read the Bible, and when of age, to give her freedom dues, wearing apparel, and a two-year old mare.

For running away, a servant of Henry Heath was to serve four months extra time, or pay 200 pounds of tobacco as the cost of recapture.

For bearing an illegitimate child, the churchwardens ordered the sheriff to apply 25 lashes to the bare back of Elizabeth King. This punishment was because of an inability to pay a fine. For the same offense, Mary Wolf was to pay either 500 pounds of tobacco or 50 shillings in specie, in addition to the costs. Also for the same offense, Mary Flood, an indentured servant, was to serve one year extra time. This signifies that her master was not adjudged to be the father of her child. When such was the case, the servant was not thus detained. In spite of the severity authorized by the law, bastardy was of frequent occurrence in colonial America, and infanticide is occasionally mentioned.

Values were reckoned in pounds, shillings, and pence, but these terms were not equivalent to what was true in England. There had been a depreciation in all the colonies, though in unequal degree, and this had driven English money from circulation. A shilling, for example, is never to be understood as an English shilling, unless it is explicitly mentioned as a shilling stirling. The hard money used in America was of Spanish, French, and Portuguese coinage, and came here through the trade with the West Indies. This is why there is mention of the doubloon, the joe (johannes), the loodore (louis d' or), the pistole, and the pistareen, worth, respectively, $7.84, $13.71, $3.96, $3.92, and $19\frac{1}{2}$ cents. Excepting the last named, these were gold coins. Aside from the pistareen, the silver in common circulation was the "piece of eight' and its subdivisions. The Spanish-American dollar was so called because equivalent to eight reals, the real having the same value as the Virginia ninepence. The dollar was also equivalent to six shillings. In fact, the readiness with which this foreign dollar subdivided into terms of colonial currency was the compelling reason that made it the basis of the subsequent Federal currency. It also gave Jefferson a coveted opportunity to have a decimal division of the dollar legalized, and thus cause the cumbrous English monetary notation to be disenthroned. Yet so strong is the force of usage, that until the war of 1861 the older people constantly spoke of the shilling, the ninepence, the sixpence, etc., although no coins of these names were in use in the United States. Nearly as recently as that event, the real and half-real circulated freely under the names of the "levy" and the "fip." They ceased to be legal tender only in consequence of a law against them.

The larger foreign coins were reckoned by weight, and moneyscales were a necessity to any prosperous man. The process of computing their values in Virginia currency must have been at times a little tedious. In 1776, Mr. Fithian describes the collection after two sermons at Stephensburg as, "34 pieces of silver in cut money, quarters of dollars, pistareens, and half-bits," the whole, by the author's computation, being $6.75.

The depreciation from the British standard was least in Virginia and New England and greatest in New York. In our money, the Virginia pound was $3.33, the shilling 16 2-3 cents, and the penny 1 7-18 cents. In 1752 we find the Frederick court entering an order that Maryland money shall be rated the same as Pennsylvania money.

Until 1794 tobacco was legal tender in Virginia. Tobacco certificates did not need to be indorsed, and they passed from hand to hand like banknotes at the present time. After the Revolution, five pounds of the weed had the money value of one shilling in currency, and 100 pounds were equivalent to one pound in currency. But in the period covered by this chapter, the ratio of tobacco to specie was much lower.

Until the French and Indian war, paper money of colonial issue did not appear in Virginia, nor was there any coinage of copper coins. And as the bank had not arrived, there were no checks.

It is very interesting to compare the prices of a former time with those of the present. An invaluable sidelight is thus thrown on economic conditions. In colonial Frederick the prices set upon land, labor, and livestock seem absurdly low. But the purchasing power of the dollar was several times greater than in our day. In a new country, it is expected that low values will attach to land and domestic animals, and yet neither was as cheap as will at first sight appear. The monopolizing of choice land all along the frontier had very much to do with pushing people westward at a speed more rapid than was desirable. Sugar, molasses, and condiments all came from the West and East Indies, and were luxuries. Imported cloth was not woven in great factories, for steam power had not been introduced. The only machines known, even in England, were hand machines, except to the small degree in which waterpower was in use.

The prices below are taken from the account books of Colonel James Wood. Since the denominations of the colonial money tell a story of their own, we use them in the list, placing the modern equivalents in a column by themselves.

Sugar, double-refined, per pound		1s 6d	$0.25
Sugar, single-refined, per pound		1s 3d	.21
Tea, per pound		7s	1.17
Chocolate, per pound		1s 4d	.22
Pepper, per pound		2s	.33
Raisins, per pound		9d	.12½
Allspice, per pound		1s 4d	.22
Muscovado (brown sugar), per pound		6d	.08
Butter, per pound		3 3-4d	.05
Beef, per pound		2d	.03
Pork, per pound		1 1-2d	.02
Cheese, per pound		6d	.08
Mutton, per pound		1 1-2d	.02
Gunpowder, per pound	3s	3d	.54
Writing paper, per quire	4s	7d	.76
Shoes	14s		2.33
Canvas, per yard	4s		.67
Tablecloth	4p 15s	5 1-4d	15.90
Handkerchief	1s	3d	.21
Wig	1p 6s		4.33
Pumps	7s	6d	1.25
Weaving linsey, per yard	1s	3d	.21
Thread, per ounce	1s	3d	.21
Ribbon, per yard	1s	3d	.21
Cambric, per yard	9s		1.50
"souling" shoes	2s		.33
1000 shingles	1p 7s	6d	4.91
8 sash lights for schoolhouse	5s		.83
Mauling 1000 rails	1p		3.33
Ditching, per rod		6d	.08
Plank, per 100 feet	7s	6d	1.25
Door	8s		1.33
Labor, per day	1s	6d	.25

Plastering and whitewashing, per yard		1 7-12d	.02¼
Well bucket	2s	3d	.37½
Carpenter, per day	2s	6d	.42
Chair	2s	3d	.37½
Reaping grain, per day	1s	3d	.22
Liquor for a funeral	2p 1s	1 1-2d	6.85
Whiskey, per quart	1s	3d	.22
Peach brandy, per gallon	1s	5 1-4d	.24
Lead, per pound		6d	.08
Corn, per barrel	7s	6d	1.25
Wheat, per bushel	2s	7 1-2d	.43
Oats, per bushel	1s	1 1-2d	.19
Rye, per bushel	2s		.33
Iron, per pound		3 3-4d	.06¼
Steel, per pound	1s	1 1-2d	.20
Hops, per pound	1s		.17
Paper of pins		9d	.12½
Bridle	4s		.67
3 "Dyche" spelling books	5s	7 1-2d	.99
Harrow	5s		.83
Coffee pot	10s		1.67
Salt, per bushel	2s		.33
Timothy seed, per bushel	1p 1s	6d	3.58
Boarding invalid five weeks, 1747	1p 5s		4.17
Coffin for same	10s		1.67
Digging grave for same	2s	6d	.41
Coffin for negro	1s	6d	.25
School tuition, per quarter	5s		.83
Town lot	11p		36.33
Board, per month	1p		3.33
Slave man, 1753	42p 18s	9d	143.12
One year's shaving at barber shop	1p		3.33
"Virginia Gazette", one year	1p 10s		5.00
Rent for old courthouse, 1757	4p		13.33
Slave woman, 21 years old, 1747	60p		200.00
Two slave girls, 2 years old and 7 months old, children of above	20p		66.67
Rent of house one year to Jacob Fry, 1751	5p		16.67

From the account-books of Colonel Wood we learn that the marriage license cost one pound, the ordinary license, 15 shillings, and the pedler's license, 10 shillings. In 1750-1751 eight ordinary licenses were given in the county, and in 1754, ten. At the former date, four licenses were given to pedlers. The only two-wheeled "chairs" in Frederick—by which was meant a form of gig—belonged to Lord Fairfax, Colonel Wood, Marquis Calmes, and John Hill. There is mention of a barn 20 by 48 feet, weatherboarded, and supplied with double doors and thrashing floor.

The revenue of the county in 1754 was 95,717 pounds of tobacco, equal to 299 pounds, two shillings, five pence, three farthings, or $997.08.

There would seem to have been considerable illness in the colonel's family, since there is rather frequent mention of alteratives, Peruvian bark, pills, jalap, liniments, and salivating. On an otherwise blank page is a recipe for ink with directions for making it. The ingredients are galls, copperas, gum arabic, alum, salt, and water.

And last, but not least, Colonel Wood, in 1748, speaks of putting up 10 bushels of keeping apples in "ye loft, "and 22 more in "ye hole." If these apples were grown in Frederick, the settlers must have been very prompt in setting out orchards.

Supplementary to the above are these items from a ledger by Charles Smith in 1759:

75 pounds brown sugar	2p	10s	$ 8.33
1 pair woman's stays	3p	10s	11.67
2½ gallons wine	1p	5s	4.17

To give more completeness to the items from Wood's account books, we add some others gleaned from the public records for the years 1744-1750.

Broadcloth coat and breeches	$15.00	Steel trap	1.33
Silk damask waistcoat	6.67	Copper still and appurtenances	66.67
Leather breeches	$ 1.25	Crosscut saw	2.33
Broadcloth, per yard	1.67	50 acres of land	50.00
Calico, per yard	.33	1000 feet boards	62.00
Blue stockings	.33	Linen, per yard	.31
Frying-pan	.41	Horse	12.50
2 sides leather	1.50	Cow	4.17
16 harrow teeth, weighing 24 pounds	2.00	6 calves	5.00
		9 sheep	5.00
Servant man to serve about 2 years more	33.33	10 hogs	5.00
		Washed wool, per pound	.11
Axe	.87	Hemp, per pound	.03
Rifle	8.33	Nails, per pound	.08
Smoothbored gun	2.50	Deerskin in the hair	.50
Grindstone	2.33	Wagon and chain	28.33

Mould for making pewter spoons	1.25	1000 feet redoak plank	5.00
		2 stocks of bees	2.00
Arithmetic	.67	3 acres standing corn	
Man's saddle	4.17	(Oct. 3, O. S.)	7.50
Brass kettle	4.17	8 glass bottles	.33
Money scales	.41		

The items in this final list were taken from inventories, and must necessarily include some second hand articles. We may expect that the prices named were lower than would be the case in the open market. Yet everything seemed to sell at a colonial "vandue." The country was new and therefore it was not well supplied.

Since the age of labor-saving machinery was yet in the future, manufactured goods were relatively dear. One wonders how a pioneer household could afford a tablecloth that cost more than a horse, or a woman's corset of nearly equal value, but one does not wonder why the people of that day were extremely economical in the use of writing paper.

Winchester was incorporated in October, 1779, by an Act of Assembly. The same Act established the offices of mayor, recorder, sergeant, aldermen, and councilmen. It was really the first charter of the town, and though it became a law while the colonies were struggling for independence, it remained in force, with certain minor amendments, for ninety-five years. An Act of 1874 created the city of Winchester, and with subsequent amendments is the existing charter of the city.

Colonel James Wood, the actual founder of this city, was born in Winchester, England, in 1707. According to an unverified family tradition, he was a lieutenant in the British navy. While still a young man he came to Virginia, and in 1734 was appointed a surveyor of land, receiving his credentials, according to a practice of the colonial period, from William and Mary College. At this time, or shortly afterward, he settled in what was then the District of Frederick, and having a quick perception of all that constitutes a good choice of land, he selected a minor grant that includes the heart of the present city of Winchester. As a prospector of public lands, he acquired a number of valuable holdings in "New Virginia." Usually acting in partnership with Robert Green and William Russell, he entered a number of large and choice tracts far up the west side of the Shenandoah Valley and on the South Branch of the Potomac, above the line of the Northern Neck. Wood, who became a colonel of militia, was the first county clerk of Frederick, holding this office until his death, November 6, 1759. He gave the name Glen Burnie to the stone house he built on the western border of Winchester, and which is still in use. This frontier home, with its adjuncts, was doubtless as commodious as many of the mansions in the older communities along the seacoast. Wood's wife was Mary Rutherford, who survived him thirty-nine years. Their children were Elizabeth, James, Mary, John, and Robert, all of whom married. The elder daughter wedded Alexander White, a member of the Continental Congress. The younger daughter married Colonel Matthew Harrison, who became a judge. James Wood, Jr. was an officer in the Revolution and rose to the rank of brigadier general. He was governor of Virginia in 1796-1799.

VI

WAR WITH THE FRENCH AND INDIANS

Indian Visitors — The Braddock Expedition — Washington in Command — Annoyances — Fort Loudoun — Declaration of War — Washington's Election — A Review — The Washingtons.

> I would again urge the necessity of a large and strong fort at this town. It being the center of all the public roads, it will be the sole refuge for the inhabitants upon any alarm — Washington (writing from Winchester, 1756).

Supposing that the policy of William Penn would hold good in the Lower Shenandoah, the Indians did not at first resist the coming of the whites. The only natives actually living here were those of the little village at the Shawnee spring. But war or hunting parties continued to come through by way of the Indian road, and they camped at the springs. The fountain near the house of Joseph Carter, about five miles northeast of Winchester, was a favorite camping ground, the red men sometimes remaining several weeks. At times they are said to have assembled here to the number of 200, but this looks like an exaggeration.

The dusky visitors picked up a serviceable knowledge of English. The Shawnees were exceptionally good linguists, some members of the tribe being able to converse in several languages. Nevertheless, the relations between paleface and redskin were not cordial. The Indian was the soul of hospitality, when entertaining a stranger at his cabin, and thought the white man should reciprocate. The latter often did reciprocate, but unwillingly, and the man of the woods pronounced him a "tight wad." The frontiersman was vexed at the visits he did not ask for nor welcome, and when a party of the "heathen" came along, expecting to have their stomachs filled, he thought he was being eaten out of house and home. He wished the men of the forest would stay away.

At first the Indian thought the white came as a joint occupant, and he could see how this status might be of advantage to both colors. But joint occupation was never in the mind of the immigrant. His numbers increased year by year, and the outcome was to give one more application to the fable of the Arab and his camel.

In America, the camel was the white man and the Arab was the Indian. The native soon came to see that the English-speaking settler, unlike the Frenchman, proposed to have the whole country for his exclusive use. The Indian, being only a "heathen", was expected to go on; and to keep going on, so long as it might suit the white to crowd westward. The Indian retired, step by step, and he was sullen and resentful. If there were any chance to get back at the British-Americans he would use it.

For almost a generation there was peace in the Lower Valley. The region was prospering, and had become comparatively populous. Winchester had grown into a town. So many people had moved west of the Valley that the county of Hampshire was organized in 1753. As originally laid out, the new county comprised all the Northern Neck west of North Mountain, and therefore touched the Alleghany summit at the source of the North Branch of the Potomac. There was a trapping station at Will's Creek, where now is the city of Cumberland, and in its vicinity were several permanent settlers.

"King George's War," closing in 1748, did not affect the Shenandoah in a very appreciable degree, because no French were then nearer than Lake Erie. But in five years another war-cloud was forming. The French had come into the northwest of Pennsylvania, and showed every inclination to extend and strengthen their hold. The tribes were very generally aligning themselves with the French. So the Shawnees on the Scioto sent word to the little band at the Shawnee Spring to join them, and in the spring of 1754 the latter went away very abruptly.

The presence of French on the Alleghany River was construed as a distinct trespass on Virginia soil. The Old Dominion claimed all the interior country west of a line drawn due north from the Fairfax Stone at the source of the North Branch. In looking about for a messenger to carry his letter of protest, Governor Dinwiddie hit upon George Washington, then only twenty-one years of age. The young man came from a prominent Tidewater family, and had an influential friend in the person of Lord Fairfax, for whom he had done much land surveying in the preceding five years. Washington had a very intimate knowledge of the frontier, this fact alone making his appointment very appropriate. Furthermore, he was already in charge of the northernmost of the four military districts into which the colony was divided.

In the period 1748-53, Washington had spent a good deal of time in Winchester and Frederick county. "A valuable acquisition in his forest experience," remarks the Schroeder-Lossing biography, "was his familiar acquaintance with the habits and opinions of the backswoodsmen. He took part with them in their hunting excursions, camped with them in the woods, sat with them in their log cabins, partook of their coarse fare, and formed from his own observations a just estimate of their true character, so that afterward, when they became soldiers of his armies, he thoroughly understood the secret of commanding and directing their best energies. And in his surveying expeditions and in his intercourse with borderers and red men, he enjoyed very favorable opportunities for gaining a knowledge of Indian life in its best and its worst phases. He ascertained that combined with the worst traits of the wild men were some of a far less repugnant nature. A knowledge of their social habits, their opinions, their prejudices, their artifices in war, and the best modes of conciliating and controlling them, or of contending with and overpowering them, he acquired in the very regions where they made their haunts."

The events of the dangerous winter journey to Venango, and the attempt the following year with a very inadequate force to drive the French from the Monongahela are outside the scope of the present volume. They are familiar to the reader of any school history of the United States. We therefore dismiss the topic with the mention that the prisoners of the party under Jumonville were brought to Winchester and here released; also, that nine of Washington's companions for the perilous trip to Venango were gathered in at Winchester.

It being necessary to make a stronger effort to expel the French from their vantage ground, the task was assigned to General Edward Braddock, a veteran of the wars in Europe. It was assumed in America that this officer was capable as well as experienced. But Braddock had certain English traits in extreme form. Fairfax, who had known him in England, told Washington the new leader was a great fool. Convinced that he knew all things military that he needed to know, and full of contempt for all things American, Braddock would listen to no advice. He was totally lacking in adaptability, and would make war as it was made in Europe or not at all.

The march of Braddock's column from the landing at Alexandria began April 20, 1755. The Forty-eighth regiment, under Colonel Dunbar, took the Maryland side of the Potomac, but recrossed the river at Shepherdstown and passed within six miles of Winchester. Six companies of the Forty-fourth regiment, under

Sir Peter Halkett, came direct to this town, reaching it in five days. With this wing were the military supplies and a force of Virginia provincials, the whole army being about 2000 strong.

Why the army was temporarily divided is not explained. Braddock accompanied Dunbar, riding in a chariot, and according to Washington, he spent at least one night in Winchester. It is also stated that Benjamin Franklin was here on business connected with the expedition.

Sargeant, in his history of Cumberland, says the expedition kept south of the Potomac from Winchester because of a new road completed nearly as far as Will's Creek. From that point eleven weeks were consumed in advancing 140 miles. Washington made the sarcastic comment that in building a road 12 feet broad Braddock ordered every ditch to be bridged and every mole-hill to be leveled.

The overthrow of Braddock by a much smaller force of French and Indians who expected only to delay him a while, need not here be retold. Led by Dunbar, the boasted invincibles made a tumultuous flight to Philadelphia, leaving the frontier to defend itself as best it could. Had Braddock been able to comprehend that war could not be carried on in America in the way that was customary in Europe, and had he shown the resourcefulness of Colonel Bouquet in the war with Pontiac, the American phase of the Seven Years War might have ended in 1756, the frontier of Virginia might have been spared the horrors of the Indian raids of four successive seasons, and the frontier would not have lost by massacre or captivity 3000 of its settlers, to say nothing of the other thousands who sought new homes in the Carolinas because of the corrupt and inefficient government presided over by Dinwiddie. General Braddock did not earn a memorial in the towns and streets that have been named for him.

The British officer of the eighteenth century wore a sash which could be used as a litter in carrying him to the rear in case he were wounded. The silk sash worn by Braddock, and in which he was borne from the scene of his defeat, was woven in 1707. He gave it to Washington, from whom it passed to his nephew, Colonel Lewis, and next to Mrs. Butler, a daughter of Lewis. After the war with Mexico, the relic was presented to General Zachary Taylor, who accepted it with some hesitation, and bequeathed it to his daughter, Mrs. Bettie Dandridge, a resident of Winchester. She refused an offer of $3000 by the Coldstream Guards, in which regiment Braddock had been an officer. The blood-stained sash is now at Mount Vernon.

Since the French at Duquesne were only 200 miles away, Winchester, the metropolis of the Shenandoah, was now in peril. The cowardly flight of Dunbar to the seacoast made it necessary to extemporize a defense for the frontier. This could not be done in a day, and the foe took prompt advantage of the opportunity.

In August—the month following the defeat of Braddock—Washington was made commander-in-chief of the Virginia forces. He was now a colonel, this being the highest rank in military service which the colonial government was competent to bestow. No one else seems to have been thought of. Washington had served on Braddock's staff, and though that general would not listen to words of caution from him, or anyone else, he formed a favorable opinion of the abilities of the young officer.

Winchester was necessarily Washington's headquarters. He was promised a regiment of 700 men, and with it he was expected to defend a frontier 350 miles long.

Next in command were Lieutenant Colonel Adam Stephen and Major Andrew Lewis. The captains under Washington were George Mercer, Thomas Colt, Joshua Lewis, William Peachy, Robert Stewart, William Bronaugh, John Mercer, and David Bell.

But for some time, the regiment existed only on paper. At the outset scarcely any other men were available than the militia of Frederick county. October 10 he arrived at Winchester to take command in person, and the following extracts from a letter written the next day will give the reader some idea of the trying position in which he was now placed.

"I found everything in the greatest hurry and confusion, by the back inhabitants flocking in and those of the town removing out, which I have prevented, so far as it was in my power. I was desirous of proceeding immediately, but was told by Colonel Martin that it was impossible to get above 20 or 25 men, they choosing, as they say, to die with their wives and families. I sent off expresses to hurry the recruits from below (east of the Blue Ridge), and the militia, which Lord Fairfax had ordered out, and hired spies to discover the numbers of the enemy and to encourage the rangers, who, I believe, are more encompassed by fear than by the enemy. I have impressed wagons, and sent them to Conococheague for flour, flints, powder, and trifling quantity of (cartridge) paper, bought at extravagant price... In all things I meet with the greatest opposition. No orders are obeyed, but what a party of soldiers, or my own drawn sword, enforces—to such a pitch has the insolence of these people arrived, by having every point hitherto submitted to them. They threaten to blow out my brains.... I have invited the poor, distressed people (refugees) to lodge their families in some place of security, and to join our parties in scouring the woods in which the enemy lie, and believe some will cheerfully assist.... I see the growing insolence of the soldiers, the indolence and inactivity of the officers.... I recommend to have the inhabitants liable to heavy fines or corporal punishments for entertaining deserters, and a reward for taking them up.... As things now stand, they are not only seduced to run away, but are also harbored."

In a postscript written Sunday, October 12, Washington reports that an express rode into town the night before, saying that Indians were at Isaac Julian's, twelve miles from Winchester, and that the people of that neighborhood were in flight. In the morning another express came in, vastly more terrified than the first. He said the Indians were within four miles, and that he had heard constant firing and shrieks. The commander marched out with 41 men, no more being available, and found the scare to proceed from three drunken, cursing soldiers, who were firing their pistols. The alleged foe were two colored men hunting cattle. Meanwhile, Colonel Fairfax sent for a "noble captain" to report for duty with his company, but the reply was made that he could not come because his corn had to be gathered in.

There had been a raid, however, and about 70 people were missing.

After a tour of inspection extending as far as Fort Dinwiddie on Jackson's River, Washington posted the following notice at Winchester, October 13:

"Whereas, divers timorous persons run through the country, and alarm its inhabitants by false reports of the Indians having attacked and destroyed the country—even Winchester itself—and that they are still proceeding: This is to give notice to all people, that I have great reason to believe that the Indians who committed the late cruelties (though no lower than the South Branch) are returned home, as I have certain accounts that they have not been seen nor heard of these ten days past. And I do advise all my countrymen not to be alarmed on every false report they may hear, as they keep to their homes, and take care of their crops, as I can venture to assure them that in a short time the frontiers will be so well guarded that no mischief can be done, either to them or their plantations, which must of course be destroyed, if they desert them in so shameful a manner."

There were many things to tax the patience of the young commander. The recruiting of his regiment progressed very slowly, ten officers returning with only twenty new men. The dilatoriness of the newly appointed officers in coming to the rendezvous at Winchester made him say that, "if these practices are allowed, we may as well quit altogether." The camp kettles furnished him were of tin and soon wore out.

In the spring of 1756, Washington was eager to lead an expedition into the enemy's country, but without a much larger number of men than there was "a visible prospect of getting," all he could do was to act on the defensive. It was impossible to get wagons or horses until the people were paid what was due them for the vehicles and animals supplied for the Braddock expedition. Some of the stores intended for him were embezzled at Alexandria by the captain of the ship bringing them. The clothing of his men was nearly worn out, and he saw no other way of getting a new supply than by sending North. The clothing that did at length reach him from Tidewater was unfit for use because made by dishonest contractors.

As if to make his annoyances almost unbearable, one Captain Dagworthy was in command at Fort Cumberland. Because he held a British commission, and because his stockade was a "king's fort," Dagworthy heeded Washington's orders no more than he pleased, and was upheld in this by the governor of Maryland. He even claimed that Washington should be subordinate to him. Saying he would resign sooner than serve under this punctilious captain, Washington secured a leave of absence to go to Boston and lay the matter before Governor Shirley, commander-in-chief of the British forces in North America.

Washington was gone two months and was successful in his errand. Shirley, whom he had met in a conference of six governors at Alexandria, received him kindly and issued an order requiring Dagworthy to give obedience to the orders issued by Washington. In Philadelphia he was told by Gist that his name was more talked of in that city than that of any other person in the army, and that there was a general willingness to serve under him. Immediately after his return in April, he wrote as follows to the governor of Virginia:

"The enemy have returned in greater numbers, committed several murders not far from Winchester, and are even so daring as to attack our forts in open day. Unless a stop is put to the depredations of the Indians, the Blue Ridge will soon become our frontier. Orders are no longer regarded in this county. It is impossible to continue on to Fort Cumberland until a body of men can be raised. Five hundred Indians have it more in their power to annoy the inhabitants than ten times their number of regulars. I do not think it unworthy the notice of the legislature to compel the inhabitants (if things thus continue) to live in townships, working at each other's farms by turns, and to drive their cattle into the thickly settled parts of the country. Were this done, they could not be cut off by small parties, and large ones (of the enemy) could not subsist without provisions."

During the whole winter the recruiting officers had secured only 600 men. It may have been for this slow response in a time of urgent need that the legislature favored a chain of forts along the frontier. Washington was vehemently opposed to a passive defense, comparable in its idea to the Great Wall of China. He believed, with the foremost of the world's generals, that the best defense is the offensive. He wanted to carry the war home to the enemy and give them little or no opportunity for stealthy raids which they could plan and execute at their leisure. He insisted that the proposed chain of forts could be effective only if held by "an inconceivable number of men." But because of the wretchedly inadequate support given him, the much desired offensive did not become possible. Yet the Maryland governor who had gone far to make necessary the trip to Boston requested Shirley to appoint Washington second in command, "in case these colonies shall raise a sufficient number of troops for carrying on an expedition or making a diversion to the westward this summer."

By the close of April, 1756, Thomas Slaughter, commander of the forces for Culpeper, marched to Winchester with 300 of the 400 men he was to raise. Thinking these were more than were necessary, Washington retained two companies and they served through the summer. A letter of July 20 says that 117 militiamen marched from Stafford and that others deserted.

In April Washington wrote that, "the people of this town are under dreadful apprehensions of an attack, and all the roads between this and Fort Cumberland are much infested.... Our detachments have sought them diligently, but the cunning and vigilance of Indians in the woods are no more to be conceived than they are to be equaled by our people. They burn plantations, etc. in defiance of the small parties, while they dexterously avoid the larger. Indians are (the) only match for Indians; and without these we shall ever fight upon unequal terms.... I was in high hopes of being by this time at the head of a large party scouring the Alleghany hills. But the timidity of the inhabitants of this county is to be equaled by nothing but their perverseness. Yesterday (April 15) was the time appointed for all to meet who were inclined to join for this desirable end, and only 15 came, some of whom refused to go but upon terms such as must have rendered their services burthensome to the country."

In answer to a complaint by Dinwiddie that the "Assembly is greatly inflamed at reports of greatest immoralities and drunkenness countenanced and discipline neglected," Washington says he has combatted these evils in every possible manner.

The sufferings of the people on the frontier wring from the commander the following impassioned statement, also in a letter to the governor:

"I see their situation, know their danger, and participate in their sufferings, without having it in my power to give them further relief than uncertain promises. I see inevitable destruction in so clear a light that unless vigorous measures are taken by the Assembly and speedy assistance sent from below, the poor inhabitants that are now in forts must inevitably fall, while the remainder are fleeing before the barbarous foe. In fine, the melancholy situation of the people, the little prospect of assistance, the gross and scandalous abuse cast upon the officers in general, which is reflecting upon me in particular, for suffering misconduct of such extraordinary kinds, and the distant prospect, if any, of gaining honor and reputation in the service, cause me to lament the hour that gave me a commission, and would induce me at any other time than this of imminent danger, to resign, without one hesitating moment, a command from which I never expect to reap either honor or benefit, but, on the contrary, have almost an absolute certainty of incurring displeasure below (east of Blue Ridge), while the murder of helpless families may be laid to my account here. The supplicating tears of the women and moving petitions of the men, melt me into such deadly sorrow that I solemnly declare, if I know my own mind, I could offer myself a willing sacrifice to the butchering enemy, provided that would contribute to the people's ease.... Colonel Fairfax has ordered out the militia from below, but no one knows if it will have any effect. Three days incessant efforts have produced but 20 men. The woods seem to be alive with Indians who feast upon the fat of the land."

The reader will by this time perceive that Washington had to deal with a corrupt, incompetent legislature, and a meddlesome, inefficient, punctilious governor. The Tidewater was the seat of political power in Virginia. The planter-legislators looked upon the Valley as a colony of the Old Dominion, which in effect it was. They did not appreciate the fact that the Valley was a buffer state between the Tidewater and the common enemy. The Valley people were not like themselves and did not have their sympathy. They held that if the new immigration chose to settle such an exposed region it should take the consequences. Being themselves "below the Blue Ridge," and therefore remote from the enemy, they deemed they were safe, and only something like an earthquake could move them. When the legislators did vote measures of defense, it was with a child-like ignorance of the geography of the frontier, and in the handling of appropriations graft was rampant.

As if to make the situation as bad as possible, the governor was without any military knowledge, although he made liberal use of his military prerogative. From his secure mansion in the distant capital, he was incessantly issuing commands, now to one effect and now to another. He was avaricious, he extorted from the people illegal fees, and he failed to account for large sums of money. Consequently it is not strange that he was a cheese-parer when he dealt out supplies, and that he was constantly harping on the need of being "frugal" with them.

This was not all the trouble emanating from Williamsburg. The Scotch governor was surrounded by a knot of Scotch friends, who sought to fatten at the public crib. By underhanded methods they tried to create dissatisfaction in the army, and thus induce the higher officers to resign in disgust. False rumors were given publicity, especially in the Virginia Gazette, the only newspaper of the colony. The petty-minded governor was piqued at the popularity of Washington, and sought to supplant him with Colonel Innes, a Scotchman like himself.

Partial relief came when Governor Shirley was succeeded as commander-in-chief by Lord Loudoun. Washington was present at a conference of governors at Philadelphia, and was favorably regarded. He asked that the Virginia troops be taken into the royal establishment, so that discrimination might be avoided. This was not done, but Colonel Stanwix, the new commander for the Middle and Southern colonies, was of vastly better sense than Braddock. Washington could work in harmony with him, but Dinwiddie continued to make confusion by issuing military orders.

Near the close of April Washington made this report to the governor:

"Not an hour, nay, scarcely a minute passes, that does not produce fresh alarms and melancholy accounts; so that I am distracted what to do. Nor is it possible for me to give the people the necessary assistance for their defense, upon account of the small number we have, or are likely to be here for some time. The inhabitants are removing daily, and in a short time will leave this county as desolate as Hampshire, where scarce a family lives. Three families were murdered the night before last within twelve miles of this place, and every day we have accounts of such cruelties and barbarities as are shocking to human nature. Nor is it possible to conceive the situation of this miserable country. Such numbers of French and Indians are all around, no road is safe to travel; and here we know not the hour how soon we may be attacked. I have written for the militia of Fairfax, Prince William, and Culpeper, but how they are to be supplied with ammunition and provisions, I am quite at a loss. The inhabitants leaving their farms will make it impossible for the militia to subsist without provisions, which are now very scarce and will be more so. I have been just now informed that numbers about the neighborhood hold councils and cabals to very dishonorable purposes, and unworthy the thoughts of a British subject. Despairing of assistance and protection from below, they talk of capitulating. My force at present is very weak, and unable to take the necessary measures with those suspected; but as soon as the militia arrive, be assured I will do my utmost to detect and secure such pests of society."

To John Robinson, Speaker of the House of Burgesses and the recognized political chief of Virginia, Washington wrote to this effect:

"The deplorable situation of this people is no more to be described than my anxiety and uneasiness for their relief. And I see in so clear a light the inevitable destruction of this county without immediate assistance, that I cannot look forward but with the most poignant sorrow. You may expect, by the time this comes to hand, that without a considerable reenforcement, Frederick county will not be mistress of fifteen families. They are now removing to the securest parts in droves of fifties... If we do not endeavor to remove the cause, we are as liable to the same incursions seven years hence as now, if the war continues, and they (Indians) are allowed to remain on the Ohio... If Maryland makes no provision for its frontiers, we shall have a long, unguarded space quite open and defenseless, from Wills Creek to the mouth of Shenandoah, where the enemy may have, and have already given proof of, free egress and regress in crossing the Potomac; plundering, burning, murdering, and destroying all before them. For we must secure that weak side, if our neighbors are so indifferent as to disregard their own safety, because of its connection with ours.... I would again urge the necessity of a large and strong fort at this town. It being the center of all the public roads, it will be the sole refuge for the inhabitants upon any alarm. Had such a place of defense been here, it would have hindered some hundreds of families from moving further than this that are now lost to the county. The women and children might have been secure, while the men would have gone in a body against the savages, whereas the number of men now left is so small that no assistance or defense can be made to any purpose. Winchester is now the farthest boundary of this county—no inhabitants beyond it—and if measures are not taken to maintain it, we must retire below the Blue Ridge in a very short time. Should this panic and fear continue, not a soul will be left on this side the Ridge; and what now remain are collected in small forts (out of which there is no prevailing on them to stir) and every plantation deserted. I have exerted every power for the protection and peace of this distressed, unhappy people, and used my utmost to persuade them to continue, though to little effect."

On the very same day, Washington wrote thus to the governor:

"Desolation and murder still increase and no prospects of relief. There are now no militia in this county; when there were, they could not be brought into action. If the inhabitants of the adjacent counties pursue the same system of disobedience, the whole must fall an inevitable sacrifice; and there is room to fear they have caught the infection, since I have sent (besides divers letters to Lord Fairfax) express after express to hurry them on, and yet have no tidings of their march. We have the greatest reason to believe that the number of the enemy is very considerable, and as they are spread all over this part of the country, and that their success, and the spoils with which they have enriched themselves, dished up with a good deal of French policy, will encourage the Indians of distant nations to fall upon our inhabitants in greater numbers, and if possible, with greater rapidity. They enjoy the sweets of a profitable war, and no doubt will improve the success which ever must attend their arms, without we have Indians to oppose theirs. If such another torrent as this has been (or may be ere it is done) should press upon our settlements, there will not be a living creature left in Frederick county; and how soon Fairfax and Prince William may share its fate is easily conceived, if we only consider a cruel and bloodthirsty enemy, already possessed of the finest parts of Virginia, plentifully filled with all kinds of provisions, pursuing a people overcome with fear and consternation. The inhabitants, who are now in forts, are greatly distressed for the want of ammunition and provisions, and are incessantly importuning me for both; neither of which have I at this place to spare. To hear the cries of the hungry, who have fled for refuge to these places, with nothing more than they carry on their backs, is exceedingly moving."

May 23, the commander writes Dinwiddie that, "the spirit of desertion was so remarkable in the militia that it had a surprising effect upon the regiment, and encouraged many of the soldiers to desert.... I found it absolutely impossible to go to Fort Cumberland at this time without letting matters of greater importance suffer in my absence.... At this place I have begun the fort, and found the work would not be conducted if I was away."

Washington alludes to Fort Loudoun, for the building of which the Assembly voted 1000 pounds ($3,333). Because of untoward hinderances the construction proceeded very slowly, but is said to have been practically complete in September, 1757. This fortification covered half an acre, and was a redoubt with four bastions. Each curtain, or section of wall between two bastions, was 96 feet long, and each flank or face of a bastion had an extent of 25 feet. The position of the fort was the rise of ground on Main Street just north of Peyton Street, and the larger part of the inclosure was on the west side of the thoroughfare. It was placed on an outlot, and consequently was outside the town proper. Nothing now remains of the redoubt except the bastion which may be seen at the rear of Fort Loudoun Seminary. But in 1813 the salient and re-entering angles were easily visible where Main Street was cut through, and twenty years later much of the wall was still to be seen. The intention to dig a ditch around the fort was not carried into effect because of the thick stratum of lime-rock. The well to supply the fort with water was sunk the entire distance of 103 feet through solid limestone. It is said to overflow at times, this proving that the distant source of supply is at a higher level. As late as July, 1886, in the digging of a cistern, there were found cannon-wheels, six and twelve pound balls, grenades, and some bones of a skeleton.

Fourteen cannon were mounted at Fort Loudoun; six eighteen pounders, six twelve pounders, six six pounders, four swivel guns, and two howitzers. All but one of these were removed during the Revolution to be used elsewhere. But in the Christmas season of 1824, some young men came by night from the Thespian hall and fired a dozen rounds from a six pounder. The concussions broke at least twenty panes of glass in John Peyton's house, but Mrs. Peyton declined a tender of payment for the damage. On the other hand, she treated the young men to wine and cake. This cannon is still in Winchester.

The room in the fort used by Washington is said to have been above the gateway commanding a view of Main Street. He owned a lot on the west side of the street, between Piccadilly and Fairfax Lane, and according to General John Smith, he built a blacksmith shop upon it. To make the ironwork needed in the fort, he brought his own blacksmith from Mount Vernon.

The building of Fort Loudoun insured the safety of Winchester. The redoubt was reconnoitered by French officers, who decided that it was impregnable against any force they could bring here from Duquesne.

On the Maryland side of the Potomac was Fort Frederick, near North Mountain Station and 12 miles from either Williamsport or Martinsburg. It covered one and one-half acres, the walls were four and one-half feet thick at the base and twenty feet high. The cost of this fortification was 65,000 pounds sterling.

Much of Washington's time was now engrossed in preparing the specifications for the stockades ordered built along the frontier. The governor ordered the militia discharged after harvest, they being unwilling to remain till December. As a matter of fact, they were scarcely willing to remain for any reason. Writing June 25, Washington says he is "under the greatest apprehensions that all who are now up will desert. They go off in twenties, and all threaten to return (home) if they are not relieved in a very short time or discharged."

August 4, the commander writes that, "the inhabitants have been driven so low down that the Indians do not hesitate to follow them as far as this place. I could by no means bring the Quakers to any terms. They choose rather to be whipped to death than bear arms, or lend us any assistance whatever upon the fort, or anything of self-defense."

As to the Quakers, the governor directed Washington to "use them with lenity," merely holding them at their own expense to the end of the term for which they were drafted. Among other soldiers, the evil of desertion did not abate, the commander stating that deserters were generally aided and secreted by the people, and that in consequence it was seldom possible to apprehend them.

The Potomac was a source of concern. The colonies were independent of one another, and Washington had no authority outside of Virginia. He writes that, "if we cannot take our forces across the Potomac, the enemy may mock our best endeavors.... The whole settlement of Conochocheague in Maryland is fled, and there now remain only two families from thence to Fredericktown.... When Hampshire was invaded and called on Frederick for assistance, the answer was, 'Let them defend themselves, as we shall do if they come to us.' Now the enemy have forced through that county and begun to infest this, those a little removed from danger are equally infatuated, and will be, I fear, until all in turn fall a sacrifice. I am so weak-handed here that I could not, without stagnating the public works (fort), spare a man to these people's assistance."

In America the French and the English had been fighting for two years. But in Europe there was official peace between their governments until the summer of 1756. Dinwiddie, who was as strong on etiquette as he was weak in effective performance, sent Washington elaborate directions for proclaiming the war in his department, although it could not make the least difference in the actual situation. Fortunately for us, a letter of August 17, 1756, describes the occasion in these words:

"On Sunday (August 15) Colonel Washington having received the declaration of war against France with the governor's commands to proclaim it in the most solemn manner, he ordered the three companies of the Virginia regiment here to appear under arms at the general parade at three o'clock on the eve of the next day; when, attended by the principal gentlemen of this town, they marched in regular order to Fort Loudoun, where, the soldiery being properly drawn up, the declaration was read aloud. His Majesty's and many other healths were drank."

The letter goes on to say that there were three rounds of musketry and loud acclamations of the people, after which there was a march in regular order round the town, with more proclaiming of the declaration at the cross-streets. It was again read at a grand parade, after which the soldiers were dismissed by the colonel with an exhortation.

Washington's indignation rose to the boiling-point at the complaint that the officers and soldiers who were out in recruiting service took up the stray animals they found in the woods. "Let such practices," he said, "be discouraged. Waters and Burrass behaved extremely ill when they were sent down last. If I could lay my hands on them, I would try the effect of one thousand lashes on the former, and whether a general court-martial would not condemn the latter to the life eternal."

We now give a few extracts from a letter to the governor in September.

"It (enlisting servants) is the best, most expeditious, nay, the only method I know of now to recruit the forces... Those (deserters) delivered to the constables are always suffered to escape, and no notice taken of it... People here in general are very selfish; every person expects forces at his own door, and is angry to see them at his neighbor's... The number of tippling houses kept here is a great nuisance... The Potomac is deserted on the Maryland side forty miles below Conococheague. I am credibly informed no less than 350 wagons, transporting the affrighted families, passed in the space of three days through Fredericktown... Those Indians who are coming should be showed all possible respect, and the greatest care taken of them, as upon them much depends. It is a critical time, they are very humorsome, and their assistance very necessary. One false step might lose us all that, but even turn them against us."

In October, Washington was absent from Winchester on a tour of inspection. The governor and his friends now renewed their attacks upon him, a broadside of scurrilous abuse appearing in the Gazette. This time the commander seriously thought of resigning. In November, the meddlesome governor, who had no personal acquaintance with the frontier, directed Washington to march to Fort Cumberland with 100 of the men at Winchester, and remain there. The commander replied that there were not 100 enlisted men in Winchester; that by leaving the town, the works would be unfinished and exposed. "The materials which have been collected with unspeakable difficulty and expense will be pillaged and destroyed by the inhabitants of the town. To comply with my orders, not a man will be left there to secure the works or defend the king's stores."

Washington's letter of December 2 shows that his patience had nearly failed him. He had only 81 men, including the sick and the boy drummers, and the governor's order had brought terror to Winchester. "The works lie open, untenable, and exposed to the weather. The timber and scantling will be used for fuel. By not having a garrison at this place, no convoys can get up to us. I had rather be at Fort Cumberland a thousand times over, for I am tired of the place, the inhabitants, the life I lead here."

Later in the month he thus freed his mind to Robinson:

"My strongest representations of matters relative to the peace of the frontiers are disregarded as idle and frivolous; my propositions and measures as partial and selfish and all my sincerest endeavors for the service of my country perverted to the worst purposes. My orders are dark, doubtful, and uncertain; today approved, tomorrow condemned. I look to Lord Loudoun for the future fate of Virginia."

In February, 1757, Washington wrote at some length to Loudoun, who had ruled that the fort at Winchester was to be held at any cost. The paper is a detailed review of the activities in his department, and is a very able document. He points out that his regiment has "done a vast amount of work, and has been very alert in defending the people." Since the March of 1756, there had been one constant campaign, with more than twenty skirmishes and a casualty list of nearly 100. He closes his letter with his respects to the "chimney-corner politicians who are thirsting for news, and expecting by every express in what manner Fort Duquesne was taken and the garrison led away captive by our small numbers."

In June, 1757, Lord Loudoun ordered Washington to detach 200 men for service in South Carolina. His regiment was thereby reduced to a strength of 420. A few days later he reports that, "we work on this fort (Loudoun) night and day, intending to make it tenable against the worst event.." In July, 24 of his drafted men deserted after receiving their money and clothes. The same month he wrote Stanwix that out of 400 men drafted, 114 had deserted, and that to inspire terror he had built a gallows 40 feet high. July 30, he reported that out of 22 deserters recovered, he had hanged two, but one month later he wrote that he found the example of little weight. In September he says that, "one of those who were condemned to be hanged deserted immediately upon receiving his pardon. In short, they tire my patience and almost worry me to death." In October we find him complaining of the "lawless thieving practiced by the tippling-house keepers, receiving and concealing stores, arms, etc., belonging to the regiment, and of the rascally, illegal conduct of the justices in giving no redress through the courts."

Near the end of this year Washington was compelled to listen to the repeated remonstrances of his physician. He was nearly worn out with his many vexations, and was so reduced by dysentery and fever that he had to go to Mount Vernon and stay there till the next April. But if his repeated remonstrances could not move an incompetent governor and an imbecile commander-in-chief, they directed the public mind to the urgent need of wresting Fort Duquesne from the enemy.

While Washington was recuperating, Virginia was happily rid of an executive of whom the young leader made this remark to Robinson: "I am convinced it would give pleasure to the governor to hear that I was involved in trouble, however undeservedly, such are his dispositions toward me." In January, 1758, Dinwiddie sailed for England, unlamented in Virginia except by the satellites who had basked in his sunshine. He had been recalled by the new premier, William Pitt, a man of energy and good judgment.

Full support for our estimate of Dinwiddie is given by Trevelyan in his History of the American Revolution. This author observes that the governor grudged Washington his rank and pay and stinted him in both men and means; that he lost no opportunity of reminding Washington that he was not a royal officer but a mere provincial; and that he made himself a center of military intrigues which gave Washington a foretaste of what he was to endure at the hands of Gates, Arnold, and Charles Lee.

Another and much needed item in the colonial house-cleaning was the recall of Lord Loudoun. In population and resources, the English colonies were incomparably superior to the French, but with such failures as Dinwiddie and Loudoun at the helm, the defense of British America was a thing of derision in the eyes of the Gallic adversary. There was now good leadership, and the French power in North America was soon demolished. The titled nonentity who was a laughing-stock to Franklin and other men of affairs in America did not deserve to have his name perpetuated in a county in Virginia and a street in Winchester.

In April, Washington returned to his command, and took part in the successful expedition of 1758 against Fort Duquesne. He led one of the Virginia regiments and Colonial William Byrd the other. He desired an early start, but he was compelled to visit Williamsburg in the interest of his regiment, the soldiers grew impatient, and nearly all the 700 Indian allies who had assembled at Winchester went home. So it was not until June 24 that the Virginia contingent began its march from the capital of Frederick county.

Washington was given leave to attend the election in Frederick on July 24. Although his home was Mount Vernon, his ownership of real estate in this county and town qualified him to be a candidate for office. The preceding year he had been a candidate for the House of Burgesses, but was overwhelmingly defeated by the pro-liquor vote. Only 40 ballots were given to him, against 271 to Hugh West and 270 to Thomas Swearingen.* He had wished for an election, and it has been suggested that Mrs. Custis, whom he was about to marry, favored a honeymoon at the capital of Virginia. But "walkovers" have not been in favor in Frederick, and two men who stood in with the drinking element entered the race and bore off the prize.

---

* The names of this "old guard" are as follows:

Robert Ashby	Henry Heath	William Russell
William Bethel	Adam Hunter	Robert Rutherford
Joseph Borden	James Lemon	Edward Sniggars
Henry Brinker	John McCormick	Edward Stevenson
John Briscoe	William McKee	Taliaferro Stribling
James Burns	Alexander Mathews	Levi Swearingen
William Calmes	Henry Moore	Magnes Tate
John Calvey	Ryley Moore	Alexander Vance
William Cochran	Elisha Parkins	Augustus Windle
Edward Corday	Reuben Patchett	Thomas Waddington
Valentine Crawford	Robert Peans	Colonel James Wood
William Crawford	Thomas Perry	Robert Worthington Jr.
Meredith Helm	William Potter	
Thomas Helm	Nicholas Princelear	

At the next election, Washington bent to the breeze. James Wood, who seems to have been an astute politician, was his campaign manager, and he attended to the disbursing of $39 for a dinner and bar-room drinks. Washington was triumphantly elected, receiving 310 votes. Colonel T. B. Martin, Hugh West, and Thomas Swearingen received, respectively, 240, 199, and 45 votes. Being absent from Winchester on the election day, Colonel Wood acted as proxy, and as such was triumphantly carried through the street on a chair, in honor of Washington's election. The commander served as a burgess from Frederick during the years 1758-1761. The following comment by the historian Sparks seems very just:

"Considering the command which he had been obliged to exercise in Frederick for near five years, and the restraints which the exigency of circumstances required him occasionally to put upon the inhabitants, this result (election) was deemed a triumphant proof of his abilities, address, and power to win the affections and confidence of the people."

After the capture of Duquesne Washington resigned from the army, and during the next sixteen years was quite steadily at Mount Vernon. For ten years he had been very much of the time in Winchester and the region around, and he continued to be an owner of real estate in Frederick, partly by purchase and partly by inheritance from his half-brother Lawrence.

In a review of the three years that Washington was at the head of the Virginia forces in the French and Indian war, it is impossible not to discover a startling parallelism between his military career in the Shenandoah and his military career in the much broader field of the American Revolution. Concerning those three years, the usual books on American history are strangely deficient. They speak of this period in a very few lines if they speak of it at all, whereas they devote pages to the picturesque trip to Venango and to Braddock's defeat, where he was present only as a staff officer.

The things with which Washington had to contend in 1755-1758 were of the same nature as those confronting him in 1775-1783. In each instance he had fewer men than could have been provided. Those few were half-clothed, half-fed, and poorly equipped, although there was no lack of clothing and provisions in the country. In each war his men were militia to a considerable degree, and the militia of colonial America were notoriously un-

CHAIRING COLONEL WOOD AS PROXY FOR WASHINGTON.

Celebrating the Election of George Washington to The Virginia House of Burgesses by "Chairing" James Wood, His Campaign Manager and Proxy

dependable. On the Virginian frontier, Washington was steadily hampered by that meddlesome martinet and public nuisance, Governor Dinwiddie, and by a legislature that failed woefully to rise to the occasion. In the Revolution, he was hampered by a fussy Congress that had little power, and that lost ground in efficiency, year by year. In the former field he had an enemy behind his back in the form of the cabal led by Dinwiddie and Innes. In the latter field he had to contend with the Conway cabal. In 1756, he was to be superseded by the foreign-born Innes. In 1778, he was to be superseded by the foreign-born Gates, who was ignominiously defeated at Camden. We used to read of what the patriots of '76 would do in the "glorious cause of liberty," but human nature was the same in the eighteenth century as it is in the twentieth, and the men of 1755 and 1775 were slow to move unless the danger were very near, and even then they would compromise their cause by narrow-mindedness and petty jealousies.

In 1757 Washington was but twenty-five years old, yet he had become ill through the hounding of men in high position, who thought more of place, pelf, and dignity than of the public danger; by the selfish clamor and the lame support of the men on the frontier; and of being unable to secure that frontier, when he had only one or two men to the mile. Had he been less patient and long-suffering, the memories of 1754-1757 could not have induced him to lead the American armies in 1775-1783. But the severe apprenticeship of the earlier period enabled him to win in the latter. Had it not been for the experience gained in the military district of which Winchester was the center and the danger-point, there is room for grave doubt whether Washington would have been victor in the war for Independence.

An observation by John Esten Cooke, written in 1859, is very much to the point. After remarking—figuratively, of course—that Washington was born in Winchester in 1756, he says, "it was here that his supreme powers of endurance and resistance were developed. After this time he seldom thought of amusement. On a smaller theater he rehearsed the great contest of the Revolution."

We have devoted considerable space to this neglected yet highly important episode in Washington's career, and we feel that the space is justified. Winchester is as closely associated with this period in his military life as Mount Vernon is with his home life. We have quoted freely from his letters, since these help to tell the story, and in a most graphic and forcible manner. Washington is not ranked as a literary artist, yet he possessed in a high degree the gift of writing tersely and to the very point.

We have purposely excluded from the narrative more than slight mention of such occurrences as are not of a local character. Had these been interwoven, the account would be more comprehensive and valuable, but space did not permit.

Certain clauses in the story may not be pleasant reading to the Winchester people of today. And yet there are some grounds of extenuation. The America of 1755 was exceedingly unlike the America of 1924. The two are not to be measured by the same yardstick. The things that vexed Washington so deeply were not at all peculiar to the Lower Shenandoah. They were true without exception of all the American colonies. The frontiersman had an inveterate love of personal liberty and independent action. This was fundamentally a good thing, yet it often blinded him to a just perception of civic duty, and it stood sadly in the way of his becoming an efficient soldier. The colonials had a deep-seated distrust of standing armies, and were not without considerable excuse. It was this feeling which led the county court to refuse Washington permission to put unruly soldiers into the public jail. He was thus compelled to build a military prison on the west side of Main Street a little north of the corner occupied by the Shenandoah Valley Bank. Yet the court saw no inconsistency in asking Washington for a guard when some Indians were thrown into the county jail. The guard was supplied.

Furthermore, "New Virginia" had but recently been settled. Very many of the adult inhabitants were not native to the soil. They felt that in a very real sense they were a colony of the Tidewater, and it is a well known fact of history that it is not easy for a colony to get the ear of the parent country. Between the people of the Valley and the people "below the Blue Ridge" there were strong points of divergence. They knew little of one another, and that little did not make for comfortable relations. And whom people do not know they do not like.

Although George Washington was never a bona fide resident of Winchester, it is very probable that he would have made the Shenandoah Valley his permanent home, had he not inherited from his half-brother Lawrence the plantation of Mount Vernon.

In doing so, he would have followed the example of his brother Samuel, who lived in what is now Jefferson county. It was sentiment that caused him to make his home on the infertile and unhealthful estate of Mount Vernon. To the end of his life General

Washington owned two plantations in Frederick county and a lot in Winchester. He considered the Shenandoah as the Garden of Virginia, if not of all America.

Lawrence Augustine Washington, a son of Samuel and a nephew to the general, was a resident and prominent citizen of Winchester from the time of his marriage in 1797 until his removal to Kanawha county in 1811. His wife was Mary Dorcas, a daughter of Robert Wood, and in Winchester they lived at "Hawthorne," originally a part of the Glen Burnie estate. In 1820, when he was forty-five years of age, Mr. Washington wrote for his four children the story of his courtship and marriage. It is a story of love at first sight, and the woman of his choice was only fifteen years old when he first met her at Berkeley Springs.

VII

LATER COLONIAL PERIOD

A Time of Stress — Descriptions by Visitors — Winchester in 1775 — Morgan and His Soldiers — Prisoners of War — Quaker Exiles — End of the Period — James Wood, Jr. — Daniel Morgan.

> "May 10, 1771 — Daniel Morgan having been summoned, appeared before the Justices and took the usual oaths to his Majesty's person and government and was sworn Captain in the militia of Frederick County". — (Minutes County Court of Frederick County, Virginia).

The thirty years closing with the peace of 1783 were years of stress. A period of prosperity was to begin immediately afterward.

Just after the period opened, Winchester fell into what was practically a state of siege lasting until the expulsion of the French from the Ohio Valley in 1758. But for the exertions of Washington and the building of a strong fort, Winchester would with little doubt have been captured and burned. This would have meant a temporary blotting out of all settlement west of the Blue Ridge.

As soon as the menace of the French and Indians appeared to be removed, the settlers returned to the devastated valley to reoccupy their farms and rebuild such of their homes as had been destroyed. This process of recovery consumed several years. But immediately after the war with France came the long quarrel with England, culminating in the revolt of 1775. This quarrel was complicated by the attitude of the Indians, with whom there were wars in 1763-1764 and in 1774. And the Revolution itself, because of the hazards of trade with Europe, was a period of hard times.

Our first pen-pictures of Winchester in these thirty years are by two British visitors.

Lord Adam Gordon, who was here in 1755, describes Winchester as built of limestone and "inhabited by a spurious race of mortals known by the appellation of Scotch-Irish." He adds that the people enjoyed most of the necessities of life, but had almost no books. Though Lord Gordon was a Scotchman, it is very clear that he did not think well of the immigrants from the north of

GENERAL DANIEL MORGAN

Ireland. He does not allude to the war, and as his visit was probably before the defeat of Braddock, the capital of the Northern Neck was not yet injuriously affected by the cloud lowering over the Ohio Valley.

Burnaby, an Englishman traveling in the colonies, spent a week in Winchester, entering the Lower Valley through Ashby's Gap at the end of May, 1760. His description is also brief, but he says there were 200 houses in the town. Because Winchester had been made a military rendezvous, there had within a few years been a rapid increase in its size and business was flourishing. He mentions the barracks in Fort Loudoun as sufficient for 450 men. The redoubt was "built of logs filled up with earth," the limestone in Fort Hill preventing the construction of a dry ditch. Although 9000 pounds had been spent, the legislature refused to appropriate the additional 1000 pounds needed for its completion, saying that the capture of Duquesne had made further effort unnecessary.

The Moravian visitors of 1753 found about 60 houses in Winchester. The great expansion in seven years was largely because of the refugees who had flocked here for safety. Many of the new houses were undoubtedly small and hastily constructed, like the soldier-huts with which Washington had dotted the slope of Fort Hill. The prosperity mentioned by the traveler was of that artificial sort that accompanies heavy expenditures for military purposes.

Burnaby speaks a good word for the German settlers of the Lower Valley. He praises their industry, thrift, and physical vigor, and remarks that they export butter to the "low country."

Although the militia of Frederick were no more than 923 in 1777, Kercheval says Winchester had 800 inhabitants.

Since Williamsburg had but 1000 inhabitants at the time of Burnaby's visit, it follows that the metropolis of the Shenandoah Valley was as large in 1760 as the capital of Virginia.

Neither in the war with Pontiac's confederacy, which suddenly broke out in 1763, nor in the Dunmore war of 1774 did the hostilities directly affect the Lower Valley. But in the latter contest this town was the rendezvous for the right wing of the army that marched against the tribes on the Ohio. It was led by Governor Dunmore in person, the left wing, assembling where now is Lewisburg, West Virginia, being commanded by Colonel Andrew Lewis. It was the left column which did all the fighting of the campaign. Two companies of the regiment raised in Frederick were led by James Wood and Daniel Morgan.

But the blue, three-cornered hats, knee-breeches, and silver buttons and buckles that were so much in evidence in the Braddock campaign were now in retirement. The men in the armies of 1774 were garbed in hunting shirts of various colors. The officers were attired much like the men under them and they carried rifles instead of swords.

Kercheval remarks that before the war had actually begun, Colonel Angus McDonald went from near Winchester to survey military grants on the Ohio and the Great Kanawha. After his surveyors had been driven back, he made a personal visit to Dunmore who authorized him to raise 400 men. With these he crossed the Ohio in June and burned some villages, but saw little fighting.

The campaign in the fall of 1774 was quickly followed by the Revolution. Premonitory mutterings had already been heard. It was by way of Winchester that Augusta county sent a contribution of 137 barrels of flour for the relief of the people of Boston, when that city was closed to commerce by the autocratic harshness of the Boston Port Bill.

Mr. Fithian, an observant Presbyterian minister, visited the Lower Valley in 1775. His diary is so interesting and of so much historic value that we wish his contact with this region had been much longer. He visited the nearby town of Martinsburg May 19 and speaks of it as "founded two years ago in high woods," and as now having about 30 houses, a stone jail, and also a good courthouse in process of erection.

Winchester is described as "a smart village nearly half a mile in length, and several streets broad and pretty full. The situation is low and disagreeable. There is on a pleasant hill northeast from the town, at a small distance, a large stone Lutheran church with a tall steeple. North of the town are the ruins of an old fort wasted, and crumbled down by time. The land is good, the country pleasant, the houses in general large."

Writing June 8, he observes that "we see many every day, traveling out and in, to and from Carolina, some on foot with packs, and some in large covered wagons. The road here is much frequented, and for 150 miles farther west (south) thickly inhabited." The writer goes on to tell of the lynching, toward Augusta county, of a thief who had killed a man and taken 110 pounds from him. The nervousness engendered by the political situation appears in his statement that many servants (white) and negroes were running away.

Two days earlier—the day before election—Mr. Fithian gives us a vivid glimpse into the war feeling in Winchester.

"The court was sitting. Mars, the great god of battle, is now honored in every part of this spacious colony, but here every presence is warlike, every sound is martial—drums are beating, fifes and bagpipes playing, and only sonorous tunes. Every man has a hunting shirt, which is the uniform of each company. Almost all have a cockade and bulltail in their hats to represent that they are hardy, resolute, and invincible natives of the woods of America."

The diarist adds that "one S—— was backward this morning in attendance," and resisted the file of soldiers sent to bring him in. Tar and feathers were talked of. It was drill-day, and every able-bodied male between the ages of sixteen and sixty was summoned to attend.

Four days later the diary relates that the office of Lord Fairfax was broken into but no money found.

The war feeling was stronger in "New Virginia" than in the Land of the Tuckahoe. The Stamp Act resolutions introduced into the legislature by Patrick Henry would have been lost had it not been for the votes of the burgesses from behind the Blue Ridge. But with the short-sighted and brutal malice that was so often shown by the British leaders in the Revolution, the expelled governor burned Norfolk to the ground causing a loss of $1,500,000, and at the end of the war not 12 houses had been rebuilt. The effect on the Virginians was the exact opposite of what had been looked for.

Heinrich Ringer of Winchester solicited his townsmen of German speech for subscriptions for "Der Staatsbote," a Pennsylvania journal, that favored independence.

The first soldiers from Virginia to join the besieging army before Boston were a company of riflemen under Daniel Morgan. They left Winchester July 14, 1775, and arrived at their destination August 7. Their progress over the bad roads and bridgeless streams which were then almost universal in America was fully eighteen miles a day. This march deserves to rank with the phenomenal speed of some recruits in going from Marseilles to Paris in the days of the French Revolution. But those enthusiastic soldiers were stimulated by the newly written Marseillaise. Morgan used a conch shell when calling his men, every one of whom wore a hunting shirt and had a bucktail attached to his hat. There were no desertions from the 96 men, and at the close of the war 65 of them were accounted for. The brilliant exploits of Morgan's riflemen, particularly in the Saratoga campaign, are familiar to readers of the war for Independence.

Morgan's bodyguard was known as the "Dutch Mess." It was composed of George Grim, Henry Heiskell, George Kurtz, Peter Lauck, John Schultz, and Peter Sperry, although another account adds the names of Robert Anderson, Adam Kurtz, and Simon Lauck, and makes the given names of Grim and Sperry to be Charles and Jacob. These men were present at the battle of Great Bridge, near Norfolk, December 9, 1775, where the British left 31 of their number on the field and carried off others, although there were no casualties among the Americans. The Dutch Mess used turkey bones with which to call one another. All of them returned to their homes after the war, and all survived their leader, Peter Lauck living until October 2, 1839, and Schultz until about 1841. Schultz was a wagon-maker. His stone house and his shop were on the ground where the Handley Library now stands. Sperry lived opposite on Piccadilly. The mess chest of these men remains as a war relic in the house where Morgan died.

Peter Helphinstine, a major in the Eighth Virginia under Colonel Muhlenburg, fell sick in the Carolinas, came home on furlough, and died in the fall of 1776. He had commanded a company under Colonel Adam Stephen in the Dunmore war, and among his men were John Grim, Peter Lauck, and George Snapp. In a petition to the legislature, dated November 21, 1833, these men say they never had any compensation for their services in the Dunmore campaign and ask relief.

The company of Captain Joseph Bowman served under George Rogers Clarke in 1778, and helped that zealous officer conquer the Illinois country. Had this not been accomplished, the treaty of 1783 might have excluded the new republic from the region beyond the Ohio. Captain Bowman died at a fort in 1779.

In the spring of 1781 Morgan left the army because of disability. But in June he was called upon to quell the tory insurrection on the South Branch. He marched from Winchester with 400 men in the middle of the month, and performed his duty in about ten days. The county lieutenant had been authorized to loan him 140 muskets.

Because of its remoteness from the coast, Winchester was chosen as a camp for the prisoners taken from the British armies. So far as we know, the first to be sent here were some of the Hessians captured at Trenton. On the last day of September,

1777, 300 were parceled out among the farmers at the rate of $7.50 a month each. Two weeks later 300 more arrived under a guard of about 75 men. For boarding them Philip Bush was allowed twelvepence a day (17 cents).

After the surrender of Burgoyne, General Morgan conducted many of the prisoners to this place, others being sent to Staunton and Charlottesville. Many of the privates were at once permitted to work on the farms. Some of them married here, after paying a ransom of $80. When it was necessary, this money would be advanced by the farmers of the Lower Valley.

The camp for the prisoners who were not thus fortunate was four miles west of the town. Von Elking, one of the Hessian officers, complained that the food was scanty and poor, and that the huts, built of wood and canvas, were wretched. But Baron Riedesel—called "Red Hazel" by the Americans—in a letter of March 19, 1781 gave Colonel Wood very warm thanks for his kindness to the prisoners.

About March 1, 1780, Colonel James Wood arrived to take charge. In his journal he says he found matters in very unsatisfactory shape. There was not an ounce of flour on hand and salt pork for only eight days. The scarcity of provisions and the exorbitantly high prices charged were partly owing to the exceedingly cold winter of 1779-1780, and partly to a deficiency of commissary funds in the preceding fall, thus preventing the purchase of beef and pork. The hardships did not fall wholly on the prisoners. Of the 12 officers and 36 militia privates present when he took command, not one-half were sufficiently clothed. The prisoners had been pulling down the pickets around their camp, presumably to use as fuel. In one letter he speaks of recovering 40 prisoners. In another he says he has retaken more than 150 in a few days. It would thus appear that the guarding was much less strict than in the war of 1861, when both combatants established a dead-line inside of each prison stockade, and the guards might shoot any prisoner presuming to cross it.

In the June of 1781 there was much concern for the security of the 1600 prisoners at Winchester. The section of the state east of the Blue Ridge was almost defenseless, and Cornwallis was marching where he pleased, plundering and destroying as he went along. His cavalry made threats of forcing their way into the Shenandoah. Just after the return of Morgan from the South Branch, two expresses rode into Winchester, bringing word that "Tarleton and his devils" were coming to rescue the prisoners.

Colonel Wood was empowered to call out the militia. June 8 he reported the prisoners at Shepherdstown and requested a guard of 250 men. The captives were removed to Fort Frederick, where they remained till the close of the war. There was an intention of sending them to York, Pennsylvania.

About this time there was a council of war at Winchester, in which Generals Gates, Morgan, and Darke were present. It recommended that magazines of provisions, wagons, axes, and intrenching tools be established at Winchester, Shepherdstown, and Stoverstown (Strasburg). At the end of June, Morgan was asked to assemble all the men he could and join Lafayette, who was resisting Cornwallis as much as his smaller army would permit.

But Tarleton did not attempt to force Rockfish Gap and brave the hot reception he would have met from the riflemen of the Valley. The whole British army moved toward the coast and Winchester was relieved from apprehension. In fact, the number of prisoners in this region was soon to be increased. At the beginning of September 136 arrived from South Carolina. Two months later came 2500 of the prisoners taken in the surrender of Cornwallis. A diary by a British officer relates that the guards were Valley men and kind to the captives, who were allowed to use fence rails for fuel during the march from Yorktown. But at this time there was little good feeling between the inhabitants of the Valley and those of the "low country."

The Winchester of 1781 is described by this officer as "an inconsiderable town surrounded at a short distance by gigantic forests." For winter weather the log huts were called insufficient. A church in Winchester with a seating capacity of 500 was to be turned over to the prisoners, but Morgan put a stop to this, saying the prisoners should fix up their winter quarters themselves. The officer says his men could not complain of their treatment while they were here, since the farmers often invited them to their homes.

Here at Winchester the eight regiments of the Virginia Continental Line were reduced to one regiment and two companies. The new command, with an enrollment of 509 men, was then called the First Regiment, and its leader was Colonel James Wood.

An episode of the Revolution was the detention in Winchester of 20 persons from Pennsylvania, charged with holding treasonable relations with the British. For refusing to swear allegiance to the state, the Continental Congress ordered them sent to Staunton. But because of better lodging accommodations, and through the influence of Isaac Zane, they were halted at Winchester, where they arrived September 29, 1777, and were taken to the inn of Philip Bush. The Executive Council of Pennsylvania ordered that the whole cost of the confinement be borne by the prisoners. The charge made by Bush appears to have been 10 shillings silver (12 1-2 shillings in Pennsylvania money) per day, the prisoners to furnish bed, drink, and washing. They were to stay within a six-mile limit around Winchester, and Colonel Smith offered not to confine them if they would promise not to run away. All but three of the number were Quakers, they would give no pledges, and as the governor of the state sent word that they be secured, they were put under guard. During the eight months that they were in captivity two of them died. One of the party, named Fisher, was the spokesman. They hired Alexander White, a lawyer living near Winchester, to secure permission for their return, and he was paid 100 pounds in gold, Virginia money. White succeeded, but was aided by public sentiment in Pennsylvania, which demanded their return.

The following are the names of the men:

Thomas Affleck	Thomas Gilpin	Edward Pennington
Elijah Brown	John Hunt	Thomas Pike
Henry Drinker	Charles Jervis	Samuel Pleasants
Charles Eddy	Owen Jones, Jr.	William Smith (a broker)
Miers Fisher	Israel Pemberton	
Thomas Fisher	James Pemberton	William D. Smith
Samuel Fisher of Joshua	John Pemberton	Thomas Wharton

To say the least, some of these men had seriously compromised themselves. The Friends are opposed to war on principle, but in a crisis like that of the Revolution it seemed impossible for them to remain "neutral in thought," to say nothing of neutrality in action. The Quakers of the Winchester district seem to have given no aid to the British, but as is remarked by Kercheval, the treasonable actions of a few individuals aroused much feeling against the denomination. It was thought that its actions did not harmonize with its professions, and some evidences of this disapproval will be seen in the next chapter. The Friends, as Kercheval further remarks, were great sufferers by the Revolution, through their refusal to bear arms and pay war taxes, and by reason of incurring the expense of hiring substitutes. Much of their property was sold by the sheriffs, but because of the industry which is characteristic of the Friends, they soon recovered from financial distress. Many of them at length moved to the new states.

A few other incidents of the period require notice.

The Journal and Baltimore Advertiser of May 17, 1775 contained the following advertisement:

"Winchester, Virginia, April 17, 1775. Now confined for debt a young man, capable of teaching and a perfect master of the mathematics .... was a bookkeeper at Bristol, England. Would sign indenture for three years to the one paying his debts (27 pounds 10 shillings plus 31 pounds 12 shillings in two years). Apply to George Roots, lawyer, Winchester."

For an indebtedness of $230.17 this young man was languishing in jail, as was permitted by the laws of Virginia for more than sixty years afterward. The principal use for a jail was that it might be a boarding house for delinquent debtors. But around the prison was a "limit" defined by the county court, and if an imprisoned debtor could rent a house within the said limit, he had his full liberty, provided he never went outside of it.

A local visitation of the smallpox in 1768 is a reminder that this disease was very prevalent in the eighteenth century, and that a pitted face was an everyday spectacle. Vaccination had not been discovered at the date just named. Inoculation was practiced, but the mild type of smallpox which it induced was liable to occasion a severe type in any individual who might be exposed to the patient.

Excepting Martinsburg and Stevensburg, there were no other statute-made towns in the Lower Valley. Berryville—long known as Battletown—Front Royal, Middletown, and Strasburg were as yet scarcely more than hamlets. Until 1776 there was no other court at Winchester than the court composed of the county justices. In that year a Court of Law and Equity was created.

James Wood Jr., born in 1741, died in Richmond in 1813. As a soldier, he rose from the rank of captain in the Dunmore campaign of 1774 to that of colonel of the Eighth Virginia regiment of the Continental Line, and in 1783 he became a brigadier general. His record in civil life is more conspicuous. He was a Burgess in 1775, one of the commissioners that made the treaty of Fort Pitt in the same year, a member of the Constitutional Convention of 1776, and for many years he served in the Governor's Council. In 1788 he was presidential elector, only one vote being cast against him. General Wood was governor of Virginia from December, 1796 to December, 1799. Wood county in West Virginia was named for him. Lawrence A. Washington paid this tribute to his character:

> I never knew a man I thought so pure,
> I never loved a man so well.

The biographers of General Daniel Morgan say that he was born in New Jersey in 1736 and came to Nineveh, Frederick county, in 1753.* He was totally silent as to his early history, and it is believed that he left home because of his stepmother. In his new home he speedily fell into a military career. In the Braddock campaign he was a teamster and was wounded. In 1763 he became a lieutenant, and in 1774 was a captain under Dunmore. He purchased land near Winchester in 1762, but after his marriage to Abigail Bailey he lived on his estate of "Saratoga" near Boyce. The stone mansion was completed by Hessian stonemasons in 1782.

Morgan's march to Boston with a company of riflemen is spoken of in a preceding chapter. In the attack on Quebec, in December, 1775, he penetrated well into the city, but was hemmed in and forced to surrender. He was offered a colonelcy in the British army, but scorned to become another Benedict Arnold, and was released from his parole a year later, by which time he was commissioned colonel of the Eleventh Virginia regiment. In 1777 he was in very active service under Washington, by whom he was sent to the assistance of General Gates at the time of Burgoyne's invasion. In both the battles of Saratoga he took a prominent part and the fire of his riflemen told most severely on the British ranks.

After the surrender of Burgoyne, Morgan rejoined Washington. Feeling aggrieved at not being promoted, he resigned in 1779 and returned to Virginia, but after the overthrow of Gates at Camden in the summer of 1780, he joined the army in the South and took command of a corps. He was now raised to the rank of brigadier general. After General Greene succeeded Gates, he sent Morgan with 900 men to operate against the rear of the British army under Cornwallis. That general detached Tarleton with

---

* Mrs. A. Bruce of Martinsburg, West Virginia, who has supplied a portion of the material used in this sketch, says that Daniel Morgan was born in 1737 and came to Virginia in 1754, settling in Berkeley county, where descendants of his brother Reese, still live.

1200 men to take care of Morgan, but Tarleton was speedily and effectually crushed in the battle of the Cowpens, March 13, 1781. Although Morgan had the fewer men and they were mostly militia, a more brilliant triumph was never won by the American arms in the Revolution. The British lost 784 men, the Americans only 72. Cornwallis with the main army of the British pursued in hot haste, but though encumbered with 600 prisoners and a great amount of spoil, Morgan crossed the line of march of his enemy and made his escape without any further loss. For this victory, he was voted a gold medal by Congress. An attack of rheumatism compelled his retirement from the army, and he again returned to the Shenandoah, where he was called upon in July of the same year to suppress the tory insurrection on the South Branch. This duty was quickly performed, and he was made commandant de facto of the Winchester military district, in which were many of the Saratoga prisoners. Finding them in a deplorable condition in their stockades, he set them at work to repair the roads and quarry stone for building purposes. Charges were preferred against Morgan for his treatment of the prisoners, but he was exonerated. In 1793 he was advanced to the rank of major general, and in the following year he commanded the Virginia troops of the army sent to put down the Whiskey Insurrection.

In 1795, General Morgan came to Winchester to live, the new home being called "Amber Hill." In 1797-1799 he was a member of Congress. In 1800, being in failing health, he went to live with his daughter Betsy, who had married Major James S. Heard. In her house, which is yet standing in Winchester, he died July 6, 1802, after uniting with the Presbyterian Church. Betsy and Nancy, the children of General Morgan, were born at "Saratoga." The latter married Colonel Pressley Neville. Both had families, and a great granddaughter of Mrs. Neville married the late Admiral Robley D. Evans. General Morgan, who was more than six feet tall and of unusual muscular strength, figured in many pugilistic exploits in his earlier years.

The remains of General Morgan were buried in the old Presbyterian graveyard, and was subsequently reinterred in Mount Hebron, where the fissured tombstone, set in a horizontal position, may still be seen. In 1865 an attempt to take the slab to New Jersey was frustrated by another removal. Several efforts have been made to erect a monument in Winchester to the hero of the Cowpens, and it is to be hoped, for the credit of the city, that another and successful effort will yet be made. A committee intended to lay the cornerstone of a monument on July 4, 1856, but nothing was done. Probably at about the same time, one-half of the proceeds of an entertainment were turned into the monument fund, but what became of the money no one now seems to know. In 1886 Congress was asked for $15,000 for a monument, but declined on the ground that it had already set up a memorial on the battlefield of the Cowpens. In 1900 the firemen of Winchester initiated a movement that did not materialize, and through the influence of Mr. Cartmell's history, the Daniel Morgan Monument Association was formed in 1911 in Portland, Maine.

The inscription on the stone at General Morgan's grave reads as follows:

MAJOR-GENERAL DANIEL MORGAN
departed this life
On July the 6th, 1802,
In the 67th year of his Age.
Patriotism and valor were the
prominent features of his character,
And
the honorable services he rendered
to his country
during the Revolutionary War
crowned him with Glory, and will
remain in the Hearts of his
Countrymen
a Perpetual Monument
to his
Memory.

VIII

THE MIDDLE PERIOD

Petitions to Legislature — Streets — Roads — Hotels — Louis Philippe Incident — Fire Companies — Descriptions by Visitors.

> Came back to Winchester with Mr. Holmes and Captain Hunter and found everything war-like, every sound was martial, from drum beating or fifes and bag pipe playing. — Diary of Rev. Philip Fithian, in his visit to Winchester in 1775.

From the petitions to the General Assembly, one may glean interesting facts on local history. We preface this chapter with mention of certain of these and some running comment.

One of April 5, 1779 says that many persons "refuse the present currency to the great inconvenience and injury of many." A law is asked for their relief. But it was practically impossible to compel people to accept a paper money that was constantly depreciating, and in two more years was of so little account that a dinner in a tavern cost $30. They exacted coin or its equivalent whenever they could.

The same complaint reappears in a petition of May 17, 1780. Twelve "traders" of Winchester say that "depreciation is so rapid that we have never been able to replace the same quantity of goods with the money received from goods sold." The signers allege that the tax of 2½ percent on goods retailed, and not of Virginia growth or manufacture, is unequal, since the farmer does not pay a tax of one percent. The merchants are Bryant Brian, James Dowdall, Charles Haynes, James and William Holladay, John Kaine, William Kincaid, Samuel May, Patrick Murray, John Reynolds, Benjamin Shreve, and Lewis Wolfe.

A petition of May 20, 1782, signed by Frederick Conrad, Philip Bush, Edward Smith, and Edward McGuire, says much trouble is given by the sellers of intoxicants, and asks that the hustings court of the borough be given the sole power to grant license. The request was granted, and tavern-keepers were excluded from sitting as judges in the said court.

Six months later, Thomas Edmondson is wanting to divide his outlot of five acres into half-acre building lots. Permission was given.

A petition a year later still says hemp is much grown to get the money for paying taxes. In April, 1783, it brought four pounds ($13.33) per hundredweight in Pennsylvania, where much of the Virginia crop was marketed. Throughout the colonial period, hemp was a very important product west of the Blue Ridge, and a bounty was paid on it by the state. It has completely disappeared from Virginia and it is disappearing from Kentucky.

A petition of 1784, written on what looks like some of the wrapping paper now in use, asks that the Quakers be excused from having to attend muster. It was rejected.

Next year, 74 Mennonites, signing their names in German, ask relief from a revisal of the militia laws which violates the exemption they have enjoyed.

A paper of 1786 says there is no direct road to Richmond, and that the route via Fredericksburg is not only 25 miles out of the way, but hilly and sandy and several of the bridges out of repair. To go through Chester Gap only 12 miles of new road are needed.

Another of the same year says that tobacco is increasingly grown, and that at Alexandria, the nearest point of inspection, the facilities are inadequate.

The document of November 6, 1787 says the freight from the head of navigation is greater than the duties which are there levied. Before the present duties came into force, the petitioners could engross in a great measure the trade of the Western country, including Kentucky. They now feel a falling off in this trade. There are 21 retail stores in Winchester and eight in the county outside. Signers: John Conrad, Archibald Magill, Robert Sherrard, Jesse Taylor Jr., William Armstrong, Thomas Owram & Company, Matthew Wright & Company, Samuel Dowdall, W. and James Holliday, Lewis Wolfe, Richard Gray, John and James McAlister, W. W. Baker, N. Cooper.

A paper of nearly the same date asks a repeal of the exemption to Quakers and Mennonites, on the ground that the exemption tends to a total relaxation of discipline.

In 1790 we learn of an established road to Moorefield, and in the following year that there is a great increase in the population of Winchester, the town flourishing in trade and manufactures.

Petitioners of October 21, 1791 have spent much money in making sidewalks on Main street, and ask that the carriage way be paved also, since it is almost impassable in wet weather, especially in winter. Many of the merchants are now in Philadelphia and therefore not present to sign.

A paper of 1792 says it is a practice for a man wishing to marry a minor to forge a certificate, and put into it the names of two fictitious witnesses.

In 1793 there is a numerously signed petition against exempting the Quakers from militia service, and in 1797 another with a still larger number of signers.

In 1799 and again in 1815 there are petitions that a new county be formed out of parts of Frederick, Loudoun, and Fauquier. It is significant that since 1738 no county line has run across the Blue Ridge, thus showing that it has been recognized as a natural boundary between two well individualized sections of Virginia.

The many signers to a petition of December 13, 1810 declare that a local bank is needed. Winchester "possesses advantages for trade and manufacture equal to any inland town in the United States." But because of bad roads produce lies dead on the hands of its owners for several months and then sells at a disadvantage. Flour is the principal product and brings cash. "The farmer who is obliged to sell his produce is under the necessity of taking such price as the few monied men amongst us choose to give."

Incorporation is asked for a turnpike between Winchester and Harper's Ferry. A second petition asks for a turnpike to Snicker's Ferry by way of Berryville. A third asks for a joint company, the road dividing at Opequon Creek. A fourth, dated December 4, 1811, and with a very large number of signers, objects to the proposed plan because of the inconvenience to the people in the northwest of the county. It wishes the pike to begin at the northeast end of Main Street.

A paper of 1812 says Winchester has over 200 freeholders; more than in some entire counties. Including licenses, the town pays the state a revenue tax of about $1200. "Particular representation" in the legislature is asked.

In the same year the Opequon Manufacturing Company (John Davenport & Company) has a capital of $12,000, manufactures wool and cotton, and asks incorporation. Its plant includes a fulling mill and is on the Opequon. The signers are John McClure, John Hoff, John Clark, John Wright, John Davenport, Jr., Lewis Hoff, George Reed, James Curl, and Christopher Frye.

In 1813 a pension is asked by Daniel Anderson, who was twice wounded at Quebec and unfitted for hard labor. There is a testimonial by General Morgan. Robert Mackey is a doctor.

In 1815 there is already a turnpike from Baltimore to Boonsboro, and a company is to continue it to the Potomac at Shepherdstown. An extension from that place to Winchester is asked.

A petition of 1817 to restrain drunkenness is identical with one from Loudoun, especially the Quaker village of Waterford. The 61 names seem to belong chiefly in Winchester.

"Particular representation" is again asked in 1818, Winchester having between 200 and 300 voters.

In 1819 it is asked that Washington and Braddock streets be extended northward, and the lands described incorporated as an addition to Winchester. This is rejected. A counter petition by the landowners involved says there are more vacant lots in town than the spirit of improvement requires.

A petition of 1822 with 200 signers says that the peddling of tinware makes tin manufacturing in Virginia impossible. Peddlers come every fall from Massachusetts, Connecticut, and New York. The manufacturer comes at the same time with hands, tools, and materials, and thus furnishes the peddlers with fresh supplies. Each concern employs from 10 to 30 wagons, and every available article of trade is picked up in exchange. In April or May they go back, taking out of the state at least $75,000, not including what is sold by other peddlers from the North. These men pay no tax and evade license. Other states tax them.

Petitioners of 1822 have subscribed some money toward a monument to George Washington. Nothing being done they ask its return. The paper was laid on the table.

Three petitions of 1815 and 1824 ask a constitutional convention and a reform of the state government. The membership of the House should be 100 instead of over 200. The suffrage should be extended to all free white males having evidence of a common interest in the community and an attachment to it. The first of these petitions has 247 signatures.

In the Fairfax and Wood additions are ends of streets and alleys that run in between the lots and never can advantageously be extended farther. These are injurious to the looks of the town and are a resort for idle boys and negroes, thus causing the people much annoyance. There is no power in the town authorities to abate the nuisance. An Act making title to such ends became a law in 1825.

In 1825 Ephraim Hawkins, John Baker, and Heriot Conrad wish to build houses on Outlot 23. A law is passed to this effect, and in future applications of this nature the City Council is empowered to act.

John Colbert, a cavalryman in 1781-1783, is now infirm (1827) and asks a pension. It is not allowed because he was not in the Continental Line.

In the same year—1827—the Quakers protest against a law of 1806 that requires emancipated negroes to be sold as slaves unless they leave the state within one year.

Likewise in the same year, a turnpike is asked for the 36 miles to Stony Creek. The present road is rough and uneven, almost impassable in wet weather, and is dangerous in all seasons.

At a meeting held in the courthouse, December 27, 1827, Alfred H. Powell being chairman and Samuel H. Davis secretary, a memorial was unanimously adopted. It recites that the northwest of Virginia is cut off by mountains from the rest of the state. The produce of its people rots on their hands. "To all the purposes of commerce the territory is lost to the commonwealth and might as well be situated on the shores of the Pacific." Maryland by her enterprise has better roads and trade goes her way. On the Virginia route are ruinous villages. Virginia has given too much heed to Federal politics. A railroad without delay is urged from Winchester to Parkersburg, the navigation of the Ohio becoming surer from that point than from Pittsburg. There is a turnpike to Smithfield, 12 miles from here. To complete a pike to Washington, 30 miles of prepared road are needed, the four miles over the Blue Ridge being already paved. The postage on the petition, which was laid on the table, was 18¾ cents.

A memorial of 1822 says that "we have long viewed with regret and dissatisfaction the present seat of government for the state." It is not centrally located and is too vulnerable in time of war.

In 1830 the road from Berryville to the Shenandoah River is pronounced exceedingly bad.

A petition of the same year asks a good road to the Ohio River opposite Marietta. People now have to use the National Road, which lies in Maryland and Pennsylvania. The counties east of Winchester will be greatly benefitted. The Ohio will not need to be crossed. The northwest of the state asks that from $100,000 to $150,000 be applied.

In 1831 a road to Berryville is wanted.

In this year it is said that freedmen are "degraded, vicious, discontented, a burden to the community, and their presence objectionable." There is a memorial in favor of sending them to Liberia.

A petition of 1834, with many signatures, asks that Randolph Evans be permitted to remain. He bought his freedom of the late Captain Edward McGuire and keeps a confectionery shop and a refectory (restaurant). He is a useful citizen, but his wife and children are slaves, and if he can have the money to buy them he will go to Liberia.

Barbara, widow of Daniel Miller, a Continental in Lee's Legion, asks a pension in 1833.

In and about 1834 there are voluminous petitions for and against some proposed new counties. One of these required 75 cents in postage.

In 1834 is asked the incorporation of the "Winchester Infirmary" on the John Taylor estate, purchased for $2,000. The capital stock is not to exceed $10,000.

In 1830, "West Frederick" (the present county) had 9858 white inhabitants and 2088 slaves.

In 1835 it is declared that the Northwestern Pike will cost not over $1,000 a mile. The sections in it are 20 miles long. The tolls are too high, being based on roads costing $4,000 to $5,000 a mile. On a load of produce selling at $20 to $50, the tolls consume from 15 to 20 per cent.

Permission is asked in 1836 that Jonas Baker, freedman, be allowed to remain, but in the same year it is declared that "next to the existence of slavery, the partial emancipation of slaves is the greatest evil amongst us."

Piked roads are wanted in 1836 to Moorefield and Harrisonburg. If the Northwestern Road is extended to Berryville to connect with the turnpike to Washington, much trade will come to Winchester.

In 1838 a turnpike to Bath, distant 36 miles, is asked.

There are several other petitions in the same year. A good road to Moorefield is much needed. There is a huge petition for a turnpike to Staunton, but the Winchester and Potomac Railroad has lessened the interest of the people of this town in the road to Berryville, although there is now a piked road from that place to Washington. Liberia is the only available outlet for free negroes, other states excluding them. There is a petition against the annoyance by hucksters in selling cider, beer, candy, cakes, and other articles at places of worship. Liquor is secretly retailed and a disorderly crowd attracted.

Even before the Revolution the original Frederick county had been very greatly reduced in size. Hampshire, comprising at first all that lay west of North Mountain, was formed as early as 1753. Berkeley and Dunmore, each extending entirely across the Shenandoah Valley, were created in 1772, but as the tory governor of 1771-1775 became anathema to the patriot element, the county of Dunmore was renamed Shenandoah. The county of Clarke is the only further subtraction that has been made from Frederick, and it did not come into existence until 1836.

Since Winchester was at first very small it had very few streets, about the only ones being those now designated as Piccadilly, Market, and Water. In 1761, and by means of a lottery, Main Street was opened from Piccadilly to Cork. This section of the street was then a marsh, and in fact the basin comprising the business quarter of the town was long known as a marsh, from its liability to flood after heavy rains, and from the tanneries beyond Market Street. Mr. Russell mentions the high waters of 1795, 1818, 1838, 1839, 1846, and 1855. In 1855 two men took a swim in Main Street, and in the Planters' Bank the water was fifteen inches deep. Before 1811 he saw loads of wood drawn by eight horses stalled in the streets. But since all the hills have been reduced and the low areas raised, such inundations have become little more than a memory. In 1791 the sum of not more than 200 pounds ($667) was to be raised by a lottery for the purpose of paving Main Street; a sum which now would make only a respectable beginning. The proposition was accepted about 1804.

It was expected that Market would be the leading business street, but the lead was taken by the narrower Main Street from the fact that it lay in front of Fort Loudoun.

An explanation of the names of the principal streets may appropriately be given at this point.

Market was first called Cameron, from the title, "baron of Cameron," which Fairfax never failed to write into his deeds. Piccadilly is a namesake of one of the most beautiful and important of the streets of London. Main was first called Loudoun Street from the idol of clay who was military commander-in-chief in America in 1756. As such he brought contempt upon himself and the British government as well. Braddock was of course named for General Braddock, and Washington for General Washington. Boscawen—now Water Street—was named for Admiral Boscawen, who convoyed Braddock's army to Alexandria. Cork Street is alleged to be so called from the Irish families who located in that part of the town, and Germain was named for Lord Germain, a member of Lord North's cabinet. Cecil was named for Sir William Cecil, Lord Treasurer of England in the reign of Elizabeth. Gerard was named for Lord Charles Gerard, and Monmouth for the Duke of Monmouth, one of the dozen bastard children of Charles II. Leicester takes its name from the Earl of Leicester, a foul libertine in public life in the days of "good Queen Bess." Clifford is thought to have been named for Sir Thomas Clifford, an unsavory character in English history in the disgraceful reign of Charles II. He was the first in a group of five men who were a power behind the throne, the initial letters of their names spelling the word "cabal," a term always of sinister significance. Amherst and Wolfe streets were named, respectively, for Lord Amherst and General Wolfe of the French and Indian war. There was once a Duffield Street, but it is uncertain what street it was. Kent, in some manner, commemorates the county of Kent in England. Pall Mall is named for a street in London.

It will be observed that the names of several of the streets of this city have unfortunate associations, although the names, as names, are unobjectionable.

Mention of the streets naturally leads to mention of the roads tributary to Winchester. During the first nine years in the history of Frederick county—until 1753—the county court ordered 68 roads to be opened, and in the year and a half between March, 1788, and October, 1789, which was a time of prosperity, about 50 new roads were opened. Although the colonial roads were poor, the laws relating to their construction were rather minutely drawn. At every fork it was required that a guide-board in the form of a hand be set up.

As Pennsylvania, partly because of its German element, was the first state to have improved roads, so the Shenandoah was the first section of Virginia to move in the same matter, the abundance of limestone giving a very obvious hint. Distances were so great in the America of 1800 that good roads were a matter of the most vital need. Mr. Beveridge in his life of John Marshall mentions that it took 20 days to haul a ton of freight from Philadelphia to Pittsburg, the cost being $120, and it cost more to haul tobacco from Staunton to Richmond than the load would bring in the market.

When macadamizing began in the Lower Valley we do not know. The earliest recognition of turnpikes that we find is a one-column article in the Constellation for 1811. In speaking of

Winchester as the "metropolis of New Virginia," the editor says that pikes ought to diverge from the town, and that the people of the vicinity must positively act soon. The rapid growth of the Western and Southwestern states shows the necessity of better roads.

Even after railways began to appear there was quite a furor for piked highways, and for building them many companies were incorporated.

The more important of the macadamized roads radiating from Winchester in the pre-war period were the Valley Pike and the Northwestern Road, both being finished about 1838. The former was begun on an authorized capital of $300,000, the State taking three-fifths, and Winchester being authorized to subscribe for 400 shares of $25 each. But the actual cost of the 92 miles to Staunton was $425,000. The Northwestern Road, touching the Ohio at Parkersburg, was put forward by the western counties as a counterpoise to the Valley Pike, and until the construction of the Baltimore and Ohio railroad was the avenue of a heavy traffic. So long as it was under the care of the State Board of Public Works it was well kept up. In 1884 it became a public road.

In 1838 the Martinsburg Pike had cost $60,000.

During the fifties Virginia was building quite a mileage of planked roads. The Front Royal road was planked for four miles out from Winchester, and the North Frederick road for two miles. In 1858 the Berryville road was reported in excellent condition. In 1877 the county had spent on turnpikes $60,213.

The proprietor of the Taylor Hotel operated stage lines but had no monopoly of the business, and there was sometimes war between rival lines. In 1825 the stage fares were $2.50 to Harper's Ferry, $2.00 to Martinsburg, $6.00 to Staunton or Alexandria, and $8.00 to Baltimore, three days being required to make the distance to that city. In 1839 and 1840 the fares to Alexandria and Washington are advertised as reduced to $3.00 and $3.50, but in 1841 it was costing $4.00 to go to Washington. A stage left the Taylor Hotel at four o'clock in the morning, three times a week, arriving at Washington at seven in the afternoon. There was also a stage to Staunton three times a week, leaving at five in the morning and being due at Staunton at 1:30 p. m. the next day. In 1839 there was a stage twice a week to Parkersburg. Four days were required for the 235 miles and the fare was $15.50.

The hotels of Winchester make an interesting theme. There were already five or six at the close of the French and Indian War.

Three of these were the hostelries of Henry Heath, Philip Bush, and John Lindsay.

For more than a century the hotel of Winchester had a painted sign. The patron might not always be able to read, but he could always understand a picture.

The leading hotel was the one leased by Edward McGuire about 1765. He was followed by Bushrod Taylor. In 1846 a joint stock company was formed and the hotel was remodeled. At first there were two weatherboarded log houses, each 50 feet long with an alley between them. This hotel was considered the best in the town and army officers put up here. General Wilkenson, a man who tried to carry water on both shoulders, one shoulder standing for the United States and the other for Spain, was one of the frequenters of the Taylor House. His blue coat was faced with yellow where it was turned up in the corners of the skirt. The collar was trimmed with gold lace and on the shoulders were gold epaulettes. He wore a rosette in his hat, and from his belt hung a gold-hilted sword. Many noted Americans have been guests of this hotel. Henry Clay was here in 1849. Daniel Webster came in 1851 and addressed an audience from the upper porch. On the night of the presidential election of 1840 the building was stoned, but by which political faction we do not know. Thirteen men were presented by the next grand jury because of this affair. In the war of 1861 it was a headquarters for officers, both Federal and Confederate, and it was used by General Banks as a hospital. After a period of disuse as a hostelry it was reopened in 1905, but six years later it was sold to J. C. McCrory, and the ground story was converted into one of his ten-cent stores. In 1860, board and lodging cost $200 a year, and board alone, $150. Lodging for one day cost 50 cents and meals, $1.25, or both combined, $1.50. In the olden days the sign was plain and square, and bore the two words, "Coffee House." But before the recollection of Mr. Russell it carried the name, "General Washington."

The "Indian Queen," the sign representing a squaw, stood next to the Taylor House. In 1811 it was under the management of Pendleton Hironymus. Other proprietors were William McSherry and one Brady.

Opposite the Taylor House was the "Winchester Inn," which opened before 1800 and was running in 1838. One of its managers was Daniel Linn. The sign was a golden sheaf of wheat, carrying the legend, "May our Country never want Bread."

The "Virginia House" of 1838, at the corner of Main and Water, had taken some other name in 1841. The proprietor at the former date was Frederick Aulick.

The stand now known as the City Hotel sprang up before 1800, its first proprietor being William Van Horn. In 1861 it was carried on by Philip Hoover. Of the existing hotels this is by far the oldest.

The "Red Lion" at the southeast corner of Main and Cork, was a hotel at least as early as 1783. Soon after 1800 it had one large room for shows and exhibits, such as wax-works and Punch and Judy. This hotel enjoyed a widespread reputation, General Washington being one of its guests. It was conducted in different years by Peter Lauck, Edmund Pendleton, James Bryarly, James Kiger, Josiah Massie, and Mrs. Myer, the last named being here in 1811.

The "Columbian Inn", south of Town Run, was kept by Captain Peter Prince, who went to Zanesville, Ohio, in 1824. The "Traveler's Stand" was on Main near the Valley Bank, and was kept in 1838 by Andrew Bush. Henry Bush, a son of Philip Bush, kept where the present Presbyterian church stands, and he was succeeded by E. E. Russell. The Hollabeck House was on Main at the corner of Girard. Dalby's was on the east side of the street below Cork. Peter Kurtz was keeping a hotel on the same street in 1800 and after. At the corner of Main and Monmouth Elijah Walker had a wagon stand, his sign being a wagon and four horses. It is said that he was previously keeping a tavern on the site of the Planter's Bank. Later landlords here were Benjamin Richards and William Harr. The place was otherwise known as the "Negro Trader's Jail," and it seems to be referred to in an advertisement of 1856 which says that a hotel and negro jail are for sale in the south end of the city, the former containing fifteen rooms and having been in use twenty years. The notice adds that there is a "large and safe brick enclosure with the necessary arrangements for the safe keeping of slaves. It would consequently be a desirable property for a person dealing in slaves." Opposite Walker was the tavern of Philip Amick.

In the stage-coach days the hotel entertaining teamsters and drovers could not hope for any patronage from the upper crust of society.

In 1868 the "European Hotel" had lately been opened at the corner of Main and Piccadilly.

We have now enumerated all the taverns that we definitely know to have stood on Main Street. There were nearly as many on other streets.

Perhaps the earliest of the remaining hotels was the "Golden Buck" on the west side of Market just south of Town Run, the watercourse running through the lot. This fashionable hostelry was fifty feet long, and in front of the door was a large English walnut. After it ceased to be a hotel, the stone building was used as a house of worship by the Presbyterians. In 1842 it was used as a jail. Still later it was torn down to give place to a sawmill, the latter being burned by drunken soldiers in the war of 1861. Philip Bush, the proprietor of the "Golden Buck," came from Mannheim, Germany—as did also Lewis Wolfe the merchant—and he was a sworn enemy to royalty, having seen enough of it in his native land. Of him an interesting incident is related by John Esten Cooke and C. Toler Wolfe.

Louis Philippe, who had an unquiet tenure of the French throne for eighteen years, was in 1796-1800 a refugee in the United States, where he was joined by two brothers. His extensive travels in this country included a visit to Winchester. He and his brother, the Duke of Montpensier, and their servant arrived in a carriage, asked for lodgings, and were shown to a room. Dinner was announced by the rattle of a triangle, and though the seats were soon filled, the aristocratic guests did not appear. A servant was sent upstairs to call them and brought back the message that the Frenchmen wanted their dinner sent to their room. Bush replied that if they were too good for the common table they might go on. The future king pointed to the sign, and now, as it would appear, he disclosed his rank. Bush boiled over. He said he would not entertain such guests under any consideration, and, calling for his axe, said he would chop his sign down first. The guests paid their bill and drove on and the sign was saved.

"Rust's Hotel" was on Water Street in the rear of the establishment of Captain Kurtz. It was an old building with high roof and dormer windows, and was remembered by Mr. Russell as a great resort for the humorous men of the town. The "Union Hotel," a rival to the Taylor, was at the corner of Market Street and Fairfax Lane and therefore near the station. In 1838 Michael Price was keeping a hotel close to the station. It was destroyed by the Federal soldiers. The "Hart House" was on the site of the Graichen glove factory. The "American," also on Market Street was running in 1855. Another hotel on this street, on the west side, was started by Conrad Kremer, a deserter from the Hessian troops, and was afterward conducted by L. T. F. Grim, Henry Fridley, and finally Robert Brannon. It had a high reputation and in the rear was a wagon-yard.

"Osborne's Hotel" on Water Street had a local patronage. The "Blackhorse," which seems also to have been on the same street, was an ancient tavern. The landlord just after the Revolution was John Walters.

Another tavern was opened very soon after the Revolution by A. M. Edmondson. According to one account it was nearly opposite Fort Loudoun. Another and more probable statement is that it stood on Braddock and was pulled down to make room for the Episcopal college. It was a two-story building with a porch, and the sign was a full-rigged ship on a dark ground. In 1789 the landlord advertised that he had a newly opened billiard room. But Mr. Russell speaks of a log and frame house on Braddock, once occupied by Edmondson, as one of the buildings destroyed by the Union soldiers.

On the site of the Braddock Street Methodist church was the hostelry of Henry Heath, afterward a lieutenant in Daniel Morgan's company of riflemen. Washington boarded here prior to the building of Fort Loudoun. A very evident reason for doing so was the fact that the drill-ground for the militia lay on the other side of the street, and therefore within very convenient distance. Other hotels, whose location we are not able to give, were the "Winchester Hotel" and "Stubblefield's," existing in 1838; the "Tremont," conducted by E. A. Hibbard in 1841; and a long building back of Dr. Love's, which was kept by Frederick Aldridge, a bachelor. He had a still and sold whiskey, beer, and cakes. A hostelry of 1786 was the "Peyton House," probably on North Main Street. Although it was not a hotel, mention should be made of "Taffytown" on Piccadilly east of Kent, where a woman sold 20 inches of fine taffy for a penny. She had a monopoly in this species of candy, but after her time the business passed to the colored people. When C. Toler Wolfe was a printer's "devil" in Winchester, he used to gather up the exchanges in the office and trade them to her for eight or ten sticks.

In our account of the hotels it is possible that there are a few instances of duplication. Many of the taverns of Winchester ceased to exist long before the recollection of any townsman now living.

The "Winchester Inn," long since pulled down, was one of the ventures of the Equity Company about 1890. Of the modern houses of entertainment, Hotel Jack was opened in 1914. During the compilation of this volume, the George Washington has been in process of construction at the corner of Piccadilly and Market and was opened in June, 1924. The Hotel Evans formerly at the corner of Main and Piccadilly was razed to provide a site for the Commercial and Savings Bank.

The question of a water supply has been rendered easy by the copious limestone springs just within the town limits. When Colonel Wood caused Winchester to come into existence, he was required by Fairfax not to stop or alter the watercourse issuing from the "Federal Spring" near his house. This was so that the people of the town might be supplied with water from it. Because of the springs an ordinance against hogs running at large was enacted in 1791. In addition to the springs wells were formerly much in use. Among these were four public wells, and for many years they were carefully guarded. It is supposed to have been about 1808 that water was brought into town from the Tidball Spring, wooden pipes being used. These pipes were bored by horsepower. Every joint was secured by an iron ring sharpened at each end, and against these the pipes were forced. For further security there was also an outer ring. Sections of these wooden pipes with their collars are still dug up here and there. In fact, there appears to be some authority for the statement that Winchester is the pioneer town in the United States to install water works. A petition to the legislature, dated December 13, 1828, says it has been found necessary to substitute for the wooden tubes iron pipes from $1\frac{1}{2}$ to 6 inches in diameter. A fund of $10,000 was needed, and it could be redeemed in ten years. Accordingly, in 1829, iron pipes were put into position. About 1890, at an expense of $60,000, one-half of which was met by the city, the Hollingsworth Spring was purchased, and the water distributed from a reservoir.

A Gas Company was organized in 1853 with a capital of $60,000, and in May, 1889, it began lighting the streets. The corporation was succeeded in 1906 by the Winchester Gas and Electric Light Company.

The first fire company in Winchester had no other equipment than ladders and leather buckets. Each house of one story was required to have one of these, and every two-story house had to have two. There were tubs holding at least 50 gallons, but no hose. When the fire bell rang, every householder was expected to seize his leather bucket and run to the scene of action, where the emptied buckets were returned to the tank by women and children. The first engine was of the "gooseneck" pattern and very small, and came from England in 1788. A larger and better one was afterward supplied. In 1829 the Union engine was purchased. After the civil war, when the Shenandoah engine was put into use, there were three efficient engines.

The present fire department of the city is of the volunteer type. It has long been a source of pride to the community and has exerted great influence. The separate companies are four: the Friendship, the Charley Rouss, the Sarah Zane, and the South End Hose Company. The memberships, respectively, are 636, 481, 214, and 136. The captains, in the order of mention, are F. W. Forney, W. E. Huntsberry, H. H. Willis, and C. H. Grim.

The oldest companies are the Friendship and the Charley Rouss, formerly the Union. As to which of these was first in the field there has been no little controversy. The matter was carried into court and not decided for three years owing to the loss of all early records. It was there adjudged that the Friendship was organized in 1831 and the Union in 1833. But since that time the Rouss company has brought forward the following notice, which appears in the Winchester Gazette of May 10, 1789: "The members of the Union Fire Company are notified that their meeting was adjourned to the first Saturday in the present month, then to assemble at the Market House." But the Friendship counters by producing a helmet of an early member of the company bearing the date 1771.

The Union was first quartered in the building immediately west of the Lutheran church that was taken down in 1923. Because of a donation of $10,000 from Mr. Rouss, it changed its name to the Charley Rouss Fire Company, and was incorporated as such, May 20, 1896. In its present home, still on Water Street, the birthday of Mr. Rouss is observed every year with banquet and speeches. October 5, 1917, the Rouss Hook and Ladder Company was consolidated with the Charley Rouss Fire Company. The equipment is very modern and includes hose truck and pumper, the former driven by a motor of 118 horsepower and the latter having a capacity of 350 gallons per minute. Its city service ladder truck, with a 130 horsepower motor, was also built by the Seagrave Company.

The Friendship Fire Company is on Cork Street, and was also befriended by Mr. Rouss. It has an American La France fire truck and an engine of the same type, the latter having a delivery per minute of 800 gallons. Its La France combination hose wagon has a 100 horsepower motor.

The Sarah Zane Fire Company appeared in 1840 and was named for Miss Sarah Zane, who presented it with its first hand-pumping engine. This is still preserved as a relic. The Zane was the first local company to use horses, the Friendship coming next. Horses were never used by the Union. Its present engine house was completed in 1879. This company has a Seagrave combination hose wagon with 130 horsepower motor and pump of 600 gallons capacity.

The South End Hose Company, organized in 1895, has Dodge motor and American La France hose truck.

Fire alarms are not infrequent in Winchester, but in nearly every instance the flames are brought under speedy control. In 1894 a fire opposite the Taylor House caused a loss of $50,000. Since this volume was begun the hospital of the city was nearly ruined by a conflagration, which, through no fault of the firemen, could not promptly be subdued.

It was remarked in a preceding chapter that when two Moravian missionaries passed through Winchester in 1753, they found about 60 houses in the place. Staunton at the same time had only one-third as many, and it may astonish the reader to be told that Baltimore, though founded in 1729, had in 1752 only 25 houses and 200 inhabitants. Whether Philadelphia or New York was then the metropolis of the colonies is a point in controversy, but in 1753 the population of the former city was 14,563, or less than twice the present size of Winchester. Alexandria, the nearest point to navigable water, was not laid out until 1749.

When this town was visited in 1786 by a foreigner, Count Castiglioni, he speaks of its having about 200 houses. The chief traffic was in wheat, flour, and hemp, which were exchanged in Philadelphia and Baltimore for European manufactures. From Winchester these goods were expedited over the mountains to the West. Land in the vicinity could be bought for three to four pounds per acre, and twelve miles away for 50 shillings ($8.33.)

The fairs, already alluded to and which now lasted three days, were much like the Western Fourth of July in the seventies in addition to the commercial features. People came to pay debts, buy land, trade horses, and get bills of exchange. Goods were displayed in booths and on tables. Pocket money was saved up for the occasion, and a part of it was spent for gingerbread and sweetmeats. For the amusement of the crowd, and incidentally for fleecing it, there were greased pigs, slow horse races, fortune-telling, fakirs, and vendors of quack medicines.

In 1796 Isaac Weld found 350 houses in Winchester. The same year Le Rochefoucauld, a French traveler, says there were over 30 stores in the place and 10 or 12 inns. By this time the population of the Shenandoah Valley had become almost stationary. The farmers were turning their attention to wheat and had begun to pasture their cattle in the Alleghanies. This Frenchman observes that "the habitations are in this district more numerous than on the other side of the Blue Mountains, but the mean, small log houses are inhabited by families that swarm with children and eat salt fish, pork, and greens." But perhaps this specimen of the European nobility was not fair or sympathetic in reporting what he saw.

Morse's American Gazetteer of 1810 says that "Winchester, or Frederickstown, is a handsome and flourishing town standing on low and broken ground, and has a number of respectable buildings, among which are courthouse, jail, Presbyterian, Methodist, and new Roman Catholic churches. The dwelling houses are about 350 in number, several of which are built of stone. It is a corporation and contains 1780 free inhabitatants and 348 slaves. It was formerly fortified, but the works are now in ruins."

Morse does not speak of brick buildings, but if there were none as yet they soon began to appear. It is said that the first brick house in the Valley was built in Stephensburg in 1785 by John Hite. The enumeration of the churches could not have been accurate, since there were five in 1812.

Kercheval's description in 1833 is very complimentary. He says there are 4000 people, 30 to 40 retail stores, six or seven large warehouses at the station, many lawyers and doctors, several taverns, confectionaries, and merchant tailors, and that nearly every kind of business found in a seaport occurs here, Winchester being a place of deposit of vast quantities of merchandise. The Taylor Hotel, 90 by 130 feet, contains 70 rooms and does an immense business. The writer adds that the health of the town is good, that the place is very fortunate as to fires, and that there are many hydrants. The Valley Turnpike has just come into operation, and the Northwestern Road has lately been finished.

In the Rockingham Register of February, 1840, an Alabama visitor says the streets of Winchester are lined with wagons from Pocahontas, Pendleton, Augusta, Hardy, and Hampshire, filled with produce of all kinds. There are 10 or 12 commodious warehouses and immense trains of loaded cars. This Southerner says the change from what he saw on a former visit is magical. In his comment on the letter, the editor of the Virginian declares that Winchester is "destined to become the center of trade for all the vast section of the state west of the Blue Ridge."

For a long while there was a great amount of wilderness in the country to the westward, and special attention was thus given to the fur trade. For a century and a half tanning was an important and profitable business in Winchester.

When David H. Strother, otherwise "Porte Crayon," left this town in the summer of 1851 to travel to the Canaan of the upper Potomac at the rate of 10 miles an hour over the Northwestern Road, he remarks that Winchester has 5,000 inhabitants. And yet only 87 miles westward lay a wilderness nearly as large as the state of Rhode Island in which elk had lately been killed.

Mr. Russell speaks of an unchartered bank in 1815, which, in consequence of a law enacted about two years later, was compelled to close; and that most merchants of the preceding period had been issuing individual notes, which, by the same law, were called in. He may refer to the Bank of Winchester, chartered in 1804, Winchester being allowed to take 525 shares of $100 each.

The first local bank of a bona fide nature was the Winchester Branch of the Farmers Bank of Virginia, established in 1812 with a capital of $250,000; or, by another statement, 1,666 shares of stock of a par value per share of $100. In 1818 the directors of this bank, as appointed by the Executive, were Beatty Carson, Isaac Hollingsworth, Daniel Lee, John Mackey, Archibald Magill, William Morris, John Smith, and Edward J. Smith. Those appointed by the stockholders were Jacob Baker, Daniel Hartman, Godfrey Miller, Robert Page, and Edward Smith. Miller was succeeded the next year by John Baker. The heaviest stockholders were H. W. Baker with 126 shares, Daniel Gold with 100, John Miller with 50, Robert Gray with 30, and Godfrey Miller with 24.

A petition of 1835 asks an increase of $360,000 to the capital stock of the Bank of the Valley, $150,000 being assigned to the mother bank, the branches at Leesburg, Charlestown, and Romney each receiving $70,000. Lewis Hoff was the cashier of this bank from the time of organization until his death.

In 1816 there was a proposal to divide Virginia on the line of the Rappahannock and Great Kanawha rivers. Had it been carried into effect, Winchester would almost certainly have become the capital of the new commonwealth.

In speaking of the industrial and mercantile establishments in Winchester a century ago, Mr. Russell names 13 cabinet and chair makers, 13 wagonmakers, 13 boot and shoe makers, 12 blacksmiths, more than 12 hatters, 9 saddlers, 7 tanners, 7 tailors, 6 tinners, and 5 weavers. The dealers in ready-made clothing were Leonard Baum, Benjamin and Richard Bushnell, John Harrison, Frederick Aulick, Jacob Sherer, William McFee, Michael Fitzsimmons, and Alexander Gibson. Baum, the pioneer in this line, opened his store about 1820. The jewelers were James Meredith, Thomas and William Campbell, Samuel Johnston, Daniel Hartman, William Phillips, George B. Graves, Goldsmith Chandler, and one Evard.

IX

AN ANNALISTIC CHAPTER

> At 12 o'clock the different crafts, consisting of upwards of two hundred, with Capt. Heiskell's Company of Light Infantry, commanded by Maj. McGuire, assembled at the court house from whence they marched in procession through the principal streets to the Federal Spring, at Gen. Wood's plantation, whence an elegant Barbequi was prepared for their reception. — Winchester Centinel, July 9, 1788, on the celebration of the ratification of the Federal Constitution.

In this chapter we are giving the newspapers of Winchester an opportunity to present their version of the story of the town for the period of nearly three-fourths of a century intervening between the making of the national constitution and the war of 1861. But certain topics, discussed in other chapters, are excluded from the present one.

At the beginning of the era the War for Independence had very lately closed. The times were prosperous and trade with Europe was unimpeded. Winchester was enjoying a "boom" of a very real kind and more normal than the artificial spurts of 1889-1890.

Yet long-visioned people did not see bright colors throughout the picture. The hard money thrown into circulation by the French and British armies was stimulating the importation of articles of luxury and creating a fever of speculation. Another effect of the war was a marked drift toward infidelity fostered by such writers as Thomas Paine and the French skeptics.

Our running narrative is not continuous, the gaps being occasioned by the fact that for some years the newspaper files are entirely missing. Our first glance begins in the summer of 1787 and continues four years.

George Newsam and Edward Slater have begun business in Winchester as carpenters, joiners, and cabinet-makers. They hail from London and Dublin and come with "long experience in the first cities of Europe." No doubt they toned up their "ad," but by reading between the lines we can understand that they decided upon Winchester because they believed it had a bright future before it.

One Wells makes clocks and watches. In other words, he is not simply a repairer of those necessary articles.

Daniel Norton & Company, whose store is on the corner of Main and Piccadilly, have a long advertisement, in which they not only enumerate the goods they have just received from Europe, but name the ship in which they were brought.

The store of John & James McAlister on Main opposite the bridge has a tobacco hogshead for a sign. The firm operates a nail factory. The store of the McAlisters was one of the largest in Winchester. Leaf tobacco, ginseng, deerskins, and military certificates were purchased. The stone nail factory was probably at the east alley, where it enters the public square. It was afterward used as a bakery. This firm built the Greenwood Mills about 1785.

Another advertiser has an elegant double chair with steel springs and it is almost new. A fourteen year old negro girl will be taken as payment.

Frederick Conrad offers a reward of $15 for eight calfskins taken from his place by night. One guinea ($3.50) is offered for the return of a gold ring that has been lost, and a reward of six guineas is offered for the return of two slaves. For the recovery of a horse the sum of $5 is offered. We read that the watchmaker shop of William Richardson has been broken into, but that two of the villains have been caught. In fact, runaways, burglaries, and other forms of theft seem to be of rather frequent occurrence.

Somebody wants rags; probably for the paper-maker, rather than for carpets.

Persons fond of tropical fruits may purchase pineapples, oranges, lemons, and figs.

James Ridley is a maker of stays, an article that now is called a corset.

A letter on "The Fatal Consequences of Luxury" is published, and in 1788 the editor remarks on the unusual number of families that pass through Winchester on their way to Kentucky.

In language suggestive of the sharpness of old vinegar, several persons free their minds with respect to stories circulated to their disadvantage.

Nathaniel Burwell, miller, will trade salt for wheat, bushel for bushel. Edward Powers, "taylor and habit-maker," will give 12 months credit to old customers. Martha and Catharine Mackay, mantua-makers, have learned their business in Europe.

In May, 1788, the Gazette says that Rumsay has made his steamboat run upstream at Shepherdstown at a speed of four miles an hour. This experiment was destined to work wonders in navigation.

November 3, 1789, a bear strolled into town, but was shot before he could exhibit a written permission for his visit.

E. S. Deegin, who has learned his trade in Europe, has a scythe factory on Duffield Street and wants apprentices.

E. Smith advertises apple trees large enough to set out.

A bachelor is defined by some local genius as "a whimsical being which nature never intended to create."

M. Twigg proposes to establish a cotton factory employing 50 to 60 hands and some boys and girls. The business is to have a capital of 100 shares of 10 pounds each.

A tavern sign representing an Indian chief is for sale.

Sherrard & Alexander at the new stone house advertise wet and dry goods, but fail to say whether the former are articles that have fallen into Town Run.

Joseph Hollingsworth has built a fulling mill. Raw cloth designed for it may be left at the store of Amos Jolliffe, sign of the Blue Ball.

Rye and barley are wanted at the brewery.

William King, turner and cabinet-maker, is on Market Street opposite the sign of the Bear.

Dr. Scott will inoculate gratis not more than 25 poor persons.

In 1790 Frederick will produce more than 50,000 barrels of flour; more than any other county in the Valley.

A wife has eloped with another man, but no reward is offered.

20 barrels of peach brandy are wanted.

A negro man has run away from General Morgan.

Daniel Miller wants at once five or six journeymen tailors and will pay weekly 18¾ shillings ($3.12) in addition to board and washing. There will be no charge for board when work is slack. The frequent calls for journeymen indicate that business is generally good.

Thomas Owram & Company employ workmen from Europe in their hemp and flax factory in Piccadilly, and pay $6 per hundredweight for good, clean hemp. They complain of depredations by boys but want eight or ten apprentices.

A certain advertiser offers a reward of one cent for the return of a runaway white servant, but one liberal man offers $2. Apprentices used to be noted for idleness, and the inference is that their masters were willing to be rid of them.

Some of the business men not already spoken of are the following:

L. M. Christophe, a portrait painter, is on Market Street near the Market House. His name indicates that he is a Frenchman.

Perry & Huston are clockmakers.

Richard White is a bookbinder.

Peter Kehoe, opposite the "gaol," makes boots, shoes, and slippers.

The store of Jacob Kahn is near the Market House. That of Joseph Tidball carries the sign of the umbrella, while Kinzing & Harbeson, who exchange merchandise for country produce, have a tea canister as a sign. William Holliday's store is opposite John Donaldson's tavern. O'Neal & O'Loughlin, opposite the jail, have the sign of the spinning wheel and carry a general assortment of European and West India goods. Thomas Cantwell is a successor to Joseph Holmes. John Murphy, near the Run, has groceries, hardware, dry goods, liquors, and he carries on a baking business. Jonathan Swift & Company, in a ten-inch space of double column breadth, advertise New England shoes among many other articles. Still other general merchants are Henry Baker, Hamilton Cooper, Richard Gray, and William Lowry & Company.

Daniel Miller, a tailor and habit-maker, is opposite Thomas Edmondson's tavern on Federal Hill.. William Richardson, a "watchsmith," lives two miles from town. Robert Wills and John Smith are also jewelers. Philip Bush is another jeweler and his sign is a golden urn. Hugh Jordan has a boot and shoe factory opposite the church on Main Street. Edward Brackenson, John Miller, and Richard Riordan are in the same line. William Hall is a hatter, and Frederick Hass is a tanner. George Hardesty keeps a tavern, and W. Haycock is a soap-boiler and tallow chandler.

Our next glimpse is in the summer of 1800. The Gazette is issued every Wednesday from its office on Main Street opposite the Episcopal church. The Fourth of July is celebrated by a dinner with sixteen toasts at Henry Bush's tavern, and in the evening by a ball at Captain A. McDonald's. There is mention of Bell's bookstore. Robert Gray deals in dry goods, hardware, and cutlery. Runaway negroes and apprentices are advertised. We are told that for forty years there has been no ferry in the Shenandoah above the main fork; also that Berryville was laid off a few years ago adjoining Battletown, on the land of Benjamin Berry, and that it has since rapidly grown.

In October, 1802, the executors of General Washington offer

for sale a half-acre lot adjoining Dr. Mackey. There is a good post and rail fence around it. They will also sell a farm in this county of 571 acres. We further learn that rags are in keen demand and cash will be paid for them.

We now come forward to the period of the war of 1812, our file of the Constellation beginning in January, 1811. But we are helped out by the reminiscences of Mr. Conrad and Mr. Russell, their boyhood recollections beginning a few years earlier.

An extraordinarily wet period began in May, 1804 and continued eight weeks. We are told by Mr. Conrad that it rained every day, and that for two years following there was much sickness.

The same authority relates that until about 1810 British halfpennies were in general circulation, the value of the coin being the same as our cent. Packhorses bringing ginseng came from as far as Tennessee. Companies of Indians visited Winchester every year about this time. In their target practice they would hit a mark for a silver coin, but scorned to do so for a copper penny. Soon after the expedition by Lewis and Clark in 1803, a delegation from the tribes on the upper Missouri passed through this town.

Mr. Russell describes the type of carriage he used to see in his boyhood. The wheels were low and strong and the running gear was very heavy. On the hounds were two springs fifteen inches high in the form of a J turned upside down. A similar pair in front did not rise so high, and to these were attached strong leather braces made by stitching several pieces of leather together. The braces supported a coach with an elliptical bottom. In the door on each side was a large oval glass, and at the rear was a larger door. At the end of the running gear was a flat board to support a trunk. There was no seat in front. The driver rode and used neither whip nor lines.

The first circus to visit Winchester came about 1810.

In 1813 the salient and reentering angles of Fort Loudoun were easily visible, and the stone magazine was still in place.

We now turn to the short file of the Constellation, and one of the first things we learn is that in 1811 there was a society in Winchester for the encouragement of domestic manufactures. It undoubtedly came into existence because of the depredations of England and France on American shipping. Philip Nelson was president and Lawrence A. Washington secretary. Premiums of from $5 to $50 were offered on wool and woolen goods of home production. The society was still in operation in 1813. The third annual meeting was at the Friendly Grove Factory by the residence of Joseph C. Baldwin. The pieces of woolen, cotton, and linen goods exhibited were larger than ever yet. An improvement in sheep is noted and several premiums are given, Mrs. Edward McGuire winning a prize of $10 on a piece of cotton cloth.

Nicholas Fitzsimmons, a tailor, wants two journeymen and two apprentices, and is prepared to make a man's suit in twelve hours. His prices are $2.50 to $3.50 for "great coats," $2 to $3 for common coats, $1.00 to $1.25 for breeches or pantaloons, and $1 for a waistcoat.

Philip Hoff, a merchant, advertises for furs.

Bound boys who run away are still in poor demand, the highest reward we find being "100 cents," and the lowest one cent. Whoever takes up a fifteen-year old bound girl of "low statue" and wearing a striped linsey petticoat will be paid six cents but will receive no charges or thanks. But for a negro man $10 is offered.

Two girls and one man are to be sold from McGuire's tavern.

Wax figures are one of the attractions at the Red Lion, and among the curiosities brought into town are a baboon and a guanaco.

General merchants are James Roberts & Company, Throckmorton & Holliday, James Little, Hoff & Morris, William A. Baker, Joseph Evans & Company, and Joshua & B. Aydelotte.

James Little has a warehouse for wheat, Nathaniel Perkins is a rectifier of spirits, David Russell has a chair factory, Adam Kurts Jr. is a maker of boots and shoes, Jeremiah Bowling has a tobacco factory, and Robert Gray is bookseller and stationer. John Wall has a brickyard, Jacob Kiger is a blacksmith, John Hasfeldt is a confectioner, and John C. Clarke is a skin dresser and maker of buckskin breeches. Robert Campbell and Joseph Massie are hatters, William Jones is a chair maker, Sommerville & Poland are saddlers, William Washington Vernon is a tailor, and Thomas Roberts Company have a "constant supply of split-bottom'd chairs." F. Kimmelmyer is a sign and portrait painter and he teaches his craft to others. S. & D. Hollingsworth have a fulling and dyeing mill. Charles Potter is glazier, house painter, and paper-hanger. Lauck & Coyle have a hat factory, Hening & Barhart are coach-makers, Newbrough & Hendricks are cabinet makers, Lewis & John Young are tailors, R. W. Kent handles dry goods and hardware, and kettles and stills may be had at the copper and tin warehouse of Davison & Richardson.

Against the good order of the community are several debits. Elopements occurred a century ago as well as now. The mail stage between Winchester and Frederick was robbed of two trunks. One white man and two negroes broke jail, one of the latter having given his freedom papers to a slave.

Among the orderly occurrences are a meeting at the Coffee House (McGuire's tavern) in favor of turnpike roads. In 1811 the Fourth of July is celebrated with a barbecue and eighteen toasts. On the next anniversary the speech delivered in the Presbyterian church is printed in the Constellation.

In 1811 the events of the war in Europe between Napoleon and the allies are given much space, but attention is soon directed to the prospect of war between our country and England. The Federalist party, especially in New England, was much opposed to the clash, and bitter language was exchanged by political editors. The Constellation says of some remarks in a Federalist paper that 'they should have come from Canada." In 1813 it reprints from a Boston paper an editorial on "infernalism," the Northern editor complaining that, "we are in a condition no better in relation to the South than that of a conquered people."

The Constellation notes that in his defeat of the Indians at Tippecanoe, General Harrison captured 90 new rifles and muskets of British manufacture. Ever since the Revolution the British officers in the Northwest had been instigating the red men to raid the border settlements. And yet English writers seem to wonder at the dislike of England which had not died out in 1917.

The day after the news of the burning of Washington was memorable in Winchester. There was a levy en masse, and every able-bodied white male from sixteen up to old age was asked to fall into the ranks. But as the British hastily retired from the capital, then consisting only of scattered groups of houses, the militia did not march beyond Harper's Ferry.

For a while the Twelfth United States Infantry lay in camp at Winchester. There are seemingly contradictory statements as to the position of its camp, one placing it on Camp Hill between Leicester and Monmouth streets, and the other placing it at the Shawnee Spring. Perhaps both localities were used. Its commander was Colonel Thomas Parker, whose military district took in all Virginia west of the Blue Ridge. He drilled his men twice a day. The private soldier received $8 a month, a bounty of $40, and the promise of 160 acres of public land. Dr. Scott, the regimental physician, offered his services to the people of Winchester. Before the regiment began its march to the Canadian boundary, its band played the dead march before a snow figure in a sleigh. The effigy was understood to represent General Hull, the officer who had just disgraced the American cause by surrendering at Detroit.

Winchester was the recruiting station for the companies of Captains Thomas Roberts, Willoughby Morgan, William Morris, Henry Beatty, and Michael Coyle. Morgan's company was in the artillery service, and that of Roberts was a rifle company. Roberts had great influence with his men, who were six months in the service. Their blue uniform was trimmed with white cord. To the fur hat was attached a bucktail, and in front was a white plate on which appeared an eagle armed with arrows. Both commands proceeded to Norfolk, as did also a cavalry company under Henry St. George Tucker. Some of the soldiers from this district were present at the battle of Craney Island, July 26, 1814, when 4000 British soldiers and marines were repulsed with a loss of 200 men, the Americans sustaining no casualties. Yet several from Winchester and vicinity lost their lives in the war. William Bell and John Schultz died at Norfolk, the former being killed by accident. David Hunter and Natty Ryan, probably members of the Twelfth Regulars, were killed in the battle of Williamsburg on the St. Lawrence.

There were desertions from the troops that rendezvoused at Winchester, and there is an advertisement for the recovery of a "deserter and villain." On the other hand, the Constellation publishes an interesting letter two columns long, written by a soldier in camp.

A riot in Baltimore in 1812 has a local bearing, since one of its victims was the printer Lingan, who had followed his trade in Winchester. It was in the same riot that General Henry Lee, father of the Confederate chieftain, received injuries from which he never fully recovered.

February 20, 1815 was a day of thanksgiving in this town because of the news of the conclusion of a treaty of peace with Britain. There was a speech at the Presbyterian church by the Rev. William Hill. But there was a business depression the same year. Land in the Lower Valley depreciated 50 per cent in value, and money became very "tight."

The next turn of the kaleidoscope carries us forward ten years, but the picture presented is very meager. The times are hard and the plan for a new courthouse is much opposed. Beef is four cents a pound and the cost of a trip to Baltimore is twice what it is now. Lafayette, who was touring the United States, was expected to visit Winchester, but he failed to do so.

AN ANNALISTIC CHAPTER 123

Beginning in January, 1838, the newspaper files become nearly continuous, and we examine those closing with 1840.

The business houses are seemingly more numerous than ever, and we find the following dealers in general merchandise:

Clark & Windle	John Harrison
Henry P. Ward	William Sherman
Samuel Rea	Frederick Aulick
William Miller	N. S. Long & Company
Jacob Senseny	Rhodes & Smith
Henry F. Baker	Thomas Allen
Hupp & Machir	Brannon & Forney
M. Hite	William D. Holliday
James M. Richards	James B. Taylor & Company
Lloyd Logan	William T. Wall
Joseph McIntosh	

Long is at the corner of Piccadilly and Main. Wall, who is in the Golden Temple, otherwise known as Solomon's Temple, has hats for sale at $2.50 to $8.00; figures with a very modern appearance. J. & G. Baker have 2000 pounds of loaf sugar in stock. One merchant has received 500 bushels of Maine potatoes. A certain class of customers are gladdened at the news that in one store are 600 bottles of Scotch snuff.

But there are other stores and offices. The druggists are Dorsey & Bowly and William Miller, the latter three doors south of the Taylor Hotel. The jewelers are Robert W. Reed and Thomas B. Campbell. Reed's sign is a gold watch and is opposite the Eagle Hotel on Main. The bookstore is kept by John N. Bell. John G. Smith keeps hardware, and Simpson & Barley have a shoestore. The special dealers in dry goods are Michael W. Reed and John M. Lupton & Company. The barbers are James Enders, Robert Simmons, and Frederick Williams. Ginn & Stackhouse have an iron and brass foundry, and George Barnhart has a coach factory. Thomas McGlennan is a dyer and James H. Burgess a draper and tailor. William Sherman keeps ready-made clothing as well as groceries. John D. Seaman is a coach and harness maker. L. Wilson & Company are commission merchants. The milliners are Mrs. Thomas, Mrs. Tipping, and Mrs. Searle. The dentists are M. Smith and M. Overfield, the latter giving Winchester ten days each month. The photographer has not arrived as yet, but James McCoughtry, a native of Jefferson county who has studied in Europe, will paint portraits. Landreth's seeds are for sale in some of the stores, and there are many advertisements of patent medicines and lotteries. That cooking stoves are already known appears in the advertisement of one of them for sale. A

Front Royal firm advertises a thrashing machine which is probably of that early pattern known in industrial history as a chaffpiler.

Thomas Allen, proprietor of the Winchester Gardens, will furnish cream and sugar to those who wish to eat his strawberries on his grounds, the charge being 12½ cents a quart. Like Robert Steele of the same line of business, Allen was a Scotchman. His garden was near the Wood spring.

In Frederick county are 12 subscribers to a 12 volume Life of Washington at the price of $3.25 a volume.

The postoffice advertises about 160 letters, and papers issued in Richmond on Friday do not arrive until the Tuesday following. In 1810 and for a long time after, William Davidson was postmaster. Mail was delivered through a window opening upon an alley, and callers had to take the weather as it came. The postage from Baltimore or Washington was 10 cents. Davidson was followed by Thomas Roberts.

With Tygert, Tidball, and others, Roberts started about 1815 a cotton factory on Abraham's Run, a little more than two miles from town, but the enterprise did not succeed.

In the Virginian is a letter from Liberia written by a free negro.

There are just four pianos in Winchester, on which music is executed; sometimes literally, it may be. Other items of local news are that one merchant has 600 oranges; that in the year ending July 15, 1840, 163,000 barrels of flour were shipped from this town; that in August of the same year the Valley Pike is nearly finished and the Northwestern Road completed; that James M. Carson commands the Sixteenth Brigade; that the cost of admission to the circus and menagerie of 1838 is 50 cents; and that in one column of the Virginian are nine advertisements for the hiring out of slaves.

That newspapers are much less plentiful than in our time is shown by the statement that in all Virginia there are 52, and 10 of these are published in Richmond. And it is of interest to note that in the United States there are 1555 papers, including 116 dailies. Of the 1555 only 33 are foreign language journals.

Theatrical entertainments were much in vogue, both before and after the war of 1812. The Thespian society performed in the Market House. In 1825 another society was formed that used Daniel Hartman's building. A third, organized soon afterward, performed in the old Methodist church. The customary admission appears to have been 50 cents.

An Annalistic Chapter

The Virginian of 1841 is heavily charged with national politics, and yet it reserves a little space for local occurrences. In its columns are numerous liquor and lottery advertisements, and there is a very long list of advertised letters, the rule requiring prepayment not yet having come into force. In accordance with a proclamation of President Tyler, the mayor, Obed Waite, appoints Friday, May 14, as a day for national humiliation and prayer. To the recently organized Washingtonian Temperance Society, 70 members were added at the close of a temperance lecture in June. There is complaint of disorderly conduct by negroes on the streets at night. The Fourth of July falling on Sunday, there was a parade on Saturday by the Winchester Artillery and the Highland Blues, and an oration in the new Presbyterian church by George F. Thornton. There was another parade on Sunday and a special sermon in the Kent Street Presbyterian church. Finally a Sunday school procession wended its way to the Methodist church and was there addressed by the minister. And last but not least, those who can afford to do so may eat fresh oysters every day.

Although the railroad fare was lower in 1841 than it is now, it cost $4.50 to go to Washington, because the trains had to go by way of Relay. The Metropolitan Branch, from Point of Rocks to Washington, was not built until 1872.

Home manufactures still thrive. John Kerr, a cabinet and bedstead maker, has a place of business at the Virginia House on the corner of Main and Water. That Thomas W. Grimshaw is a reed-maker, proves that the hand looms have not been retired from service.

The paper money of that era was of uncertain quality. A copy of "The Bank Note Detector," costing $1, was as likely to be seen on the merchant's desk as the mammoth catalog of a mail order house is now likely to be seen in a private home. The Virginian remarks that the "country is flooded with noted thieves, counterfeiters, and swindlers of every description." Baltimore and Ohio notes are a larger part of the circulating medium in Winchester. They are 10 per cent below par, and the people are much concerned about it.

The census of 1840 reports 3454 people in Winchester, which is the eighth place in the state in point of size.

Early in the year the editor says the young people of the town are moving for a library. The movement must have succeeded, for a letter written in September remarks that there is an excellent library and free use of the town hall for public discussions. But the correspondent puts this question: "Is not mental improvement too much neglected by the young gentlemen of Winchester?"

In 1842 a temperance convention, representing nine counties and 5000 members, was held on Washington's birthday. There are 300 members in the Winchester Total Abstinence Society.

There are special trains to the Halltown camp meeting, yet railroad notes fall to 75 cents on the dollar.

Newton Boley, whose headquarters are at Danner's Hotel, wishes to buy 40 to 50 negroes.

Fitch & Evans have begun making candies at the corner of Main and Water streets. Sugar is six cents a pound, coffee $12\frac{1}{2}$, and molasses $37\frac{1}{2}$.

Twelve Indians visit this town in December.

The Republican of 1848 is a Democratic newspaper, the full name of the party being "Democratic-Republican." In common usage the first part of the hyphenated name was dropped. Members of the Whig party, the one then in opposition, were called "Coons." The paper has much to say on the war with Mexico and on John Q. Adams, that statesman having been stricken with apoplexy at his seat in the House of Representatives.

In 1855 Winchester has two daguerreotype galleries, by which we may conclude that the portrait painter has been thrown out of business. Next year this kind of picture costs 75 cents. In 1857 there are ambrotypes and photographs as well as daguerreotypes.

Winchester gives employment to four merchant tailors and John B. Hart has a "wheat fan factory."

Apprentices are still in low esteem, since there is a reward of six cents for the capture of a runaway. If the question is asked why the advertiser did not offer a nickel instead of six cents, the answer is that the nickel was not yet in circulation. The advertiser was offering a "fip," a Spanish coin worth $6\frac{1}{4}$ cents.

Beginning in October, 1830, the "Miscellany and Literary Chronicle" had an existence of at least one year, and the editor gave some attention to local events, as well as to the war in Poland and other striking events in Europe. The smallpox is in town and one death has occurred. The Fourth of July oration for 1831 was delivered in the Methodist church by John D. B. Smith. Alfred H. Powell, Delegate-elect, died in the courthouse August 3, 1831.

In 1852 we begin to read of the naturalizations of foreigners. Immigration, particularly from Ireland, had lately become very active.

Mr. Russell mentions the hanging of Crane for the murder of one Van Horne as probably the first civil execution in Winchester. This he states was in 1791. But seemingly in the same year, Dr. James Medlicott, who lived on Fairfax Lane, was hanged for killing William Hefferman. The cost of the gallows was $10. In 1790 Solomon Watson and James Ridley were under sentence of death for horse stealing. In 1798 Ralph, a negro, was hanged for poisoning James Strother and his wife.

The next executions we read of were those of three negroes, one of whom was a woman, and these took place about 1817. In 1838 William Brent was mortally stabbed by a runaway slave from Rappahannock. Three days after Christmas the assassin was hanged on a commons near the present Catholic cemetery. It would thus seem that another spot was chosen, since Crane was hanged at the south end of Braddock Street. Another negro was executed about the same time. In 1856 Isaac Smith was murdered in the Massie tavern by William H. Spurr and Andrew J. Copenhaver. The former was sentenced to 18 years imprisonment and the latter to 15, but both men were pardoned by Governor Wise. In 1858 James Catlett was executed for the murder of Samuel Brock, another negro who was highly esteemed.

The executions we have named appear to be all that took place under the civil law prior to the war of 1861.

The general muster of Monday, October 22, 1787, reminds us that muster day was an annual event nearly to the time of the civil war, and that as a means of attracting the notice of the public, it vied with the old-time fair or the modern circus.

The Shenandoah Herald speaks of a fair at Winchester "last Tuesday, Wednesday, Thursday"—November 30---December 2, 1824. The prizes aggregated $175.

X

WINCHESTER'S RAILROADS

The Baltimore and Ohio — The Winchester and Potomac — The Cumberland Valley — The Washington and Ohio; a Blighted Promise — The Winchester and Western.

> The train runs ten to fifteen miles an hour. One engine can carry four hundred barrels of flour to Harper's Ferry in four hours. Travelers reach New York in one and one-half days, and flour is delivered to the seaports in forty-eight hours. Four thousand people have traveled on the railroad. — Winchester Virginian, 1838.

The first line of railway to link the American seaboard to the Great West was the Baltimore and Ohio, begun in 1828. It could not do otherwise than pass the Blue Ridge by the water-level gorge at Harper's Ferry. Whether it should then take the Shenandoah Valley or the valley of the Upper Potomac was for a while an open question. The management inclined to the northern route, but the National Road, scenting a dangerous competitor in the new-fangled iron track, fought it tooth and nail and kept it outside the Pennsylvania border. Railroad engineering was a very amateur science in the decade of the thirties, and this may explain why the decision was finally against the Shenandoah route. Had the southern course been chosen, the oldest town in the Valley of Virginia would today be situated on a through line of railroad and it would be a much larger place than it is.

From what is said in the above paragraph, there is much significance in a petition from Winchester dated December 6, 1827. It asks the legislature that the Baltimore and Ohio railroad be not restricted to a route lying to the north of the Little Kanawha. This proves that the signers were quite awake to the situation. Another proof is seen in the incorporation of the Winchester and Potomac almost as soon as the Shenandoah route was rejected.

Railroad construction proceeded slowly for some time, and Harper's Ferry, only 81 miles from Baltimore, was not reached until December, 1834; about six years after work was begun at Baltimore. Cumberland was not reached until the close of 1842, and not until ten years later did the iron horse throw its steam over the waters of the Ohio. The first train from Harper's Ferry to Martinsburg made its trip May 22, 1841. While Harper's

Ferry remained the terminus, there were two lines of stages daily to Winchester, where might have been seen hundreds of covered wagons that had journeyed all the way from the southwest of Virginia and even from Tennessee.

A charter was given by the legislature of Virginia to the Staunton and Potomac Railroad, but for some reason that is not now clear it was superseded after only nineteen days by the charter to the Winchester and Potomac Railroad, dated April 8, 1831. Nearly all the distance of 32 miles was under contract early in February, 1834, and by the August of the following year the grading was nearly done. The arrival of the first train in Winchester was in the spring of 1836; earlier by five years, it will be observed, than the first train from Harper's Ferry to Martinsburg. The editor of the Virginian gleefully observes that a seaboard market is virtually brought to Winchester. He adds that the closing of the turnpike gap to Harrisonburg will, with the early completion of the Harrisonburg and Warm Springs pike, provide a line of good road to the Ohio river at the mouth of the Guyandotte.

The capital stock authorized by the charter was $300,000 in shares of $25. A petition of December 28, 1831, announces that all but $10,000 is subscribed. The first president of the company was John Bruce. The first board of directors was made up of Henry W. Baker, Henry M. Brent, John Brown, M. B. Cartmell, John R. Cooper, John Gilkeson, John Heiskell, Alfred H. Powell, Joseph H. Sherrard, and Alexander S. Tidball. A petition of 1838 tells us the enterprise has cost a little more than $12,000 a mile, and that an additional sum of $50,000 is needed.

Could we only see it, the roadbed of 1838 would look crude as well as strange. The car wheels rolled on strap-rails bolted to wooden sleepers, and when one of these thin, flat rails broke loose and buckled it might cause a serious accident.

For the year ending July 15, 1838, the receipts of the new road were $46,256.48, about 30 per cent of this coming from the passenger fares of the 4000 persons who had used the road. Passenger trains were making a speed of 10 to 15 miles an hour, which undoubtedly seemed rapid to the people of ninety years ago.

In 1841 the passenger train left the station in Winchester at 5:15 a. m., reaching Washington by way of Relay—a distance of 143 miles—in a little less than 13 hours. Arrangements were on foot whereby a person leaving Philadelphia in the morning might reach Winchester the same day, even though it was necessary to go by steamer as far as Wilmington.

For the fiscal year closing July 15, 1841, the receipts of the Winchester and Potomac had risen to $62,110.76. The barrels of flour taken to market were 105,784. But in 1859-1860, there was a slight falling off. Flour was still first in the volume of railway tonnage. Merchandise came next and produce third, these three classes of freight comprising five-sixths of the total. The freight on a barrel of flour was 33 cents to Harper's Ferry, plus a charge of two cents for receiving and forwarding.

As late as 1861 the roadbed was not so strong as that of the Baltimore and Ohio, since it was feared that the freight engines used on the latter would break down the trestles. From the midsummer of that year until the midspring of 1865, the Winchester and Potomac, except when the Union army was in possession of the southern terminal, was on a vacation. At the close of the war, trains could not run above Stephenson's.

As an individual road the Winchester and Potomac was never extended above Winchester, although in 1856 there was an effort to connect it with the Manassas Gap railroad at Strasburg. In February, 1861, a bill to continue the road to Strasburg passed the lower house of the legislature, but ten weeks later there was war and the building of iron roads was no longer thought of, save for urgent military necessity. Shortly after the return of peace the line was rebuilt, and in 1868 was able to declare a semi-annual dividend of three percent. There were now in daily service two mail trains and one mixed train. In 1870 further repairing was done.

In March, 1899, the Winchester and Potomac was purchased by the Baltimore and Ohio Company, and in 1913 the general offices of the Valley Division were moved from Winchester to Brunswick.

The Winchester and Strasburg, a link in the Baltimore and Ohio system, was chartered April 23, 1867 and reached Strasburg Junction in May, 1870. The Manassas Gap railroad had been built to this point in 1856, but instead of continuing to the coalfields of West Virginia, as was originally planned, it was turned southward to Harrisonburg. The section lying above Strasburg was leased by the Baltimore and Ohio, and it was the intention of that company to build southward to the Tennessee line. For this purpose the Valley Railroad was incorporated, and it reached Staunton April 1, 1874. But the country was then in the throes of a severe financial panic, and the road was never completed farther than Lexington, although construction work was carried as far as Roanoke. The Baltimore and Ohio corporation fell into trouble, and control of the Strasburg-Harrisonburg link was resumed by the Southern Railway November 30, 1896. For its lease, the Baltimore and Ohio had been paying $89,250 a year, much had been spent in improvements, and Baltimore had invested $1,000,000 in the Valley Railroad. Since that date, the last-named link has been a disconnected and not very important member of the Baltimore and Ohio system. For a long while the Baltimore and Ohio and the Southern railways did not get on very well at their junction points, but in 1913 a through passenger service from Baltimore to Lexington was installed.

In 1909 there had been much complaint for several years relative to poor service in the Shenandoah Valley, and a circular letter was sent out by R. E. Byrd of this city. Two years later, the Baltimore and Ohio service was still far from satisfactory, there were many unsound ties in the roadbed, and it was not felt that this locality was being given a square deal. But in 1912 there was begun the laying of 90 pound rails to replace those of nearly one-third less weight.

The year 1885 witnessed the completion of the Martinsburg and Potomac Railroad, an extension of the Cumberland Valley division of the Pennsylvania system. In its capital stock Winchester invested $20,000. Early in the fall of 1889 the road was continued to Winchester, and thus the efforts of 20 years were crowned with success. As early as September, 1870, there was a vote on aiding this road to the extent of $133,500, and a mass meeting of the citizens of Winchester was held January 15, 1877 to induce the Martinsburg and Potomac to come here. But in 1906 there was complaint that the new road, as well as the Baltimore and Ohio, was discriminating against this place. A public meeting to express the protest of the citizens was held October 1. The station of the Cumberland Valley road is quite far from that of the Baltimore and Ohio, and during the latter part of the period of the World War it was closed, its trains arriving and departing from the other station.

In 1913 the Shenandoah Valley Railroad was chartered to build an electric line from Williamsport to Winchester, but in consequence of the World War the project was suspended, and it has never been revived.

A possibility of much promise to Winchester, yet which was utterly lost, lay in a railroad which was on the horizon as early as 1842, although not begun until 1855. In the latter year the Alexandria, Loudoun, and Hampshire Railroad was started from Alexandria, and at the outbreak of the war of 1861 it had come at least as far as Vienna, a distance of 15 miles. Aid was voted upon in Frederick May 22, 1856. The proposition carried in Winchester by a vote of 45 to 35, which seems incomprehensibly light. In Frederick county it was defeated by a vote of 1203 to 335. The plan was for stock in two railroads, a dividend of six percent being guaranteed. The new road was to cross the Winchester and Potomac at a right angle. In Clarke and Hampshire the vote was affirmative. In the former county, the ratio of aid to valuation was one to forty, and in the latter it was one to seventy. Frederick, which at this time had an assessed valuation of $8,000,000, was asked for $30,000. In 1857 it was proposed to vote aid to the extent of not more than $70,000. In 1858, the new road was confidently expected to come to Winchester, but nothing more was done until after the close of the war of the sixties.

In 1868 the road had reached Clark's Gap, and was operating two passenger trains daily and one mixed train. The cost of going from Winchester to Alexandria by this route was $5. Next year the Washington and Cincinnati railroad was projected to Point Pleasant, and a contract was drawn for building the road to Winchester, the name being now changed to Washington and Ohio.

Collis P. Huntington, who had won fame as a railroad magnate on the Pacific coast, would have taken the Washington and Ohio in preference to the Virginia Central but for the obstacles in his way. In his hands, the latter road, renamed the Chesapeake and Ohio, and extended to Newport News on the east and Cincinnati on the west, became a line of great importance. Had Mr. Huntington done a corresponding work with the Washington and Ohio, the record of Winchester during the last forty years would have been very different.

So it is very natural that in the seventies the Washington and Ohio was much discussed in Winchester. In 1871 it had reached Hamilton, and it was to arrive in Winchester in the following May under the penalty of forfeiture of its charter. Hardy county voted aid to the extent of $150,000. Gilmer, Upshur, and Calhoun also voted affirmatively. In the fall of 1873 the road was still under contract to build to this city. Round Hill was reached the next year, but there was now financial panic, and it was not until long afterward that the Washington and Ohio was carried four miles farther to Snickersville, since known as Bluemont. It was possible to cross the Blue Ridge on a grade of not more than 92 feet to the mile, or, by piercing the mountain with a tunnel 4200 feet long, a grade of one degree—53 feet to the mile—could be secured. But nothing more has been done.

In 1881 there was still a prospect that the road would be extended. The Baltimore, Cincinnati, and Western was to be built from Baltimore to Leesburg, crossing the Potomac at Edwards Ferry. The Washington and Ohio was to become a part of the new line. But this project fell through, and in 1911 what was known as the Bluemont Division of the Southern Railway was leased by the Old Dominion Company, and has since been operated as an electric line.

But for the untoward history of the Washington and Ohio, the city of Winchester would not now be served merely by two branch lines of the Baltimore and Pennsylvania systems and by a lumber railroad. It would be directly on an east and west line of importance. An opportunity was lost, and seemingly forever. A general and practical support by this locality might have turned the scale.

The Winchester and Western, the newest of the city's railways, runs west and southwest 40 miles to Wardensville on Capon river in Hardy county. While it traverses an agricultural region for the greater part of the distance, it has opened up a district highly important because of its forest resources. Timber products accordingly supply the leading amount of freight. It is estimated that there are 200,000,000 feet of virgin timber along the route.

XI

THE PUBLIC SQUARE

The Public Lots — Courthouse — Jail — Market House — Other Buildings

> The courthouse square was inclosed with posts and rails; in the center of the yard stood "Black Betty," the whipping-post, and also the pillory with a platform; below and some ten feet higher up there was another platform and pillory. — William G. Russell, speaking of 1810.

In laying out the town of Winchester, James Wood set aside four lots for public uses. In approving what Wood had done, Fairfax dedicated them to the use of the county. This is the true source of title, as was decided in the lawsuit between the city of Winchester and the county of Frederick. But as Fairfax would give only leasehold titles, it was discovered after his death that the county had no legal title to the public square. By a special Act of Assembly, James Marshall, as purchaser of the Fairfax interest, was empowered to grant the necessary deed. But this deed was merely to rectify a technical defect, and this was accomplished in 1801.

Since each of the four lots surveyed by Wood is 119 feet by 188 feet 9 inches, the total area is nearly two acres and one-fourth. When the square was laid out, and for near a century afterward, the ground was not level. There was an upward slope from both Main and Water streets, so that toward the northeast corner the surface was fifteen feet above the present level of Market Street, or quite as high as the knoll on which stands the residence of the late Holmes Conrad.

In its primeval state, the square, with perhaps the exception of its west and south borders, appears to have been wooded, but we have no information as to how long any of the forest trees were permitted to remain.

The first buildings on the square were the courthouse, the jail, and an Episcopal church, all of very primitive construction. If a photograph could have been taken of the public lots at the time of the French and Indian war, it would show practically nothing that is now familiar. In fact, for about a century after the founding of Winchester, the appearance of the square was almost entirely different from what it is now. At one time there were eleven buildings on the public property, not one of which is any longer in existence.

The first courthouse was a little log cabin, and was soon followed by a larger and better one of the same material. In 1757 the account book of Colonel Wood speaks of the "old courthouse" being rented for four pounds ($13.33) a year. Mr. Cartmell says that the second courthouse seems to have been 40 feet square. There were trees around it, and the front was toward Water Street. He adds that in 1827 the building was remodeled and repaired. Outside it was boarded and inside it was plastered. The entrance was changed from the south side to the west, and a steeple was built. For a clock there was an appropriation of $750. A bell had been hung at least as early as 1795. This courthouse was 15 feet east of the present one, and was entered by large stone steps on two sides. There was a bull's-eye in the gable, and according to Mr. Russell the roof projected 10 feet.

By the removal of the hill under the Market House in 1821, the courthouse was undermined and became insecure, yet there was much opposition to a new building.

Around the year 1825 there was much opposition to a new courthouse, and seemingly on the ground of hard times. But by a petition of June 9, 1834, we learn of a new brick courthouse, 40 by 50 feet on the ground and two stories high. It was built with a levy of $3000, to which was added the proceeds of the old courthouse and lot. But to the date of the petition, the total expenditure for courthouse purposes is given as $11,977.51. In the office of the county clerk hangs a weather-vane in the form of a fish and carrying the date 1840. It was once on the top of the tower of the courthouse, and the date may be that of the year in which the tower was built.

In the war of 1861 the courthouse was used as a hospital.

The first jail was of logs, only 12 feet square, and the sheriff was not held answerable for the escape of prisoners. Mr. Cartmell says this jail fronted Water Street and stood nearly opposite the southwest corner of the City Hall. A stone addition was built to it about 1759. In 1790 it was unsafe, and apparently in the same year a new one was built immediately to the north. The new jail, which fronted Market Street, was 50 feet square, and stood back from that street. The yard, which ran 100 feet on Water Street, was built on the north side against a bank five feet high. Elsewhere the wall was 15 feet high. In 1821 the building was damaged by fire, and though restored, it burned to the ground at noon on a January day in 1843. The present jail, also on Market Street, but some distance south of the public square, was built in 1845 and remodeled in 1907.

The colonial jail was supposed to need the adjuncts of a whipping post, a pillory, and a ducking stool. According to Mr. Cartmell, the whipping post, known as "Black Betty," was set up in 1806 at the center of the public square. But there was certainly a predecessor, unless, as in some other counties, a tree was used. Monday was the regulation day for warming a prisoner's back with a lash and thereby stimulating the capillary circulation.

The ducking stool, modeled after that at Fredericksburg, was near the large coal window in the basement of the City Hall on the plaza side. It was six feet square and seven feet deep, was walled with stone, and roofed. The date of the last order referring to its use is 1790. When a prisoner was punished by means of this contrivance, the culprit was tied to an end of a long plank working on a pivot, and then soused in the pit. As in this instance there was no running water, the content of the tank could not have been of the purity that a washerwoman would deem desirable.

There were two pillories, accompanied by a platform. Probably one was for the feet, the other for the hands only. A pillory consisted of two planks, fitting edgewise, the lower one being stationary. Openings were notched into each plank, so as to hold the prisoner by the ankles. Sometimes the hands were similarly confined. The position could not have been enjoyable when flies and mosquitoes were about, or when scurrilous epithets were hurled at a person who was helpless except as to his tongue. The barbarous English practice of pelting the prisoner with sticks, brickbats, and superannuated eggs we do not hear of in America.

For two years after the organization of Frederick, James Wood, the first clerk, had an office on his lawn at his mansion, which he named "Glen Burnie." A log office was then built south of the courthouse and adjacent to the Episcopal graveyard. It stood partly on the site of the present office, and was 11 feet from the southwest corner of the courthouse. In 1780 it was succeeded by a one-story brick building, the cost of which was $1100. But it was cold and damp, and the books mildewed. The brick office now in use was finished in 1832. Brick vaults were added on the south side in 1886. In 1905 the entire building was remodeled, the two rooms on the ground floor being thrown into one.

The Market House torn down to make room for the Rouss City Hall was the second one of the name. When the first was built we do not know positively, but it was before the Revolution.

In the "Maryland Gazette" of December 16, 1760 is the advertisement of a lottery in Winchester for the purpose of building a Market House. The drawing was to begin May 1, 1761, and the 300 tickets were to sell at 15 shillings each, or $2.50. Since this was in a time of peace and a fair degree of prosperity, it is probable that the construction of the original Market House soon followed the drawing. It is described by Mr. Russell as looking like an old castle, this effect being emphasized by the circumstance that it stood on a knoll, like the Conrad residence on the opposite side of Market Street. The building was two stories high and 60 to 70 feet long. The walls, rough and rugged, were of stone. The front, facing Market Street, displayed six heavy, open arches, and above each arch was a window. The ground floor was used as a town market. Above was one long, plastered room with a fireplace at each end. This hall was used for public entertainments, especially by the Thespian Society, one of whose handbills, dated October 3, 1820, tells that the admission was 50 cents. Through the joint exertions of the corporation and Hiram Lodge, the Market House was extended to the north, the addition being completed in the fall of 1810. This increased the frontage of the building by 20 feet, but the addition was on a lower level. The first Market House was sometimes called the "old fort house," and by tradition it was once—near the close of the Revolution—a magazine for ammunition.

The "Winchester Gazette" of March 17, 1821 publishes a town ordinance for removing the old Market House, leveling the site and building a new one. This was completed in the same year. Seemingly, the fort had fallen into disuse as a market place, since at this time a large yard on Water Street south of where the Lutheran church now stands was used for that purpose. A second was the Rust wagonyard, which was on the north side of Rouss Avenue and occupied the space now partially taken up by a row of law offices.

The new Market House was also two stories high, but was built of brick. Beginning at Rouss Avenue it extended southward to a point on Market Street opposite the lockup window in the City Hall. Like its predecessor, the walls of the ground floor were built up in a series of arches, and the arches were closed with lattice-work. The first story, which had a brick floor, was used for displaying market goods. In 1840 and 1848 wooden annexes were built westward from the two ends. A stairway, approached from Market Street led to three upper rooms; the Masonic Hall in the north end, and the town hall and council chamber in the middle and south. The building was used by the Federals during their occupation of Winchester. Just after the war it was repaired, and continued to be used for market purposes until about 1880. It then began to deteriorate and was torn down in 1900.

The cornerstone of the Rouss City Hall was laid May 16, 1900. The cost of this fine building was $60,000, one-half of which was met by Charles Broadway Rouss.

Northward from the old jail was an era occupied by the "public scale of weights and measures." After these scales were removed, which seems to have been not later than about 1840, an open courtway was left in the rear of the Market House. Here pigs, poultry, and other livestock were exposed for sale, and it was where Charles Broadway Rouss sold pins and needles when a schoolboy.

Fronting on Water Street and beginning 24 feet from the wall around the jail, was a tobacco warehouse 100 feet square. The permit for its building was granted April 6, 1825, at which time tobacco was the leading money crop in the Lower Valley.

Fronting Water Street and next the churchyard was an Engine House. It was removed in 1829 and a new one, 12 feet by 21, was built between the wall of the old jail and the tobacco warehouse, leaving an alley 12 feet broad, running from Water Street to Market Square. The new home was called the "Watchtower Building." It was ordered to be removed in 1844. The upper room was a lodging place for vagrants.

Still another building on the public square was the "Golden Temple," nicknamed "Solomon's Temple." The name was suggested by the yellow-painted bricks. In 1832 a permit was issued for putting a new engine house in the northwest corner of courthouse square. The plan was amplified, and the structure was made 30 by 38 feet. The two rooms of the first floor were used as engine houses till 1849. The upper room in the east end was the office of the city clerk. The "Golden Temple" was removed about 1850 and the bricks were used to build the engine house that until the winter of 1923-1924 stood immediately west of the Lutheran church. Toward the last it was used as a store and for various other purposes, and objection was made thereto.

Even a blacksmith's shop was one of the many buildings that once stood on the square.

From the beginning of Winchester as a town, the vacant spaces east and south of the courthouse and the clerk's office were used as wagon yards and hitching places. There was also a stable at the corner of Market and Water. After Mr. Rouss made his offer to assist in building a City Hall, there was a stubborn contest between the city of Winchester and the county of Frederick for the continued use of what is now the plaza as a wagon-yard. This is the suit mentioned in the beginning of the present chapter. An agreement was reached in October, 1899, whereby the hitching posts were removed, the plaza paved, and the Grim lot in the southeast corner of Market and Water was purchased for a yard at a cost of $10,000.

About 1800 a stone wall was built to inclose the square. In 1826 the city fathers voted for a brick wall five feet high and one and one-half feet thick. Mr. Russell affirms that this was built in 1829 and was surmounted with a locust railing. Gates were placed in front of the courthouse entrance. This was more ornamental than the stone wall, but in 1851 it gave way to an iron picket fence. During the war it seems to have been badly used, for it was in poor condition by 1871, and was finally removed. Since then the square has been open. The sidewalk from Main Street to the courthouse door was laid in 1908. Later additions are the Confederate monument at the entrance to the above mentioned walk and the historical markers in front of the courthouse steps. The Fairfax marker reads as follows:

"At sometime prior to the incorporation of Winchester, Thomas Lord Fairfax Baron of Cameron, and at one time a Justice of the County of Frederick, dedicated to public uses the square which is bounded by Court House Avenue and the streets known as Main, Water and Market. The northwestern quarter was adopted as the site of the first court house. Thereafter the market house and jail were erected upon the eastern half. At an early date the southwestern portion of the square was appropriated to the use of the Established Church and its burial ground.

"The corporate limits of the Borough of Winchester, as defined by its first charter granted in 1752, embraced not only the original site laid out by Colonel Wood but also the large addition thereto laid out by Lord Fairfax, as shown by the survey and plat thereof made by John Baylis of record in Deed Book No. 24 of the County Clerk's Office.

"His residence was at "Greenway Court" near White Post then in Frederick County. Shortly after the surrender of Cornwallis, in October 1781, he died and was buried in the church yard, a few feet from the spot where this tablet is erected. About 1827, upon the removal of the Episcopal Church to its present site, his remains were carried there and now rest under the chancel of that church."

The neighboring marker, to Colonel James Wood, reads thus:

"Colonel James Wood, the founder of Winchester, was a native of the ancient city of the same name in England. He laid out and founded the new town prior to 1743. It received a charter of incorporation from the Colonial Legislature in February, 1752.

"Colonel Wood was the first surveyor of the County of Orange, from which the new county of Frederick was carved by authority of an Act of the House of Burgesses passed in 1738. Upon the formal organization of Frederick County in 1743, he was commissioned by the Governor of the Colony of Virginia to act as the first Clerk of Frederick County, an office which he held till his death on November 8, 1759.

"Under his supervision the first court house for Frederick County was built. It stood upon the site of the present structure, and was, in fact, the first court house erected west of the Blue Ridge. During its construction the office of County Clerk was held in a building on the lawn of his residence, "Glen Burnie," built by him in the western suburbs. This mansion, still in the possession of lineal descendants, illustrates one of the types of Pre-Revolutionary architecture in Virginia. The first seal of the Court of Frederick County, still in occasional use, is represented upon this tablet."

Rouss Avenue, to the north of the square, was formerly Courthouse Avenue. A lane on the other side of the courthouse was known as Church Avenue. Market Street was not opened over the hill in front of the Market House until 1819. Before that time, teamsters had a driveway through the Rust wagonyard around the limestone ridge, and across Market Square, entering Water Street at the west end of the wall of the old jail. When the hill was graded down to a level between Water Street and the entrance to Rouss Avenue, Mr. Russell related that boys earned 50 cents a week. When the Winchester and Potomac railroad was built, its track came down Market Street to the south end of Market House, and the ticket office was in the building. When this was moved to the new station, the track remained until after the beginning of the war of 1861 because of the large flour mill on the south side of Town Run, that was burned by drunken soldiers about 1864.

The southwest quarter of the public square was first the churchyard and burial ground of the Episcopalians. It was inclosed by a stone wall that boys used to jump over. The stone church, built about 1762, was not so large, according to tradition, as the log edifice that preceded it. It was not in use at the time Mr. Balmain arrived to become its rector.

Charles Broadway Rouss was born near Woodstock, Maryland, February 11, 1836, and when he was four years old his parents moved into Berkeley county, West Virginia. In 1846 the boy came to Winchester, where he received his school training and displayed the nature of the man in the making by peddling various small articles among the people who frequented the Market House. At the age of fourteen he entered the Senseny store as a clerk and on a salary of $150 a year. Yet in only four years he had saved up $500 and he went into business for himself. The youth visited Baltimore for a stock of goods, and told Mr. Abell of the "Baltimore Sun" that he was going to revolutionize business in Winchester. The advertisement writer of that paper prepared this statement: "We will keep everything calculated to make a man fashionable, a lady irresistible, and a family comfortable." This advertisement was put into the journals of Winchester, and it was also scattered by means of handbills. The success of the young man's methods was immediate, and when war came, seven years later, he was the heaviest business man in Winchester and was worth $60,000. Mr. Rouss then disposed of his stock of goods in Richmond, enlisted in the Confederate army as a private, and served until the end. When he again became a private citizen, he had only two horses, and he owed $8000 to merchants in the city of New York. He farmed a short while, but this calling was alien to his temperament.

In 1867, Mr. Rouss went to New York with $28 in his pocket, and though heavily in debt, he asked for a supply of goods and was granted them on a short credit. He now located in the American metropolis, but for several years the road to prosperity was thorny. The panic of 1873 made him a bankrupt, yet he got on his feet once more, and eventually paid all his creditors in full. In 1876 he opened a store on Broadway, and was either entire or part owner of 36 stores in all. His employees came to number 500 and he carried on a business of $15,000,000 a year, his trade motto being "Quick sales and small profits." He became worth $10,000,000 in his own name. Mr. Rouss was eminently a philanthropist. He was accessible to all callers and turned no charity away. His benefactions aggregated a million dollars; and those of which the town of Winchester was the recipient amounted to about $200,000. He gave the city $30,000 toward a new city hall and an equal sum toward new waterworks. He provided new quarters for the Union Fire Company, and in its hall his birthday is regularly observed with a banquet. For the iron fence around the Mount Hebron and Stonewall cemeteries he gave $7500. One of his final bequests was a gift of $1000 to the poor of Winchester. The philanthropic spirit of the millionaire merchant is exhibited in the instructions sent with a check of $250 toward providing a Christmas dinner for the poor of Winchester in 1887. "All I ask," he said, "is to give them, male or female, black or white, Democrat or Republican, a good, hearty dinner." To the city of New York he gave statues of Washington and Lafayette costing $25,000. These were placed in Morningside Park, where, in the time of business reverse, he had slept in the open air. Mr. Rouss was a student as well as business man, and all the leisure moments that he could spare were given to reading. But he made his hours of sleep too brief and overstrain wore out the optic nerve, causing blindness in the last years of his life. In religious questions, Mr. Rouss was an agnostic, though not an infidel. He died in New York, March 5, 1899. Interment was in the Rouss mausoleum in Mount Hebron cemetery at Winchester. The following maxims by Mr. Rouss relate to personal conduct:

"Keep good company or none. Never be idle. If your hands cannot fully be employed, attend to the cultivation of your mind. Always speak the truth. Make few promises. Live up to your engagements. Keep your own secrets, if you have any. When you speak to a person look him in the face. Good company and good conversation are the very sinews of virtue. Good character is above all else. Your character cannot be essentially injured except by your own acts. If any one speaks evil of you, let your life be so that none will believe him. Drink no kinds of intoxicating liquors. Ever live (misfortune excepted) within your income. When you retire, think over what you have been doing during the day. Never play at a game of chance. Avoid temptation, through fear that you may not withstand it. Earn money before you spend it. Never run into debt unless you see a way out of it again. Never borrow if you can possibly avoid it. Do not marry until you are able to support a wife. Never speak evil of anyone. Be just before you are generous. Keep yourself innocent if you would be happy. Save when you are young, to spend when you are old. Read over the above maxims at least once a week."

XII

WAR AND ITS FORERUNNERS

The John Brown Raid — The Election of 1860 — Winchester Strategic — Harper's Ferry — Confederate Leaders — The Romney Expedition — Kernstown — The First Valley Campaign — Defeat of Milroy

> We spent as happy a winter as ever falls to the lot of mortals upon earth. — Mrs. Stonewall Jackson, on the winter of 1861-1862, spent in Winchester.

On the morning of October 16, 1859, the telegraph sent broadcast the startling and entirely unexpected news that the business quarter of Harper's Ferry was in the control of men whose avowed aim was to free the slaves in the South. Within forty-eight hours all but five of the twenty-two raiders were killed or captured, and after what is conceded to have been a fair trial, the leader and four of his men were convicted of treason and murder, and after about seven weeks were hanged at Charles Town.

"Coming events cast their shadows before," and in the long contention between North and South one of the shadows was this raid by that picturesque character, John Brown of Ossawatomie.

The affair caused great excitement, particularly in the Lower Shenandoah, for it brought the people face to face with the possibility of a servile insurrection. The Nat Turner uprising in Southhampton, in 1831, was not so remote in time or place as to have been forgotten. And as free state soil lay only thirty miles away, it was feared that there would be an attempt to rescue Brown. In the general alarm and uncertainty, this fear seemed reasonable, yet it was unfounded. In the North there was no previous knowledge of Brown's object, except among the few conspirators themselves, and only by the unthinking was it condoned. Not a Virginian, white or black, joined the raiders, and the feeling it brought to the colored population was one of alarm and terror.

To the number of 3000, the Virginia militia were called out for duty at Charles Town and its neighborhood. In this force were men from Winchester and Frederick, serving in the Winchester Rifles, the Morgan Continental Guards, the Marion Riflemen, and the Boomerangs. All these military organizations were uniformed and well drilled. The Winchester Riflemen, under Captain W. L. Clark, scouted a week in Berkeley. The Marion Riflemen, under Captain J. H. S. Funk, were under arms several days, patrolling Winchester by night. But the Continental Morgan Guards were five weeks at Charles Town, their whole term of service being two months. They wore out their uniforms, and the citizens were asked for $400, with which to replace them. This uniform was like that worn by General Washington and his staff in the Revolution, and therefore was buff and blue in color. The company had been organized in 1855, and its first captain was Hugh Low. John Avis was captain when the war broke out, and was succeeded by George W. Kurtz, who still survives as an active business man of his native city.

Since the mad attempt was not actively abetted by those most inclined to sympathize with it, there was presently an ebb in the excitement. The crazy raid had as little practical effect in ending slavery as Brown's murders in Kansas had practical influence in making that territory a free state. Mr. T. A. Ashby relates that the effect on the slaves in this region was transient only. There was no more than a slight degree of insubordination, some distrust of the masters, and an inclination to assemble after dark. In no long time the colored people became quiet. But among the whites the occurrence stimulated the organization and drilling of military companies, and after the election of the next fall this became yet more active.

During the forty-seven days between the seizure of Harper's Ferry and the execution of the seven captured raiders, the newspapers of Winchester had much to say on the burning topic.

An after-result of the occurrence was the destruction of the Medical College of Winchester. Just after the capture of the surviving raiders, several students drove to Harper's Ferry, and finding near the bank of Shenandoah River the corpse of one of the assailants, they put it into a box and took it to the college as a subject for dissection. Papers in a pocket then identified the body as a son of Brown. It was preserved and kept in the college museum. When this fact became known to the Federals, upon their occupation of Winchester in March, 1862, the buildings were promptly burned by order of General Banks.

Richard Parker, the judge who presided at the trial of Brown, was a resident of Winchester and the third man in his family line to fill a judicial seat. In his reminiscences he states that among the men on the street there was a general sentiment in favor of a lynching, but after all sides of the matter had been presented to them they were willing for the law to take its course.

By the census of 1860 there were 701 families in the city, the number of individual persons being 4403. Of these 3040 were whites, 655 were freedmen, and 708 were slaves. John W. Pifer, the deputy marshal who took the census, said that the great majority of the free negroes could give no definite account of their subsistence, many of them giving rude answers to the questions asked. He added that they were too lazy to earn an honest living and prowled around after night. But the very fact that the freedmen were nearly equal in number to the slaves shows that slavery was a decaying institution in the Valley of Virginia, as was more the case in Maryland and still more in Delaware. Where staples were not produced on a large scale, American slavery never gained a strong foothold and was of the domestic rather than the plantation type. It never gained the general approval of the people of the Shenandoah. As early as 1784 a statute favoring emancipation received the votes of their own delegates, although it failed to become a law. In 1852 the Republican remarked approvingly that the 50,000 freedmen in Virginia could be removed from the state at an expense of $2,500,000. When the war opened, there were several cases on the docket of Frederick county of free negroes who were staying without permission. And as late as November 16, 1860, Mary Phelps petitioned to be reduced to slavery. At that time able-bodied colored men were hired out by the year at an average of $110 each. The price for women or large boys was $50 to $60, and for girls, $25 to $40.

After the presidential contest of 1860 began, interest in national politics became intense. The campaign of that year was unique in American history. Each of the four candidates received electoral votes. In the North the only contest was between Lincoln and Douglas. In the South the only contest was between Breckenridge and Bell. Since Lincoln and Breckenridge stood for the extremes in the political controversy, the former had no votes in the South, except a few in the border states, and the latter had slight support in the North, except where there was a fusion ticket. The strength of the conciliatory candidates, Douglas and Bell, lay in the border states, Virginia giving her electoral votes to Bell. The only man in Frederick to vote for Lincoln was Joseph N. Jolliffe, a Quaker living six miles north of Winchester. For his radicalism he was never molested.

Douglas made a campaign speech in Winchester in the first week of September. C. L. Vallandigham of Ohio, very conspicuous as a "copperhead" in the next presidential campaign, lectured in the Methodist church in the winter of 1860-1861, but we have no information as to his subject.

The four months after November 6, 1860 were ominous of the coming strife, and the newspapers of this city had very much to say about it. The prevailing local sentiment was strongly for the maintenance of the Union, and in midwinter there was great indignation at the course taken by South Carolina. This feeling was voiced in a published letter by Robert Y. Conrad. "If the present Union be broken up," he writes, "I would yet look to a reconstruction at some future time. Our present difficulties could have been satisfactorily settled within the Union, but for the premature movements of the states farther South. If no attempt at coercion is made, the best course Virginia can take is to remain peaceably in the Union." A month later—February 17—he writes that, "a separate Southern confederacy of any durability I have no faith in, considering it as entirely an impracticable idea. United, we can bid defiance to the rest of the world. Split up into partial confederacies, we are doomed and doomed forever."

Money is proverbially timid, but in the first week of 1860, the farm of Meredith Jolliffe, six miles north of Winchester, sold at auction for $50 an acre, thus showing that the coming war cloud was little above the horizon, so far as Virginia was concerned. Likewise, the Singer sewing machine was selling freely at $50 to $125. A meeting held January 28, 1860, and presided over by Richard E. Byrd, passed long resolutions repudiating all efforts toward creating sectional animosity, or measures tending to a dissolution of the Union. But with a view of influencing the North, the people were urged to encourage home industry, and to boycott Northern goods until favorable action were taken.

The local delegates to the Virginia Convention of 1861 were Robert Y. Conrad and James Marshall, elected as Union men by 547 and 540 votes, respectively, their opponents receiving only 104 and 87. The address of the successful candidates is dated January 24, 1861, and contains these words:

"The John Brown raid we have no warrant for charging was approved either before or after the act by Northern citizens, respectable for number or character... The continued existence of this (Republican) party is inconsistent with the safety and permanence of our Union, because it is necessarily confined to one portion of the states, and if in a majority, would establish permanent rule over the other section.

.... All our just complaints might, we are convinced, have been within a reasonable time peaceably redressed within the Union..... With both branches (of Congress) opposed to him (Lincoln), his mere tenure of the office could do us no harm."

The candidates add the opinion that the secession of the cotton states was precipitate and without reasonable excuse.

The Republican reprinted the following declaration by Thomas Ritchie, which had appeared in the Richmond Examiner of 1814: "No man, no association of men, no state or set of states, has a right to withdraw itself from this Union of its own accord. The same power which knit us together can alone unknit."

The same paper in its issue of April 5 published a five-column speech by George W. Summers, a member of the Convention from the Kanawha valley. The speaker predicted that in five years after separation there would be a European status on this side of the Atlantic; that on either side of the line there would be a standing army of 100,000 men; that as slaves could not now be recovered from Canada, no more could they be recovered from the North, Virginia itself having 400 miles of hostile boundary.

There appeared at the top of the editorial section of the Winchester Republican, April 12, 1861, a border state flag of eight stars and thirteen stripes. Below was a leader a column long, deploring war and advocating a suspension of hostilities for sixty days, so that there might be effective meditation between the contending parties. Two weeks later there were three columns of news relative to the taking of Fort Sumter.

The events in Charleston harbor made war inevitable. The political feeling at Winchester was now to become very Southern and exceptionally bitter. Yet throughout the Lower Shenandoah were persons who held steadfastly for the Union. Quite naturally this sentiment was stronger in the direction of the Mason and Dixon line, only forty miles away. At Martinsburg, in the middle distance, there was much lack of sympathy for the Confederate cause.

The limits of this book will not permit a discussion of the causes of the War of 1861. Volume upon volume has been written on this theme alone, and to them the reader is referred.

That Winchester and the Lower Shenandoah would bulk heavily in the war until a decision was reached was predetermined by facts of geography and military science. The town was the focus of nine important highways, mostly macadamized. The country around was well peopled and productive, and could therefore supply great quantities of provisions and forage. The control of Winchester by the South was a constant threat of an invasion of Pennsylvania, and a continual menace to the security of the city of Washington. It made difficult a Federal occupation of the South Branch valley, and it made very precarious the use of the Baltimore and Ohio railway by the North. And further, the Lower Valley was and is the gateway to the upper and middle sections of the Shenandoah. According to General Johnston, the Lower Valley was able to feed an army of 40,000 men, and so long as it could firmly be held by the South, the Shenandoah Valley, taken as a unit, was a most important source of supply to the Confederate armies at Richmond. It was sound military instinct that made Stonewall Jackson say that, "if this valley is lost, Virginia is lost."

To the Federals, Winchester was of great strategic value, because of the ease with which supplies could be brought in, and also because of its radiating thoroughfares and its command of the region to the west. When they held the place, they relieved Washington from peril on its right flank, they could use the Baltimore and Ohio road, and being within one hundred miles of Staunton, they were a threat to the western lines of supply of the Confederate capital.

Since the Cumberland Valley of Maryland and Pennsylvania is a continuation of the Shenandoah Valley, and a natural highway to the Susquehanna,—almost as near to Winchester as Staunton,—this valley was to the North a heel of Achilles. With a strong Confederate army at Winchester, neither Washington nor Baltimore was safe, and Philadelphia and New York were not out of danger. The long valley crossed by the Potomac was to be a reminder of the Vale of Esdraelon in Palestine; a military road that has been trodden by the armies of Egypt, Assyria, Greece, and Rome, later by the Crusaders, the Saracens, and the French, and in our own day by the British under Allenby.

Thus it becomes easy to understand why the struggle for the Lower Shenandoah was severe and protracted; why this district was repeatedly the scene of important and sometimes brilliant maneuvers, and why at least 112 engagements were fought within its confines. No other town in the entire theatre of war changed hands so many times as Winchester, the "Northern Gate of the Confederacy," the lowest statement making sixty-eight the number of transfers between the opposing forces. No other town or city was so battered by the effects of war, unless Richmond and Atlanta be excepted. But each of those places was lost only once and finally to the South, and in each instance the destruction was mainly the result of an unhindered fire. In short, the bitter struggle for the Lower Shenandoah made it the Flanders of America. Elsewhere were heavier battles, fought by larger armies than those of Jackson or Banks, Sheridan or Early, but in no district of equal size were the actions so many and distributed over so long a period of time. The aggregate of casualties to the armies contending here was not less than 50,000; a number that equals the combined losses at Gettysburg, the greatest single battle of the entire war.

With respect to the war of 1861, no more will be attempted in this volume than to narrate the events local to the Lower Shenandoah and the districts immediately contiguous to the south and west. No more than casual mention will be given to events elsewhere.

Harper's Ferry, a railroad junction and the seat of an armory, was of military importance, and was promptly occupied by some of the Virginia militia, the men in charge of the armory setting fire to the buildings as they retired. The officer who was soon to win fame as Stonewall Jackson arrived April 29, bearing a commission as colonel and taking command. There gathered here 4500 soldiers, full of enthusiasm and energy, but poorly armed and poorly disciplined. Some of them wore hunting shirts, like their forebears of the Revolution. And like the latter, some of their weapons were flintlocks, the percussion gun not yet having come into universal use. But the four companies from Winchester were handsomely uniformed and well equipped. The white belt of the Winchester Rifles, with its large brass buckle, was soon laid aside. The weapon of this company was the minie rifle. The military suit was dark green.

The green soldiers were drilled seven hours daily, and better equipment was provided as rapidly as possible. The repaired gun factory was kept busy in converting the flintlocks into percussion muskets. Loudoun and Maryland heights were fortified. The army became 7,000 strong. Jackson wanted 10,000 men, saying that the control of Harper's Ferry meant the control of the northwest of Virginia also.

For reasons of policy, there was no interference for more than a month with the running of trains on the Baltimore and Ohio. But Jackson was very desirous that his men should sleep soundly. On the plea that night trains interfered with the slumbers of his soldiers, he brought about a congestion of cars and locomotives on the double-track line between Point of Rocks and Martinsburg. He took care to relieve this congestion by moving some of the rolling stock to Strasburg. Since the Baltimore and Ohio engines were too heavy for the Winchester and Potomac, and were liable to break down the trestles, the turnpikes had to be brought into use. Until after the war there was no railroad connection between Winchester and Strasburg.

Jackson was succeeded in chief command by General Joseph E. Johnston, who arrived May 24. The army rose to a strength of 9,000 and was named the Army of the Shenandoah. Jackson, who was promoted to the rank of brigadier general July 3, was placed in charge of the First Brigade, consisting of the Second, Fourth, Fifth, Twenty-seventh, and Thirty-third infantry regiments of the Virginia line. The Seventh Virginia Cavalry was organized June 17 by Colonel A. W. McDonald of Winchester. Turner Ashby was second in command. Jackson's brigade was 3500 strong.

Martinsburg was occupied by Jackson June 20. The railroad shops were burned and four engines were moved away by the turnpike. A Federal army, overestimated by Johnston at 20,000 men, crossed the Potomac at Williamsport. It was led by General Patterson, a native of Ireland who was no longer young, since he had fought on the American side in the war of 1812. He had little influence with his raw troops.

With an observation force of one gun, 50 cavalry under J. E. B. Stuart, and 480 of the Fifth Infantry, Jackson confronted Patterson on the very day of the crossing, and fought the engagement of Falling Waters on the Porterfield farm five miles south of the river. The affair was an inconclusive skirmish, each side losing only about ten men in killed and wounded. But through a stratagem, Stuart took 43 prisoners.

The flank movement by this Federal army caused Johnston to evacuate Harper's Ferry, which he deemed less defensible than Winchester. The railroad bridge and the public buildings were burned, and the machinery in the gun factory was removed. He states that nearly every private had a trunk, and that two-fifths of his men were ill, particularly with measles and mumps. He did not think it wise to attack the Federals at Martinsburg, but offered battle at Bunker Hill, which the slow-moving Patterson reached July 15. The Northern general permitted himself to be bluffed, and made a retrograde movement to Charles Town. He was expected to hold Johnston in the Lower Valley and keep that leader from reenforcing Beauregard at Manassas, but he signally failed to do so and was relieved of his command, being succeeded by General Banks.

Johnston was now free to move to the support of Beauregard, and he moved with promptness. Leaving Winchester the morning of July 18, he reached Paris the same day, a distance of twenty miles, and the next day helped to bring a Waterloo defeat to the Federal arms. His abandonment of Winchester was deeply resented by the citizens. He had left 1700 of his sick in the town, and the country toward the Potomac was stripped of Southern defenders. But Patterson's army recrossed the Potomac. Until the following March there were no Federals south of the river, and consequently no military operations.

Winchester soldiers killed at First Manassas were Owen Burgess, Isaac Glaize, James W. Hines, Lloyd Powell, Charles Mitchell, and William Young. Burgess and Glaize were orderly sergeants. Captain William L. Clark, Strother Barton, William Hobson, and several others were wounded.

Joseph E. Johnston was at this time fifty-four years old. He was a veteran soldier and had been a meritorious officer in the United States army. He was one of the five full generals in the Confederate service. His later campaigns are familiar to students of the war. He was greatly respected by his foes as well as his friends, and he lived to old age, although wounded eleven times during his military career. General Scott said of him that he had the bad habit of getting hit every time he went into battle.

Stonewall Jackson was not generally known in Virginia at the time he was put in command at Harper's Ferry. He had been ten years a professor in the Virginia Military Institute, where he was esteemed eccentric. But Governor Letcher was a townsman, and knew Jackson's familiarity with all things military. Jackson proved his ability at Falling Waters and Bull Run, and by the next May had fully won the confidence of the South.

Of General J. E. B. Stuart, after the summer of 1861 the foremost cavalry leader in the Army of Northern Virginia, there is related an incident of the first Valley campaign. It is given by a West Point chum, Captain Perkins of the regular army and Federal service.

Perkins, commanding a battery of light artillery, was riding carelessly a half-mile in front of his men. He was suddenly accosted by three officers, one of whom exclaimed in a familiar voice and manner;

"Hello, Perk, I'm glad to see you. What are you doing here?"

Recognizing his West Point friend, the captain returned the salute heartily and replied:

"Why, Beauty, how are you? I didn't know you were with us."

"Nor did I know you were on our side. What command have you?"

"There's my command coming over the hill," returned Perkins, pointing complacently to the well-equipped battery that was approaching with the Union colors displayed.

"Oh, the devil!" exclaimed Stuart, wheeling suddenly and plunging into the forest. "Good bye, Perk."

Jackson was promoted to the rank of major general, October 7, and put in command of the Valley District, with headquarters at Winchester. The town and vicinity were still "prosperous, gay, and happy," Jackson was joined by his wife and he found the winter a pleasant one.

At the beginning of 1862 Jackson had 9,000 men in his department. There was a much larger Federal army under Banks on the other side of the Potomac, but it was not displaying any aggressiveness. The Confederate leader was very desirous of pushing westward to Grafton and recovering West Virginia. With 2200 men he began his advance on New Year's day. The morning was most unseasonably mild, and was a weather-breeder. In the afternoon snow and hail began to fall, and the next six weeks were cold and stormy, and very unpleasant. Yet the columns pressed forward on icy roads. The three Federal regiments at Berkeley Springs escaped across the Potomac, only 16 prisoners being captured. When the town of Hancock was reached, it was shelled from the south bank, much damage was done to both railroad and canal, and some stores were sent to Winchester. It was Jackson's plan to compel Kelley and his 5000 men to evacuate Romney or fight, and by cutting the telegraph line to prevent reenforcements from being sent in from the west. Kelley retired without a battle, but there was no farther advance. Loring, who commanded a large part of the column, was not on easy terms with his chief, and there was great discontent among his men. This spirit was due, in great measure, to the attitude of Loring himself. That officer was left to hold Romney with three regiments of infantry and three companies of cavalry. The rest of the little army returned to Winchester, after an absence of twenty-two days.

In a military sense, Jackson regarded the expedition as successful. Much damage had been done, his enemy had been forced over the Potomac, and his own loss had been only 32 men. Yet it disappointed the Confederate government, and was severely criticized. The soldiers suffered exceedingly in the cold, stormy weather of the mountains, especially the men under Loring, who were from the Gulf states. The secretary of war at Richmond sent an order that Loring's command be returned to Winchester, and Romney was at once reoccupied by Lander. Jackson tendered his resignation. It was not accepted, but the plain hint was understood, and there was no further meddling with his plans by civilian authority. Loring and his men were sent to the South, and Jackson's army was thus very much depleted.

It has been said that during the Romney expedition, Jackson was stern and ungenial; that his soldiers were repelled by his air and were restive at the thought of a protracted campaign in such trying weather. One writer even compares the advance to Napoleon's campaign in Russia. This opinion is not just, but an additional march of one hundred miles to Grafton would have been a severe tax on the endurance of Jackson's soldiers, whatever good result might have come from going over the Alleghany Divide in midwinter.

Banks crossed the Potomac late in February. He was brave and was willing to fight, yet was slow in his movements and overcautious. He was one of the many political generals of the early years of the war, and had perhaps not a tenth part of Jackson's knowledge of the military art. The army at Winchester was supposed to be twice as numerous as it really was, and Banks was under orders to hold the Charlestown-Martinsburg line.

Jackson knew that with only 3600 infantry, 600 cavalry, and 27 guns, he could scarcely hope to hold Winchester. Yet he first offered battle. The invitation was declined, and Jackson purposed a night attack while the opposing army was four miles north of the city. But his staff sent his trains southward, Winchester was evacuated March 11, and Banks entered the next day. The small strength of the Confederate army was now ascertained, and when Banks was joined by General Shields, the latter at once pursued as far as Strasburg, the Southern army retreating to Mount Jackson. The discovery of the small strength of the latter may explain why Banks was now ordered to send two of his divisions to support McClellan in an advance upon Richmond. It was not believed that the little army which had retired far up the Valley could give any serious trouble. So Shields fell back to Kernstown, and the two divisions marched toward Manassas.

But Jackson immediately followed Shields. Ashby, who reconnoitered nearly as far as Winchester, was under the impression that only four infantry regiments and some cavalry were holding the line at Kernstown. Jackson intended to attack at night, but as reenforcements were supposed to be on their way to Shields, he delivered an assault without delay.

Shields, like Patterson, was of Irish birth. He was a more capable officer, and had served under General Scott in Mexico, where he was severely wounded. Because of a slight hurt received in a skirmish, he was not with his army on the afternoon of the battle, which was conducted on the Union side by General Kimball.

The first battle of Kernstown took place on Sunday, March 23, and raged from four o'clock in the afternoon until dark. The winter had been unusually wet, and the ground was still watersoaked. The Federal line lay across the pike, and mostly to the east of it. Jackson sought to turn Kimball's flank by seizing a wooded ridge to the west of the pike. This would force his antagonist to adopt a new and hastily devised plan, and therefore fight at a disadvantage. The action was very severe, great loss occurring at a stone fence used as a breastwork. But the unexpected Federal superiority in numbers made the flank movement unsuccessful, and at dusk Jackson retired from the scene of his first and only defeat. The retreat to Woodstock was in good order, and the pursuit, which was continued to Toms Brook, was not energetic. But though the engagement was a tactical reverse, the main object of the Southern leader was achieved. The bold attack made a profound scare at Washington, and had the effect of turning back 46,000 men who were on their way to join McClellan. It proved that the army under Jackson was vigilant and formidable, even though small, and it created a respect for the military ability of its leader.

In this battle the numbers actually engaged were 7000 Federals and 3500 Confederates. The loss to the former was 118 killed, 450 wounded, and 22 missing, a total of 590. The loss to the latter was 80 killed, 375 wounded, and 263 missing, a total of 718. Of the Confederate wounded, 70 were left on the field, and in abandoning Winchester, a number of sick and wounded were left behind. Though far from being one of the great battles of the war, with respect to the number of casualties, Kernstown was the first action of consequence in the lower Shenandoah, and the soldiers who fell on the Confederate side were Valley men.

It was not until near the end of April that the Federal army, 19,000 strong, reached Harrisonburg. Jackson with 6,000 men took position at Elkton, thereby checking further advance. Banks could not move upon Staunton without exposing his communications to a direct attack at Harrisonburg, or a dash down the Luray valley. And Jackson could not move to Staunton across Banks' front without advertising his purpose.

In moving from Manassas to Richmond, Johnston left General Ewell at Gordonsville with 8,000 troops to hold the line of the Rapidan. Jackson summoned this force to his aid, and Ewell occupied the abandoned camp April 30. With his own army Jackson marched across the Blue Ridge to the nearest point on the Virginia Central railroad, and then moved his army rapidly to Staunton. Meanwhile, General Edward Johnson, who had wintered in an intrenched camp on the Alleghany summit, fell back to West View, only seven miles west of Staunton. This retrograde movement was caused by the advance up the South Branch of a strong Federal column under General Fremont. It was moving upon Johnson's rear. Following Johnson from the Greenbrier River, a small Federal army under General Milroy had reached McDowell, and the advance guard was only twelve miles from West View. The head of Fremont's army was at Franklin, within supporting distance of Milroy.

Jackson picketed the roads toward Harrisonburg, so as to keep Banks in the dark as to his immediate purpose, which was to remove the menace to his own rear. Uniting with Johnson, he marched against Milroy and won a costly victory at McDowell, May 8. Milroy, who had been joined by a division of Fremont's army, was driven back to Franklin. By ordering the road between Franklin and Harrisonburg to be obstructed, Jackson compelled Fremont to return to Moorefield in order to get over the mountains to the Shenandoah Valley. Jackson then marched swiftly to Harrisonburg. He was now 17,000 strong and able to cope with Banks. But having been ordered to detach a large part of his army for service east of the Blue Ridge, Banks had fallen back to Strasburg, where he now lay with 7400 men. Two companies were at Buckton, 1000 men with two guns were at Front Royal, and 1000 more were at Rectortown, east of the Blue Ridge. At Winchester was a rearguard of 1450 men.

Jackson's present aim was to fall upon Banks and drive him out of the Lower Shenandoah before he could be reenforced by Fremont or from the east. Rapid movement was necessary, and it was now that his soldiers became known as "foot cavalry."

Banks was expecting a frontal attack at Strasburg. But throwing his army across the Massanutten into the Luray valley, Jackson suddenly pounced upon Kenly and his Marylanders at Front Royal, capturing the greater part of the force. He was now as near to Winchester as Banks was, and it would look as though that general should have fared the same as Kenly. Furthermore, Banks was slow to abandon Strasburg, since he could not for a while credit the news that the whole Confederate army was on his flank. But Jackson's men were not yet veterans, and the converging columns did not move with machine-like precision. The Federals managed to escape, although there were rear-guard actions at Middletown and Newtown (Stephens City) on May 24, the day after the attack at Front Royal. May 25, Banks made a stand with his 8000 men and 16 guns just south of Winchester, his line forming an arc of a circle. The Federals had some temporary success against the frontal attack that was made, but had to retire in haste when their right flank was turned by Ewell. There was a little fighting in the streets. The defeated soldiers ran pell-mell through the town, dropping coffee-pots, canteens, and other articles of camp equipage.

The taking of Winchester cost Jackson 398 men. The loss of Banks in killed and wounded was 305, but the large number of prisoners brought the total to 2019. The Federals escaped on the roads to Martinsburg and Harper's Ferry, and although a vigorous pursuit was not long continued, they did not halt until they were on the Maryland side of the Potomac. At Winchester Jackson captured so large a quantity of military supplies that the Federal leader now became known as "Commissary General Banks." The stores he lost equipped the army of his antagonist.

The authorities at Washington were in a panic. The military advisors of President Lincoln correctly interpreted Jackson's dash to the Lower Shenandoah as a measure to cause McClellan to relax his pressure on Richmond. Against their judgment, the president ordered McDowell, who had 40,000 men at Fredericksburg, to send troops to cut off Jackson's retreat. Three days after the reoccupation of Winchester, the advance of Jackson's army was near Harper's Ferry. But on the same day, Fremont was at Wardensville, and Shields, who had been detached by McDowell, was well on his way to Manassas Gap. Had the two columns which were thus closing in on Jackson's rear moved with the speed of the Confederates, the Southern army would have been trapped. But Jackson correctly estimated the relative speed of the several forces, and he escaped with little difficulty. A skirmish near Strasburg delayed the approach of Fremont, who pursued up the main Valley, Shields turning aside at Front Royal to take the Luray route. But Fremont was defeated by Ewell at Cross Keys, and the head of Shield's column was beaten at Fort Republic by the main army under Jackson himself. Both Federal armies now retired from the Shenandoah, and Jackson's Valley campaign was at an end. The Southern army was free to join Lee at Richmond, where it took a share in the Peninsula battles.

From May 8 to June 9, Jackson had marched 300 miles and fought four important battles, defeating in detail armies whose total numbers were 60,000 men. He had liberated the Shenandoah Valley, and kept McDowell from uniting with McClellan. He had also taken a great amount of spoil. During the month he had lost 2725 men, but had inflicted a loss of 4567. His military reputation was now secure.

When General Pope was called to command in front of Washington, he sent General White with 2000 men to occupy Winchester. But Pope was defeated at Second Manassas, and Lee crossed into Maryland. The garrison of 12,500 men left at Harper's Ferry was captured by Jackson in time to permit him to rejoin Lee and take part in the battle of Antietam, September 17. After that event, Jackson lay several weeks on the Opequon, and as he moved back to join Lee at Fredericksburg, he wrecked the Manassas Gap railroad. White was thus compelled to evacuate Winchester. He began a retreat to Harper's Ferry September 2, after spiking four siege guns. The Confederates now held the town until December 2, when they yielded its possession to a detachment of Federals under General Geary. Geary remained only a few days, but Milroy came near the end of the same month and kept possession until the middle of the following June. His rule is mentioned in a subsequent chapter.

Milroy built, or completed the Star Redoubt, two miles north of Winchester, and constructed other forts on the high ground west of the city. These forts were octagonal, and the protecting ditches were ten feet broad and twelve feet deep. The walls of one of them were constructed of bags filled with clay. The Star Fort mounted six guns, and on the heights around, especially to the west, there were rifle-pits. The citizens doubted whether the position could be taken. The works were held by 7000 men, and at Berryville were 1800 more under McReynolds. Milroy said he would stay in Winchester till hell froze over, and then he would skate out on the ice.

In June, 1863, began the Gettysburg campaign, Lee's army invading the North by way of the Lower Shenandoah, and being three days in coming through Chester Gap. The advance was by Ewell with 10,000 men, although his strength was very much overestimated by his enemy. They thought they were confronted by nearly all of Lee's army.

Edward Johnson with his division advanced by way of Berryville, from which McReynolds had withdrawn his brigade. The rest of Ewell's corps came by the Valley Pike. Early's division made a long flank movement to the west, and at length gained a position that made Winchester untenable. At a council of war held near midnight, June 14, a retreat was decided upon, and it was conducted as quietly as possible. Although the movement was favored by the intense darkness, it was foreseen by Ewell, and between the hours of three and four in the morning the retiring column came into collision with Johnson, four miles north of the city. The Federals were thrown into great confusion, continuing their retreat in two bodies and mostly by the Martinsburg route. Milroy escaped with his cavalry and some of his infantry. As in the preceding year, many stores were captured, and to guard them, the Twelfth Virginia was left in the town, the rest of the victorious army proceeding northward into Maryland.

In this battle of June 13-15, Milroy lost 443 in killed and wounded and about 4000 prisoners. Ewell's loss was 266.

In the course of this engagement a round shot was fired from one of the Union guns in Star Fort. It went through the gable of a house at the corner of Clifford and South Market. In repairing the damage the owner of the house mortared the projectile into the brick wall, where it may still be seen.

Lee retreated from Gettysburg the way he had come, Mr. Ashby observing that his army made a less brave appearance than on the advance, its morale and organization having been shaken by the great battle.

Once more, and for a long while, there was a respite to the Lower Shenandoah, so far as large military operations were concerned. The fighting around Winchester in June was, with one exception, the only affair of consequence in 1863, other engagements being skirmishes, especially between bodies of cavalry. The exception was the battle of Shepherdstown, July 19-20, during the retreat of Lee. The advantage was with the Confederates, they losing 285 men and their opponents, 383.

Late in the year, Early was posted in the Middle Shenandoah with two brigades of infantry and some cavalry. He was incessantly active, his object being to annoy the Federal forces in the Lower Valley and to carry back as much provision and forage as he could, so that it might not be used by the other side. This foraging was carried out systematically, and on a large scale.

The occurrences of 1861-63 were to be far eclipsed in 1864.

XIII

MILITARY EVENTS OF 1864-65

General Early at Winchester — A Period of Maneuvers — Battles of Opequon, Fisher's Hill, Cedar Creek — A Summing Up — Surrender of Mosby.

> The houses are crowded and the streets are strewn with dead, wounded, and dying from the battle. — From the diary of a Winchester girl after the battle of September 19, 1864.

In the spring of 1864, General Sigel, a man of German birth who was not very successful in his military enterprises, led a small army up the Valley. This advance was a feature of the general forward movement ordered by Grant, the Federal commander-in-chief. But after a defeat at New Market, Sigel was replaced by David Hunter, a general who was energetic, yet stern and harsh. Hunter won a victory at Piedmont, captured Staunton and Lexington, and then crossed the Blue Ridge to attack Lynchburg.

Early with 8,000 men was sent from Richmond to the relief of this very important point. Hunter was compelled to retire, and was pursued so vigorously that he made his retreat by way of the Kanawha River instead of going down the Shenandoah Valley. As it would take some time for his army to get back to the Lower Valley, the way was now open for a Confederate dash into that region, and Early took swift advantage of the opportunity. He reached Winchester July 2, after marching 94 miles in five days. According to Stribling, Early left Staunton with 12,500 men. Pond sets the number at 17,000. Perhaps neither writer is much in error. In the Federal service it was the custom to count all men who were connected with an army, while it was the Confederate practice to count only the men who carried muskets or sabers, or served the artillery. As the fringe enumerated on the one side and excluded on the other was a fairly constant factor in the American armies of 1861-65, it should either be included or omitted in all statements of strength, whether Federal or Confederate.

Two days after coming to Winchester, Early was master of the Lower Valley. An advance on Martinsburg led to the evacuation of Harper's Ferry, although that town could not be occupied by the Confederates because of Sigel's position on Maryland

Heights. But the Baltimore and Ohio railroad was put out of use all the way from Martinsburg to the South Branch, and the Potomac canal was damaged. Early carried the war into Maryland, where he gained a victory over Wallace at Frederick Junction. The defeated army fell back in the direction of Baltimore, and the cavalry under Jackson broke the line of railway between that city and Philadelphia. The road to Washington was left open. The line of fortifications around the national capital was thirty-three miles in extent, and was held at this time by the insufficient number of 13,000 men, only 4,000 of them being north of the Potomac. There was great alarm in the city and a real danger of its capture. Until July 5, Grant would not credit the news that Early was in the Lower Valley, and since he realized that the dash by the latter was a ruse to make him relax his grip on Petersburg, he would not budge, although he sent the Sixth and Nineteenth corps to Washington, these men reaching the city as Early was demonstrating in front of Fort Stevens. Knowing that it was imprudent to attempt to force an entrance into the city, Early recrossed the Potomac at White's Ford and returned to the Lower Valley, taking a position on the west bank of the Shenandoah at Castleman's Ferry. Here he protected Winchester and still threatened the railroad. He was followed by General Wright, in command of the troops sent by Grant.

Because of low water in the Ohio, Hunter was some time in getting back to the Lower Valley. His advance was at Martinsburg, July 11, and three days later at Harper's Ferry, where it was in contact with the troops pursuing Early. July 18 there was sharp fighting on Shenandoah River, the Southern army holding its positions.

Being threatened on his flank, Early retreated from Castleman's Ferry to Strasburg. Crook, who had succeeded Milroy in command of the Federal Eighth Corps, was joined by Averill and took position at Kernstown with 11,000 men. It was thought this force could hold the Lower Valley, and Wright began a return to Grant's army. But only two days after his arrival at Strasburg, Early suddenly attacked Crook and defeated him with a loss of 1185 men, including 479 prisoners, the Confederate loss being much smaller. Crook was pursued seven miles beyond Winchester, but the Southern cavalry was not efficient in this battle and no guns were taken. Early advanced his infantry to Bunker Hill, Crook retiring to the Maryland bank of the Potomac opposite Harper's Ferry. Wright was recalled, and he joined Crook July 29, five days after the battle at Kernstown. McCausland was sent by Early into Maryland and Pennsylvania. He penetrated as far as Chambersburg, and made requisitions on the towns visited. On his return he was surprised by Averill at Moorefield, and routed with a loss of 420 prisoners and four guns, the Federal loss being only 41. Early states that this reverse had a depressing influence upon his cavalry. McCausland was succeeded in command by Lomax.

After the return of McCausland, Early slowly fell back on Strasburg, leaving a division at Winchester under Ramseur. This officer attacked Averill at Carter's farm, near Stephenson's Depot, but the foe was stronger than he had thought, and he was beaten with a loss of 475 men and four guns, Averill's loss being 218.

For over a month, Early had been dominant in the Lower Valley. Twice had his forces been across the Potomac. The Baltimore and Ohio railroad could not be used. The Federal loss in this field had been 6000 men, and Grant was seriously hampered in his operations against Lee at Petersburg and Richmond. Early's continued presence was humiliating to the Federal authorities, and steps were taken to end an intolerable situation. Grant came on to look into the matter for himself. At this direction, Hunter advanced his army from the Monocacy to Halltown. In this strong position, occupied August 6, a turning movement against him was impracticable, and his enemy was kept on the watch. Grant seems to have been willing to retain Hunter in command, but the latter asked to be relieved for the good of the service, saying he was not sufficiently in favor with the War Department.

The Middle Military Division was now created, and General Sheridan was placed in command August 8. This officer was thirty-three years old, and by some was thought too young for the responsibility. His previous experience had been almost wholly in the West, and in a subordinate capacity, particularly as a cavalry commander. Though not used to an independent command, Sheridan had gained a high reputation for energy and aggressiveness. He was now expected to act with vigor. He had been nominated by Grant, who looked to him to destroy Early's army and then seize Lee's western lines of supply.

Early was fifteen years older than Sheridan, and his military experience had been longer. He was esteemed by Lee as one of his best generals, and he had risen to high command. He was alert, skillful, and pugnacious, and, on the whole, the present campaign had been very successful. Early used a caustic wit against stragglers and laggards. He had little use for chaplains, and could swear with great fluency, but his new antagonist had ability in the same line. The Confederate general had a weakness for liquor, and to this failing are attributed some of his errors of judgment.

Sheridan had 61,000 men in his military department, but a large number were unavailable on the firing line. He complained that some of his soldiers were inexperienced. The respective numbers of the Sixth Corps under Wright and the Nineteenth under Emory were 16,645 and 14,645. In the Eighth Corps—the Army of West Virginia—the enrollment was 14,032. In Torbert's cavalry corps were 11,048 men. Other cavalry commands were Averill's division of 3,500 men and Lovell's brigade of 1,000. Sheridan was thus very strong in cavalry, which was his favorite arm, and he had brought it to great efficiency. He sought to use his mounted men as a mask behind which he might screen the movements of his infantry.

According to Stribling, our authority for the present strength of the contending armies in the Lower Shenandoah, Early's Second Corps numbered 10,910 and Wharton's division, 2,104. The cavalry, under Lomax, were 1,700, thus giving a total under Early's direct command of 14,714. But attached to Early was Anderson, who had the 4,769 men of Kershaw's division and the 1,200 horse of Fitzhugh Lee. The Confederate army therefore aggregated 20,683. A difference in the method of enumerating military strength has already been discussed. Subject to this possible qualification, the odds against Early were three to one. With respect to cavalry, the discrepancy was still greater, both in number and quality. Early states that, "the enemy's cavalry is so much superior to ours, both in number and equipment, and the country so favorable to the operations of cavalry, that it is impossible for ours to compete with his." Brooking says the Confederate leaders had made a practice of fattening their horses in the Valley before crossing the Potomac. But so scarce had forage now become in this region that Early had to sustain his animals by grazing. It is for this reason that Fitzhugh Lee remarks that he always had to keep half his men in the rear, pasturing their horses. The Southern losses in guns and wagons were largely due to the weak condition of the teams.

By a return of August 20, there were in Gordon's division, 3,370 men present; in Rode's, 4,160; in Ramseur's 2,512; and in the cavalry brigades of Vaughan, Imboden, Lomax, Johnson, and Jackson, there were 4,091: a total of 14,233, Wharton's division not appearing in the report. Under Gordon were three brigades;

the Louisiana men under York, the Virginians with Terry, and the Georgians with Evans. Rodes had four brigadiers, Cox and Grimes commanding North Carolinians, Battle, Alabama men, and Cook, Georgians. Ramseur's brigadiers were Pegram, Johnston, and Godwin, the first commanding Virginia men, the others, North Carolinians.

Three weeks later, the number present for duty was 15,495.

But for six weeks, although there was much marching and a number of minor collisions, there was nothing decisive in the Lower Valley. Each general was sparring for time and space. In Georgia, two great strategists, Sherman and Johnston, had been fighting all summer, and the outcome was still in suspense. The campaign against Lee was thus far inconclusive, and Grant's losses had been very heavy. A presidential campaign was in progress, and to the North very much depended on the news from the front. A defeat of Sheridan might be enough to turn the scale. This was a cogent reason why the Union leader should act circumspectly in the face of an alert, aggressive, and experienced antagonist. And furthermore, the size of the Southern army was much exaggerated.

From Bunker Hill, Early was covering Winchester, keeping the railroad useless, and holding back from joining Grant a number of soldiers about equal to Lee's army at Richmond. Sheridan indeed began a forward movement just after taking command. Early declined battle on the Opequon, which the Union general considered a very formidable barrier, and on August 13 was at Fisher's Hill, Sheridan advancing to Cedar Creek. Two days later, hearing that Early was reenforced from Richmond, Sheridan fell back in a night march, retiring to Berryville, and thence to his former position at Halltown. The foe was swiftly on the move, and in passing through Winchester the Federal rearguard was roughly handled, losing 350 men out of 700. There was heavy skirmishing along the Opequon, August 21, with a Union loss of 275 men. During the next three days the armies were in contact at Halltown. Early did not venture an attack on this intrenched position, and leaving Anderson to confront all the forces holding it he marched to Shepherdstown, as if to invade Maryland once more. August 25, there was a considerable engagement at Kearneysville. The Union cavalry commands of Wilson and Merritt were driven back by the Confederate infantry. Custer was cut off, but escaped by fording the Potomac. Early indeed threw a small force across the river, but with his main army returned to Bunker Hill. Sheridan moved back to Berryville September 2, Anderson still lying across his front.

The retreat of Sheridan from Cedar Creek, and his very cautious defensive attitude beyond the Opequon, led to distinctly unfavorable comments, both by his friends and his foes. In the North the withdrawal was loudly denounced, and Sheridan's removal was called for. Early considered that his antagonist was greatly lacking in spirit and enterprise. The Union leader was covering Washington effectually, but this was all. The army opposing him remained practically intact, and the Baltimore and Ohio was still out of use. Early was as bold and audacious as though it were he himself who had the larger army. Sheridan had already thrown away several good opportunities. In his advance to Cedar Creek he had a chance to attack Early and Anderson separately, at a time when they were effectually out of touch with one another. After Early withdrew from the lines at Halltown, Sheridan could have thrown himself against his rear, a reconnoissance exposing the small size of Anderson's own army. The Federal general was not being held back by his commander-in-chief, and Grant was by no means satisfied with the negative results of September. Nearly every day he was sending letters or telegrams to Sheridan, urging the need of a prompt and vigorous offensive. Grant came a second time to look into the situation, but as Sheridan's representations looked plausible, he did not take out of his pocket the plan of battle he had prepared. There is reason to believe that Grant thought of taking personal command on this important front.

Lee was very much needing Anderson and his men at Richmond, and on September 3 they started to rejoin him, going by way of Berryville. But as Sheridan was reoccupying that position, the march was countermanded, and Anderson remained twelve days longer, leaving the second time by way of Front Royal and unmolested. After ascertaining that Anderson was finally gone, Sheridan decided on an attack. Two days before Anderson left, five cavalry regiments under McIntosh pushed forward to the vicinity of Winchester and captured 106 men of the Eighth South Carolina and about 67 others.

The time chosen by Sheridan was otherwise favorable. Only 4,000 Confederates lay between him and Winchester. Gordon's division and some other troops had been sent to Martinsburg to destroy the repairs being made to the railroad, and Rodes was at Bunker Hill. Through a spy in Winchester, Sheridan had secured quite accurate knowledge of the dispositions of the forces opposing him. This spy was a Quakeress, who with her mother and sister kept a boarding house, she herself carrying on a school for children of Northern sympathizers. The household was divided in feeling, the sister siding with the South. The letter to the spy was carried by a negro, who wrapped it in tinfoil and kept it in his mouth. The answer was conveyed in the same manner.

Grant's visit had just taken place, and having learned of it through the telegraph wires, Early knew that Sheridan would yield to the pressure to "go in." So Gordon was ordered back to Bunker Hill, and Rodes was to join Wharton at Stephenson's. These movements were carried out on the night of September 18.

At three o'clock next morning, Sheridan started his columns from Berryville. It was nine miles to the Confederate position, a mile and a half in front of Winchester, and it does not look as though it should have taken nearly eight hours to reach his objective. This slowness had an important bearing on the battle that ensued.

Yet the topography of the ground west of the Opequon affords a partial explanation. Abraham's Creek flows in a deep hollow a mile south of the Berryville pike, and the Sixth Corps crossed the Opequon near the mouth of this tributary. A mile and a half north of the pike is Red Bud Run, also in a hollow, and beyond was open ground, favorable to cavalry movements. The two-mile breadth between the Opequon and the plateau on which was the Confederate position is rising ground cut into deep hollows, and therefore of a nature to delay the marching of large masses of men.

The Confederate position was near the beginning of the drop toward the Opequon. It rested on Abraham's Creek at the right, and ran northward and finally northwestward to the Martinsburg road. Consequently, the direction of the battlefield from Winchester is east and northeast. When the action began, the only Confederate infantry on the ground were the men under Ramseur, the division being east of the town and covering the Berryville pike. A part of the cavalry of Lomax were watching the Senseny and Front Royal roads, the other part occupying the space between Ramseur's left and the Red Bud.

The Federal horse dashed up the Berryville pike, carried an earthwork at the head of the defile, and thus cleared the way for the infantry. Presently four batteries, on both sides of the pike, were engaged in a duel with the guns supporting Ramseur. But active fighting did not begin until nearly noon, and by this time Early's entire army was on the field. The action became very severe and it was long continued. There were almost no earthworks, and it was a battle in the open, except so far as shelter was given by bodies of timber.

Sheridan had his Sixth Corps on his left and his Nineteenth on his right. Lomax was forced up the Senseny road. The Nineteenth Corps attacked Gordon, and its effort to connect with the Sixth created a gap in the Federal line. Grover's division of the Nineteenth drove the brigade of Evans through a belt of woods, and came close to the seven-gun battery of Braxton. The day was lost to Early unless Grover were repulsed. But the Confederate leader was fighting what is technically known as an offensive-defensive battle. Three regiments were thrown into the gap in the Federal line, the advance of the assailants being checked also by the fire of Braxton's battery. Battle's brigade was also thrown into the fray as soon as it arrived. The divisions of Ricketts and Grover were driven back by Gordon and the rest of the division under Rodes, and the whole Union line was disarranged, the Sixth Corps having to give up some of the ground it had won, in order to cover the mishap on the right. It was at this junction that the Federals sustained their chief loss in prisoners. General Rodes was killed in this charge. The tide was turned by Russell's division, which struck the flank of the column that was sweeping away the Federal right. Russell was killed, but the Federal line was reestablished. The Confederate defense was very stubborn, and the battle was not decided until the Federal cavalry came into action on the Union right, this being the danger point. Some of the fiercest of the fighting was around the Hackwood mansion, two miles northeast of Winchester. Torbert crossed the Opequon by the Ridgeway and Locke fords, and Averill came up the Martinsburg pike. Merritt's cavalry was checked by Wharton, supported by King's battery, but by driving Imboden and Ferguson, Averill came into Wharton's rear. Gordon's line was already broken, and Patton and Lee were yielding ground to the arriving Eighth Corps, which attacked Early's left. Since Wilson was threatening the Valley pike, Wickham's cavalry was sent to cover that line of retreat. Being overborne, the Southern army retreated rapidly and in much disorder through the streets of Winchester. But sunset had nearly come, and the Federal infantry, wearied by an all-day march and battle, did not follow beyond the town. The cavalry continued the pursuit to Kernstown, where Ramseur made a stand to cover the retreat.

In this battle of September 19, 1864, the Union men actually engaged were 30,000, with 70 guns. This is exclusive of the Eighth Corps, which took no part until almost the close of the day. Early says that his force present on the field was 13,273. Kennon, following the Federal mode of reckoning, places it at "less than 17,000 men of all arms." Even without counting such brigades of the Eighth as finally participated, the Southern army was greatly outnumbered. The losses on both sides were very heavy. In the army of Sheridan, 697 were killed, 3983 were wounded, and 338 were missing, a total of 5018. The Confederate loss was reported at 276 killed, 1827 wounded, and 1818 missing, some of the latter belonging to the list of killed and wounded. The total was therefore 3921. Early lost five guns and nine colors, but saved his trains. Of his officers, Generals Rodes and Goodwin and Colonel Patton were killed, and Generals Lee and York were wounded. The Federal loss was the heavier, since Sheridan was the assailant and had the greater number of men. But when the size of the two armies is taken into account, the Southern loss was much the greater.

The immediate result of the battle of Opequon was the abandonment of Winchester by Early, and his withdrawal to the strongly fortified lines at Fisher's Hill. To the Federal cause, the further results were highly important. Thenceforward, the Lower Shenandoah was permanently held, Pennsylvania and Maryland were not again invaded, the national capital was relieved from menace, and the Baltimore and Ohio railroad was restored to use. And its influence in reelecting Lincoln was possibly decisive.

Early has been adversely criticized, by Southern as well as Northern writers, for giving battle in country so open as that around Winchester, where his smaller army was liable to be enveloped by the powerful Federal cavalry. Brooking wonders why Early did not make his stand at Fisher's Hill, after being weakened by returning Kershaw to Richmond. A Southern writer observes that he would soon have had to give up Winchester for want of supplies. But Early says he had either to fight at Winchester or give up the very purposes for which he was in the Lower Valley. It is the opinion of another writer that if Kershaw had been present, Sheridan would have lost the day. The task of the Union general would have been harder, yet his superiority in numbers, especially in very efficient cavalry, was almost certain to guarantee ultimate success.

On the other hand, Sheridan's plan of battle is condemned by Kennon as "exceedingly faulty." It was a violation of the military maxim that a general should not beat his head against a wall. He made a frontal attack on a strong position, as favorable for the Confederate defense as conditions permitted. He expected to overwhelm Ramseur, yet he could not but know that the divisions around Stephenson's Depot could be brought up soon after his own advance was detected. The plan of battle was not the one he submitted to Grant, and which was approved by the latter. He then proposed to strike Early's rear at Newtown. This was also Grant's idea, and had this plan been carried out, it would have been all but impossible for Early to get away. The Lower Shenandoah was already nearly stripped of provisions and forage. To escape starvation, Early would have had to move into enemy country, and then attempt to force his way back by a circuitous route and at very great disadvantage. It was the move on Newtown which Crook urged upon his chief on the very day of the battle. Sheridan afterward admitted that it should have been done, and believed it would have resulted in the capture of the bulk of the Southern army. But Crook was thrown into action on the Federal right to break the counterstroke of Gordon and Rodes. Notwithstanding the reverse in that quarter, a move by Crook against the Southern right would have been very disastrous to Early. Wilson alone had almost reached the Valley pike. Knowing that Early's line stretched from Winchester to Martinsburg, Sheridan would have done well to deliver his attack at Stephenson's, where he would have had the advantages of better ground and converging roads. Also, he could have got into action earlier in the morning. He would not have had the whole opposing army to fight, since Early could not afford to uncover Winchester by summoning Ramseur to Stephenson's. In choosing another and faulty plan, Sheridan added one more to the opportunities he failed to take advantage of. The Confederate officers noticed this and wondered at it.

Two days later the armies were confronting one another from opposite sides of the deep valley through which flows the well-named Tumbling Run. In the center and on the right, the Confederate position on the plateau of Fisher's Hill was exceedingly strong, but on the left it was vulnerable. In this direction— toward Little North Mountain—were the cavalry of Lomax, dismounted. Then, in succession, came the divisions of Gordon, Ramseur, and Pegram. Two skeleton brigades of cavalry under Wickham had been dispatched to Milford, thirteen miles south of Front Royal, in order to defend the Luray valley. Rickett's division of the Sixth Corps demonstrated against the Confederate center. It is alleged, though it seems incredible, that Sheridan intended to send Crook against Early's right on the Shenandoah River. This might have resulted like Burnside's assault on Marye's Hill at Fredericksburg. Sheridan yielded to the joint protests of Crook and Hayes, and reluctantly adopted their plan, which was to turn the Southern left at the base of North Mountain. The commander did not think this was practicable, but Crook had already reconnoitered the ground. While batteries on the Federal center were keeping up a noisy cannonade on Fisher's Hill, the Southern guns replying, Crook carried out his flanking movement unobserved and with complete success. He advanced from the mountain rapidly, striking the Valley pike a little in the rear of Early's first position. In attempting to form a new front, the Confederate commands became confused. The Sixth Corps pushed across the defile and connected with the flanking column. Early's army was stampeded and streamed up the Valley, regardless of the roads. As actually fought, the battle of Fisher's Hill is regarded as one of the best examples of grand tactics in the American war. Sheridan's loss was 528 men. Early's was 1235, mostly in prisoners, and not inclusive of a small loss to his cavalry. He also lost 16 guns.

Campbell says that Early intended to abandon his position after dark. He further states that the feeling was general among the private soldiers that Fisher's Hill could not be held against a vigorous assault, and that this explains the rout. He adds that if Sheridan had begun his pursuit the morning after his victory at Winchester, no stand would have been possible.

Torbert and Wilson, who had been sent against Wickham, did not act with energy and failed to get into Early's rear by way of Harrisonburg.

Out of his much smaller army, Early had now lost nearly as many men as Sheridan, and he was no longer able to prevent an advance by his enemy. He retired rapidly to Brown's Gap, where he was reenforced by 3000 men from Richmond under Kershaw, and by 600 cavalry under Rosser. The Federal pursuit was swift. The infantry advanced as far as Mount Crawford. Torbert's cavalry reached Staunton and Waynesboro, where the railroad line was broken and government property destroyed. Sheridan began a return October 6, taking a position at Cedar Creek four days later.

Meanwhile there was taking place a very painful episode of the war. The Shenandoah had been a provision house to the Confederate armies. To make it such no longer, and therefore to make it impossible for a Southern army in the Valley to subsist itself from this region alone, there was a wholesale burning of mills, granaries, and barns, and a general removal of the livestock. This havoc accomplished the object intended, and it led to much desertion from the Confederate ranks. But it caused very great loss and hardship to the non-combatant population. From a strictly military viewpoint, it does not look as though the devastation was justified. Already the Shenandoah had been swept nearly bare by the appetites of at least 60,000 soldiers and their horses. If Sheridan had obeyed Grant's explicit orders, he would have pushed across the Blue Ridge, compelling Early to do likewise, and then broken Lee's lines of supply as completely as he did the following spring. This farther advance was as practicable in the fall of 1864 as it was in the spring of 1865, and the fall of Richmond would have been hastened by several months. Taking the Shenandoah out of the field of military operations would have removed the excuse for its devastation.

At Cedar Creek Sheridan made his headquarters the mansion of Belle Grove. In his retirement, he was so closely followed by Rosser that he ordered his cavalry to drive the latter back or get whipped themselves. The desired result was accomplished in the action of Tom's Brook, October 9, Rosser losing 400 men, 11 guns, and many wagons and the Federals 57 men.

Early lost no time in reoccupying his old position at Fisher's Hill. His reenforcements made him about as strong as before, and because of the destruction that had just occurred, he was eager to strike and strike hard. But the Federal leader did not take Early's return very seriously. He did not think his antagonist capable of an offensive. He went to Washington to consult the Federal high command with reference to the movement he had been ordered to make against Lee's lines of supply. During his absence General Wright was left in command.

Early returned to Fisher's Hill October 13. Because of a scarcity of provisions and forage he could not long remain, and he determined upon an attack. His first thought was to move by his left against the Federal right, but this flank was found to be well defended. Neither Early nor Sheridan seems to have thought a movement by the other flank could succeed, because of the steep Three Top Mountain. But to assure himself, Early sent Gordon and Hotchkiss, the latter a topographical engineer, to the signal station on the summit. From the lofty promontory the entire Union position could be studied. The report of the observers being favorable, Early adopted it with some modifications. He therefore decided to attack Sheridan's left wing, the most vulnerable part of the line. There were no pickets on the river. The Union general had been very negligent in watching the return of Early. A reconnoissance which had just been made toward Fisher's Hill induced the belief that Early had again fallen back.

MILITARY EVENTS OF 1864-65 171

On the contrary he had even occupied Hupp's Hill, north of Strasburg.

The Eighth Corps of the Federal army, much reduced by detachments, lay east of the Valley pike. Thoburn's division, now only 2000 strong, was on a fortified bluff, a mile above the mouth of Cedar Creek and a half-mile below the turnpike bridge. Against a frontal attack the position was good, but on the flank toward the river it was weak. Some distance in the rear of Thoburn was the brigade of Colonel R. B. Hayes, afterward president of the United States. At Buckton was Moore's brigade, and at Front Royal was a detachment of Averill's cavalry. West of the pike and extending to Meadow Brook was the Nineteenth Corps. Beyond, and somewhat back, was the Sixth Corps, the left of its line being two miles from Thoburn. In the rear of the Sixth was Merritt's cavalry. One and one-half miles to the right of Merritt was Custer's cavalry brigade watching the fords in Cedar Creek. The entire Federal line was at least five miles in extent, and was not heavily manned at any one point. The Sixth and the Nineteenth corps had each about 12,000 men on the day of the battle, and the Eighth Corps was 4,000 strong. The cavalry numbered 7,000, so that the aggregate strength of the Union army, present on the field, was about 35,000. The artillery included 84 guns.

On the Confederate side were the cavalry brigades of Rosser and Lomax, numbering 1200 and 1700 men, respectively. The infantry divisions of Kershaw, Ramseur, Gordon, Pegram, and Wharton numbered, in the order of mention, 2700, 2100, 1700, 1200 and 1100. In the batteries were somewhat more than 40 guns. These figures are taken from the narrative by Campbell, who doubtless follows the Southern practice of counting only muskets, sabers, and bona-fide artillerists. His summary is 12,000. Federal historians, following their own method of counting, put the Confederate strength at 17,000. This is undoubtedly too high. The entire number of the men under Early may be conservatively stated at 14,000. The relative proportions of the armies were therefore two Confederates against five Federals, the latter being at first on the defensive.

Lomax was sent to Riverton, from which point he was to strike the Valley pike in the rear of the Federal line. Crossing Cedar Creek a little above its mouth, Kershaw was to attack Thoburn at 4:30 in the morning. Wharton, descending from Hupp's Hill, was to attack the Nineteenth Corps. The divisions of Gordon, Ramseur, and Pegram, and the cavalry under Payne were to execute a very important flank movement, which necessitated a night march. The Shenandoah was crossed by an improvised bridge on the upper side of Sandy Hook. Thence by a wood-path skirting the base of Three Top Mountain the march continued to a ford below the mouth of Cedar Creek. This flanking column was under the immediate command of Gordon. Because of the narrow path, it almost had to move in Indian file, and it was therefore several miles long. Canteens were made noiseless and orders were given in whispers. The night was frosty, and it was cold business to wade a river waist-deep. The attack by this flanking column was to be simultaneous with that by Kershaw.

By throwing 8000 men against 4000, Early expected to make short work of the Eighth Corps. He would then defeat the Nineteenth Corps. Next, by seizing the Valley Pike, the Federal line of communication, and by persistently flanking the Sixth Corps, he hoped to drive the whole Union army from the field. Control of the turnpike was a vital feature of the plan of battle. The Sixth Corps, the fighting qualities of which were superb, would be the last to get into action, and if kept away from the pike would be forced to a disadvantageous and perhaps disastrous retreat.

The Napoleonic maxim of bringing a superior force to the point of contact, even though the entire opposing army might be larger, was now followed by Early, as it was often followed by other Confederate leaders. Using the words of Forrest, he would "get there fust with the mostest men."

East of the pike the battlefield is broken by numerous deep ravines, and there were, as there still are, many thickets of scrubby cedar. Before daybreak a dense fog settled over the whole surface of the scene of action. These two facts had very much to do with the outcome of the first stage of the battle.

Kershaw delivered his attack at five o'clock, carrying Thoburn's position with a rush, and driving him a mile before Gordon came up. He connected with the latter at the pike. Wharton and the artillery were ordered forward at sunrise. The rough ground and the thick fog threw the men of the Eighth Corps into complete confusion, and that command was put out of action for the first half of the day. Hayes and Kitching were not intrenched, and their position was turned by Gordon, whose line connected with Wharton's at the pike. The Confederate divisions, now united, immediately turned on the Nineteenth Corps, which commanded the pike in its front with its batteries. But being enfiladed by the Confederate assault, it was likewise thrown back in great disorder.

Stragglers from the two broken corps began to pour down the pike toward Winchester.

By seven o'clock Early had gained a great advantage, but not a victory, because a decision had not yet been reached. The heavy firing added great quantities of smoke to the fog and the Union positions could not be seen. Early had to reform his lines, the impetus of the attack carrying his right wing across the pike. At eight o'clock the fog lifted, and one hour later, Middletown was reached by the Southern soldiers.

But the Sixth Corps was pushing to the pike. A heavy artillery fire was directed upon it, only causing the veterans to fall back very slowly and in perfect order to a strong position one mile north of Middletown. Wright was now in full control of the pike, and both his flanks were effectually supported by his cavalry. Attacks by Ramseur, Pegram, and Wharton were quickly repulsed.

After ten o'clock there was a long lull in the battle. Two of the Federal corps had been scattered, but Wright's infantry and Torbert's cavalry—nearly three-fifths of the Union army—were undefeated and unshaken and they outnumbered all the Confederates on the field. Their hold on the turnpike was secure. They were in a position of their own choice, and from it they could not be driven. From the artillery 23 guns had been taken, yet 60 remained. Furthermore, both the broken corps were reforming in Wright's rear.

The battle was already lost to Early. He recognized that his men had been pushed to the limit of endurance. His present purpose was to hold his ground until the spoils could be got away. Many of his soldiers were not in line, for there was much straggling, and in the captured camps there was plundering to an extent never yet witnessed during the war. The sky being now clear, the Federals could see the weakness of the battle-line in their front, and Wright intended to counterattack at noon, by which time his ammunition would be replenished. His men were known to their foes as admirable fighters, and the latter conceded that no general could have handled them better.

It is now in order to speak of Sheridan's ride, the current impression of which is rather wide of the actual facts. This is because Thomas Buchanan Read wrote a poem upon it which caught the popular fancy in the North to a wonderful degree. By reason of the poetic license that he took—probably through deficient information—the reader gets the idea that Sheridan had scarcely more than returned to Winchester when he began a daybreak rush to the scene of action, found his army in a general rout, and snatched victory from the very jaws of defeat. He was not "twenty miles away" when he started, for it is barely more than half that distance to Wright's position. Like "Barbara Fritchie", a poem that contains much fancy and only a shred of fact, "Sheridan's Ride" has even been called a myth, the factor of myth attaching not to the ride itself but to its consequences.

According to Adjutant Sinclair of Duryea's Zouaves, a defender of Sheridan, the general reached Winchester at four o'clock in the afternoon of the day before the battle and lodged at his headquarters, now the Elks' Home, at the corner of Braddock and Piccadilly. He was awakened at six o'clock, not by the sound of artillery, but by a picket officer's report. The booming of field guns was thought at first to be a reconnoissance by Grover's division of the Nineteenth Corps. It was not until nearly nine o'clock that Sheridan mounted his black warhorse, "Rienzi." When he reached the camp of the Zouaves, three miles south of Winchester, stragglers had been arriving for an hour and a half, but only the wounded were allowed to go by. That he was two hours on the road bears out the statement by General Manning, second in command in the Sixth Corps, that the general-in-chief was riding no faster than any other well-mounted officer. However, the pike was so blockaded at Newtown and some other points that he had to take to the fields. Sheridan's arrival changed nothing except to encourage his troops. The Union lines were already reformed, and a counterstroke was being arranged. Moore had come up from Buckton, but Lomax never joined Early till the end of the day and took no part in the battle. On the other hand, the demonstrations by the Union cavalry compelled the Southern commander to extend his own lines until they were perilously thin. Two years before he died, Sheridan told Manning he had done wrong in claiming the personal credit for the victory which appears in the dispatches written just after the occurrence. In his Memoirs, he concedes that the surprise of the early morning might have taken place, even if he had then been present.

Sheridan's arrival was during the lull. The last Confederate line had just been formed at the north end of Middletown. With the exception of an unsuccessful attack at one o'clock upon the Nineteenth Corps, on the Union right, there was until half-past four, no other activity than skirmishing and some artillery firing. Sheridan then ordered a general advance. Once more the fighting became severe, but under the heavy impact the Southern line crumbled, and at length dissolved in a rout, which was the greatest that had been seen since First Manassas. Early's trains were halted by a broken bridge just below Strasburg. All the captured cannon were retaken, and 24 others. Several flags were also captured. Darkness was now coming on and the pursuit was not pressed any farther. As at Fisher's Hill, Sheridan delayed his attack too long to gather in the full results of either victory.

The losses on both sides had been very severe. In the Federal army, the killed were 644, the wounded 3430, and the missing 1591, including 1429 prisoners taken in the surprise of the morning. The total was therefore 5665. Nearly half of the loss—2488—had fallen on the Nineteenth corps. Early reported his killed at 320 and his wounded at 1540. The prisoners—taken in the last stage of the battle—bring the total of Confederate casualties to about 3200.

Each commander made a serious error. Early remained too long on the battlefield. When he found it no longer possible to make any impression on the opposing army, he should have retired before a counterstroke could be delivered. He could then have got away with at least much of his spoil, and with less than half the loss he actually sustained. There would have been no real victory to either side, and another stand at Fisher's Hill might have been possible. On the other hand, Sheridan did not assume the offensive until more than five hours after he arrived. Had he not taken the ride rendered spectacular by Read's poem, Wright would have advanced very early in the afternoon, and undoubtedly with more disastrous effect to the Southern army.

Concerning the battle of Cedar Creek, there have been several controversies and misapprehensions. Gordon speaks of a "fatal order" to halt, given about seven o'clock in the morning. McKim says it was not Sheridan's ride, but the alleged halt, that lost the battle, and that with Gordon in command of the whole Southern army, there would have been a complete victory. But Campbell, writing from a Southern viewpoint, and, with the aid of both Federal and Confederate documents, canvassing the topic exhaustively, proves that the order to halt was a myth. Early continued to press the attack until his men were too jaded for further effort. He pushed back the Federal line four miles, but was then brought to a standstill by the Sixth Corps and the cavalry. A minor portion of the Federal army had been routed, but there could be no victory so long as a larger and undefeated portion not only barred the way to Winchester, but made retirement necessary. Early's army scored a temporary advantage, but was too light to achieve a complete victory. In his book, Early says the straggling of his men was the chief cause of his defeat, but Campbell shows that the straggling, great as it was, did not of itself lose the battle. This writer observes that never did the plundering of a captured camp have better excuse. Early's men were but half-clothed, and had been on half-rations for weeks. Half of them were barefoot. They had been out in the cold nearly all night, and 5000 of them had waded the chilly waters of the Shenandoah. They fought three hours before they had any breakfast. The privates felt that the battle was lost when, after two hours had been used up in pressing the Sixth Corps back a short distance, it was seen to be impossible to move it from the position of its choice.

The Union victory was decisive, and there was no second battle of Fisher's Hill. Early's broken army moved some distance up the Valley, pursued by Sheridan, who, however, again fell back, going into winter quarters at Kernstown. Once more Early followed, reaching Newtown November 11. There was fighting the next day, Sheridan massing cavalry on both his flanks. McCausland was routed and driven up the Luray valley, losing two guns, two colors, and 245 men. The Federal infantry advanced three miles and were under orders to be alert the next morning. But in the night Early retired toward New Market and was pursued to Rude's Hill. Early's Second Corps was sent to Richmond early in December. About the same time the Federal Sixth Corps was sent to rejoin Grant.

The Valley Pike now ceased to be a racecourse for armies. An Alabama officer wrote in his diary that, "we have walked the pike road so often that we know not only every house, fence, spring, and shade-tree, but very many of the citizens, their wives, and children." But Fisher's Hill has become one of the largest and best known of the Confederate picnic grounds.

The net result of three months of effort and a loss of nearly 17,000 men was little more than the expulsion of Early from the Lower Shenandoah. Sherman would have accomplished this result by maneuvering and without fighting any large battle. But Sheridan's success, exaggerated at the time and for years afterward, electrified the North. Opequon made him a brigadier in the regular army, and Cedar Creek advanced him to the rank of major general. "Little Phil" had an excess of caution, yet he was a fighting general, and as such his power of personal magnetism was exceptional.

Lee had underestimated the size of Sheridan's army, and in view of the condition of affairs at Richmond, a victory at Cedar Creek was wellnigh a necessity to him. Yet until the closing days of the campaign, he thought his subordinate had accomplished all that could reasonably be expected. In twenty weeks Early had marched 1670 miles and fought 75 engagements. He had held back 70,000 men from joining Grant. He had kept the Baltimore and Ohio railroad broken for three months, and had threatened both Washington and Baltimore with capture. He had sent across the Potomac large amounts of provisions, livestock, and clothing, and by holding the Lower Valley throughout the summer he enabled its grain harvest to be secured. The requisitions levied on the towns beyond the Potomac he used in purchasing supplies for his men. All this had been done with an aggregate strength, according to Campbell, of 18,000 poorly clothed, poorly fed, and poorly equipped soldiers, although Anderson, who was not subordinate to Early, is evidently not included in this estimate. He had inflicted a loss about equal to the entire Southern army, though not without great loss to himself. Campbell observes that at least a half of Early's men had been wounded at one time or another, and that many had been wounded more than once. The brigade of Smith was reduced during the campaign from 2100 men to 400, and that of Echols from 2150 to 275. The Southern army in the Shenandoah was in fact made up of remnants. In Terry's brigade of Gordon's division were, on September 13, 963 men from 14 Virginia regiments. Under York were 803 men of 10 Louisiana regiments. Once again, the season was unusually hot until into the month of September. This excessive heat turned the scale in the proposed attack on Washington.

On the contrary, the Northern soldiers were well fed, well clothed, and well equipped. They had rifled muskets, Spencer carbines, and revolvers. They had remarkably little sickness. At Cedar Creek they went into battle on full rations and unfatigued.

But in war, more than anywhere else, nothing succeeds like success. Early was severely censured for his ultimate failure, and he became the target of sarcastic jibes. Cedar Creek lost him the confidence of the Southern public, and as had not been the case in Jackson's Valley campaign, his army was not thanked by the Confederate Congress. He tempted fate too far, and became soured and embittered, his attitude after the war contrasting unfavorably with that of such men as Lee and Johnston. A writer of Winchester remarks that, "the nineteenth of September and the nineteenth of October combined made up his Waterloo, and his subsequent life was spent in the Saint Helena of disappointed ambitions and wrecked hopes."

At the end of February, 1865, Sheridan began a forward movement with 10,000 mounted men and 100 guns. Early's little army at Waynesboro was mostly captured and with very little loss to himself. He then crossed the Blue Ridge, struck the James River canal, and took a share in the Appomattox campaign. Within six weeks from leaving Kernstown, Lee had surrendered and all Confederate resistance in Virginia was at an end. The last military event in the Lower Shenandoah occurred April 21. Colonel Mosby then surrendered his 600 men to General Hancock, who was now in command at Winchester. The preceding fall Mosby had been a great annoyance to Sheridan by persistently raiding upon his rear. It was the practice of both armies to make short work of civilians acting as guerrillas, and on the plea that they were such, several of Mosby's men were executed at Front Royal. This was put an end to after Mosby proved that his men were regularly enlisted soldiers.

XIV

BEHIND THE SOUTHERN LINES

The Early Months — The First Winter — Recapture by Jackson — Milroy and His Rule — Conduct of Soldiers — Privations — Spies — Battles of 1864 — Winchester at the End of the War.

> It is to the everlasting honor of the men of this country that so few women were molested, when so many were absolutely unprotected, and even the law powerless to protect them or to punish those who might harm them. And this was true of the men of the North as of the South. — Kate McVicar (writing in the Winchester Evening Star.)

After the middle of April, 1861, war within the United States became a reality. And yet it was only a very few who were able to foresee a long and devastating contest. On either side of the Mason and Dixon line was the impression that the other party was playing a game of bluff, and that a determined display of military force would be enough to clear the air. Consequently, in the late spring and the early summer of 1861, the clash of arms was regarded far more lightly than was the case, one, two, and three years later. Free state soil was exceedingly close to the Lower Valley, yet there was a hopefulness that any attempt at its invasion would be beaten back.

In the superficial aspects of military preparation there is something hypnotic. A parade by men in uniform, with colors flying and bands playing has a mighty power to thrill the spectator and stir his deepest feelings. And when the parade is in time of great public danger, there comes into general play the will to do one's utmost.

In the latter half of the spring there was the hurry of preparation. Gray cloth, woven in the mills close to Winchester, was in urgent demand for uniforms. Firearms, some of them very old fashioned, were brought from their resting-places, which perhaps were deer-antlers fastened to a wall, and as rapidly as possible the flintlock was changed into a percussion musket gun. Tournaments had been very popular in this region, and they now proved their value as a training school, especially in cavalry service.

In the Shenandoah, as everywhere else in the South, horsemanship was very general, and it required but a minimum of effort to turn the young civilian into a very efficient mounted soldier. His steed was usually his own, and if he were not familiar with the district he happened to be in at a given time, some comrade was nearly certain to be able to supply the lack.

Some one with a fondness for parallels has compared the Great American War with the Wars of the Roses in English history. And at the time when the partisans of the White Rose of York and the Red Rose of Lancaster were exterminating one another in hand to hand combat, the institution of chivalry was in the forefront. The idea of chivalry had been kept alive among the Southern people by reading the romances of Sir Walter Scott. And as knighthood and chivalry are still very familiar terms, it is safe to affirm that for generations yet to come the exploits of the Confederate cavalry leaders will continue to be to American literature much the same as the exploits of the knights depicted in the Waverley novels.

Despite the briefness of his career as a soldier, no Southern horseman is a more picturesque character than Turner Ashby. Though a native of Fauquier, he became fully naturalized to the Shenandoah Valley. He was a man of medium height and wiry, and his long black beard added to his martial appearance. He was in the prime of life, being but thirty-three years old, and could ride eighty miles within twenty-four hours, using two mounts. Thoroughly familiar with the Lower Valley, Ashby's scouting service with the Seventh Virginia Cavalry was invaluable to his superiors. He attained the rank of brigadier general, but a career of great promise was cut short by his fall in a skirmish, only twelve months after the opening of hostilities. Had he lived through the war, he would probably have become one of the best known of the leaders in the Confederate cavalry.

Less conspicuous, because of lower rank, was a younger brother, Captain Richard Ashby, killed near Romney, June 7, 1861. The Ashby brothers have had many namesakes in the Shenandoah. They are buried in the cemetery at Winchester.

As soon as the war had become a reality, Winchester was made a rendezvous for the new soldiers, and after his abandonment of Harper's Ferry, General Johnston made the town his headquarters. The war was poetry as yet. The girls read the poetry of Thomas Moore, and were more sentimental than their successors of the present decade. Gold lace and brass buttons were everywhere in evidence, and uniforms were new, spick, and span. The wearers of the same bulked large in the minds of the maidens. Throughout the war the soldiers courted and married whenever opportunity offered.

In the summer of 1861 the exigencies of war had not much dislocated the usual activities of Winchester, although the churches were turned into barracks. The women and girls took to carding, spinning, weaving, and knitting. Such arts were not lost arts, as was the case in 1917, and one-half of the Southern recruits came to camp wearing homespun. Yet the factory system, aided by the extending lines of railway, was already relegating these activities to the background. Knitting, however, was still practiced by women and girls generally. Sewing and knitting circles immediately sprang up, and they met every few days. Outside of the town, the female element assumed in large degree the care of the garden and the dairy.

After Johnston moved back from Harper's Ferry, Fort Collyer was thrown up around the house of Isaac Stine, who went to his farm in Clarke county. Prisoners of war were set to work on this fortification, much of which is still visible. Camp Stephenson, the leading rendezvous of the Southern soldiers was one mile from town.

Mass psychology is a thing of curious interest. People in crowds are more excitable and inflammable than is true of the average individual, and are easily swayed by vague alarms. It has been said that the "crowd-mind is the child-mind." Thus in the early months of the war, before the people had become somewhat used to the new and abnormal status, there was often a local panic. One of these occurred June 15, more than two weeks before Patterson's army crossed the Potomac. There was wild commotion at a report that the Federals were coming. The militia swarmed into Winchester, armed with shotguns and other private weapons. If no firearm was available, the man brought a club, or perhaps a hay-knife; anything with which it might be possible to hurt an enemy at close quarters.

Patterson did not come much nearer than Martinsburg, and after three weeks his army returned to the Maryland side of the Potomac. The incursion was little else than a farce. All fighting was confined to a few insignificant skirmishes, and Johnston was not kept from reenforcing Beauregard at Manassas. But at the moment, the citizens were indignant at being left in a defenseless condition, and with a host of sick or wounded soldiers to care for. Johnston, however, had taken the measure of his adversary and was justified in the risk. One of the results of the victory at

Manassas was the return of Patterson's army to the north bank of the Potomac. During the next seven months, the Lower Valley lay behind the Confederate front.

As the crow flies, the battlefield of Manassas is little more than forty miles from Winchester, and the roar of artillery, continuing several hours, was distinctly heard. The news of the Southern triumph was dimmed as the casualty lists were examined and found to include several young men of Winchester and its vicinity.

For more than half a year there was a fair sense of security. The armies did little more than observe one another across the Potomac, although behind the lines, in both directions, mighty preparations were in progress to compel a decision in the following year. Stonewall Jackson came to Winchester as commander in the Valley, and made the town his headquarters. His military home was in the Moore house near Peyton Street, but he boarded with Dr. Graham, pastor of the Kent Street Presbyterian church, and was a regular attendant at that house of worship. He was joined by his wife, who survived him more than fifty years, attaining the age of eighty-three.

While Jackson was here, the commissary department was on the east side of Market Street, on the site of the Baker warehouse. The quartermaster's office was on the opposite side. The fairgrounds became a camp for the militia, who complained of their privations in being away from home. It was the volunteers for whom the girls reserved their smiles.

Except during the three weeks consumed in the expedition to Romney, Jackson was in the town throughout the winter, which was exceptionally wet and unpleasant.

With the opening days of spring came the approach of the Federal army under Banks. Because of the much larger number of his enemy, Jackson withdrew from Winchester, after burning in Shawnee hollow tobacco of the value of $75,000. This was done to prevent its capture. Mrs. Macon, from whose interesting book we derive much of the material for this chapter, relates that it was not supposed anyone would be safe with the "Yankees" about. She and her sisters were accordingly sent to Milford, more than thirty miles away. Mr. Powell, a teacher, was in so great haste to get out of town that he left his dinner on the table.

Banks was in possession of Winchester nearly three months, but his rule was less severe than that of the year following. Because of putting an incorrect inference on the finding in the medical college the preserved body of a son of John Brown, the building was immediately burned, and it seems to have been at this time that "Selma," the residence of James M. Mason was destroyed in the same way. Mr. Mason, who had for many years represented Virginia in the Senate of the United States, had been ordered to England on a diplomatic errand. The British steamer Trent, in which he took passage from Havana, was overhauled by Commodore Wilkes of the Federal navy, and Mr. Mason was imprisoned at Fort Warren in Boston harbor. But as Wilkes had exceeded his right, under the law of nations, the captive was released and proceeded to England. This affair had very recently occurred, and it doubtless instigated the burning of the Mason house. In the hall of the Turner Ashby Camp of Winchester is a chest that belonged to Mr. Mason. It contains also a chest that belonged to General W. N. Pendleton.

Banks soon moved southward to Strasburg, leaving a rearguard in Winchester. However, it was before the occupation of Strasburg that the battle of Kernstown was fought. Taking place only four miles away, the sound of the firing was far more distinct than in the case of Manassas. The action closed at nightfall, and as soon as it could be done, the scene was visited for the burial of the soldiers killed and the relief of the wounded. Thus for the first time was the grim reality of war brought to the immediate notice of the townspeople. In the two armies 1200 men had been struck by bullet or shell, and yet Kernstown was a small affair compared with some battles that came afterward, even in the Valley itself.

The two battles of Kernstown and the first battle of Winchester were fought on Sunday, as was also, in part, the retaking of Winchester in 1863.

Just two months later, an engagement began in the southern border of the town, and as the Federals were driven, there was some firing in the streets. The Union soldiers ran pell mell to the northward, dropping canteens, coffee-pots, and other articles of camp equipage.

An incident in the entry by the pursuing Confederates is related by General Taylor, whose soldiers were from Louisiana, many of them using French as their mother tongue. A buxom, comely woman of about thirty-five made the remark, "Oh, you come too late!" A tall Teche at once stepped out of the ranks, threw his arms around her, and said with a kiss, "Madame, je n'arrive jamais trop tard!" (Madame, I never arrive too late.) In the general laughing, the woman, with a rosy face but a merry twinkle, got out of the way. The same day, Colonel Bradley T. Johnson was the recipient of a kiss. He did not object to the salute, but he did not think well of the odor of homemade soap that clung to the woman's clothes.

It was in the course of this battle that General David H. Strother narrowly escaped capture in a town where for some years he had been well-known. As an artist, and signing his drawings "Porte Crayon," he had gained a national reputation. Strother's sympathies were with the North and he was in the Northern army.

In his hasty retreat, Banks fired the town in several places. Several warehouses burned to the ground, but elsewhere the flames were put out.

Another incident in the retaking of Winchester was the number of colored servants who joined the fleeing Federals. They believed, or had been led to believe, that they would be put to death if they remained. Before leaving, they loaded themselves with plunder, one woman striding down the pike with a feather bed on her head. These refugees were a handicap to the retreating army, and by encumbering the roads caused many of the Union men to be captured. Some of the negroes lost their bundles, and when they came back with the subsequent return of the Northern army, they were a source of much trouble to the townspeople. They secured search-warrants, which were executed by provost guards, and in this way many things were taken from the houses which did not belong to them at all.

When the war came on, there was a strong undercurrent of antislavery feeling, but it was not considered that the time had arrived for a general emancipation. The buying and selling of negroes had almost ceased. In Winchester some of the house servants ran off when Banks was driven from the town, but in the farming neighborhoods the greater number of the slaves remained at work. Had they also decamped, the pinch with respect to food and fuel would have been much more acute.

In this campaign General Taylor remarks that the Southern cavalry exhibited every good quality but discipline. Because of their elation at the successful advance, and the wish to visit the private homes and the friends living in them, they scattered over the Valley like a cloud of locusts.

A numerous portion of the Confederate forces in the Valley were the men from North Carolina, not a few of whom succumbed to homesickness as well as enemy bullets, and they filled more graves in Stonewall Cemetery than the soldiers from any other state of the South. While here, they became fond of apple butter, a novelty to them but plentiful in the Shenandoah, since it was a common practice for a family to put up from twenty to thirty gallons. So a frequent request of the Tarheel was this: "Will you-uns give we-uns some red-spread?"

With large forces trying to close in upon his rear, Jackson could stay but a few days in the Lower Valley, and Winchester again passed into the hands of the Federals. General White came with a brigade and began throwing up some earthworks. On the Gainsboro road, two miles north of town, and in full view from the highway, is the Star Fort, built by Milroy, or at least completed by him. It is still well preserved, and cannon tracks may yet be seen in the bastions.

But when Lee crossed the Potomac, just after the second battle of Manassas, White was flanked and had to retreat to Harper's Ferry. In the evacuation, which took place September 1, the railroad station, the commissary stores, and the warehouses on the west side of Market Street were burned. At two o'clock the following night there was a tremendous explosion that shattered many windows. In what is now known as Milroy's Fort, northwest of the city, was a magazine, and a small detail of soldiers was left behind to explode it. This was accomplished, and a yawning hole is still to be seen. In performing their duty, one or two of the soldiers lost their lives.

The fall and early winter were a period of Confederate control. After the great battle of Antietam, Jackson's corps was encamped for several weeks on the Opequon. Its march to Fredericksburg emptied the Lower Valley of Southern troops, and General Milroy came from West Virginia to take command. Winchester was his headquarters from late in December, 1862, until the middle of the following June. This general has been characterized as the "Weyler of the Civil War," the memory of his administration having come down through the half-century as a reign of terror.

Milroy, who had been a lawyer of Indiana, was a harsh, narrow, uncompromising man, of a type often seen while the two great sections of the land viewed one another with a prejudice born of a lack of acquaintance. When a man of this kind was given command in a region alien to his point of view, he was severe and unsympathetic and sometimes brutal.

The Sunday school training of this general seems to have been very deficient, or to have fallen into eclipse. He could swear with great readiness and unction, especially when giving his opinion of the more obnoxious "rebels" in Winchester, and the "devilish rebellion" they were helping to support. His temper was violent and was easily ruffled, yet there was a tender side to his rough nature, and discerning individuals of the gentler sex learned how to manage him. Mrs. Macon relates that he told General Torbert that her family were the "only decent damned secesh in town." On one occasion her aunt said to her, "Emma, go down and ask Milroy to give me a permit to go to the mill. Tell him the old cow has eaten rosebushes till the thorns are sticking out of her sides."

We are told the trouble with Milroy was not so much a cruel spirit as his "intolerable meanness." With only a very few hours' warning, citizens were forced to give up their dwelling houses. Sentinels were posted at nearly every street intersection. No one might get a pass without taking an oath, and even then he was searched at the first picket post he came to. A man coming to town with a load of fuel had to throw off the wood at the demand of a sentry, so as to ascertain whether anything were concealed in it. Only two physicians—Baldwin and Holliday—had remained in town, and they were forbidden to make professional calls outside. Sutlers had opened stores in Winchester, as was always the case when the Union army was present for any length of time; but under the Milroy regime no citizen might buy from a sutler. Even with his own soldiers Milroy was stern and rigid.

Milroy's outposts up the Valley were much annoyed, and on one occasion they met with a sharp reverse. The general said he would hang a certain "bushwhacker, if Jeff Davis and Halleck would not make too much fuss about it." Because of some assessments that he levied upon Winchester, General Lee recommended that some of the prisoners taken from his army be detained as hostages.

In March a number of Southern sympathizers expelled from West Virginia came through Winchester on their way to places of refuge, and were treated harshly by the commandant.

Some Northern women were here during the occupation by Banks, and a still larger number were present under Milroy's rule. Because of the fortifications around, it was not supposed that the place could easily be taken. The evacuation was stealthy, and in the dead of night. Three hundred women, many of whom were wives or relatives of Federal officers, were left stranded. Their plight was all the worse because of the exasperating severity shown by Milroy, and they were given little sympathy or help by the inhabitants. They were taken to Richmond, and there exchanged for Southern women in Northern prisons.

In the political campaign of 1868, General Milroy, then in

command at Winchester, was made to feel the odium of his military rule. He tried to address a large audience in the courthouse, October 21, but there was so much confusion from invective and catcalls that it was impossible to hear him until Mayor Conrad quieted the uproar with a caution as to the effect that might be produced in the North. A taunt several times hurled at the speaker related to "John Arnold's cow." Mr. Arnold had a cow and pasturage for the animal was refused by Milroy. Yet by a clever exercise of strategy his daughter outwitted the general and secured for the animal something to eat. At the meeting inquiries were also made about some spoons that had disappeared from the house used by Milroy as his headquarters. It would thus seem that General B. F. Butler was not the only Federal officer whose fingers became adhesive when silver spoons were lying about.

Mr. Ashby tells us that the Union officers of the earlier campaigns were nearly always gentlemen, and the privates the best type of Northern citizens. But in the later campaigns were officers who had come up from the ranks, while into the ranks the working of the draft had introduced a considerable amount of riffraff. Soldiers liked to avoid their army rations, and in the first half of the war the Union men gave money in return for the bread, cakes, and pies they had from the private homes. In 1863 they began to display a propensity to pillage. This was sometimes forestalled by telling the would-be looters that smallpox, or some other contagious ailment, was in the house. This subterfuge was called "strategy."

Miss Kate McVicar assures us that there was no authentic instance of any woman or girl being molested by either Northern or Southern soldiers, unless insult had been invited.

But of course there were differences in the Federal soldiery. Children screamed in terror at the sight of the Zouaves from New York in their gaudy, fantastic uniform. "Blenker's Dutch" in the army of Milroy are remembered as a "holy terror," their rough, disagreeable manners and their propensity to loot being unpleasantly suggestive of the conduct of the Hessians in the Revolution.

As campaign followed campaign, there appeared a degree of coarseness among the soldiers of either army that was little in evidence at the start, because warfare was then something unfamiliar. There grew up a feeling that the lengthening out of the conflict was distinctly the fault of the other side, and therefore deserving of brusque treatment.

The local sentiment for the Southern cause was not quite unanimous, and there was an occasional person who sympathized with the Union. Mr. Ashby observes that not all the non-combatants of this class were spies or renegades. Some of them were entirely sincere, and when the Federal army was in control, their services in behalf of their neighbors were invaluable.

Yet there were spies, and through them each contestant found help. Sometimes the spy was a real or pretended Quaker. The Friends are opposed to warfare on principle, but in the war of the sixties, as in the war of the American Revolution, there were individuals who found it impossible to remain "neutral in thought," and thereby exposed themselves to the criticism that their actions were not in harmony with their professions. A few days before the battle of the Opequon, a Quakeress of this city sent important information to General Sheridan. His letter to her was wrapped in tinfoil and sent by a negro. The answer was conveyed in the same manner. After the war, this person was rewarded with a government clerkship in Washington. In the fall of 1864 she was carrying on a school for loyalist children, and her mother kept a boarding house. Her sister was of Southern sympathy. On the other hand we are told of an assumed Quaker who visited Sheridan's camp and reported his observations to General Early.

The spy who gained the greatest notoriety in the Lower Shenandoah was Belle Boyd, a native of Martinsburg. She was attractive in manner and appearance and of magnetic personality. She possessed dash, energy, and courage, and was a skillful rider.

Mr. Ashby calls attention to a deceptive prosperity in the early years of the war. Any man in commercial business might, and often did, issue "shinplasters" in denominations of five, ten, twenty-five, and fifty cents. Paper money became exceedingly plentiful as compared with the supply before the war. Every man had money, and values rose. Confederate bonds were extensively purchased, and, in the sequel, with unfortunate results.

In the third year of the war the vitality of the South was being sapped by the unequal contest. Visible trade with the North was of course suspended, and as the only imports from Europe were such as made out to run the blockade, "store goods" became scarce. Fields and orchards yielded well, so far as they could be looked after, and game and nuts were as abundant as usual; but so very many were the men taken into military service, the conscript age-limits being 16 and 60, that the normal yield of the soil could not be attained. Home economies became compulsory, and they grew into a kind of religion. Rye was substituted for coffee, sassafras for tea, and sorghum sirup for sugar as well as for West India molasses. Leather grew scarce. The foundations of meat houses were dug up to eke out a deficient supply of salt. To get soda corncobs were burned. Wallpaper was cut into strips for use as writing paper. The uniforms abandoned by Federal soldiers were dyed black. In making a "Confederate candle," a wick ten to twenty inches long was dipped in tallow and wax, and then coiled round a stick eighteen inches long. The stick was nailed to a block, and one end of the wick rose one inch above it. The "molasses pie" was made of sorghum sirup and lemons stewed together and baked three minutes with pastry. But this makeshift was enough to tax the digestion of an ostrich.

Three salt agents were appointed, December 1, 1862, to allow seven pounds of salt to each member of the community, and to collect for the same six cents a pound. For this purpose the sum of $7000 was borrowed. August 31, 1863, the agents were authorized to borrow $12,000 additional.

The long frontier between the warring sections was only a few miles away, and was so extensive that it could not be rigidly guarded at every point. There were Southern sympathizers to the north, and there were Northern sympathizers to the south. There was no little amount of smuggling across the border, particularly in medicines. The balloon-like hoopskirts worn by the women of the period now became highly serviceable as screens for contraband goods. On a smaller scale, the same was true of the poke bonnets and hairnets which were then in fashion. But in spite of such relief as came from this source, quinine sold at one dollar a grain in 1864 and bacon at ten dollars a pound. Just prior to the fall of the Confederacy, flour sold at six hundred dollars a barrel and a military coat cost six hundred fifty dollars.

It was the fate of Winchester to be one great hospital throughout the conflict. When Johnston marched to Manassas he left behind 1700 of his men in hospital. When Jackson evacuated the town the next March, he left his sick and wounded, and before the month had expired, very many of the men disabled at Kernstown were brought here. In September of the same year, great numbers of Confederate wounded were brought to Winchester from the bloody field of Antietam. And in July of the succeeding year came 6000 wounded from Gettysburg. For days after that titanic struggle, trains of ambulances passed through the town. Hundreds of the injured soldiers walked, many of whom gave out from exhaustion, and some died. All the churches, hotels, and public buildings were filled with the wounded, and others lay on the grass in the courthouse inclosure. And anaesthetics were scarce.

Even these successive influxes were to be rivaled in the summer and fall of 1864.

After Gettysburg, the Boomerangs—Company H, Thirteenth Virginia Infantry—did provost duty at Winchester. George McDaniel of this command was transferred to Morgan's cavalry in Kentucky, and died of homesickness in Camp Chase.

The fall of 1863 was comparatively quiet, but the twelve months which came after it proved to the people of the Lower Valley the most trying period of the entire war. The raiding and marching became almost incessant, and the frequent engagements created a never-ceasing fear and apprehension. When General Hunter advanced, at the close of the spring of 1864, it was understood that he meant to burn Winchester, and he did intend to burn Newtown, excepting the few loyalist homes.

In the southern outskirts of Winchester, cannon roared on May 25, 1862, and some bullets flew about in the streets. But this display of the destructive side of the military art was far exceeded during the entire afternoon of September 19, 1864. The armies which then came together in battle-shock were twice as large, and ten times as many were the killed and wounded. The firing lines, on the plateau to the east and northeast, were distant only one mile and a half, and women and girls watched the fighting from the fence around the cemetery of Mount Hebron. But when Early's soldiers were pressed back, they had to retire in haste. Both shells and bullets rained upon the town, driving the civilian population to cellars and other places of refuge. Certain units of the beaten army marched through the city in good order, but concerning others, an entry in a Confederate diary says that, "I never saw our troops in such confusion before." Wounded men staggered along, often falling from weakness in the street or on the sidewalk. The night which was fast coming on was a time of horror. The surgeons were operating all night, and the air was rent with the shrieks and groans of the sufferers. An old well out of town was filled with amputated limbs and afterward covered over.

The next day the wounded still on the field were brought in to the hospitals, but no civilian might visit the scene unless he had a permit to look after the dead of his side. The Southern soldiers who had been captured were placed in the courthouse and yard. Food and delicacies were brought them by the ladies of the town.

The women of the little city were living at high tension. They gave little thought to their own safety, and did not shrink from the horrible sights of the battlefield and the hospital. One of these was Miss Matilda M. Russell. She came to a desperately wounded soldier, and sat down by him to give such aid as seemed possible. A Federal surgeon passing by told her that if he could remain as he was there was a chance for him, but that a change of position would be fatal. Miss Russell did not hesitate for a moment, and held the unconscious man hour after hour, scarcely daring to move a muscle. Her care was rewarded and the soldier's life was saved, though at much cost to herself, because of the nervous and physical strain. This incident made Miss Russell the heroine of the story, "A Night on the Battlefield," by John Esten Cooke. It was also the subject of two paintings, one of which, by M. K. Kellogg, found its way to the gallery of a Northern millionaire. The other, entitled, "An Angel on the Battlefield," was executed by Oregon R. Wilson in 1869. Miss Russell died in 1897.

There was no more fighting very close to Winchester, but exactly one month later came the equally heavy battle of Cedar Creek. The booming of cannon fifteen miles away began to be heard about daybreak. There was a rumor in the town that Early was strongly reenforced and was forcing his way back. The picket guards in Winchester were doubled, and horsemen dashed through the streets in wild excitement. But the end of the day brought tidings of another defeat, and once more were the hospitals filled with the wounded. Among the slain officers was General Ramseur of Early's army, who left an infant daughter he had never seen. He died in the Belle Grove mansion.

A story is associated with the Hillman tollgate, built in 1840 and standing a short distance beyond the southern line of Winchester. When Sheridan was in pursuit of Early, after the battle of Opequon, Charlotte Hillman stood at the gate and demanded payment. Sheridan replied that he would pay for himself and staff, but could not answer for his men. Entirely undaunted, the young woman cut a notch in a stick for every ten men who passed through.

When Early finally retired in November, the war was over in the Lower Valley, but it was still five months to the return of peace, and Winchester was still under military rule. Social life was dormant, except as affected by the presence of the Union army. Civil government had long since collapsed. Courts seldom met, stores and shops were closed, very little teaching was done, and the mechanics were almost out of work. In 1862 the records of county and city were sent to Luray, and when returned in June, 1864, some of them were missing.

We here quote some observations taken from the war diary of W. S. Tyler, a soldier of a Massachusetts regiment. The entries are from just after the battle of the Opequon and within the six weeks following:

"Winchester is a beautiful place, or, rather, has been, and is very compactly built. Now the stores and public buildings are all deserted, and there are very few male inhabitants that are not over sixty years of age. They have some of the prettiest girls here I ever saw, and any quantity of them... Only the Episcopal church is open... The lights were pretty much all smashed out of the windows when we came here... The marks of war are indelibly written in the appearance of every family in the town...There are some people here who boast that they have never spoken to a Yankee since the war commenced, unless they were obliged to."

The diarist speaks very kindly of Dr. Graham, to whom he several times listened in the Kent Street Presbyterian church.

When the Federals were here they sought to visit the homes where girls were to be found, and they displayed a preference for those of outspoken Southern sympathy. They knew where the latter stood, and they could not always feel certain as to the sincerity of the loyal element. A tragic event was the killing of Millie Forsythe, who lived near the corner of Braddock and Cork. The fatal shot came from a revolver, and was believed to have been fired by a jealous Federal. Another shooting, but with a happier ending, occurred January 15, 1865. As a troop of the First Vermont Cavalry was going by the home of Mrs. John W. Ridings a carbine was accidentally discharged, and Mrs. Ridings received a flesh wound above the knee. Captain Woodbury of the regiment was much shocked, and went into the house, remaining until help came. He corresponded with the lady until she died in 1896.

Apart from the surrender of Mosby, of which mention has been made, the chief military event of 1865 was when 1200 of the Confederates captured at Waynesboro were marched through Winchester.

The surrender of General Lee was celebrated by the army of occupation. There was playing by the bands, and the booming of cannon continued all night. There was an order for an illumination, some of the citizens refusing to comply, but at half past eight the streets had a pretty appearance. All at once the lights went out and the bands ceased playing, telegraphic news of the assassination of President Lincoln having arrived. The people of Winchester could observe that the crime had very unfortunate results. Until now there was a spirit of conciliation among the Northern soldiers and in the Northern newspapers. This feeling at once gave way to fierce threats of retaliation.

Among the officers under Sheridan were two men who subsequently filled the presidential chair; General Hayes and Major McKinley. On the upper floor of the brick store building on the east side of Main next to the recently erected home of the Commercial and Savings Bank, McKinley was initiated as a Mason into Hiram Lodge by J. B. T. Reed, a Confederate chaplain. This ceremony occurred May 1, 1865, and two days later the initiate completed the Blue Lodge degrees. During his presidential term, McKinley visited Winchester—May 20, 1899—and when the tidings came of his death, the lodge held an appropriate service. Resolutions were also passed by the city council.

According to a diary by a townsman, Winchester was tossed back and forth between the two armies no fewer than seventy-two times, four transfers taking place in one period of twenty-four hours. The citizens could not always feel any assurance, on looking out in the morning, whether the Stars and Stripes or the Stars and Bars would be floating in the breeze. The Taylor Hotel must have been very popular to both sides, for we are assured that on one particular day it changed hands five times. Another statement increases the number of changes of control in Winchester to eighty-four.

The sorry appearance which had increasingly come to the battle-scarred town in the four years of war reached a climax in the spring of 1865. In and close around Winchester more than 200 houses were missing. Some had been demolished, and some had been burned. On Main Street a hundred homes had been turned into stables or slaughter houses, or put to some other exceptional use as a consequence of military urgency. The churches had fared harshly. The Catholic and the Reformed houses of worship were so badly wrecked that repair was almost out of the question. Some years later, damages were paid by the national government to several of the congregations.

Writing from Winchester, October 31, 1865, an English visitor says that all the way up from Harper's Ferry the Shenandoah Valley looked like one vast moor. There were few trees and no fences. In every direction were the ruins of burned houses. The fields were lying idle, and in many of them were the graves of soldiers. Around Stephenson's Depot was the height of the desolation. There was scarcely a family but had lost one or more of its members, and for months the people had been in almost a starving condition. There was still at Winchester a small Federal force, and although its commander was a person of tact and delicacy, the people would not receive into their homes either himself or his men.

The material havoc of the strife is graphically summed up in an editorial of the Times, appearing December 11, 1895.

"Within the limits of the county of Frederick and the city of Winchester", writes the editor, "fighting was almost incessant during the civil war, and during that period no portion of the South suffered more, comparatively, than our sturdy old county and city, and no people ever bore the outrages of war with more unshaken fortitude and courage, or since the return of peace have displayed more energy and enterprise in repairing the ruinous effects of war. The farmers had lost nearly all their stock, wagons, and farming implements, and many of their homes, and nearly all their barns and other outbuildings were destroyed by the Federal soldiery. Every building that survived the torch, both in the city and county, was more or less out of repair. All business and financial institutions were wrecked. There was absolutely no money, either in the city or county. Both communities have more than recovered from their losses, and are thoroughly solvent as corporations, and in respect to their honest, thrifty, energetic, and enterprising citizens."

Another writer supplements the above statement by saying that fences and barns were generally gone, and that four-fifths of the personal property had disappeared; that farm land had grown up to weeds and briars, and that the tools of the farmers, blacksmiths, and mechanics had become well-nigh worthless. He adds that in the summer of 1865 the stringency began to be relieved.

It has been very truly remarked that, "the worst phase of the war (to the people behind the lines) was the terrible suspense, the hoping against hope, the long, weary days waiting for better news." The strain, severe and long-continued, on the vitality of the non-combatant population, bore fruit in a very abnormal degree of mortality. It was observed that "there was never a time, as during those four years, when there were so many deaths of old people and girls. It took but little illness to terminate fatally."

Recollections of those trying years are thus alluded to by John Esten Cooke, whose boyhood was spent in Winchester: "Is it wrong to remember the past? I think of it without bitterness. God did it—God, the All-wise, the Almighty—for his own purpose. I do not indulge in repinings, or reflect with rancor upon the issues of the struggle. I prefer recalling the stirring adventures, the brave voices, the gallant faces."

Robert Y. Conrad of Winchester had five sons in the Confederate army. His townsman, David W. Barton, had six sons in the same service, two of whom were killed and another died of his wounds. These two facts are indicative of the degree to which the homes of the Lower Valley were stripped of their members of military age.

XV

BENCH, BAR AND LEGISLATIVE

Judges — Attorneys — Legislators — Local Statutes

> It was therefore ordered that the sheriff take him and at the Common Whipping Post give him thirty-nine lashes on his Bare Back well laid on and also that he confine the said Wm. Earle two hours in the Pillory. — Minutes of County Court of Frederick, year 1746.

As the oldest, and for some years the leading town of the Shenandoah Valley, Winchester early became a judicial center, thus attracting some of the most conspicuous practitioners of Virginia.

John Marshall, Chief Justice of the Supreme Court of the United States, was never a resident of this city, but made visits to it in an official capacity, and an incident in one of these may be of interest. It was published in the Winchester Republican, and runs substantially as follows:

An old gentleman in somewhat rusty looking attire and traveling in a gig almost broken down became a guest of the Taylor Hotel. When he and the writer of the narrative were seated in the public room, they were joined by three or four young men whose conversation turned to an eloquent speech delivered that day in the local courthouse. A sarcastic comparison being made with the pulpit eloquence of the time, the merits of the Christian religion were brought into the discussion. After a long debate, an appeal was made to the old gentleman, who was supposed to belong in some country neighborhood and had until now kept silent. The effect was like that of a thunderpeal. For an hour the man in the rusty suit, who was no other than Chief Justice Marshall, gave an unanswerable argument in favor of Christianity. Every attack by the young skeptics was met in the order in which it was delivered. An attempt to describe the speech, said the narrator, was like an attempt to paint the sunbeams.

Until the Revolution there was no higher court of law in Winchester than the Old Justices Court. After 1776 a Court of Law and Equity had jurisdiction here, but districts were not apportioned until 1802. With 1809 came a Superior Court of Chancery, and a judge was to hold terms twice a year in every county, the records being kept at some central point. After 1811,

Winchester was such a point for many years. The first judge of this court was Robert White, and he was succeeded by William Brockenbrough and John Scott. Dabney Carr was judge in 1812, and continued in office till 1824, when he was followed by Henry St. George Tucker, Daniel Lee being clerk of the court all this while, who held till 1831.

A law of 1831, provided for a Court of Law and Chancery in each of the counties. Under this change, Richard E. Parker was judge from 1831 to 1836, Isaac R. Douglas from 1836 to 1850, and Richard Parker, son of Richard E., was then judge until the civil war disarranged the administration of justice. After the end of the reconstruction period, Joseph S. Carson was judge in 1870-71. He was followed by Joseph H. Sherrard. William L. Clark became judge in 1883, William M. Atkinson in 1891, and Thomas W. Harrison in 1904.

One of the most famous cases in the annals of local litigation was that of Hunter v. Fairfax, which originated in the Superior Court at Winchester. The Life of John Marshall by Albert J. Beveridge gives a full account of this case, which called in question the legitimacy of the Fairfax title.

Robert White, who was born in 1759, was one of the soldiers who marched from Winchester to Boston under General Morgan. In the battle of Short Hills in New Jersey, in 1777, his thigh-bone was splintered by a ball, and he was left on the field. A British soldier brutally struck him on the head with the butt of his musket. After the enemy had gone on, some country people took him to a hospital, where he endured a living death for seven months. In the fall of 1778, he returned to Virginia, his wound still unhealed, but after the removal of some fragments of bone the wound closed and he returned to the army, although permanently lame. In 1783 he began the practice of law in Winchester, and was a judge from 1793 until 1825.

James M. Mason became a resident of Winchester when twenty-two years old. He was fourteen years a member of the Senate of the United States. Robert Y. Conrad, who died in Winchester in 1875, at the age of sixty-eight, was a State Senator and a member of the Virginia Convention of 1861. Holmes Conrad, son of Robert Y., a very eminent local attorney, was Solicitor General of the United States under the Cleveland administration and was special attorney for the national government in the postal cases under Roosevelt. Jonathan D. Carlile, who lived on Piccadilly, the house-lot being now covered by the George Washington Hotel, was the father of John S. Carlile, also a lawyer and very instrumental in the formation of West Virginia. John Randolph Tucker, Congressman, Attorney General of Virginia, and professor in Washington and Lee University, was born in Winchester in 1820. He was the author of "Tucker's Commentaries" and other works on various branches of jurisprudence. R. T. Barton is celebrated as the author of the well known law books, "Barton's Law Practice" and "Barton's Chancery Practice."

Did space permit, interesting mention might be made of still others of the local bar.

The following is as complete a list as we have been able to gather of the attorneys of Winchester down to a recent period. The year following a name is the earliest mention. Where a name is starred, the year is not earlier than 1858.

Alexander, William A.*
Armstrong, Maxwell—1790
Arnett, W. W.*
Ash, James—1791
Atkinson, William M.*
Baker, John—1819
Balch, Lewis P. W.—1819
Barnes, C.*
Barnes, W.*
Barton, Daniel W.—1833
Barton, Robert T.*
Barton, Randolph *
Berry, Henry—1819
Blincoe, Sampson—1819
Bliss, Oliver—1812
Botts, Lawson *
Boyce, N. L. *
Boyd, Elisha—1819
Boyd, E. Holmes *
Boyd, Holmes, Jr. *
Bragonier, D. H. *
Brent, Charles L. *
Brent, George W. *
Brooke, Walton*—1833
Brown, John—1794
Byrd, Richard E.—1833
Byrd, William *
Byrne, Henry—1833
Caldwell, Joseph—1801

Caither, Elijah—1794
Campbell, B. C. *
Carlyle, Jonathan D.—1819
Carson, James H.—1833
Carson, Joseph S.—1833
Chilton, William—1819
Chipley, James—1799
Clark, William L.—1819
Clark, William L., Jr.*
Cochrane, James—1791
Conrad, Robert Y.—1833
Conrad, Robert Y.*
Conrad, D. H.*
Conrad, Powell*
Conrad, Holmes*
Cook, Edward E.—1833
Cook, Giles—1833
Cooke, John R.—1812
Daingerfield, Henry—1801
Dandridge, E. P.*
Denny, J. W.*
Dixon, John—1789
Dougherty, —— —1825
Faulkner, Charles J.—1825
Fauntleroy, T. T., Jr.*
Fowke, —— —1825

Furman, A. Treadwell—1788
Ginn, Charles L.*
Glover, Lewis—1833
Green, John L.—1833
Grey, —— —1825
Griggs, Thomas—1800
Harrison, Burr W.—1833
Harrison, Thomas W.*
Henderson, Richard H.—1833
Hoge, J. B.*
Holliday, Richard—1799
Holliday, F. W. M.*
Holmes, David—1791
Holmes, Hugh—1789
Hopkins, John—1819
Huck, Lewis N.*
Hunter, Moses T.—1819
Hunter, Edmund P.—1833
Hunter, Andrew *
Hunter, R. W.*
Jenkins, J. W.*
Johnston, William R.—1833
Jones, Gabriel—1743
Kennedy, Andrew—1833
Kercheval, Samuel, Jr.—1812

Kern, Asbury *
Lacy, Horace *
Lauck, William *
Lee, Daniel—1805
Lee, Richard H.—1819
Lee, Edmund I.—1833
Lodge, Matthew—1800
Lucas, William—1825
Lynch, Maurice M.*
Lynch, Harry
McCann, William *
McCormick, Province—1833
McDonald, Angus W.—1833
McGuire, David H.—1833
McMechen, Samuel—1800
McPharlane, John—1819
Magill, Charles—1785
Magill, Archibald—1819
Magill, Charles T.—1833
Magill, John S.—1833
Mantor, E. B.*
Marshall, Charles—1787
Marshall, Thomas—1819
Marshall, James M.—1833
Mason, John T.—1788
Mason, James M.—1820
Maund, John J.—1788
Moore, Lewis T.*
Moore, S. J. C.*

Murray, George—1819
Naylor, William—1812
Nelson, Charles M.*
Nicholas, George—1787
Page, Robert—1788
Page, John E.—1819
Page, Robert, Jr.—1833
Parker, Richard—1833
Pendleton, A. R.*
Porteus, James—1743
Powell, Alfred H.—1801
Powell, Humphrey—1819
Powell, Charles L.—1825
Randolph, James J.—1833
Reed, Samuel—1786
Riely, J. P.*
Robinson, W. J.*
Roots, George—1775
Samuels, —— —1825
Seivers, Robert E.*
Sexton, Joseph—1799
Seymour, —— —1825
Sherrard, Joseph H.—1833
Shields, J. Hayes *
Shumate, T.*
Singleton, W. G.—1833
Smith, Augustus C.—1812
Smith, John B.—1824
Snickers, Beverly—1833
Snodgrass, J. L.—1833
Stephenson, W. Roy *
Stickley, E. E.*
Strother, Joseph—1819
Swan, Thomas—1791

Tapscott, —— —1825
Tate, William—1799
Thomas, Daniel—1799
Thompson, John A.—1833
Throckmorton, Warner —1812
Thruston, Buckner—1787
Tidball, Josiah—1805
Tidball, Alexander S.—1819
Tucker, Henry St. G.—1812
Tucker, John R.*
Turner, Robert *
Waite, Obed—1812
Walton, Carroll *
Walton, M.*
Ward, George W.*
Ward, George W., Jr.*
Ward, Robert M.*
Watrous, C. L.*
Wells, Morgan*
White, Robert—1781
White, Alexander—1795
White, Robert B.—1812
White, N. S.*
Whiting, Francis—1785
Whittaker, James P.*
Williams, Isaac H.—1794
Williams, Philip—1833
Williams, J. J.*
Williams, J. H.*
Williamson, —— —1825
Wolfe, Lewis—1812
Wright, Uriel *
Yancey, C. A.*

To bring this chapter 15 up to date:

Hon. Frank B. Whiting of Berryville, Virginia, is Judge of the Circuit Court of Frederick County and of the Corporation Court of the City of Winchester.

The members of the Bar at this time are:

Barton, Robert T.	Frazier, Lake J.	Rice, Warren
Cather, T. Russell	Larrick, Herbert S.	Steck, John M.
Kern, Harry R.	Newlin, Joseph B.	Williams, R. Gray
Lynch, Maurice M.	Reardon, James P.	Williams, Philip

FREDERICK LEGISLATORS

During the colonial period only the members of the lower house of the legislature were chosen by popular vote. In the modern sense the legislature was unicameral. Its members were styled Burgesses, this term remaining in use until 1830.

BURGESSES

Samuel Earle	1743-1747	Thomas Swearingen	1756-1758
Andrew Campbell	1745-1747	George Washington	1758-1761
George Fairfax	1748-1750	Thomas B. Martin	1758-1761
Gabriel Jones	1748-1754	George Mercer	1761-1765
George W. Fairfax	1752-1755	Robert Rutherford	1766-1772
Isaac Parkins	1754-1755	James Wood	1766-1775
Hugh West	1756-1758	Isaac Zane	1773-1775

MEMBERS OF COLONIAL CONVENTION OF 1775

Isaac Zane   Charles M. Thruston

STATE SENATORS

Until 1800 Frederick was in a district with Berkeley and Hampshire. Hardy was then added. From 1817 to 1836 this county was united with Jefferson, and Clarke was then added. In 1851 Frederick was joined with Warren and Clarke. In 1869-1870 it was joined with Clarke and Shenandoah. Warren was then substituted for Shenandoah, but in 1896 Frederick and Shenandoah became a senatorial district.

Robert Rutherford	1776-1791	John S. Gallaher	1844-1847
John Smith	1792-1795	H. L. Opie	1848-1850
Hugh Holmes	1795	Oliver R. Funsten	1851-1858
John Smith	1796	James H. Carson	1862-1863
Charles McGill	1799-1800	S. W. Thomas	1864
Lewis Wolf	1804-1811	Nathaniel B. Meade	1865-1867
A. H. Powell	1813-1818	William D. Smith	1869-1870
H. St. G. Tucker	1818-1822	G. W. Ward	1871-1878
William B. Page	1823-1826	John T. Lovell	1879-1882
Augustus C. Smith	1827-1829	J. T. McCormick	1883-1885
Hierome L. Opie	1830-1839	Marshall McCormick	1886-1887
Robert Y. Conrad	1840-1843	T. W. Harrison	1888-1894

Thomas D. Gold 1895-1896
J. G. McCune 1896
S. L. Lupton 1900
F. S. Tavenner 1904

R. M. Ward 1908-1910
Frank Tavenner 1912-1914
H. F. Byrd 1916

MEMBERS OF HOUSE OF DELEGATES

James Wood and Isaac Zane
.... 1776
Isaac Zane and John Smith 1779
Joseph Holmes 1781
Alexander White and C. M.
Thruston 1785
C. M. Thruston and S.
Woodcock 1787
Joseph Holmes and Robert
White 1789
Joseph Holmes and Mann
Page 1790
Matthew Page and Robert
White 1792
Matthew Page and Archibald McGill 1794
Archibald McGill and Robbert Page 1795
William McGuire and
James Singleton 1796
William McGuire and Archibald McGill 1797-1798
William McGuire and
George Eskridge .. 1799-1800
George Eskridge 1800-1801
Archibald McGill 1800-1801
Hugh Holmes 1802
James Singleton 1806-1807
Charles Brent 1808-1811
Jared Williams 1812-1815
William B. Page 1820-1823
Richard W. Barton ......
.... 1823-1825, 1832-1839
James Ship 1824-1828
James M. Mason 1826-1831
William M. Barton .. 1827-1828
William Castleman, Jr. 1828-1831
William Wood ....
.... 1830-1832, 1838-1844
John B. D. Smith ... 1831-1837

James G. Bryce 1831-1832
James Gibson 1833-1835
John S. Davisson 1835-1836
James Bowen 1835-1836
Edgar W. Robinson .. 1836-1837
Robert L. Baker 1839-1840
Richard E. Byrd ....
.... 1839-1844, 1850-1851
James Cather ....
.... 1840-1841, 1845-1846
James H. Carson ....
.... 1844-1847, 1859-1861
Jonathan Lovett 1844-1845
John F. Wall ....
.... 1845-1851, 1865-1866
Algernon R. Wood .. 1847-1850
R. M. Sydnor 1848-1851
Lewis A. Miller 1852-1854
Edwin S. Baker 1852
John B. McLeod 1853-1854
Thomas T. Fauntleroy 1857-1858
M. R. Kaufman 1857-1860
George W. Ward ....
.... 1859-1860, 1862-1865
M. R. Kaufman 1862-1865
J. S. Magill 1865-1867
David J. Miller 1869-1870
John F. Wall ....
.... 1867, 1870-1877
William D. Smith 1869-1871
E. M. Tidball 1871-1873
George W. Ward 1871-1873
R. W. Hunter 1874-1875
James H. Williams .. 1874-1875
P. B. Williams 1876-1877
Nimrod Whitacre ... 1877-1878
T. T. Fauntleroy, Jr.. 1877-1878
E. P. Dandridge 1879-1880
Holmes Conrad 1881-1882
Robert T. Barton 1883-1884

John V. Tavenner	1886-1887	E. C. Jordan	1898-1905
John M. Silver	1888-1891	Richard E. Byrd	1896-1912
Joseph A. Miller	1892-1893	John M. Steck	1914-1916
Charles F. Nelson	1894-1895	Richard L. Omps	1918-1920
James K. McCann	1896-1897	Boyd R. Richards	1922

We now give the substance of Acts of Assembly relative to Winchester and prior to 1875.

The Act of incorporation, of October, 1779, includes the city of Alexandria. Each second Tuesday in February the freeholders and housekeepers elect twelve men, who choose from their number a mayor, a recorder, and four aldermen, the other six forming the Common Council. The mayor holds not less than one year and not more than two. Mayor, recorder, and aldermen are justices of the peace within the town, and can appoint clerk, sergeant, clerk of the market, etc., and can make by-laws and ordinances. Their jurisdiction extends one-half mile beyond the town boundary. Each Wednesday and Saturday are market days. Vacancies are filled by the twelve members. The court of hustings is held once a month. With several amendments this Act remained in force until April 2, 1874.

May, 1782. The court of hustings has sole and exclusive power of granting ordinary licenses. Tavern-keepers cannot act as judges in the said court.

October, 1782. Five acres owned by Thomas Edmondson annexed and laid out into half-acre lots.

December, 1816. The mayor and twelve have discretionary power to appoint such and so many market days as they deem necessary.

January, 1819. Act of incorporation is amended. Four wards are created, each to elect three freehold residents yearly, these to choose from themselves a President of the Common Council. Nine members constitute a quorum, and seven are necessary for any concurrence. All orders and regulations are to have three readings. At the same election, a mayor, a recorder, and one alderman from each ward are elected, who hold office three years and constitute a borough court with judicial powers. Two freeholders in each ward superintend elections. Mayor and Council have power to remove nuisances, improve streets, etc.

February, 1820. The sale of poorhouse is authorized.

January, 1825. The Common Council is empowered to sell ends of streets and alleys running between the lots of different proprietors.

January, 1826. Ephraim Hawkins, John Baker, Heriot Conrad, owners of outlot 23, are empowered to build upon and improve the same. In further instances of this sort, the Common Council can act.

February, 1828. Magistrates are no longer prohibited from being overseers of the poor. The Common Council may until the next regular election fill a vacancy in the presidency.

January, 1829. The President and Common Council may borrow money at not more than six percent interest to replace the wooden waterpipes with iron pipes; and President and Council are empowered at any future time to borrow at their discretion.

February, 1831. No one may vote in a borough election who is delinquent in tax one year. All taverns and other places of public resort must obtain license from the Common Council, which may impose a tax of not more than $20 on each tavern or resort.

February, 1833. President and Common Council may impose and collect tax from shows, theatricals, etc.

February, 1835. The town sergeant may employ a deputy.

February, 1836. Hustings court may appoint inspectors of flour and Indian meal.

April, 1838. The Common Council may subscribe for not more than 400 shares of Valley Turnpike stock, provided that said subscription is approved by a majority vote of the qualified voters.

December, 1839. The Corporation Court shall hold a session on the first Thursday of each month.

February, 1840. The County Court of Frederick may appoint inspectors of flour.

The twelve members of Common Council are now to be elected by a general vote, irrespective of wards, but there shall be no more than three from each ward. There are now two extra aldermen. This act is to be approved by a vote of the town. The public debt of the corporation is not to exceed $50,000.

March, 1841. Hustings Court is to hold on the first Saturday of each month. It may appoint one constable in each ward, he to be a police officer, and to receive not more than $20 a year.

March, 1848. The county jail is also to be the corporation jail.

March, 1849. All water rates are to be applied to the reduction of the town debt.

March, 1850. President and Common Council may subscribe to not more than $1000 to Winchester and Berry's Ferry Turnpike Company and likewise to Front Royal Turnpike Company.

May, 1852. The overseers of the poor are made a corporation, styled "Overseers of the Poor of the County of Frederick and Corporation of Winchester."

January, 1865. Indebtedness limit raised to $150,000, but reduced to $100,000 two months later.

Ordinance of January 18, 1856: The corporation officers—to serve one year beginning June 1—are these:

Sergeant at Arms.
Clerk of the Common Council.
Treasurer of the Corporation of Winchester.
Collector of the Revenue.
Superintendent of Police.
Superintendent of Waterworks.
Clerk of the Market.
Superintendent of the Town Clock.
Weigher and Inspector of Hay.

The Clerk of the Market attends the Market House during market hours, maintains order, sweeps and cleans house and benches, keeps scales and weights in order, weighs all articles when necessary, rents stalls, etc., and cleans the public square at least once a week. Market hours continue till 9 a. m., from April 1 to October 1, and till 10 a. m. the rest of the year. The north and south wings are rented to butchers and vendors of meal, vegetables, fruits, etc. The east side is reserved for butter, eggs, etc. The space between the arch of the main building and the wall of the north end is reserved for negroes and mulattoes. Market days are Wednesdays and Saturdays. Buying and selling may not begin earlier than thirty minutes before sunrise, as determined by the ringing of the town bell, and may not be carried on except at the Market House, in which dogs are not permitted. No cannon or firecrackers are to be fired off on the premises. Sunday gaming or swearing in public are forbidden. The fine for "whooping and hallowing" is $20. No negro or mulatto shall sell any intoxicants under a penalty of ten lashes for each offense. The courthouse bell is to ring at 10 p. m., and any negro then at large without a permit may be jailed and punished with not more than 39 lashes.

XVI

THE CHURCHES AND THE FRATERNITIES

Episcopalians — Friends — Reformed — Presbyterians — Methodists — Catholics — Other Churches — Fraternities.

> There is a large stone Dutch Lutheran Church with a tall steeple. In the town is an English (Episcopal) Church. North of the town is an old fort that is wasting away. Diary of Rev. Philip Fithian, on his visit to Winchester in 1775.

In our story of the churches of Winchester we give first place to the establishment and exercise of the spirit of freedom in public worship, one of the fundamental motives underlying the original settlement of the colonies and enjoyed by the original settlers of the Valley. "Under the Law any number of persons of whatsoever name might ask and should receive a license for some place of meeting where they might worship after their own way."

The Episcopal church in Colonial days was the established church of the Colonial Government and according to the old English law the vestries of the Episcopal congregations had certain governmental functions the result of which was that wherever the Government was established the church was also established.

This establishment was made in Winchester in the year of 1738, the settlements in the Valley being six years old at that time and growing with great rapidity, the records of the Court beginning in 1744 and the old Vestry book going back to 1764. Thus it will be seen that in the year of 1744 the Vestry and Court of Frederick County were organized and in action, and this relation continued until 1780 when by Act of Assembly all Colonial vestries were dissolved. In 1752 this original vestry was dissolved on the ground that it had received more than fifteen-hundred pounds for building a number of churches which were unfinished and in a ruinous condition and a new vestry was ordered elected. In the list of the vestry which succeeded that dissolved is found the name of John Hite, one of the family by that name who were the original settlers in 1732. The name of Lord Fairfax is also found in this vestry, he being the donor of the original site of the Episcopal Church and graveyard. The other names of this vestry were Robert Lemmon, James Cromley, Isaac Perkins, Thomas Swearingen, John Lindsay, Thomas B. Martin, Gabriel Jones, Charles Buck, John Ashby and Lewis Neill.

The first Church building stood on the Southwest corner of the public square at Main and Water Streets where a log-chapel was erected about the year 1740 or 1742. This was succeeded by a stone church in 1764 which was used until 1828 when this building was sold and a new building erected at the present site, northeast corner of Water and Washington Streets.

During the Colonial period from 1744 to 1780 there were ministers and vestries in existence and action. First Rev. Mr. Gordon from 1744 until he was succeeded by Rev. Mr. Meldrum, whose work ended in 1765, he being succeeded by Rev. Mr. Sebastian to 1768, whose successor was Rev. Mr. Thruston, who in 1777 joined the Colonial forces and became Colonel Thruston of the Revolution, this bringing to a graphic close the Colonial period of the church's history.

The first rector of the Parish after the war of the Revolution was Rev. Alexander Balmain who took charge in the year 1785, and whose remains with those of Mrs. Balmain rest beneath the present building near the spot to which the ashes of Lord Fairfax were removed from beneath the original church. Dr. Balmain came from Scotland to this country and became tutor in the family of Richard Henry Lee, the grandfather of Robert E. Lee.

From which position he entered the Episcopal ministry, taking charge of West Augusta Parish in 1773 and as chairman of the Committee of Safety in Augusta drafted the resolutions forwarded to the Virginia Convention held 1776 in old St. John's Church, Richmond; the first rector after the Revolution thus being a chaplain out of the Colonial Army who had taken part in drafting original resolutions embodying the spirit of the American Revolution and the foundation of our present National Liberty. Thus it will be seen that the Episcopal Church in this community, in spite of being the established Church of the English Government, gave its rector to the Colonial forces and in 1785 received as his successor a chaplain out of the Colonial Army.

The successor to Dr. Balmain was Rev. William Meade from 1821 to 1827, who became the great Bishop Meade of the Diocese of Virginia to whose untiring efforts and great statesmanship is due as much as to any one man the revival of the Episcopal Church in America after the Revolution. Bishop Meade was succeeded by Rev. James E. Jackson from 1827 to 1842, his successor being Rev. Wm. Brooker until 1847. Rev. Cornelius Walker, afterwards professor of the Virginia Seminary, was rector from 1848

THE CHURCHES AND THE FRATERNITIES 207

to 1860. The Ante Bellum history of the Parish ended in a rector as eminent in the realm of theology as the Colonial rectors were in the realm of patriotism. Rev. William C. Meredith was rector from 1860-1875; James R. Hubard from 1875-1886; Nelson P. Dame 1886 to 1904; Wm. D. Smith 1905 to 1919; R. A. Goodwin 1920 to 1921; Robert B. Nelson the present rector. Rev. Wm. D. Smith was granted a leave of absence by the vestry to become chaplain in the A. E. F. in the world war and during his absence Rev. John W. Quinton became locum tenens for Dr. Smith. Dr. Smith's immediate successor was a returned missionary and his successor was a chaplain in the Great War.*

Alexander Balmain was born in Scotland in 1740, and came to Winchester just after the Revolution, living on Market Street where afterward stood the Hart Hotel. He was an eloquent divine, and his pastorate began at an opportune moment. The Revolution had left the establishment under a cloud. Many of the clergy were tories and had fled the country. The church was at length rehabilitated, largely through the efforts of Bishop Meade, and under the name it took after the Revolution it rose to a place of great usefulness in Virginia. Mr. Balmain was childless. His pastorate was followed by that of William Meade, who was subsequently a bishop.

By including the environs of Winchester with the town itself, it follows that the Friends are the pioneer denomination, both in organizing a congregation and in building a house of worship. Hopewell meeting house was built in 1739, or according to other statements, in 1732 or 1733. The stone building was erected about 1789 by Hessian stonemasons, and some ten years later was enlarged. At times the churchyard is thronged. About 4000 people were present May 14, 1899.

The presence of a large Quaker settlement in this vicinity is primarily due to one Ross, who came from Cecil county, Maryland, which itself is Quaker territory. In 1732 he secured a grant of 100,000 acres, chiefly northward of this town, and located a large number of his co-religionists.

Long before 1861 the Friends living in Winchester had built Center meeting house on the west side of Washington Street, between Leicester and Monmouth. This was succeeded about 1870 by the brick meeting house at the west end of Piccadilly. It is shared by both the Orthodox and the Hicksite wings of this de-

---

* This chapter, down to the paragraph beginning "Alexander Balmain," was not written by the compiler of the book.

nomination, although, as a whole, the Friends are not now numerous within Winchester.

East of the Baltimore and Ohio track, and within the short compass between the beginning of National Avenue and the entrance to Mount Hebron were once four churches: the Catholic, the Presbyterian, the Reformed, and the Lutheran. They were all on the very edge of the town. Until after the Revolution only a church of the establishment might stand at the center of a town.

The oldest of the four church buildings was the Reformed. A congregation of this sect was organized in the Kernstown neighborhood probably somewhat earlier than 1741, and worshiped there until about 1753. The deed to a lot in Winchester was given by Fairfax, May 15, 1753, but the grant was not gratuitous. A quit-rent of ten shillings was due every "feast day of St. Michael," and a forfeiture of the ground might be declared if it were thirty days in arrears. The numbers of the lots were 82 and 83, and are defined in the deed as bounded north by Abbchurch Lane, west by East Lane, south by Philpott Lane, and east by the line of the addition. In compliance with the law, the deed was issued to the trustees, Philip and David Bush, Henry Brinker, Jacob Sowers, and Frederick Conrad. After 1804, and until February, 1840, there seem to have been no services by the Reformed Church in what was commonly known as the "old log church," which was of a type that cost in the colonial period from $100 to $150. There was some thought of repairing it in 1840, but it was decided to build a new one, to be called Centenary Reformed church. The log church burned to the ground February 13, 1844, or, according to another statement, December 14, 1846. Both accounts agree in saying the fire started in the earlier part of the night, that the air was calm, and that the earth was covered with snow. For near ten years, beginning about 1816, the old church was used by the white Baptists and afterward by the colored Baptists.

The pastors at Centenary prior to the war were D. G. Bragonier, Robert Douglass, G. W. Williams, A. J. Miller, P. S. Davis, and J. M. Filzel. M. L. Shuford came in 1867, and in his pastorate repairs were made.

The Reformed congregation was revived in February, 1840 by G. A. Leapold. The new church, completed about 1841, suffered terribly during the war, being used first as a hospital and then as a stable. In 1865 nothing was left but the walls and a shattered roof. Yet the ruin was repaired, and was used until 1905 when the present building took its place. In the same year damages were paid by the general government.

The Presbyterians also had services at Kernstown before there were any at Winchester. So far as known, the first preaching at that point was by Samuel Galston in 1735. James Anderson, who came in 1739, organized the Opequon congregation. John Craig, afterward pastor of Old Stone Church in Augusta county, preached to it in 1739. There was no settled minister until 1754, John Hoge being the first and remaining until 1772. Under his pastorate, Opequon was the most important Presbyterian congregation in the whole Shenandoah. When Washington had his headquarters in Winchester in 1755-1758, he often rode out here for worship. As he was an Episcopalian, this would seem to indicate that the services of his own communion were not regularly held in Winchester. Mr. Hoge was promised a salary of 70 pounds ($233) from the entire field. After a vacant period, John Montgomery followed in 1781 and returned to the Cowpasture in 1789. He was succeeded by Nash Legrand, a famous revivalist, who remained until about 1798, and died while visiting Winchester in 1814.

The third home of the Opequon congregation burned a few years after the civil war. After the first battle of Kernstown it was not used until the return of peace. The present church was dedicated in 1897.

In 1741 there was a schism in the Presbyterian Church, lasting until 1758, and in the Shenandoah it was quite pronounced. The opposing wings were the Old Lights and the New Lights, the latter preferring extemporaneous preaching. They arose as a result of the theological writings of Jonathan Edwards. Through his influence the New Light preachers dropped the heavy European style of discourse and adopted a manner that was warm, vivid, and direct. In 1775 Mr. Fithian remarks that the congregation at Opequon would not tolerate read sermons.

The "Gazette" has mention of a meeting, July 26, 1788, for the purpose of building a Presbyterian church in Winchester. The house was ready for use in 1790, but not until ten years later was there a distinct local organization. The first house of worship was a stone building in East Piccadilly, adjoining the Catholic lot. In 1834 it was sold to the white Baptists, and by them to the colored Baptists. It was completely dismantled in the civil war, being used as a stable by the Federal soldiers. It is now the schoolhouse for the colored children of Winchester.

It was in this church that the Winchester Presbytery, cut off from Lexington Presbytery, was organized December 4, 1794. It was practically coextensive with the 25 counties of the Northern

Neck, and it began with five ministers and sixteen churches, all the latter being either in the Shenandoah or on the South Branch. Its limits remained unchanged until 1854. The General Assembly of 1799 was held in Winchester.

The boundary of Winchester Presbytery, as ordered September 26, 1794, is thus described: 'The dividing line shall begin on that part of the boundary of the Presbytery of Redstone, on the Alleghany Mountains, where Hardy county is divided from Pendleton, running thence with the said line until the same reaches the corner of Rockingham; from thence a direct course to the place where the great road through Keizeltown to Winchester crosses the river of Shenandoah; from thence to Swift Run Gap on the Blue Ridge, which reaches the boundary of the Presbytery of Hanover."

In 1828 the Presbyterians of Winchester divided into the Old School and New School branches, the former building a home of its own at the corner of Kent and Water streets. There was a reunion in 1832, but a second schism followed in 1839, and though it did not outlive the period of the civil war, the two churches continued as separate congregations of the same Presbytery until 1900. The 30 to 40 seceders of 1828 followed the lead of the Rev. William Hill, and used the stone house on Market Street that had belonged to Philip Bush. After the division of 1839, the New School congregation built the church that became known as the Loudoun Street church. The Kent street church, which was where Stonewall Jackson worshiped, suffered severely in the war. The last service held in it was on March 27, 1900. In that year the two branches consolidated, using the church in Main Street. It was remodeled in 1908.

The pastorate of James B. Graham appears to be the longest in the history of Winchester. It began in the Kent Street church October 5, 1851, and continued until the merging of the congregations in 1900. Dr. Graham died April 7, 1914 at the age of eighty-nine.

In 1753 the Lutherans purchased two half-acre lots of Fairfax, and the cornerstone of their church was laid June 16, 1764. The following are the names of the founders:

Altrick, Christopher	Franckel, Stephen	Helfenstein, Peter
Becker, Heinrich	Friendly, Andreas	Heneckel, Christopher
Berger, Imanuel	Gluck, Michael	Koppenhaber, Jacob
Braun, Jacob	Haenh, Joh. Sigmond	Lambert, Christopher
Deitrick, David	Heintz, Christopher	Laubinger, George
Doring, Eberhard	Heizel, Donald	Lemley, Johannes

Lentz, Johannes	Schmidt, Thomas	Trautvein, Jacob
Otto, Tobias	Schrack, Nicholas	Waring, Michael
Po, Balthasar	Schumacker, Christian	Wendel, Samuel
Roger, Michael	Spickert, Julius	Wetzel, Christopher

The list, made out in Latin and placed in the cornerstone, was signed by the minister, Johannes Casper Kirchner, by the schoolmaster, Anton Ludi, and by the scribe, or sacristan, Ludwig Adam. The minister, who was from Baltimore, died in 1773. The schoolmaster was competent to conduct worship.

By the terms of the dedication, none but evangelical Lutherans might use the building as a house of worship. The walls were not completed until 1772, and some final touches were added in 1793. In the Revolution the church was used as a barracks, and at the close of that war was doubtless very much in need of repairs. In May, 1788, the roof was taken off and replaced with a new one. Three years earlier, when Mr. Streit arrived as pastor, there were neither doors nor windows, and until 1789 the log church close by was used alternately by both the Reformed and the Lutheran congregations. Two bells, cast in Bremen in 1790, were imported from Germany, and they are said to have been of great sweetness. It was long a custom to ring them on Saturday evening. An organ, purchased about 1793, was removed to Baltimore in 1855.

No debt was incurred in erecting the church, but following a custom that was sustained by public opinion until less than a century ago, the legislature was petitioned, November 8, 1785, that the congregation might raise through a lottery a sum of not more than 500 pounds ($1667.) The memorial by the minister and elders—Christian Streit, Lewis Hoff, and Michael Albrith—recites that "before the late war your petitioners raised enough money by subscription to erect the walls and covering of a commodious church, but it is yet unfinished, because materials could not be brought in during the war. The society is small but patriotic. The depreciation (of paper money) prevents the completion." The privilege was granted, but the drawing did not take place until May 30, 1790. This may, however, have been a second drawing, since there is an indistinct mention in 1788 of 2000 tickets at $3 each. An advertisement by the managers, Henry Baker, Peter Lauck, Lewis Hoff, George Kiger, and Conrad Kremer, states that the lottery is for the "pious purpose" of completing the Lutheran church. The prizes in the first class were one of $100, one of $50, one of $25, five of $5, and 233 of $2, the surplus appearing to be $334. In the second class there were 1000 tickets at $1.50 each, and the sum total of the prizes was $1170.

The stone church burned September 27, 1854, yet the east wall remains firmly in place and the ruin is a picturesque landmark. It has evoked these lines by "H. C. B.:"

> Yes, mouldering walls may truest sermons preach;
> And death's damp ghastliness deep lessons bear;
> Whilst ruin mocks, e'en ruin's self may teach
> What sacred symbols dust and ashes are.
> All tombs have tongues, and every ruined shrine
> A still small voice whose accents are divine.

But before the destruction of the original building, the congregation determined to build a new house of worship near the heart of the city, and the result was Grace Church on Water street, dedicated on Christmas Day, 1842. Toward lifting the debt there was a collection of $650, which the "Virginian" speaks of as "good considering the hard times." There was some alteration and enlargement, including a spire 129 feet high. The rededication, January 14, 1877, was by the Rev. F. W. Conrad, who had conducted the dedication in 1843. This was followed by a great revival, and it was not confined to the Lutheran congregation. More recently the "Brevitt chimes" have been installed. These proclaim the evening hour of six every week-day, and are played several times each Sunday. At present (1924), the congregation is building a commodious Sunday school house adjacent to the church.

The Lutheran pastors in Winchester have been these:

Christian Streit	J. Few Smith	D. M. Gilbert
Abraham Reck	C. P. Krauth Jr.	L. G. M. Miller
L. Eichelberger	A. Esseck	W. L. Seabrook
N. W. Goertner	W. M. Baum	Geo. S. Bowers
G. Stork	T. W. Dosh	A. A. Kelly
J. R. Keiser		

Down to 1877 there had also been three supplies. It was remarked in that year that of the pastors eleven had been college graduates, eight had been doctors of divinity, and four had been editors of Lutheran church papers. Mr. Streit, who came in 1785 and remained until his death in 1812, was a native of New Jersey and the first Lutheran pastor of American birth. He lived in Market Street next to Bush's hostelry, and his daughter kept school in the house. Afterward there was a parsonage at the south end of Main.

The Churches and The Fraternities

Whether Methodism was first preached in America by Robert Strawbridge, who settled in Frederick county, Maryland, in 1760, or by Philip Embury, an immigrant to the city of New York, is a question that has not been settled conclusively. It is believed that Strawbridge made tours to the south of the Potomac, but perhaps only to Loudoun county. Be this as it may, Richard Wright and William Waters had visited the Valley in 1772. Kercheval is therefore in error in saying that the first Methodist preaching in the Shenandoah was when John Haggerty and Richard Owens visited Stephens City in 1774.

Furthermore, as is pointed out by the author of "Methodism and Early Days in Stephens City," Bishop Asbury had already visited this region. That dauntless and indefatigable man was in Winchester November 24, 1772. He then preached in an unfinished house, the rain falling upon him and his hearers looking on in astonishment. Thus far there were not 100 Methodists in all Virginia. June 21, 1783 he preached to a few, remarking in his journal that, "religion is greatly wanting in these parts. The inhabitants are much divided; made up, as they are, of different nations, and speaking different languages. They agree in scarcely anything, except it be to sin against God." The bishop preached again in Winchester, July 21, 1784, and his comment is more favorable: "We had many to hear at Winchester. They appeared to be orderly and solemn." June 4, 1786 he preached on a hill under some spreading trees to an audience in which there were some negroes. His text was Joshua XXIV, 19. Asbury made four other visits, the latest in 1805. June 6, 1793, when the streets and lanes were mire, he calls the new church an "excellent house."

During the first twenty years, excepting in warm weather, the Methodists seem to have worshiped in some private house, perhaps that of Christopher Frye at the corner of Cork and Market. He and his brothers George and Michael were local preachers. In 1791 a lot was purchased on Market Street opposite the Fairfax Hotel. The house there built is described by Mr. Russell as forty by sixty feet on the ground, primitive and old-fashioned. It was sold in 1818 and torn down, and a new church was built on the other side of the street. This was sold to S. P. York in 1852 and converted into a seminary for girls. The addition of a third story, a few years later, made the building look no longer like a church.

The third home of the Methodists was built at the northwest corner of Cork and Market, the laying of the cornerstone taking place September 12, 1853. It is a duplicate of Exeter Street Methodist church in Baltimore, which was built more than fifty years earlier. The auditorium was the largest in Winchester, it being possible for 1250 people to assemble in it. It is therefore often used for special services that are largely attended. In October, 1857 there were 62 conversions in this church. There was then a Sunday school of 446 members and a library of 1300 volumes.

Until 1784 the Methodists were a society within the Church of England and not an independent communion. It was the American Revolution that made a separate organization unavoidable. In the early years the Methodists had certain peculiarities that marked them off from the older denominations. And for some time their usages did not attract the more substantial classes of the people.

Berkeley circuit came into existence in 1778, and Winchester circuit in 1790. James Quinn, in charge of the latter in 1802, had to travel 400 miles to reach all his appointments. The first Methodist minister to be regularly stationed in this city was Charles A. Davis, who came in 1827. Until the war of 1861, these others preached at Market Street:

George Reed	Norval Wilson	Norval Wilson (second
Edward Smith	William Hamilton	time)
Henry Furlong	John Smith	Samuel Kepler
John I. Gibbons	F. Dorsey	William Krebs
John Miller	William R. Edwards	John S. Martin
Job Guest		

The schism that divided the Methodist Episcopal Church into two great branches did not appear at Winchester until 1858. A number of the members then withdrew, and were organized by William R. Denny as a congregation of the Methodist Episcopal Church, South. Their church home on Braddock Street was dedicated the next year by Bishop Granbury. After the war Federal soldiers took possession of the Market Street church, and this caused some others of the members to transfer themselves to Braddock Street. For a long while the membership at Market Street was small, but in recent years it has very much increased.

Both the church buildings of the Methodists were much injured during the war, and in each instance damages were paid by the national government. The church on Braddock Street, which had been used as a hospital, was remodeled in 1878 and an annex was built. There was a rededication, April 16, 1899. Very recently, the Market Street church has been renovated within. It celebrated its semi-centennial November 2, 1905, all the other Protestant churches of the town being officially present.

THE CHURCHES AND THE FRATERNITIES 215

Several sessions of the Baltimore Conference have been held in Winchester.

It is maintained, and probably with truth, that there were Roman Catholics in Frederick when the county was formed. The first lot belonging to the Winchester congregation was given by Edward McGuire, and lay on National Avenue immediately north of the lot containing the stone Presbyterian church. The Catholic chapel was also of stone, and tradition states that nearly all the cost was met by a wealthy Frenchman. According to the Laity's Directory of 1822 there was in that year a priest in Winchester. But from soon after this date, and until 1861, the church was seldom used. It was nearly destroyed by the Federal soldiers in 1864 and the gravestones were defaced. About twenty years later a new cemetery was laid out at the south end of Market. A new church, built on South Main, was dedicated July 28, 1878 by Bishop Kain, some Jenkinses of Baltimore contributing liberally to the expense of erection. Until now, Winchester had been an out-mission of the church at Harper's Ferry.

The first actual conference of the United Brethren was held in Baltimore in 1789. Very speedily the new denomination appeared in the Winchester region. The twin brothers and preachers, Henry and Christian Crum, settled here before 1796. The same year—October 25—Bishop Newcomer writes of preaching at night to a large congregation. Next day he visited two criminals under sentence of death. The bishop was here somewhat often, sometimes preaching in the Methodist church and sometimes in the house of Dr. Senseny, who lived where the Kerr schoolhouse now stands. Near Winchester was the home of Jacob F. Hott, a preacher of the United Brethren, as were several of his sons, one of whom became a bishop. But there was no church building in this city prior to the one built on Braddock Street by George W. Howe in 1872. It has very recently been replaced by a new church of modern architecture.

Around 1790 a Baptist minister was preaching in Winchester, at first in the Lutheran and Presbyterian churches, and later in an abandoned schoolhouse. For many years progress was slow, the intervals between pastorates were long, and there are no records earlier than 1869. In 1830 came the Rev. Joseph Baker, who taught a girls' seminary until his death in 1855. He was succeeded by one Ryland, afterward a Confederate chaplain, and under him there was further growth. After the war the Baptists began using the building which is now the Fairfax Hotel, but dedicated a church of their own on the other side of the street, December 5,

1869. This was sold to the Disciples in 1877, and for five years the local society ceased to function. The present church, on Cork Street, was dedicated free of debt in 1887.

The geographer Morse, in his gazetteer of 1810, mentions the churches of Winchester as Presbyterian, Methodist, and Catholic, the last-named being new. Why he should omit the Episcopal church is not obvious, unless it was not then in use. Kercheval in 1833 lists the denominations as Presbyterian, Catholic, Baptist, Friends, Methodist, Lutheran and Episcopalian, the Presbyterians and Methodists having each two buildings. The white people now have eleven houses of worship and the colored people four.

That the Episcopalians, as once the ruling element in Virginia, should be early on the ground will be understood from the first pages of this chapter. The presence of the Presbyterians is directly due to the Scotch-Irish immigration of the eighteenth century. An early Quaker influx explains the meeting house of the Friends. The early coming of the Methodists was due to their itinerant system, which was admirably adapted to pioneer conditions. The Catholic congregation appearing before 1800 is because in the colonial period there were more immigrants from the Catholic counties of Ireland to America than is commonly supposed. The Baptists could scarcely fail to be represented because of the strength of that communion in Virginia. The size of the German element is reflected in the Lutheran, Reformed, and United Brethren denominations, all of which used the German tongue in their services until after the dawn of the nineteenth century. The Reformed Church discontinued its use in Winchester in 1804.

The other white congregations of Winchester are of recent appearance. The handsome brick house of worship of the First Christian church on Braddock Street was occupied in 1910. The Seventh Day Adventists have a little chapel on Cork Street. The Church of God, the Pentecostal Association, and the Christian Scientists use the Odd Fellows Hall. The first named has begun a church building of its own.

The churches of the colored people of Winchester are four.

The John Mann Methodist Episcopal church is a part of the Washington Conference. It first used a log cabin on the site of the present brick building, which stands on Cork Street. The ground was given by John Mann, a white who was buried in the inclosure. The church was organized during the time of slavery, and it was a requirement of the slave code that two men should be in attendance at any religious meeting of the negroes. In this instance the men were J. R. Bowen and Joseph Nulton. The first pastor after the war was Martin Spiddle. The membership is large, though less than formerly, because of the shrinkage of the colored population of Winchester.

St. Paul's African Methodist Episcopal church was organized in 1868, and its first meetings were in the Market House. After the war a frame church was built on North Main Street, and was replaced in 1887 by a brick building. This congregation has a large Sunday School.

St. Stephen's congregation of the Colored Methodist Episcopal Church is on South Market Street, and was organized February 11, 1923. The membership is 34 and there is a flourishing Sunday School. During the first year the money raised for all purposes was $1081.54. The church has four auxiliary societies.

The Mount Carmel Free Baptist church was organized at the courthouse in 1867, and two years later it moved to its house of worship on the corner of Braddock and Leicester streets. The membership is 100. The church was organized by J. W. Dungee. The late pastor, J. W. Fisher, was in charge 17 years.

The eccentric Lorenzo Dow preached in this city in the open air, probably in the fine grove which once existed south of the corner of Washington and Cecil. Henry Boehm, son of one of the founders of the United Brethren Church, preached in Winchester in 1800 and in other years, using both German and English. He afterward joined the Methodists. He preached a sermon in the city of New York when he was one hundred years old.

A local organization of the Young Men's Christian Association was effected in 1855, and there is mention of a large picnic held by it on the fairground, September 18, 1857. After a period of eclipse occasioned by the war, it was reorganized in 1873, its library having been stored in the attic of H. S. Baker. Its reading room was discontinued in 1877, on the ground that the expense of maintenance was not generally shared by the community. But the organization remained in existence for some years later.

Until 1840 the drinking habit was so rampant in the United States as to evoke severe comment by visitors from Europe, who themselves were living in glass houses and could not afford to throw stones with a good grace. The Washingtonian movement then swept over the land, and but for the reaction caused by the war of 1861, the Eighteenth Amendment might have become law at least one generation ago.

The Republican notes that at the close of a lecture delivered June 4, 1841, 70 members were added to the recently organized Washingtonian Society. At a Temperance Convention held in

Winchester February 22, 1842, nine counties were represented, their constituency being 5000. The membership of the Winchester Total Abstinence Society was then 300. In 1868 a lodge of the Friends of Temperance is mentioned as having been in working order some time. Another temperance society was Winchester Lodge, Number 105, of the Good Templars.

Hiram Lodge, A. F. and A. M., was organized in Winchester, November 8, 1768, under a warrant from the Grand Lodge of Pennsylvania. Under the charter given by the same, the lodge in this town was designated as Number 12.

The first Master was James Gamble Doudall, a merchant. The first Senior Warden was Samuel Lindsay, and the first Junior Warden was Samuel Dobie, Jr.

December 10, 1807, the lodge, voluntarily came under the jurisdiction of the Grand Lodge of Virginia, by which it was chartered as "The Winchester Hiram Lodge, Number 21." Peter Lauck was then appointed Master, William Silver, Senior Warden, and Louis Barnet, Junior Warden.

Mr. Doudall, who, like some other merchants, imported his goods directly from Europe, was held in very high esteem in this community. He was many years a master of Hiram Lodge, and was honored with other offices therein.

The minutes of the pre-Revolutionary period show that the membership was small, but that great care was used in admitting new members, or visiting Masons. The historian of Hiram Lodge states that in 1769 a visiting brother was refused admission "for behaving so much out of character in town at different times as to put it out of our power to support our character as Free Masons in showing him any further countenance, and therefore deem him unworthy." In replying to inquiries from the Grand Lodge of Pennsylvania, the Master reported every member "an ornament to the society, nor will we suffer any other to enter in among us."

During the Revolution so few members remained in Winchester that it was thought of suspending the lodge. At the meeting of February 2, 1785, only four were present. These were J. G. Dowdall, P. M. Edward McGuire, S. W., David Kennedy, J. W., and ―― May, Master. A review was taken of the former membership. John Humphreys fell in the assault on Quebec; Angus McDonald died from the hardships of a campaign against the Indians; Major Peter Helphinstine died of a broken constitution occasioned by heat and fatigue in the Carolinas; Morgan Alexander died from the same cause; John Lewis was killed in one of the battles in the South; Thomas Craig died of wounds;

The Churches and The Fraternities 219

Robert Russell was also dead. Edmund Taylor, Dorsey Penticost, Joseph Beeler, William Campbell, ——— Dobie, ——— Howell, and ——— McBride had removed from Winchester. It was resolved to meet thenceforward on stated nights, in the hope that the membership would grow, and the hope was realized. At the next anniversary of the feast of St. John the Evangelist, the lodge visited the Lutheran church, where a special sermon was preached by the Rev. Christian Streit.

Until the close of 1785, there was no stated Tiler. John Crockwell was then appointed and he held the office many years.

February 15, 1800, the Treasurer was ordered to purchase 40 mourning aprons out of respect to General Washington, himself a Mason, and one week later, another special sermon was preached by the pastor of the Lutheran church.

In a letter received about this time from the Grand Lodge of Pennsylvania, it was mentioned that "the late war had caused great trouble among Masons, of which the Winchester Lodge had more than a common share, and its members deserved great credit for raising the lodge to its present flourishing state."

In those early years the lodge took care to enforce the attendance of its members by imposing fines on absentees unless they could show cause for absence. One of the many charities of this period was the appropriation of a considerable sum of money for the relief of Masons imprisoned at Algiers by the Barbary pirates.

In the spring of 1863 Hiram Lodge had fallen into suspended animation, but was revived at the urgent request of the army of occupation, and there were numerous initiations of men in the Federal force. Again, in the winter of 1864-1865, the lodge was in suspense, and General Sheridan was not inclined to permit it to be reopened, but yielded to the representations of a Vermont officer, who offered to be responsible for the conduct of the lodge. Until the withdrawal of the Federal army in the summer of 1865, there were initiations of Union officers or privates almost daily, the aggregate number of such from first to last being several hundred. The receipts from this source amounted to over $4400, and this fund was the nestegg from which the Masonic Temple was built. The lodge-room on the third floor is perhaps more beautifully decorated and furnished than any other in the state.

The place of so many war initiations was the upper floor of the brick building on the east side of Main Street next to the newly erected Commercial and Savings Bank. It was here that President McKinley was initiated in May, 1865. He was the second president to hold membership in Hiram Lodge.

From 1810 until after the beginning of the civil war the lodge-room was in the Market House.

The present membership of the local Masonic lodge is about 200. Auxiliary organizations are the John Dove Royal Arch Chapter, No. 21, and the Washington Commandary, Knights Templar, No. 12.

Madison Lodge, No. 6, of the Independent Order of Odd Fellows, was organized in 1836. Its membership is above 100. Its first room was in the Bantz building. It has now a three story building at the corner of Market and Water.

Shawnee Tribe, No. 5, was the fifth lodge of the Red Men to organize in the United States. An auxiliary is Minnehaha Council No. 1, the first in Virginia to organize.

The local lodge of the Elks began in October, 1903 with 65 charter members, and purchased for its home the building at the corner of Market and Water which it sold to the Odd Fellows. The present membership is 300.

Hickory Camp, No. 4, Woodmen of the World, began in February, 1901. It meets in Odd Fellows hall and has about 375 members.

Extinct organizations locally are the Good Templars and the Woman's Christian Temperance Union. Mulligan Post, No. 30, G. A. R., and Company A, Actual Survivors of the Stonewall Brigade tend to disappearance with the advanced age which is now true of all the survivors of the American civil war.

Other than those already named, Winchester has the following associative or fraternal societies:

Women's Civic League
Red Cross Association
District Nurse Association
Ministerial Association
Daughters of the American Revolution
Daughters of the Confederacy
Knights of Pythias
Loyal Order of Moose
Royal Arcanum

Rebeccas
Degree of Pocahontas
Federation of Church Women
American Legion
Patriotic Order of America
Camp Fire Girls
Boy Scouts
United Commercial Travelers
Girls' Athletic Association

The clubs of Winchester are the Fairfax, the Rotary, the Kiwanis, the Golf, and the Century.

XVII

JOURNALISM AND LITERATURE

Gazette — Sentinel — Virginian — Republican — Recent Newspapers — Books and Booklets.

> Over the sea! Over the sea!
> Where the wild waves sing the funeral dirge
> Of ships that went down in the foaming surge
> The petrel pursueth her path
> To her beetling nest on the surf-lashed shore,
> Where she reareth her young in the ocean's roar,
> Secure from the tempest's soar.
> —C. Toler Wolfe

If Winchester is not the second town in Virginia to start a newspaper, it lacks little of having that distinction. In 1787 it had a weekly journal of its own, and in the following year it had another. Yet in 1784 the only newspaper in all Virginia was printed in the state capital.

But Winchester was speedily followed by other Valley towns. The proprietor of its first paper announced in 1788 that he proposed to issue from Staunton "The Virginia Chronicle, or the Western Intelligencer." "The Potomac Advertiser," by Robert Henry, made its appearance at Martinsburg in 1789. It was nine by fifteen inches in size. Ten years later a second paper was started there by Nathaniel Willis, a Northern man who was the father of Nathaniel P. Willis and "Fanny Fern," both of whom were once noted writers.

The first number of the "Virginia Gazette, or Winchester Advertiser" is dated July 11, 1787. Why it should need this double title is not evident now, but it seems to have been a custom of the time. The publishers were Henry Wilcox & Company. Next year the style of the firm changed to Bartgis & Wilcox, and soon afterward to Bartgis & Company. Bartgis seems to have lived at Frederick, Maryland, where he had another printing office. The Gazette had four pages of three broad columns to the page, afterward increased to four columns, and was printed on thick, coarse paper. Another fashion of the day was to have a motto accompany the title, and it was imagined that the motto had peculiar efficacy if clothed in a Latin garb. The Latin, however, was not always grammar-proof. The motto used in 1800 is "Patria cara, carior libertas," which, when freely translated, means, "One's native land is dear, but dearer yet is liberty." In this year the title was carried on a streamer placed across a flying messenger blowing a trumpet. The subscription price was two dollars a year. Advertising space was sold at the rate of one dollar a square for three weeks. Bookbinding was done at the Gazette office and handbills were printed in German as well as in English. In 1789 the office was needing two journeyman printers to whom it would pay ten dollars a month, with board, lodging, and washing included. At the same time it advertised for two German boy apprentices. To accommodate the public, it offered to forward any letters that were left in its care. The printing office was on Main Street.

The reading matter consisted of foreign and domestic news and political articles, an occasional poem, and sometimes a contributed letter that might be four columns long, the print being smaller than is seen in the twentieth century newspaper. There were almost no local items whatever, and current history must be gleaned from the advertising columns, inclusive of the reading notices, some of which were in German. Advertising, as an art, was not then understood. There was little display, the business man telling his story in direct, matter-of-fact language, such as he would use in talking with a customer. Some of the reading notices are in reply to defamatory reports. The contributed articles, sometimes with a moral purpose, are in language we would now call stilted. One of them is on "The Fatal Consequences of Luxury," and by the way, there was about as much criticism of luxury a hundred years ago as there is now. An exceptional feature consists of some doggerel verses on "Charles Brainless." In the fall of 1788, the constitution of the United States, yet to undergo the ordeal of adoption or rejection by the various state legislatures, was printed in full, and there was much comment on it from week to week.

One of the papers left by General James Wood states that there was a barbecue at Federal Spring, July 4, 1787, to celebrate the ratification of the Federal Constitution and launch a "boom" for General Wood as governor. But in the date there is evidently a slip of the pen. The year could not have been 1787 and was probably 1789. The Constitutional Convention was still sitting in July, 1787, and not until about a year later was the instrument ratified by Virginia and New York. Until these states had acted the Constitution could not go into effect.

The Winchester Gazette was of the same size as the "Gazette of the United States," published at Philadelphia, but was not so well printed. In 1800 there were four columns to the page, and in 1811 there were five. In the last-named year the subscription price was three dollars with postage. The latest number we have seen is dated April 20, 1811, at which time the publisher was John Heiskell.

In 1787 the Gazette announces that Richard Bowen & Company, bookbinders on Water Street, intend soon to open a printing office. April 2, 1788, this firm issued the first number of the "Virginia Centinel, or Winchester Mercury." It was the year of the first presidential campaign in the history of the United States, and political considerations were doubtless responsible for the rival newspaper. It was an upholder of the party of Jefferson, whereas the Gazette was a champion of the Federalist party. But in size and in mechanical execution the two papers were as much alike as twin brothers. After a while, the same firm printed also the Gazette. There were several changes of ownership, and in 1827 the proprietor was J. H. Sherrard.

Bowen's office was the second floor of the stone building a little east of the Lutheran church. Richard Bowen is described as an Englishman, more than six feet tall, and of fine appearance. He adhered to the costume of the eighteenth century; short clothes, blue silk stockings, and silver knee and shoe buckles.

It will now be observed that as early as 1787 there were two book binderies in Winchester, and it is thought by Mr. Cartmell that a printing office was in existence about 1770. If so, it did nothing more than job work.

The third of the local newspapers was the "Constellation," started at the close of 1809 by Jonathan Foster, who was afterward associated with James Caldwell. Their printing office was at the corner of Main and Cork. They had agents as far away as Staunton and Kingwood, and the county seats of Pendleton and Montgomery. The "Constellation" had a page of five columns, and like its rivals it was printed on coarse material. The subscription price was two dollars, and advertising was one dollar a square for four weeks. The first and second pages were almost wholly given over to foreign news. On the third page were the news of the United States, a little literary matter, including an occasional poem by a local writer, and Alexandria and Baltimore prices. Advertising had the primacy on the fourth page. Napoleon was then making Europe a great battlefield, and the office advertised that it had for sale a map of the seat of war. In this paper we begin to find marriage and death notices, and the name of a "deserter and villain" from the American army is published. A 'slam" at the Gazette indicates that the two papers were on opposite sides of the political fence.

The "Republican" was established by Peter Printz as a continuation of the "Constellation," and the serial numbers on the title-page prove the continuity. In 1824 it was printed by Samuel H. Davis at the Sign of the Eagle on Main Street. In 1848, when its page had six broad columns, it was printed by John S. Gallaher, and it had begun to assume a modern appearance. The "Republican" survived until the outbreak of the war of 1861. Its office was destroyed by the soldiers of General Banks. It was Whig in politics, and among its editors were Henry D. Beall and George E. Senseny. The price was three dollars a year.

The "Virginian" started in 1825, and seems to have been a direct successor to the "Centinel." In 1831 it was owned by Sherrard & Robinson, in 1838 by Lewis Eichelberger, and in 1845 by J. C. Bowyer. Around the year 1840 national and state politics held the center of the stage with respect to the reading matter. An oration delivered at Middletown, July 4, 1839, by J. Smith Davison covers three broad columns. Politics was food and drink to the American of that era, and if such lengthy articles were not generally read they would not have been printed. Some space was given to world-news, and there was nearly always a poem. But there were no editorials and very little local news. More than one-half the columns were in advertising. In 1841 the "Virginian" had a large page of six columns, and the type was small. The printing was of better quality than in 1812. The price was three dollars a year, and in politics the paper was Democratic. As a victim of the war, the "Virginian" succumbed in 1861. The issue for July 12 of that year was a half-sheet.

From the summer of 1861 to the summer of 1865, Winchester was without a newspaper. In July of the latter year, George R. Henry and P. L. Kurtz began publishing the "News," H. K. Pritchard being the editor. In 1888 the paper was purchased by J. F. and R. M. Ward, and a bindery started. The "Evening Item," Winchester's first daily, was established January 12, 1895 by John I. Sloat, who sold to the Wards, and they to George F. Norton, who then began publishing the "New-Item." May 17, 1907 this daily was merged with the "Evening Star." An industrial edition was issued August 18, 1904.

The "Times," a weekly, made its advent September 17, 1865. The first owner was the firm of Goldsborough & Clark. After some years it passed into the hands of T. W. Harrison and R. E. Byrd. For a time the editor was Nathaniel B. Meade of Clarke county. The Winchester Times Publishing Company was organized in 1883, and Mr. Byrd became the editor. The "Times" was well printed, and during its continuance there were four pages of seven and sometimes eight columns, and a "patent" supplement of two pages. This newspaper was conspicuous for its large amount of general reading matter. There were many articles on Lee, Davis, Jackson, Ashby, and other Confederate leaders, and in 1873 appeared a valuable series of local history letters by the late W. G. Russell. An illustrated trade edition came out October 1, 1890.

The "Sentinel," Democratic in politics, came out in the fall of 1869. It was owned by Hollis & Company, and the editor was N. B. Meade.

The "Evening Star" was started as a daily by J. I. Sloat, July 4, 1896, and was printed at the office now owned by George F. Norton. It was consolidated with the "News-Item" May 17, 1907. After the discontinuance of the "Times" in July, 1905, it became the one and only newspaper of Winchester, although three were in existence in 1890.

The two Republican newspapers of this city were both short-lived. The "Journal," issued by A. M. Crane, began publication just after the civil war and went out of existence in 1870. It had a small page and a comparatively small amount of reading matter. The "Leader" appeared in 1884 and was conducted a few years by T. H. Goshorn.

Had the newspapers of early Winchester been published in Australia, they could not be more unlike the local journals of the last twenty-five years. The news from Europe, rather stale by the time it arrived, was given the lion's share of the reading space, and it could be adequately understood only by the person who was well read. The contributed articles showed the strong influence of the classical training of the time. It is almost solely in the advertising columns that one may collect the data for constructing a mental picture of the Winchester of the last fourth of the eighteenth century. Viewed in this light alone, the advertisements are of great value.

Even by 1812 there is no very marked change, although events within the United States receive an increasing share of attention, and the editor has something to say about the war with England. That the country is at war is seen in the advertising columns also.

Seventy-five years ago the newspapers had grown larger, but small type was still used. There is no distinction between editorials and local items, but the articles of strict local color are as yet few. A paragraph on the news of the day is not always found, and when it does occur, it is in the nature of comment. European news vacates the seat of honor in favor of Congressional news, and there are extended reports of debates on important issues. Seven and even eight columns, all in fine type, may be taken up with a single speech by some "Honorable Timothy Tremendous." The business men of Winchester were not afraid to advertise, and the space they used was almost solid matter, since there was very little attempt at display in large type.

In the late forties much is said on the war with Mexico, and in the fifties there is not a very close approach to modern newspaper practice. Yet local events now have regular recognition in some degree.

After the blank period of 1861-1865, during which no newspaper could live in the war-tossed city, there is a new era, in newspaperdom as in everything else. The journals all at once present a modern air. The editorials and local columns become very prominent. Occurrences in the United States have conspicuous mention, but seemingly the editor cares little as to what is taking place outside of North America in general and the United States in particular. And accompanying the local and telegraphic news is much general reading matter. Advertising matter is now displayed. Throughout the remainder of the nineteenth century, the county paper was a weekly, and when it came into a home it was read at leisure, no page being overlooked.

Throughout this period the political pot was boiling vigorously. The editorial ink exhaled the odors of vinegar and red pepper. The other side was denounced unceasingly and unsparingly, and without much economy in words. But this pungency was a feature of the age, and was as characteristic of the North as the South, the East as the West. If the memories of the sixties were rehearsed with comment, entire columns were devoted to topics in local history, which was now felt to have a background. And just after commencement week, whole columns were given to the seminaries.

Since the World War, American journalism has entered into a new phase, which, in fact, had already begun. The magnitude of that struggle, and the changing social and industrial life, have overshadowed the events of 1861 and the reconstruction era that followed. Political comment is now tame in comparison with what came off the editorial pen in the final quarter of the last century.

In this chapter the literary history of Winchester can be given only in a sketchy form. That the town could support two book binderies as early as 1787 is significant, since it indicates that no small amount of reading was done. And that reading begets a tendency to rush into print is a well-known fact.

In the year just mentioned, there are advertised in the Gazette as emanating from a schoolboy, "The Winchester Grammar" and "A Treatise on Education." The prices were certainly cheap, being, respectively, three farthings and one penny, or one cent and one and one-half cents. The following year there is advertised "The Virginia Almanac, or the Winchester Ephemeris, by the North Mountain Philosopher." This was perhaps an echo of Franklin's "Poor Richard's Almanac." At all events the almanac of a century ago was held in great favor. It was a repository of maxims, recipes, jokes, and miscellaneous items of general human interest.

In 1790 there was sold at sixpence an "essay on a medicinal spring near here," doubtless referring to the Jordan White Sulphur. In the same year the Gazette announces that it will publish "Spiritual Songs" as soon as there is a sufficient number of advance subscriptions. These must have been secured, since the book went to press in 1791. The price—one pistareen—is significant as proving how very well known was this foreign coin of almost twenty cents in value. In 1800 is advertised "A Serious Address to the Inhabitants of Winchester," by William Christie, the price being a ninepence (12½ cents). If Mr. Christie was giving his townsmen a scolding, we are in the dark as to the nature of it. The same year there was on sale an oration on the death of Washington at a price of one shilling and sixpence (25 cents). But this booklet may not have been printed in Winchester.

In the first and second decades of the nineteenth century several books were printed by Foster. Two of these were "The Olive Branch," by Matthew Carey, and "The Irish Emigrant," by Adam Douglass.

In after years Winchester was less conspicuous in the printing of books and booklets than in the writing of them. However, C. Toler Wolfe personally printed and bound, in 1872, his "Echoes from the Past, or Winchester and its Environs in the Olden Time." It was a little volume of 64 pages. Twenty years earlier he published in Winchester "A Book of Odds and Ends," a medley of prose and verse. Wolfe, who was born at Stephens City about

1810, was a roving, eccentric, unmarried printer, and like others of his craft, was addicted to drink. Although brilliant and versatile, his education was but elementary. He was not long content anywhere and his wanderings extended as far as the West Indies. In the earlier book, the author showed that he had serious moments of reflection, but in general he "laughed at the follies of life, satirized its vanities, and his aim was to make the world happier rather than better." It was his opinion that, "most of womankind are sheer deceit." We quote the following selection:

> To change the grave to gay—the melancholic
> Turn from their mopish moods to those of frolic,
> And so grow fat, instead of useless whinings
> At what they can't avoid, and vain repinings
> O'er ills that daily hem them round about,
> At which 'tis cheaper far to laugh than pout,
> Is my sincere intent.

Two of the works by Miss Frances Courtney Baylor are "Beyond the Blue Ridge", and "Jean and Jeanetta." Mrs. Emma C. Macon (nee Riely) wrote the very interesting volume entitled "Reminiscences of the Civil War." Local writers no longer living were the poet, Lawrence McCay Boyd, and William Lawrence Clark, the author of many works on law, including "Corpus Juris."

The following list of writers from Winchester and Frederick was compiled by Dr. W. P. McGuire.

H. St. George Tucker	Rev. Charles Krauth
John Randolph Tucker	Rev. Jas. R. Graham
R. T. Barton	Ward Lamon
F. W. M. Holliday	T. K. Cartmell
Mary Tucker McGill	Edgar Arnold
Frances Courtney Baylor	Rev. Jas. Battle Averitt
Dr. Hunter H. McGuire	C. L. C. Minor
Rev. Hunter Boyd	Willa Sibert Cather
James M. Mason	Edward C. Bruce

In 1877 the Lippencott firm of Philadelphia published "The Century: Its Fruits and Its Festival," a volume of 250 pages by Edward C. Bruce on the subject of the Centennial Exposition of 1876. Mr. Bruce, a Winchester man, was also the author of "Seekings of the South," a poem telling of Alabama.

Miss Mary Magill wrote a school history of Virginia, and in 1912 appeared "Winchester. Its Traditions and Other Verses," a volume of 145 pages by Miss Kate McVicar.

In 1905 it is announced that Prof. M. W. Swartz, now of Millsap College, Jackson, Mississippi, is the author of "A Topical Analysis of the Latin Verb."

Perhaps the first of the several illustrated booklets descriptive of Winchester is "Resources and Advantages of Winchester and the Country Contiguous Thereto," issued in 1872 by the Committee of Trade.

In his "Poets of Virginia," F. V. N. Painter gives liberal mention to two of the earlier poets of Winchester. He first names Joseph Thomas, a minister, who published in this town in 1816 a deeply religious epic entitled "A Practical Descant on the Primeval and Present State of Man." In the elaborate preface is explained the author's general idea of mankind. Prof. Painter finds his prose to be involved and pessimistic. The following selections are from his verse:

>Our land a refuge is for all distrest,
>By nature's hand most beautifully blest;
>See midland seas and broader lakes display
>Their glittering glories to the beams of day.

>Tho' war has ceased and plenty smiles around,
>Great discontent and murmurs now abound,
>Our selfish souls do avaricious groan,
>'Gainst Heaven's high will we utter out the moan.

We close the chapter with the following fine poem on "Shawnee; The Call of the Water," by the late Lawrence McK. Boyd of this city.

>'Twas blazed along the Redman's trail,
>   And carved within the rocky cave,
>'Twas whispered through the umber dale,
>   And wove in wampum for the brave.

>How that a royal Shawnee maid—
>   Dark-haired and lithe and lustrous-eyed—
>Held tryst within thy haunted glade,
>   Tryst with her lover who had died.

And when with startled night, he fled
From dawn which crept so stealthily,
Ever she cried unto her dead,
    "Come back! Come back! And drink with me!"

And still the spectral shadows fall
    On trysting place of dead Shawnee,
And still the plaintive echoes call,
    And they must heed who think of thee.

        *   *   *   *   *   *

Thy call through sombre yesterdays
    Has lingered near, oh! Rare Shawnee—
Tonight its mocking echo plays
    On trembling chords of memory:

And from dim halls of Long Ago,
    Through dusk-gray aisles of wasted years,
I hear thy singing waters flow
    Attuned to melody of tears.

A weary pilgrim at thy shrine
    I lay my staff, and kneel once more,
To fill my cup with draught divine,
    And pledge thee as in days of yore:

And ere my halcyon dream is sped
    Beyond the night, and far from me,
I drink one cup to passions dead,
    And one to home, to love, and thee!

XVIII

THE EDUCATIONAL RECORD

Early Schools — Winchester Academy — Later Academies —
Other Antebellum Schools and Teachers — Medical College
— Free Schools — The Handley Foundation — Handley Library.

> In this school the English language will be taught grammatically; Orthography, Reading, and Writing, with grace and propriety, and a complete course of the Mathematics, or any of the practical branches that may be required. Advertisement of school of Felix Kirk in Winchester, Nov. 2, 1797.

That a school was established very early in the history of Winchester may be inferred from the character of its leading settlers, even if we did not have direct verification from the journal of James Wood. About 1748 it contains an entry of five shillings for "eight sash lights for the schoolhouse." From this we may infer that the building was superior to some of the old-field schoolhouses of even a century afterward. Some of that class had only such daylight as might filter through a thickness of greased paper. Colonel Wood has also an entry of the purchase of "three Dyche spelling books," costing in our money, about 32 cents each.

The ruling class in colonial Virginia held that education is a private interest, and that schooling was to be bought and paid for like clothing or groceries. There were no free schools whatever, in the modern sense of the term. The very few "free schools" that we read of were free, simply because endowed by private individuals. They were not under public supervision any more than the others. Accordingly, it is only in the most incidental manner that we find mention of schoolhouses in the early public records. However, both the Scotch-Irish and the German settlers of the Shenandoah Valley were solicitous for the education of their children. They provided schoolhouses and teachers, even though they had to bear the expense out of their own pockets.

But beginning in 1787 considerable light is thrown on educational conditions in the advertising columns of the local newspapers. They tell us that Felix Kirk—probably a Quaker—will open a school in December, 1787. In the following year, J. H. Jones has a school and Samuel Mason is his assistant. Maria

Smith will open a school for girls October 15, 1788, if 13 patrons will guarantee tuition for one year, her terms being $3.33 a year besides an entrance fee of $1. She will give instruction in needlework. By reading between the lines we can see that the number thirteen is not a hoodoo with Maria Smith, and that teaching by women was not in marked disfavor in this community. But for some years later, female teachers were few in any state. Other teachers of this time were a Mr. Rayworth and a Mr. Cooley, the latter teaching on Main Street, although in 1790 he was teaching by the Hollabeck Hotel at the corner of Main and Gerard. Mr. Russell speaks of Henry St. George Tucker as teaching on the corner of Kent and Piccadilly the first school in Winchester, but he surely had predecessors.

Just when the Winchester Academy began its existence is not quite clear. In a petition of November 27, 1786, the trustees— Alexander Balmain, John Smith, Robert Mackey, Philip Bush, Joseph Holmes, and Rauleigh Colston—ask "the incorporation of their grammar and high school." The opening in that year took place July 10, and the tuition was four guineas ($14) a year. In this mention occurs the name of J. H. Norton as a trustee. But in an advertisement of 1787, the trustees named are Edward McGuire, Robert Wood, Samuel May, Lewis Wolf, Henry Baker, Frederick Conrad, J. G. Dowden, Isaac Sittler, and Thomas Edmondson. It is stated that the academy has been running some time, and that the principal is Charles O'Neal, a Master of Arts of Dublin and Glasgow universities. Just before Christmas week, 1788, the examination in the classical studies was at the Market House. In the afternoon there were orations by the students, and at night a theatrical entertainment, the admission to which was 25 cents. December 19, the students gave a tragedy, charging an admission of two shillings (33 cents.) In 1790, John Smith, president of the board of trustees, announces that a tutor in the classics has been engaged, that large sums of money have been subscribed, and that a five-acre lot contiguous to the town has been offered.

An early principal of the academy was Robert Heterick, a native of Scotland, who lived to the age of ninety. When Heterick was himself a student at Edinburgh he accidentally ran against the poet, Robert Burns, at a time when the streets were slippery with ice, and was made the target for a volley of words unsuited for publication. Other early teachers were John Bruce, W. L. Clark, Augustus C. Smith, and one McLemar.

In relating the general history of the Academy, Mr. Cartmell says that the school taught on Water Street near Market in 1787 seems to have developed into the Winchester Academy, because of the wording of the Act of December 9, 1789, which says a school is then in operation. The Act set apart for its use a half-acre lot in the town, as well as tracts of 200 and 520 acres, coming, respectively, from the late James Hamilton and Thomas Spear. These farm-lots were to be sold and the proceeds applied to the use of the school. The Academy migrated about and at length it found a permanent home on the hill west of the hospital. Here was erected an imposing building of stone and brick. This was destroyed and for several years after the civil war the residence of A. Magill Smith was used. Mr. Russell speaks of the Academy having once been housed on Stewart Street between Cork and Clifford, near a stone house built about 1813, subsequently burned, and replaced with a brick house by R. E. Byrd.

A rejected petition of 1826 asks a donation from the Literary Fund. The paper says there is a schoolhouse and also a house for the principal. All expenses are paid by tuition, and a lack of sufficient means prevents an expansion of the curriculum. The school has a very acceptable tutor and also an usher, but needs apparatus and a tutor in mathematics and natural and moral philosophy, so that it may be able to fit its students for college. In the preceding year there were 56 students, all but four of whom studied the classics. The average for the last eight years has been more than 50, some coming from Rockingham, Fauquier, Madison, and even from the city of Richmond.

Kercheval in 1833 says the Academy is flourishing, and that there are many classical and English schools in Winchester.

In 1838 there were two instructors. There was a full course in Latin and Greek. Other subjects taught were Spanish and German, political economy, mental and moral philosophy, surveying, civil engineering, and the higher mathematics generally. In 1839 Obed Waite was giving instruction in Hebrew, Spanish, and Italian. At this time there were lectures twice a week on chemistry and natural philosophy, and these were well attended by the townspeople. In 1841 the charge in board and lodging for a term of five months was $62.50. Tuition was $12.50 in the English branches and $16.50 in the classical. In 1856, when the Rev. William Johnson, A. M. was principal the yearly expense for board and tuition was $150.

The Shenandoah Valley Academy is the direct descendant of the old Winchester Academy, which, according to local tradition, was founded in 1764. Except for the interruptions caused by the wars of 1775 and 1861, Winchester Academy was in continuous session until 1865, when it assumed its present name. Thirty years later, R. A. Robinson of Louisville, Kentucky, donated the present site of 21 acres and most of the school buildings. Dr. Brantz M. Roszell, the principal now in charge, came in 1908, and military training was introduced. The cadet commissioned officers, who form the Honor Committee of the school, are in matters of government a part of the faculty and are the backbone of the system of discipline. The physical features of the school are quite modern and complete, and include one of the best gymnasiums in the South. There are eight instructors, and the enrollment for the current year is 86.

The record of this school in the World War cannot be surpassed. The students and ex-students of the period 1908-1918, who were eligible for military duty numbered 178, and every one of these went into the army. Nine were decorated for bravery by the allied governments. Every member of the faculty also entered the service.

During the pastorate of Mr. Streit, the Lutheran church had a parochial school near where is now the entrance to Mount Hebron. But a daughter of Mr. Streit taught in their home on Market Street. Mr. Russell speaks of the first German school in this town as taught by a man living in one of the earliest houses in Winchester. It stood in Piccadilly next to Coe's tavern. When German ceased to be used here as a medium of instruction we are not informed, and it would not seem to have been later than the early years of the last century.

Angerona, the large, conspicuous building at the west end of Piccadilly, has a conspicuous place in the educational history of Winchester. Built in 1794 as the parish house, it became four years later a seminary for girls. The roseate language of the managers in 1821 describes the house as "beautifully situated on a truly enchanting, airy eminence, from where there is a charming, delectable view of the whole town, the Blue Ridge, North, and other mountains, together with the circumjacent country and its scenery. Water is brought to the house from a noble and pellucid, unfailing, limestone spring." In 1839 Angerona Seminary, then conducted by A. M. Smith, charged for board and tuition $85 for a term of five and one-half months. The Virginia Female College was established here in 1854 by the Odd Fellows. Two years later the instructors were C. D. Elmer and J. L. Cross, both of whom were college graduates. Their charge for tuition varied from $10 to $20. Other men who taught here were Thorpe and Magill. The school ceased with the coming of the war of 1861 and did not afterward rally.

It is claimed by Mr. Russell that General Cass, Democratic candidate for the presidency in 1848, taught in Winchester, but his biography does not appear to confirm this. One of the undoubted teachers at the beginning of the last century was one Caldwell, whose room was at the corner of Market and Piccadilly.

In 1810 there was a Lancastrian school in Winchester, conducted by Mrs. Selim Nicholls at the corner of Braddock and Amherst, and according to Mr. Russell in a building that was once Edmondson's tavern. Her charge was only $10 a year. The leading peculiarity of the schools that followed the method of Joseph Lancaster, an Englishman, was the use made of the oldest pupils as assistant teachers. When these were bright and willing, and well supervised, such schools gave quite good results, and they were relatively inexpensive.

About 1830 Joseph Baker, a Baptist minister, came to this town and not only preached to the local Baptist congregation but established the Winchester Female Academy where is now the Fort Loudoun Seminary. Instruction was given in Latin, Greek, French, botany, chemistry, geometry, mental philosophy, and the other branches usual at that time, in addition to drawing, painting, and music. For tuition in the English studies the charge was $10.50, and in the classical studies, $14.50. Board and lodging for a term of five months cost $75 in 1838, and $85 a few years later. The essays read at a public exhibition in 1841 include some topics that would nowadays be shunned. The titles are these:

Death	Disobedience to Parents
Humility	The Liberty of Our Country
Friendship	The Degraded State of Africa
Amiability	The Advantages of an Improved Mind
Mental Application	

Mr. Baker carried on the school until near the time of his death in 1855. That he stood high as a teacher seems to be indicated in these lines, taken from a leaflet of 1848:

> It always has and ever will
> Be an established rule,
> That on the top of old Fort Hill
> Is taught the finest school.

By 1838 the schools of Winchester had become numerous. In this year James I. and Miss Randolph are teachers, the former having a seminary. Lucinda Morrow has a girls' school and charges $2.50 to $3.00 a quarter. In a brick building at the corner of Market and Water, John W. Marvin, a Quaker, teaches the English branches at $60 per session for board, lodging, and tuition. At the seminary for girls conducted by the Rev. Abner W. Kilpatrick, the total cost for five months is $75. Stephen F. Smith has a night as well as a day session. On Water Street W. Wilmarth has the Winchester Academical Institute. Three years later, James R. Coburn seems to have succeeded Marvin at the corner of Market and Water, but the same year he moved to the basement of the new Lutheran church. He taught English and mathematics. In 1855 there is the Ambler Hill Seminary. Newman's Seminary began in 1835 with an attendance of 47 girls. In 1845 is advertised the ninth session of the Winchester Institute, a school for girls, under the care of Dr. and Mrs. Togno. The John W. Marvin, already named, opened the Winchester Seminary about 1850, and it is mentioned in 1875 as still in existence. In 1841 is advertised the seventh session of the Wickliff Academy, A. H. Evans being the principal, and the tuition ranging from $10 to $20. In 1856 the Winchester Juvenile Academy was one of the local schools.

In 1841, J. N. Bell was keeping in stock the following textbooks:

Readers .... New York, United States, Cobb's, Emerson's
Geography .... Mitchell's
Arithmetic .... Pike's, Colburn's, Smith's, Emerson's, with keys
Grammar .... Murray's, Kirkham's
Natural Philosophy .. Comstock's
Algebra .... Day's, Davies', Colburn's
Geometry .... Legendre's
History .... Parley's—United States and Universal
Bookkeeping .... Marsh's

In 1854, Sidney P. York, a Northern man, and a graduate, like his partner, Lamont, opened the Valley Female Institute as a Methodist school in the old Methodist church on the east side of Market Street. A third story was added two years later. In 1857 they had 94 students and there was a reading room. Being out of sympathy with secession, York and Lamont had to leave Winchester very hurriedly in the early spring of 1862. By reason of inventing the green-tinted paper on which the old greenback currency was printed, Lamont became wealthy.

In 1869, Silas Billings opened in the same building a Presbyterian school which he called Fairfax Hall. Mr. Billings was assisted by his daughters, Cornelia and Mary, and by George C. Shepherd, a son-in-law. They opened with 35 students, but the average during the next 15 years was about 100. In the second year there were 126. Some of the students were from other states. Mr. Billings died in 1881, and the school was continued by his daughters until 1899, when Mr. Shepherd took charge. Three years later he moved it to the Winchester Inn, and after a few more years it was discontinued. After Shepherd left, the building became the Fairfax Hotel.

The Episcopal Female Institute was incorporated by J. C. Wheat, D. D. in 1874, and its home was the historic building at the southwest corner of Braddock and Piccadilly. This school was in operation at least 35 years.

James B. Avirett, chaplain of the Fourth Alabama, settled in Winchester after the war as principal of Dunbar Female Institute, the eleventh session of which began in the fall of 1869.

Benjamin Arbogast, a native of Pocahontas county, was a graduate of Dickenson College, and entered the ministry of the Methodist Episcopal Church, South, in 1857. In 1872 he established the Valley Female College in the Angerona building, removing at length to Fort Loudoun. It was a Methodist school and it prospered. Mr. Arbogast died in 1881 at the age of sixty-two, and was succeeded by John P. Hyde, but the institution was at length closed.

In 1905, Misses Glass and Gold, graduates of Fairfax Hall, opened the Fort Loudoun Seminary, a school for girls. With the exception of the Shenandoah Valley Academy, it is the only private school for secondary instruction that remains in Winchester.

Broaddus College, a Baptist institution, was established in 1871 at the east end of Cork Street by E. J. Willis. Five years later, the school was moved to Clarksburg, West Virginia.

In 1866 Mrs. Ann Magill, a daughter of Henry St. George Tucker, opened a seminary for girls in the brick building at the intersection of Main and Cork. This school, which was very successful, was removed to Angerona. Mrs. Magill was assisted by her daughters, Mary T. and Eva, of whom the former was the author of a school history of Virginia.

In 1856 a high school was quartered under the Main Street Presbyterian church. The term was one of five months, and the tuition varied from $10.00 to $16.50.

A law school organized in Winchester in 1824 by Henry St. George Tucker, continued for a number of years, and had about 50 students.

The Medical College of the Valley of Virginia was chartered in 1822 but suspended five years later. In 1846 it was revived and rechartered as the Winchester Medical College. The new site chosen was west of Stewart Street where there had been a garden and orchard. The building was of red brick with stone trimmings. To the support of this school $5000 was loaned from the Literary Fund and some help was given by the town. The tuition was $100 for the session of eight months. There were two or three lectures each morning, and the instruction was very practical. The school was suspended in 1861, and as mentioned elsewhere, the building was burned in March, 1862, by order of General Banks.

In the faculty of the Medical College were the following physicians: H. H. McGuire, J. Philip Smith, William Bradford, J. H. Straith, and Daniel Conrad. Bradford was succeeded by Bushrod Taylor and Conrad by J. W. Walls.

Before coming to the modern period, it may be permissible to mention some teaching that was not altogether of an educational nature.

In 1811 Albert Sweet was teaching penmanship, charging $5 for his course of lessons and 75 cents for the stationery used.

As early as 1789 J. Smith Wales was giving lessons in music at 12 shillings per quarter. In 1838, Don Marcelino Perez—a Spaniard as his name indicates—was giving lessons on the piano, guitar, and other instruments, charging $15 for a quarter of 24 lessons.

In 1789 Jeremiah Moriarty advertised that he would teach dancing on Fridays and Saturdays if 12 patrons would subscribe. In 1811, J. Xaupy and M. Guillou, both of whom were Frenchmen, gave instruction in French as well as dancing.

Until 1870 all the educational training received by the young people of Winchester came through the private schools. So far as these were of academic grade, the instruction was too bookish and there was an undue emphasis on Latin and Greek. The teaching was in fact more ornamental than practical. Its avowed aim was to impart culture to the youth of both sexes rather than to fit them for specific lines of employment in a workaday world. But though deficient in the latter particular, the exacting drill did impart a good degree of mental discipline and mental grasp. And if the training in the schools of lower grade seems like the Dark Ages to the pedagogue who tries to follow the niceties insisted upon by present educational authority, such schools were nevertheless quite practical in their day and time. The teaching was not sugar-coated. It was switched into the pupil whenever the teacher deemed the switching necessary, and his use of hickory oil was sustained by public opinion.

In the antebellum government of Virginia, the Eastern District had the "say." In that quarter the opposition to free schools was bitter and was sometimes expressed in intemperate language. In the Western District there was much less prejudice, and the active opposition was more largely due to indifference. Under pressure from the western counties, a law was passed in 1846 permitting individual counties to inaugurate a free school system provided two-thirds of the voters expressed themselves in its favor. By 1860, several of the Valley and transalleghany counties had done so.

In Frederick county the sentiment in favor of free schools was considerable, yet insufficient. As early as December, 1841, a citizens' meeting in Winchester appointed R. Y. Conrad, R. E. Byrd, and William Wood delegates to an educational convention at Richmond. This meeting declared for "a liberal system of education throughout the state."

The county was at this time receiving $1000 yearly toward the support of its district schools, but as all this was expended on the tuition of "indigents," such state aid was not well thought of in the western counties.

In this county the question of free schools was voted upon June 3, 1847, and the result was adverse. The Virginian advocated the measure, pointing to the fact that in all Virginia there were 80,000 illiterates.

After a fierce newspaper war in 1856, free schools in Frederick were again voted down. The Richmond Examiner of this year declared that "free schools are of the same brood of damnableness whose mother is sin and whose daddy is the devil."

During the four years of war there was scarcely any teaching done in Winchester, the local conditions being peculiarly unfavorable.

The state constitution adopted in the reconstruction regime provided for a general system of free schools, and it went into effect in 1870. In Winchester and Frederick the new order of things was organized by Colonel A. M. Smith a lifelong educator. In a one-column letter published in December of the same year, Colonel Smith as the first county superintendent, stated that although he had hitherto been opposed to free schools he was now convinced that they were advisable and very necessary. The public school system went into effect in Winchester in February, 1871, two private schools and their courses of study being taken into it. These schools had four rooms and three more were rented. The first principal was Captain J. C. Vanfossen, and he taught in the basement of the Braddock Street Methodist church. For several years, the Fort Loudoun building was used.

In 1870 the children of school age in Winchester were 778 whites and 268 blacks, a total of 1046. The enrollment for the first year was 285 of the white children and 117 of the colored. The daily attendance averaged 259. In 1873 the yearly cost of the city schools was $4500, coming in about equal amounts from the state, the city, and the Peabody fund. In 1875 the school year was 40 weeks. In November, 1884, the enrollment had risen to 420 white children and 166 colored. Four years later the respective numbers were 531 and 174, and of the former 91 were in the high school. In 1887 the salaries of the teachers varied from $20 to $87. In 1907 the school population was 1281 and in the following year the schoolrooms were overcrowded.

Textbooks a long while in use in the closing quarter of the last century were McGuffey's Readers, Harvey's Grammar, Maury's Geography, White's and Venable's arithmetics, and the Eclectic History of the United States.

In the opening year of the present century, the cost of the schools of Winchester was $6927.52, inclusive of $374.75 in tuition fees. The enrollment was 579 white children and 191 colored, and there was an average of 51 to each teacher.

A permanent home for the city school came in 1883. John Kerr, a local philanthropist, provided for this purpose a fund of $7000, and when it became available it had grown to $10,000. The city council added $6000, although in 1875 that body had refused to build a schoolhouse. The cornerstone was laid May 31, 1883, the day being very pleasant, and in 1884 the new building, containing 10 rooms, to which 6 were at length added, was occupied. But in 1917 the congestion was such that five rented rooms were in use, none of them very well adapted to school purposes.

Mr. Kerr, a native of England and a cabinet-maker, came to Winchester about 1825, remaining here till his death, November

15, 1874, at the age of approximately seventy-six years. Because childless, he left his property to provide a schoolhouse for his adopted town.

In 1871, two rooms and two teachers were provided for the colored pupils. In 1876 the old stone church of the Presbyterians was leased, and more than half the expense of fitting it up came from the sale of the lot on which the Medical School had stood. Further repairs and extensions have been made, yet in 1917 the accommodations were pronounced inadequate, although the commission observed that there is a progressive shrinking in the colored population of Winchester.

Until a few years ago the schools of Winchester held no exceptional rank among those of the towns of similar size in Virginia. A quite advantageous circumstance placed them upon a very advanced footing.

The will of John Handley, a man who never lived in Winchester and visited it only a few times, contains the following paragraph:

"All the rest and residue of my estate I give, devise, and bequeath to the city of Winchester, to be accumulated by said city for the period of twenty years. The income arising from said residual estate to be expended and laid out in said city by the erection of schoolhouses for the education of the poor."

Agreeably to the above provision, the Handley Board, created by the Virginia legislature in 1896, received in 1917 from the Handley estate the sum of $1,640,000. About the same time an educational survey of this city was made by the General Education Board of the United States, as a basis for carrying the bequest into effect. A summary of this report has an interest that is by no means confined to its educational aspect.

In the year of the survey—1917—there were found in Winchester 5561 white people and 908 people of color. Two-thirds of the former were natives of Winchester or of Frederick county. Of the remaining third, one-half were born in other counties of Virginia and one-half in other states of the Union. The foreign-born were only one percent. The colored element was as homogeneous as the white.

The number of active breadwinners was 2260, mainly grouped in the following lines:

Agriculture 105
Skilled workers 487
Semi-skilled workers 378
Common labor 441
Trade 394
Public service 36
Professional work 156
Domestic work 236
Clerical work 127
Army 61

It was noticed that 19 percent of the white women and 43 percent of the colored women were employed outside of their homes; that of the skilled workers only one in nine was under the age of 25; that of the common labor, nearly six-sevenths was colored; and that few persons were in any one special line of employment.

The investigators noted the lack of minerals and waterpower in the region tributary to Winchester, the close economic relation between the town and the county; the slow growth of the town, because of the lack of labor-employing industries; and a steady movement of the younger people to localities more attractive industrially. The general conclusion reached was that the instruction given in the existing schools was too bookish; that the instruction indicated should closely correlate with the local economic conditions; and that this instruction should include training in the household arts, manual training, farm training, and the training of teachers.

At the time of the survey, there were 19 rooms for the white pupils and 3 for the colored. Of the 20 white teachers, only 14 were deemed adequately prepared, and the superintendent was in large measure a teaching principal. The average salary—$514— was lower than in the average city of Virginia. The white enrollment was 929, including 142 in the high school department. The colored enrollment, wholly in the elementary grades, was 182. The cost of the schools for the school year 1916-1917 was $16,601.71, the share raised by local taxation being $11,500. In 1871-1872 the cost was $3912.05, the local tax supplying only $1486.58.

The commission arrived at these conclusions: that a college was inadvisable, and contrary to the intent of the will; that a technical high school would serve too few of the pupils; that to take over the high school would injuriously affect the general control and responsibility; that the displacing of the public school by a private one was not only legally impossible, but a pauperizing spirit would be created and the Handley income would be insufficient. Cooperation between the Handley Board and the city was found to be the only alternative. Observing that no other town of its size in Virginia had spent so little on its school plant, the commission recommended that the Handley Board erect new school buildings and apply the income from the remainder of the fund to the schools, the city adding at least $15,000 a year. A complete reconstruction of the course of study was also advised. The recommendation was for a kindergarten, and elementary department for grades 1 to 6 inclusive, a junior high school for grades 7-9, and a senior high school for grades 10-12.

The lot purchased by the Handley Board in the south of the city and devoted to the use of the high school for whites covers 72 acres. The new building, occupied in the fall of 1923, cost about $800,000, including the expense of grading the grounds. It contains 60 recitation rooms, an auditorium, a nature study court, a gymnasium, and two offices. The seating capacity of the auditorium is 1500. The 14 rooms in the John Kerr building are also used for recitation purposes. The white enrollment is 1624—758 males and 866 females—of whom 603 are in the high school. The school year includes 200 teaching days, the session for the current year opening September 10, 1923 and closing June 12, 1924. The white instructors in the city schools are 47, of whom 40 are women. The colored teachers are one male and three females. For the year 1922-1923 the entire cost of maintenance of the public schools of Winchester was $83,673.58.

The new building for the colored pupils has not yet been erected.

Archibald Magill Smith was a grandson of General John Smith, ten years a Congressman, and a son of Colonel Augustus C. Smith, lawyer and state senator, who was at the head of Winchester Academy a century ago. He was himself a lifelong educator, and was seventeen years principal of the same academy. He also for a while conducted the Episcopal Female Institute. It was he who organized the public school system in Winchester and Frederick county. He died in Louisiana in 1918.

While still a youth, John Handley came to America from Enniscorthy, county Wexford, Ireland. In the city of Washington, where he earned his living as a carpenter, he began the study of law, entering upon its practice at Scranton, Pennsylvania. In 1875 he was elected a judge. Judicious investments in coal lands made him a millionaire, and since his last years were those of a childless widower, he decided to make philanthropic use of his estate.

James Jifkins, a friend and neighbor, settled near Winchester in 1869, and was several times visited by Judge Handley. These visits laid the foundation of an enduring attachment to this city and its people. During his lifetime he founded the Handley Library. His will created the Handley Foundation of $1,641,000, the beneficiary being the public schools of Winchester. Judge Handley was six feet four inches tall, stately in manner, and of distinguished appearance. He died at the age of sixty, February 15, 1895, and his grave is in Mount Hebron Cemetery.

The Handley Library, begun in 1910, and opened August 21, 1913, stands at the northwest corner of Braddock and Piccadilly. The cornerstone was laid with Masonic ceremonies, May 26, 1908. There was an oration by Major Holmes Conrad and in the evening a banquet. The maintenance fund provided by Judge Handley is $150,000. A head librarian, two assistants, and a janitor are all busily employed. The lot, 180 by 250 feet, is not excelled in attractiveness by any other in the city. The lawn is finely sodded, and is adorned with numerous varieties of trees, shrubs, and evergreen plants. The building, of Indiana limestone, is massive, monumental, and ornate, and its cost without equipment, was $150,000. Both building and lawn are kept in faultless order.

The rotunda is suggestive of that in the Library of Congress. The north wing is a commodious reading room, and is amply supplied with magazines, daily newspapers, and other journals. The west wing is devoted to a well chosen assortment of reference books, inclusive of six general encyclopedias, atlasses, globe, and wall maps.

In a smaller room, opening from the rotunda, is a large collection of Virginiana. The lecture hall, seating 300 persons, is equipped with a Bausch and Lomb dissolving stereopticon and screen. There are also conference rooms and smaller rooms for special study.

The volumes in the stack-room for free circulation among the residents of the city number 15,000, and are increased by about 1,000 new volumes each year. The visitors in the first year were 43,000, and the circulation of books was 24,341. It has been found that the loans of books for any given month have invariably increased with each successive year, so that in 1923 the circulation rose to 56,297. This uninterrupted increase speaks volumes for the success of the institution. Twenty daily newspapers from ten leading and widely distributed cities of the United States are on file. The magazines, including ten English periodicals, number seventy-five.

Circulating books are sent regularly to patrons in the counties of Clarke, Warren, Shenandoah, Fairfax, and Alexandria in Virginia, and to Berkeley, Jefferson, and Hampshire in West Virginia. Children living in the city come numerously every school day for help in their essays, debates, and projects.

For the use of the colored people of Winchester a branch library was opened in October, 1921, in the Douglas School, and it is proving of much service to the colored element, especially the school pupils.

XIX

THE CEMETERIES

Church Burial Grounds — Mount Hebron — Stonewall Cemetery
— National Cemetery

> What they were all know.
> Who they were none know.
>
> Inscription on monument to 829 unknown Confederate soldiers buried in Stonewall Cemetery, Winchester.

Throughout the first century in the history of this city, all interments were in the graveyards attached to the various churches. The Episcopal church-lot covered the southwest corner of the public square. Just east of the Baltimore and Ohio grade were the burial grounds of the Lutheran, Reformed, Presbyterian, Methodist, and Catholic communions, all within a very short compass. The southernmost was the Lutheran, immediately to the rear of the ruined church-wall. The northernmost was the Catholic, fronting National Avenue where the Berryville Pike begins. The Friends had a graveyard at the Center Meeting House, but they had another near the Hollingsworth mill and a third near where the paper mill formerly stood.

All these became filled, the Episcopal cemetery ceasing to be used about 1820, when another ground was opened southwest of the present hospital. This site being unsuitable for long-continued service, a company was chartered and Mount Hebron was the result. Of the first board of trustees, Thomas A. Tidball was president and Joseph S. Carson secretary.

This handsome inclosure of sixty acres is on the level plateau in the east of the city. The dedication took place June 24, 1844, the impressive ceremonies being conducted by the Rev. A. H. H. Boyd of the New School Presbyterian Church. The prayer of dedication was by the Rev. W. M. Atkinson of the Old School Presbyterian Church, and the first interment was that of his wife in the following August. There was an address by William L. Clark, a paper by the Rev. D. H. Bragonier, and the singing of a hymn written for the occasion by M. S. Lovett.

Very many removals were soon made from some of the older places of burial, and by 1908 the number of interments had grown

THE CEMETERIES

to 4485. The yards attached to the Lutheran and Reformed churches were included in Mount Hebron, but the spaces covered by the other church cemeteries have in part been taken over for building purposes. Inscribed headstones were not in general use in the eighteenth century, and hence many of the graves could not be identified. One of the unmarked graves was that of Nash Legrand, a once noted Presbyterian divine. One of the historic graves in Mount Hebron is that of General Daniel Roberdeau, an officer of the Revolution who died in Winchester January 5, 1795 at the age of sixty-eight. The general was of Huguenot ancestry and his descendants are numerous. This cemetery is also the final resting-place of the remains of General Daniel Morgan of the Revolution. John Handley and Charles Broadway Rouss, both noted for their philanthropies, are likewise interred here.

The lodge and chapel of Mount Hebron, and the iron fence which includes also the Stonewall Cemetery, were provided for by Mr. Rouss, whose mausoleum is one of the conspicuous features of the silent city. Mount Hebron is high and level and commands an extensive outlook. It is a beautiful place, although many of its fine shade trees were uprooted in the gale of March, 1914.

Immediately east of Mount Hebron, and likewise high, level, and sightly, is Stonewall Cemetery, five acres in extent, where have been reburied nearly 3000 of the Confederate dead, collected from a radius of about fifteen miles. The summer of 1865 found graves of Southern soldiers scattered numerously and promiscuously about the Lower Valley, and already some of them were being disturbed in the resumption of farming operations. A war cemetery was planned, and the following appeal was issued by an organization of the women of Winchester:

To the People of the South:

The frequent battles around Winchester, Va. have left their traces in the many graves scattered broadcast over an area of twelve miles radius. The dead were generally buried where they fell, and their rude graves are fast disappearing beneath the feet of men and beasts, free from the want of enclosures, to go where they will.

Those who died in the hospitals were mostly buried in the old Episcopal graveyard, but its enclosures have long been destroyed and cattle graze over its whole extent.

The farming operations of next season, the wear of the winter, and the disappearance by removal and death of those who were present at their burials, will in a few months leave no knowledge of the resting places of many martyred dead.

Impelled by these considerations, some of the citizens of Winchester and its vicinity have determined to endeavor to collect these scattered remains in one cemetery and surround them by a substantial enclosure. This, of course, will require a considerable amount of money. The means of our citizens are very much diminished by the war and its results, we are therefore induced to appeal to you for aid in this matter, encouraged by the belief that you will feel it a privilege as well as duty to pay this tribute of respect to the memory of those who fell in your cause.

Every Southern State has its representative among these fallen heroes; we ask all then for such contributions as they feel able to give.

Should we succeed in raising the necessary funds it is proposed to remove the remains on the first of April, 1866, and would respectfully suggest to all whose friends lie under these battle-fields, to disinter them before that time if they wish to do so. In the removal every precaution will be taken to preserve all identifications, and an accessible record will be prepared of every grave.

All subscriptions may be sent to Mrs. Philip Williams, or Mrs. Dr. A. H. H. Boyd, Winchester, Va.

At a meeting held February 22, 1866, the following persons were named as a general committee to superintend the removal: J. H. Sherrard, W. R. Denny, N. M. Cartmell, J. Z. Jenkins, C. L. Crum, and J. J. Williams. There were appointed eight sub-committees of five to eleven men each, and the territory to be examined for soldier-graves was apportioned among these eight committees. A card of instructions was also issued.

The appeal we have quoted brought in a fund of $14,000. Ground was purchased, and the task of removal was immediately begun. Within twelve months the remains of 2494 soldiers were collected and reinterred. Preference was given to the bodies found in miscellaneous places. In the second Episcopal cemetery were the graves of 1400 men who had died in hospital. The reinterring of these took place somewhat later. For some time afterward, other graves had to be dug for the bodies that continued to be found in various localities. Colonel Denny laid off the grounds and superintended the reburial, J. Z. Jenkins procured the coffins, and Charles Crum attended to the removals. From Alabama came a contribution of $1200 to the expense.

A central and striking feature of Stonewall Cemetery is the monument to the 829 unknown dead. The base is of Virginia granite. The shaft, of Italian marble, is nine feet square at the base, rises to a height of 49 feet, and is surmounted by the statue of a soldier. The cost of this fine memorial was $10,000.

All the states formally included in the Southern Confederacy, and Maryland and Kentucky also, are represented in Stonewall Cemetery, each state being allotted its own section, and in the annual observances of Memorial Day the individuality of these several states is likewise acknowledged. The state monuments are those of North Carolina, South Carolina, Georgia, Florida, Louisiana, and Maryland. The interments by states are as follows: North Carolina 447, Virginia 415, Georgia 290, South Carolina 149, Alabama 71, Louisiana 69, Mississippi 66, Florida 38, Tennessee 29, Arkansas 20, Maryland 14, Texas 6, Kentucky 3.

In 1873 there was remark that Stonewall Cemetery was in a neglected condition. Until after 1886 wooden headboards were still in use. These have since been replaced by marble slabs and the present condition of the grounds is quite exceptional.

The formal dedication of Stonewall Cemetery occurred June 6, 1866, this date being chosen because it is the anniversary of the death of General Turner Ashby. The procession that marched to the grounds was the longest yet seen in Winchester, and it was escorted by 300 men who had seen service in the Confederate army. The reburial of the Ashby brothers was on October 31 of the same year, with an oration by Henry A. Wise. The flag in the neighboring National Cemetery was lowered to half-mast.

The sixth of June is Confederate Memorial Day in Winchester. Business is suspended, and the town fills with visitors, sometimes to the number of 10,000. In 1911 the crowd was the largest yet known, although it was a full half-century since the beginning of the war. There have been occasions of more than average interest, one of which was the dedication of the monument to the soldier dead of Maryland in 1880. July 1, 1896 was signalized by the unveiling of the Louisiana monument.

So long as prominent actors in the great drama of the sixties were to be had, the oration on June 6 was by some general of the Confederate armies. Among these have appeared General J. A. Early of the campaign of 1864, General J. A. Walker of Virginia, and General J. T. Morgan of Alabama.

It is claimed for Winchester that this city has the priority over all other places in the United States in the custom of strewing flowers over the graves of soldiers. It is at least certain that it was observed June 6, 1866.

Facing National Avenue and separated from Stonewall Cemetery only by an alley is Winchester National Cemetery of five acres, dedicated April 8, 1866. It is the resting-place of 4491 Union dead, 2381 of whom are unknown. The number of Pennsylvania graves is 800, and the Ohio graves are 500. The square and almost level spot is inclosed by a very substantial stone wall, and as in all the national cemeteries, the space within is well grassed and well shaded. From time to time handsome monuments have been set up, the unveiling usually taking place the Fourth of July or on the anniversary of the battle of Opequon. These special monuments are by the states of Pennsylvania, Massachusetts, and New Hampshire, besides the memorial to the Sixth Army Corps, and the regimental monuments of the Third and Thirty-fourth Massachusetts, the Twelfth, Thirteenth, and Eighteenth Connecticut, the One Hundred and Fourteenth New York, the One Hundred and Twenty-third Ohio, and the Eighth Vermont.

National Memorial Day comes just one week earlier than the Confederate, and since this cemetery is on Southern soil the occasion is less largely observed. But on the anniversary of 1880, the Times remarks on the plentiful display of the national colors, and in 1899 that more were to be seen than in any previous year. Ex-Confederates participated for the first time in 1884, largely through the efforts of J. A. Nulton and John J. Williams. In the preceding year there was a large visiting delegation of Federal veterans, accompanied by members of their families, the purpose being the dedication of some monuments. They were given a public welcome, although there was considerable opposition among the townspeople, particularly by the female element and the ministers. In 1917 the monument to the unknown dead in Stonewall Cemetery was for the first time draped with the national colors.

We close this chapter with two verses, the first by C. Toler Wolfe, the second by Kate McVicar.

> A star and a crown for the young renown,
>   Who in honored graves lie low;
> A tear and a knell for the braves who fell
>   In the strife with a Northern foe.
> They died as heroes die—
>   Beneath the triple stars;
> With a warrior's brand in each good right hand,
>   For the glorious Southern Stars.
>
> For amidst the battle's surging,
>   Then such glorious deeds were done;
> That the victor and the vanquished
>   Have alike their laurels won.

> Linked are now their hearts together,
> Hand is clasped in friendly hand,
> North and South their barriers merging
> In the glory of our land.

Orrick Cemetery for the colored residents, where the Valley Pike makes its southward exit from Winchester, carries a story in its name. Robert Orrick was a mulatto of stalwart size, who for years had almost a monopoly of the livery business in this city. He owned much real estate, both within the town limits and without, and for his day and time was a wealthy citizen. But in his last years he was financially embarrassed.

XX

THE RECENT PERIOD

A Retrospect — The Equity Company — Apple Industry — Old Houses — Winchester in the World War.

> August 7, 1747: It is ordered that no person or persons presume to strain, either by pacing or racing thro' the street by the court house in the time of holding court, or at any other public time whatever, under the penalty of a severe fine, and it is further ordered that the sheriff give public notice of the said order.—Minutes of Frederick County Court. Evidently the first speed ordinance.

The Recent Period, in the annals of Winchester, admits of four sub-divisions. The first begins with the return of peace in the spring of 1865 and ends with the civil restoration of Virginia in 1870. The second reaches forward to the industrial activity of 1889-1890. The third carries us forward to 1917, when the United States entered the World War. The fourth, with its unsettled questions, is yet in progress.

The first sub-period was a time of gradual recovery from the terrible devastation of 1862-1864. The process was more rapid here than in the broad belt fought over by the Army of the Potomac and the Army of Northern Virginia. Because the labor of the Lower Valley was predominantly white, the economic dislocation was much less severe than in the section of the state east of the Blue Ridge. Normally, the Valley has always yielded a surplus of food staples, and though there was little wheat to harvest in the summer of 1865, the other crops of that year were generous. Nevertheless, it was a heavy task to remove the wreckage of four years of war, repair damaged houses or build new ones, and get the local industries once more on their feet.

The ruin in the South was so great that in the very mistaken opinion of some observers the smitten section was never going to recover. During the quarter-century following Appomattox, vast numbers of her people moved into the North and the West. This locality was no exception to the rule, and in 1870 there was still some comment on the number of young men who were moving West to better themselves. Yet the drain was not enough to cause more than a very temporary ebb in the size of the white population. On the other hand, there was soon a call for immigrants from the northward-lying states, and the invitation was coupled with the assurance that the newcomers would be treated right. This speaks well for the magnanimity of a people who had suffered so severely during the years of military operations. In discriminating in favor of immigrants from other American states, the South has shown itself far-sighted. As a rule, this section has viewed promiscuous foreign immigration with disfavor, and as a result of this feeling only one person in one hundred of the people of Winchester is of foreign birth.

Another fact worthy of note in the same connection is that although the war-feeling of the sixties caused Independence Day to fall into eclipse in the South, the suspension in Winchester was very temporary and very partial. In 1867 we learn that the Fourth of July was "fairly observed." Twenty years after the battle of the Opequon there was a "big Fourth" and 10,000 strangers were present.

The usual respect of the American for law and public order is reflected in the circumstance that no homicide took place in Winchester for eighteen years after the close of the war. There was, indeed, no small amount of disorderly loafing, especially by insolent negroes, but the source of this evil was largely external. It was one of the ills of the reconstruction regime.

When we come to the second period the evidences of progress are distinctly manifest. In 1870 the census-taker found in Winchester 751 houses, 873 families, and 4477 persons. There was some shrinkage from the pre-war enumeration. But in 1880 there were 4958 people, and in 1890 the number was 5240. This was a slow growth, but it was much better than marking time.

In 1872 the value of the taxable property in the town was $2,004,829.10. In 1869 it had been only $1,279,445. A gain of nearly 60 percent in three years is eloquent as to the speed of the industrial recuperation. And yet money was still scarce and local manufacturing had not come into its own. In August, 1871, the editor of the Times makes the following appeal:

"Money is so scarce that it may seem like mockery to talk about the establishing of manufacturing enterprises in our midst, but what is to be done? We must look to manufacturings for its (the town's) future development. Railroads will be of little avail without them. Something must be done, else our mechanics will be compelled to cast their lots with other communities, where there is more life and activity. Upwards of $150,000 has been paid out by our citizens since the war for boots and shoes, which could have been made here at a smaller cost, and $250,000 has been paid for freight alone upon agricultural machinery used in the Lower Valley."

In the following year, the citizens of the town were taking steps to remedy the conditions complained of. Mayor Huck issued a call for a public meeting to take action in advancing the business interests and general prosperity of Winchester. The gathering in the town hall, February 3, was large and enthusiastic.

A committee of five headed by Major Holmes Conrad drafted a report closing with these resolutions:

And whereas it is also apparent that these advantages (location, climate, suitability for manufacturing, present and prospective rail lines) are now unsought, and these inducements withstood, as well from the want of capital and skill at home, as from the widespread though unfounded apprehension felt abroad, of local prejudice and sectional hostility—

Therefore Resolved, That we do now invite, and will cordially welcome, any who may come with an honest purpose of engaging in any lawful business, and we do guarantee to all such, of whatever political or religious faith, the fullest protection of person and property.

Resolved, That to any such persons who may establish in our midst manufactures of any kind, we will extend such reasonable immunity from municipal taxation as may be necessary or desirable to stimulate and foster the enterprise.

Resolved, That a committee be appointed from the citizens of Winchester with authority to use such means as they may think proper to induce immigration; to encourage the establishment of manufactures in our midst and consider and facilitate our railroad connections.

R. T. Barton, in showing how Winchester had fallen from her first estate explained that the great trade of the Southwest and East Tennessee had been tapped by Southern roads making a shorter exit than the Virginia Central and Manassas Gap roads. The Baltimore and Ohio had greatly narrowed the back country, and the projected Shenandoah Valley railroad threatened to take off another slice. A network has been formed that the very roads which have injured us can be used with a little extension of those not far from our town to restore the lost trade. The narrow extent of country left for agricultural resources makes it necessary to foster manufacturing interests.

Gen. W. S. Calohan, who came from Pennsylvania after the close of the war, said he felt as much home here as there. He had

THE RECENT PERIOD 255

told Northerners writing him that there was no more peaceful and hospitable people under the sun, and that life and property were more secure here than in most of the Northern states he was acquainted with.

Mr. R. I. Kurtz recalled the time when 50 journeymen were making hats and nearly as many were engaged in tailoring; when all the furniture and cabinet work used here and for many miles around was made in Winchester, to say nothing of large wagon-making and turning establishments. About 1820 two paper mills and two nail factories were supplying Pennsylvania and Tennessee in a large degree. Living is cheap and raw materials are cheap, yet within three years 95 industrious young men have left Winchester.

The growth of an optimistic spirit would appear to have cropped out in the holiday week of 1873, when the Times relates that never since the war was so much powder burned as on Christmas Day. There was an increasing fusillade from before daybreak until late at night. Public behavior was of the best and there was little intoxication.

In 1874 Mr. C. M. Gibbens was collecting material for a history of Winchester to the close of the civil war. Had this intention been carried out, the present volume would in a great measure have been anticipated by 50 years. It has been the observation of the writer that nearly every community has, or has had, its would-be local historian, who, however, seldom gets to work. In practice, the very fact that he is a resident counts heavily against him.

In honor of the Confederate chieftain, who had just passed away at his post of duty as president of Washington College, the citizens of Winchester numerously assembled, October 22, 1870, to adopt resolutions on the memory of General Robert E. Lee. Very nearly eleven years later—September 26, 1881—the courthouse and other buildings were draped, and there was an almost entire suspension of business, because of the funeral of President Garfield. In the morning there was a tolling of bells, and there were union services in the Lutheran and Episcopal churches.

In the course of our story we have given the brief pen-portraits of Winchester that have been left by early visitors. The town is thus mentioned in 1871 by a correspondent of the New Orleans Picayune:

"Winchester is a quaint old town of the antique English type. Prim, yet comely, stiff yet graceful, as though proud of its prestige and glorying in the hereditary honors that have come down to it from past times, it looks like one of the oldest of the progeny of the venerated Mother of States."

Beginning in 1889 an epidemic of town booming spread the entire length of the Valley of Virginia. With a touch of sarcasm, one of the editors of this region remarked that the time seemed to be near when passenger trains could make only 10 miles an hour between Harper's Ferry and Bristol, since the distance of nearly 400 miles was in prospect of becoming one continuous string of municipalities.

The Equity Improvement Company of Winchester was chartered January 25, 1890 with an authorized capital of $1,000,000. The president was John Handley of Scranton, Pennsylvania, and the secretary was Charles L. Crum of Winchester. The directors were Albert Baker, W. H. Baker, R. T. Barton, Dr. W. A. Bell, T. J. Cooper, P. C. Gore, S. H. Hansbrough, P. W. Hunter, Dr. W. P. McGuire, J. B. Russell, and R. W. Stone. The company was a little late in the field in view of the general collapse of town booms that soon occurred. But 1500 acres of ground were purchased and the Winchester Inn was built on the south side of Stewart Street near the Cumberland Valley station. The hotel proved a white elephant, and though it cost $100,000, it was sold after ten years for a little more than one-third of that sum, and was subsequently torn down.

The list given below of the business houses of 1880, when compared with a list of the present year, goes to prove that long life under a given management is not usually true of mercantile institutions.

M. D. Albin & Bro.	W. T. Gilbert	F. F. Oehm
Baetjer & Co.	J. D. Goshert	M. H. Reardon & Bro.
Baker & Co.	Mrs. C. A. Harman	W. Mason Robinson
Battle & Wheat	P. Heller	Rosenberger & Grove
Bell Bros.	C. A. Helm	Russell & Bro.
T. M. Bantz	Keating Bros.	A. N. Ryan
——— Blakner	G. W. Keller	Shoemaker & Griffith
Boon & Tolley	Henry Kenzel	Sibert & Denny
F. H. Bowley	Nathan Kohn	German Smith
Louis Bowley	G. W. Kurtz	John Vilwig
G. W. Bowley	Lloyd Logan	T. T. Wall
——— Calvert	John T. Lupton & Co.	J. C. Wheat
H. W. Clemm	T. N. Lupton	D. H. Wolfensparger
R. Colinsky	C. W. McVicar	Frederick Woolfert
Conway & Spellman	J. C. Maxwell & Co.	Henry Woolfert
J. R. Edmonds	Joseph A. Nulton	

In the antebellum era Winchester was eminently a commercial and manufacturing center. In the industrial revival following the war, the town still made a considerable showing. Among the industries of 1886 were four glove factories, three furniture factories, five tanneries, two foundries, one shoe factory, one flour mill, one farm implement factory, one soap factory, and one sumach and bark mill. The list does not include a paper mill, which was employing 50 hands in 1890, nor a broom factory, in operation in 1876. The glove industry was far in the lead, the four factories in this line employing 600 hands. The Graichen Glove Factory alone, which opened in 1852, was employing 450 persons, and its yearly payroll was $100,000. Winchester had long been famous for its gloves, and F. August Graichen, a native of Germany, brought with him the best technical knowledge of the industry that Europe could supply.

In 1900 there were still 72 plants, employing 635 hands. Their capital was $561,640 and their output for the year was $890,493. But though some of the old-time industries have either declined or have wholly disappeared, the newer manufactures, few in number, are nevertheless of much importance.

The story of the Valley apple has become increasingly intertwined with the story of Winchester.

In relating this development, the name of George Washington appears almost at once. The first president was primarily a farmer, and he spoke of agriculture as the "most noble and most useful employment of man." A deed given by him in 1776 required the purchaser to set out 100 winter apple trees and 100 peach trees. This orchard was the largest in the Valley at that time, and is said to have been the first one on Apple Pie Ridge. The position of it is a little to the north of the line separating Frederick from Berkeley.

A few years later many trees were planted on the same ridge by Hessian prisoners of war. Some endured for a century or upward, and yielded a hundred bushels to the tree. It was thus that the famous ridge acquired its name.

Before the war of 1861, Charles J. Faulkner predicted that the Lower Valley was destined to become one of the greatest apple-growing regions in the world. The first commercial orchard was begun in 1871 by John S. Lupton, and his friends wondered whether he were not a fit subject for an examination by an alienist. But as in the case of the Nebraska "blockhead" who planted a field to popcorn, and thereby revolutionized the agricultural interest of a whole county, the venture of Mr. Lupton was amply justified by the result. He started with 50 acres, but his orchard grew until it embraced 4000 acres, and brought an income of from $150,000 to $300,000.

In 1871 the merchantable apple crop of the Winchester district amounted to only about $25,000. In 1899 the yield was 240,000 barrels, the largest ever yet known. Three years later the sales amounted to $1,500,000. In 1905 there were 100,000 trees, and the shipment of the season was 1,000,000 bushels. In 1912 the number of trees was reported at 758,067, and nearly one-half of these were in bearing. In 1923 the apple crop of Frederick was more than four times greater than that of Augusta, its nearest competitor in Virginia.

Before the close of the nineteenth century, it was seen that Mr. Faulkner was entirely correct in his forecast. The soil and climate of the Lower Valley are exceptionally well suited to apple culture, and it is one of only three districts in the Atlantic States where the pippin thrives. The apple industry has become the leading agricultural interest, and is largely participated in by the citizens of Winchester themselves. The cold storage of apples, the canning and evaporating of the medium grades, and the making of vinegar, have gone very far to compensate the town for the partial or complete disappearance of tanning and some other lines of manufacture.

Within the Winchester district are now 355 commercial orchards, containing almost 700,000 trees, and representing a capital in this line of $7,000,000. In an average year the amount paid to apple pickers is $500,000. Winchester has become the largest apple storage center in the East, and it possesses the largest apple by-products plant in the world. The magnitude of the orchard interests has led to the inauguration of "Apple Blossom Day," the first observance of which took place May 3, 1924, and was witnessed by 30,000 spectators. The parade of floats was two miles in length. The success of the spectacle was such as to call out the admiration of the visitors who had witnessed exhibits of similar character in other states of the Union.

The leading industrial concerns of Winchester, given in the order of the number of persons they employ, are these:

Virginia Woolen Mills.
National Fruit Product Company.
Winchester Cold Storage Company.
Robinson Ice and Cold Storage Company.
Lewis Jones Knitting Company.

THE RECENT PERIOD 259

Shenandoah Valley Apple, Cider, and Vinegar Company.
Winchester Woolen Mills.
Owen and Trenary Glove Company.
Winchester Milling Corporation.

The voting record of Winchester, when compared with that of Frederick county, shows a tendency to cleavage in the party affiliations of the two communities. The county has always been the more pronounced in its adhesion to the Democratic fold. After the war, and until the going into effect of the constitution of 1902, the city was sometimes debatable ground. Even yet, in important elections, the minority party has the support of about two-fifths of the present electorate. As was generally true of the Valley of Virginia, the Constitutional Convention of 1902 did not have the cordial support of this community, and it was opposed by the local convention of 1900.

The first homicide in Winchester, subsequent to the civil war, was the murder in 1883 of Caroline Lee by John E. Barbour. The next was the killing of one McFall by two negroes, both of whom were hanged. The crime was committed in the jollification following the election of 1884. The most recent homicide appears to have been the shooting of C. J. Carpenter by a negro in May, 1913. The victim was an Ohio man domiciled in Winchester as an agent. But in 1885-1891, the docket of the court was loaded with felony cases.

An aftermath of the war of the sixties was a recession of the temperance wave that was sweeping the Union in the preceding decade, and that did not reassert itself in earnest for twenty years. In 1869 the Times bitingly remarks that, "the distillery of Mr. Guiselman near the Opequon is now turning out twenty barrels of whiskey a day. We suppose it requires nearly this much daily for Winchester and Berryville, from the number of drinking houses they support." Nearly forty years later, when the city was maintaining eleven saloons, one of the local pastors wrote that, "I had seen more drunkenness and had heard more profanity in the streets and public places of Winchester during the two days preceding Christmas, than I had seen or heard during a four years pastorate in Baltimore." But in August, 1910, when 943 of the 1043 voters went to the polls, local option carried by a majority of 151. The vote in 1913 was still more decisive. With the coming in of the dry regime, the Evening Star at once excluded liquor advertisements from its columns, and thereby set an example in the upholding of law that has not been followed by certain metropolitan journals.

From the viewpoint of historic architecture, Winchester probably contains more of interest than any other American town not on the seaward side of the Appalachians. There are the very old, the old, the near-new, the new, and the ultra-modern, and all these variations in housebuilding may sometimes be observed within a short compass. The log houses of the type described in the Act of 1752 have perhaps all disappeared, yet some log houses remain, even though the walls are weatherboarded. Likewise very few specimens remain of the roughly built stone houses that accompanied the early log structures. But of the solidly built stone houses reared by Hessian stonemasons, a number yet stand and some of them will long remain. Next in point of age are the brick mansions of a cream-white or pale-lilac hue. Somewhat more recent are the antebellum brick houses, where the red color of the brickwork is retained. Of varying grades of modernity are the cottages of brick or frame which are most numerous on the borders of the city. In the older quarters, one may soon pass from a series of commodious houses of brick, concrete, or frame, each within an ample lot, to a series of very unpretentious houses of wood, differing widely in structural designs, but nearly always on very narrow lots.

The old buildings are slowly yet steadily giving place to others of modern design. But for many years to come, the visitors to the old Capital of the Northern Neck will undoubtedly see a number of colonial mansions where the windows and doors in front may not be of the same pattern as those at the rear, because modernized. On the door is a well-polished brass knocker, yet there may also be a call bell at one side. The windows of the third story are of half-height, or there may be dormer windows in the roof. Where the gable-end is perhaps a blank wall, it may be overgrown with ivy, even to the broad summits of the twin chimneys. And a few business houses may long remain where twelve large lights appear in each window-sash.

Possibly the oldest house in Winchester is the one on the northeast corner of Cork and Braddock. In part the walls are of undressed limestone, and in part of log. For the better preservation of the narrow building, the log-end is faced with planed boards. Although the claim has been questioned, the evidence appears conclusive that this is the place where Washington says he worked out his surveying notes while in the employ of Fairfax. In 1908 the property was purchased for $2460 by the city of Winchester, to be preserved as a historic memorial, under the control of a commission elected by the city council. The lot, 78 by 150 feet, lies open and may be regarded as a miniature park. In it are three field cannon, one of which, pointing toward Cumberland, was left at Alexandria by Braddock. The ten marking stones came from the Blue Ridge, the Opequon Presbyterian church, the old Lutheran church at Winchester, the Shenandoah River, Glen Burnie, Fort Loudoun, Shawnee Spring, Greenway Court, Yost Hite's fort, and the grave of General Adam Stephen. The tablets on the wall bear these legends:

"While in the employ of Lord Fairfax, of Greenway Court, this building was from time to time during 1749-1753 used by George Washington as a surveyor's office.

"While engaged in supervising the erection of Fort Loudoun, 1756-57, Lieutenant Colonel Washington, then in command of the frontier, occupied this building. At this time the adjoining lot, extending from Wolfe Street to Cork Street, was used as a stockade, within which were quartered three companies of militia, detailed from the Virginia line and stationed at Winchester, then the principal frontier post in the Shenandoah Valley.

"During the years 1758-61 Colonel Washington represented Winchester and Frederick County in the House of Burgesses, the sessions of which were then held in Williamsburg, the colonial capital of Virginia."

Another very early dwelling is the now vacant stone house built near the Shawnee Spring by Abraham Hollingsworth in 1754.

On the rise of ground on the north side of Amherst between Washington and Stewart, is the big, yellowish, stuccoed mansion in which General Daniel Morgan breathed his last. The western portion was built in 1790, the eastern side being more recent. Still older is the massive stone house in the southeast angle of Cork and Main. It was completed in 1783 or the year previous, and was known for two generations as the Red Lion Hotel. The three-story brick building with many-paned windows which lies diagonally opposite, is much more recent, as is indicated by the date—1827—in the gable.

In his reminiscences on early Winchester, William G. Russell speaks of a number of ancient houses, but as he wrote fifty years ago, some of them have disappeared. Others are mentioned in the next paragraph.

Judge Robert White lived on Washington near Cecil, in one of the earliest of the brick houses. In the block by Washington,

Stewart, Germain, and Pall Mall, was the stone house of General James Singleton, built about 1805. The stone house at the northwest corner of Main and Germain was built about 1790. In the corner of Main and Leicester a house stood the same in 1873 as in 1773. North of the old Lutheran parsonage, on Main at its south end, was the fine stone house of John Prince. Hessian prisoners were quartered here in the Revolution, and it was a rendezvous for the soldiers of 1812. A brick house on the east side of Main at the corner of Water was built in 1797 by William Holliday. One of the first homes in Winchester was that of Jacob Lantz on the south side of Piccadilly near Market. The mansion on the hill east of the City Hall was built by Dr. James Conrad about 1790. Until 1820 it was the home of the first bank in Winchester. When the goods arrived and were unpacked, it was found that all the twenty dollar notes had been stolen.

Still other ancient houses are spoken of in some of the preceding chapters. In the western border of the city is Glen Burnie, the home of Colonel James Wood, the founder of Winchester. Two miles north is Glengary, once the home of John R. Cooke, a lawyer of this city and the father of the two authors, Philip Pendleton Cooke and John Esten Cooke.

Jordan White Sulphur Spring is five miles northeast of Winchester, yet may not inappropriately be mentioned. Until after the coming of the paleface it was a favorite resort of the red men. The large brick house built here by Branch Jordan in 1834 burned in 1876. Burnt Factory, nearby, was once a village, being created by Carter's paper mill. There was afterward a woolen mill also.

The census of 1920 gave Winchester a population of 3200 males and 3683 females, a total of 6883, or almost exactly twice the number in 1840 and at least eight times as many as in 1760. But the enrollment in the public schools appears to indicate an increase in the present year to quite 8000. The additional growth is due mainly to the Handley School and the apple industry.

In conclusion, it can be said of the "Queen City of the Valley", for the close of the first quarter of the twentieth century, that it has an exceptionally low tax rate; that its bank resources are $8,500,000; that in 1923 the sum of $700,000 was spent in new buildings; that its industrial plants employ 1000 persons; and that the completion of a new macadamized road places Winchester within 75 miles of the National Capital.

From the manuscript report prepared for the Virginia War History Commission, we compile the following summary relative to the share taken in that great event by the city of Winchester.

The city and county exceeded their quotas in both men and money, and an unusual number of their men received commissions in the Army and Navy. The women of both communities rendered service that was very energetic and very successful. And this record stands against the fact that here as elsewhere there were some pacifists and obstructionists.

Company I, recalled from the Rio Grande, and mustered out of service at the end of February, 1917, was summoned to the colors within a month, and attached to the One Hundred and Sixteenth Infantry. The company was on the battle-front October 4 to December 25, participated in six engagements, and sustained a loss of more than 100 men out of a maximum strength of 251. Its training began at Camp McClellan, Alabama, and was continued four months in France.

In the successful attack on Malbrouck Hill, October 8, Robert Y. Conrad, captain of Company I, was mortally wounded. His death was deeply regretted. Harold R. Dinges succeeded him as captain.

April 18, 100 Boy Scouts, under the lead of Scoutmaster L. Marshall Baker, marched to the plaza and formally dedicated their services to the Nation. Through their own efforts there were sales of Liberty Bonds to the extent of $145,900.

A little earlier in the same month, two corps of high school cadets went into training that they might become the nucleus of a Home Guard. But in March a home guard of men above the draft age was organized under the leadership of Captain Logan R. Fay. Its services were several times called upon, and always with good result.

The war activities of the various churches of the city were largely in the nature of team-work. All the congregations were very active, yet to a great extent separate records have not been preserved. The Rev. William D. Smith, rector of Christ Church, headed one of the Liberty Loan drives, was chairman of the local Red Cross, and went to the front as a chaplain.

So many of the teachers and older pupils went into the military training schools that the problem of keeping open the public schools became serious. In the one military school of Winchester, every single member of military age was in some branch of the service.

The consolidated Registration Board for Winchester and Frederick was composed of Luther Pannett, chairman, Joseph B. Newlin, and Dr. W. P. Boyd. There were many letters of commendation from the War Department to the chairman and secretary. All the members of the local bar served on the Legal Advisory Board, assisted in filling in the questionnaires, and gave such professional advice to the Boards and the registrants as was necessary. When a draftee was exempted, it was only because such individual had proved his claim to exemption or to be placed in a deferred classification.

One of the home activities was the creating of a War Chest of $60,000, the fund being in charge of H. B. McCormac.

The city and county oversubscribed all their quotas in Liberty Loans, and contributed much more than their quotas in every activity calling for money and supplies. With a population of less than 20,000 in 1920, the aggregate of subscriptions by the two communities to the five Liberty Loans was in excess of $5,000,000. Important help in the financial drives was given by the school children.

The conservation of both food and fuel was stressed in every way. The flower garden became a potato patch; the old men, the boys, the wives and the sisters took the places, in an economic sense, of the men who had gone to the camps; and as a result, crops in greater abundance than ever before were harvested. Even the great apple crop of 1918 was secured, though with the help of men detailed from the camps, and women who came as volunteers from other states. And this achievement was in spite of the epidemic of influenza in the fall of the same year. The scourge was hard to deal with, since only three physicians remained in Winchester and the trained nurses had volunteered for hospital work overseas. Hundreds of the population were smitten, yet among the townspeople the fatalities were few. On the other hand, there was no small number of deaths among the soldiers detailed to save the apple crop.

The activities of the Red Cross chapter were many, varied, and arduous, and great quantities of supplies were sent overseas.

An incident of much more than local effect was furnished by Erasmus Baker, an aged mountaineer. On a cold day he walked from his home to Winchester, a distance of more than fifteen miles, and put $3000—his entire life savings—into Liberty Bonds. The old gentleman did not think he was doing any more than his plain duty, but the story of his patriotic act was scattered widely by the metropolitan press, and served as an inspiration to many.

The only soldier from Winchester who was captured and held as a prisoner by the Germans was Charles L. Worthington, who enlisted in a Canadian command. He received many comforts and delicacies from his friends in Winchester, Canada, and elsewhere. While a prisoner of war he subscribed for $500 in Liberty Bonds.

APPENDIX

A

INHABITANTS OF 1788

The following is the list of the holders of taxable personal property in Winchester in 1788, according to the return by John Conrad, commissioner.

In the first column are the names of the persons chargeable with a tax on personal property. In the second column are the names of other tithables in the household. Where a name is starred, it belongs also in the second column. In the third column is the number of horses owned by the householder, and in the fourth is the number of the slaves.

Albert, Adam *	Simon Albert, James Welch	1	
Aldridge, Henry *			
Aldridge, Michael *	Frederick Aldridge		
Alexander, William *		1	
Anderson, Adam *	Jacob Anderson	1	
Anson, William *			
Armstrong, Maxwell *			
Armstrong, William *	John Boyle	1	
Anderson, Joseph	cleared by the court	1	
Anderson, Nathan *	Solomon Yocum	1	
Bailey, Abraham *			
Bailey, John *	Adam Howling		
Baker, Henry *	George, Jacob, John, Joseph Baker	3	2
Baker, Andrew *			
Baker, Henry William *		1	
Baldwin, Cornelius Dr. *		1	2
Ball, William *	David Little, John Everly		
Balmain, Alexander *		2	2
Barclay, John		1	
Barnhart, Peter *			
Beatty, Henry *		1	2
Benart, Frederick *			
Bennet, Robert *			
Berger, Jacob *			
Bost, George *			
Bowen, Richard *			
Bowen, Philip *			
Bowman, John *		2	

Appendix

Brady, John (tavern)*		1	3
Brown, Frederick *			
Brown, William *			
Bunker, Catharine	Peter Coleman	1	
Burger, Jacob *			
Burk, John *			
Bush, Henry *	Thomas Helm, Lewis Huff, Thomas Morrow	2	
	Samuel Hartings, Jonas Hauge, Thomas Glover		
Bowman, George Adam *			
Bush, Philip, Sr. (ordinary)*		4	2
Bush, William *			
Calvert, Samuel *		1	
Carkmore, Edward *			
Carron, Joseph *			
Carter, Robert *			
Carter, Hugh *		2	
Carter, Ezekiel *			
Caster, Michael *			
Chandler, Goldsmith *	John Whipple	1	
Chisler, Michael *	John Chisler	3	
Christie, Archibald *			
Clark, Thomas *			
Conrad, Frederick, Sr. *	Frederick Conrad Jr., Daniel Conrad, Joe Taffs, Nicholas Sink, Mathias Bush	7	4
Conrad, John *	Robert Gray	1	
Cook, John *			
Cooley, Joseph *			
Copenhavner, John *		1	
Copenhavner, Michael *			
Coyle, John *			
Craford, Hans *			
Craigen, Robert, Sr. *		7	2
Crockwell, John, Sr. *	John Crockwell, Jr.		
Cromwell, Margaret		1	
Crosby, William *			
Cooper, Hamilton *	Francis Givan	1	
Cooper, Spencer *			
Craigen, Robert, Jr. *			
Dalby, Philip *			
Deadrick, Thomas *			
Delaplain, Benjamin *		5	
Dobbins, Thomas *		2	

Donaldson, John (ordinary)* 5 5
Dowdall, James Gamble * ...Edward McGuire, Gabriel Nurse, William Worthington, John Dowdall ....
Duffield, John * ....Abner Jones—chaise 3 2

Edmonson, James * ....
Edmonson, Mary ....Magnus Tate—ordinary and billiard table 1
Edmonson, Thomas * ....Samuel Edmonson—ordinary 4 3
Egin, James * ....Marcus Nooler 1
Egin, Thomas * 2 1
Ellis, Leonard * 1
Ellison, Robert, Sr. * 6
Evans, Thomas * 2 1

Fleming, John * ....
Fridley, Henry * ....
Fry, Christian * 6 1

Gibson, Andrew * ....
Goodnight, John * ....
Gray, Richard * ....John Tidball, Patrick Dougherty .. 2 1
Grim, Peter * 1

Haas, Frederick * ....John Haas, Joshua Baker, Amos Haas 7
Haymaker, John * ....
Haymaker, John, Sr. * ......Adam Haymaker ....
Haymaker, Adam * ....John Haymaker ....
Hazelwood, Robert * 1
Headley, Isaac * ....
Holding, Elias * ....
Hollensworth, Libediah * ....
Holliday, James * ....William Holliday, Edward McGarey 3
Holmes, Joseph * ....Alexr. King, David Holmes 1 1
Holtzel, Henry * ....Charles Holtzel 2
Hoover, Philip * ....
Huff, John * (post) 2
Huffman, Jacob * 2
Hulet, Charles * ....
Hyskill, Adam * ....John Walters ....
Hyskill, Christn * ....Joseph Willert, James Wood 1
H———? ....Jacob Harmon, William Rutherford, Peter Michler ....
H———? ....William Holliday, Adam Butler, Adam Douglass 2 wheeled chaise 8 2
(Both the above places blank in record book)

Appendix

Japson, George * ....
Jenny, Abel * ....Joshua Baker, Amos Jenny 1
Jones, Joseph H. * ....
Jones, Peter * ....
Justice, Michael * ....

Kearn, John * ....Richard Boyce 3 2
Kennedy, David * ....James Cunningham ....
Kertchavel, John * ....2 wheeled chaise 2 2
Kiger, Adam * ....
Kiger, Andrew * ....
Klipstine, Philip * ....doctor 1
Kreamer, Conrad * 1
Krebs, Conrad * ....
Kurts, Adam * ....
Kurts, Frederick * ....
Kiger, George * ....John Quaker 2 1
Kennedy, Patrick * ....

Laubinger, Barbara 1
Lauck, Peter * ....Henry Upt, Jacob True—ordinary 1
Lent, Conrad * ....
Lindsey, James * ....
Lindsey, Michael * ....
Liney, John * ....
Linty, John * 1
Long, Robert * ....Thomas Long 2
Loughridge, George * 3
Love, Samuel * 1
Lynn, George * ....William Clinter 2
Lauck, Simon * ....Henry Stair 1

McAlester, James * ....John Curtis 2
McAlester, John * ....Nimrod Gresby 1
McDonald, Archibald * ....
McDougle, Thomas * 1
McGuire, Edward * ....John Walker—ordinary 5 2
McMullin, William * 1
McMun, George * ....John Murrell, John Aldridge 1
Macky, Robert * ....doctor 6 5
Magill, Archibald * ....
Magill, John * ....Humphrey Murphy 2
Magson, Marmaduke * ....
March, Michael * ....
Mason, Samuel * ....
Maugholt, F. L. * ....
May, Samuel * ....Samuel May, Jr., William Henry .. 3 3
Medlicott, James * ....doctor ....

Messmore, Nichs * ....William Grossett 1
Millburn, Robert * 1
Miller, Daniel * ....
Miller, Godfrey * ....apothecary 1
Miller, Michael * ....
Miller, William * 1
Murphy, Duncan * ....
Magill, Charles * 2 1

Nealis, John * ....
Newman, John * ....William Babcock, William Kean ..
Nolden, John * ....
Norton, Daniel * ....John Summerville, Charles Grimes 1
Norton, George L. * 1
Norton, John H. * ....John Norton * 2 7

O'Neal, Charles * ....
Osburn, David * ....Thomas Hollis 1
Overacre, George * ....Thomas Overacre 1
Overacre, Daniel * ....Godlove Boyer ....
Owram, Thomas * 1

Passmore, Joseph * ....
Payton, John * 2
Pealing, John * ....
Pearce, James * ....
Poe, Balser * ....
Poker, Jacob * ....John Will 1
Powers, Edward * ....Robert Inman 2
Pringle, George * ....
Pue, Jesse * 1
Pulley, Christian * 1
Pyles, William * ....Henry Burkhart, Christian Burkhart, Samuel Ball 1

Reandle, John * 3
Richardson, William * .....2 wheeled chaise 1
Righter, Christian * ....
Riley, Martin * ....Michael Riley, Robert Curtis 1
Rise, Christn * ....
Ritter, George M. * ....
Russell, David * 1
Rutter, Jacob * 5

Sherard, Robert * 1
Shrock, William * ....
Shultz, John * ....Thomas More 2 wheeled chaise .. 1
Sitler, Isaac * ....Joe Delaplain ....
Slater, Edward * ....Robert Morrow ....

Appendix

Smith, John * .... John Bogan ....
Smith, John * ....
Smith, Thomas * ....
Smith, Mahlon * .... Lewis Reese 2 wheeled chaise ..
Sommer, Michael * ....
Sommerset, Thomas ....
Sowers, Daniel * .... 14(?)
Sowers, Jacob * .... 12(?)
Sperry, John * 1
Sperry, Michael * ....
Sperry, Jacob .... David Smith 2
Stewart, Thomas * ....
Streit, Christn * .... 2 wheeled chaise 3
Swords, William * 1
Shuller, Conrad * 1
Sherar, Philip * ....

Thomas, John * 1
Thompson, John * 1
Thrasher, Richard * ....
True, William * ....

Updegraff, Nathan * .... George Craft, John McKinney ... 1

Vanhorn, Abraham * .... stud horse—15s 1

Wade, Thomas * ....
Walker, James * .... Henry Clough, Andrew Sprecher,
                            William Star 1
Waller, Benjamin * ....
Walters, John * .... ordinary 2
Warior, Daniel * ....
Weedon, Nathaniel * 1 1
Welch, Thomas * ....
Wells, Robert * 1
Whetsel, Christopher * ..... George Runner 1
White, Robert (exempt) ... John Baker 3 2
Willey, Allen * 1
Williamson, Thomas * ....
Willis, Nathaniel * .... Henry Willcocks ....
Windle, Peter * 2
Windle, Samuel * ....
Wolf, Lewis * 1 1
Woodrow, Isaac 1
Young, Adam * ....

B

LOT-OWNERS, 1782

The following is a list of the owners of lots in Frederick county for the First Battalion of the local militia, and for the year 1782. At that time the territory covered by a company, battalion, or regiment of the militia was treated as a political subdivision of a county. Each person had one lot unless the number is otherwise specified. The list, however, does not distinguish whether the property were in Winchester or elsewhere. But nearly all, at least, of the lots were situated here.

Albert, Adam		Friedley, Elizabeth	
Aldred, Michael		Fry, Christopher	6½
Allison, Robert	2	Gilkeson, Samuel	2½
Anderson, Adam		Glazier, Christian	
Anderson, Henry	½	Grim, Charles	
Anderson, Jacob	2	Grim, Jacob	
Anderson, Peter		Grim, John	
Ashby, Edward		Haas, Frederick	2
Baker, Henry		Harden, George	
Beatty, Henry		Haymaker, Adam	
Boyd, Andrew		Haymaker, John	3-4
Brinker, Catharine		Heiskell, Christopher	3
Brown, Jacob		Heiskell, Adam	½
Bruin, Bryan	4	Helm, George	
Bush, Philip	6	Helphinstine, Catharine	
Calms, Lucey	1-3	Helphinstine, Philip	3
Campbell, William	½	Hoff, Lewis	
Cain, John	2	Holding, Elias	½
Carleton, Hugh		Holliday, James	
Chisler, Michael		Holliday, William	4
Chandler, Gold	½	Holmes, Joseph	1-3
Copenhaver, Michael	2	Hoover, Philip	½
Craigen, Robert	2	Hutchinson, James	
Conrad, Frederick	9	Kennedy, David	3-4
Curts, Adam	2	Kiger, Andrew	
Curts, Frederick		Kiger, George	
Deaderick, David	1½	Kirk, Robert	3
Dearing, Henry	½	Lantz, John	
Denny, Henry		Lemley, John	2
Dent, Arthur		Lindsey, James	2½
Dick, Peter		Lobinger, Barbara	½
Donaldson, John	2-3	Louck, Peter	
Dowdall, John G.	8½	Lynn, George	
Dromgoole, Alexander	½	McCord, Arthur	
Duffield, John	4	McDonald, Ann	
Eagen, Thomas	1-5	McDugal, Thomas	

McGuire, Edward	4	Shoemaker, George	
Mackey, Robert (doctor)		Sidler, Isaac	½
May, Samuel		Smith, Edward	
Messmore, Nicholas		Smith, Thomas	½
Michler, Peter	3	Sovain, Abraham	3
Miller, Michael		Sowers, Daniel	½
Miller, Godfrey	3	Sowers, Jacob	½
Mitchell, Robert		Sowers, John	1-3
Murray, Patrick		Sperry, Michael	2
Neill, Abraham		Sperry, Catharine	
Neill, John	½	Sperry, Jacob	
Otto, Catharine	2	Steer, Isaac	½
Overacre, George		Strowl, Adolph	3
Pancoast, Daniel		Sowards, William	
Peyton, John		Troutwine, George Jacob	2
Poker, Jacob	1½	Underboome, Thomas	
Pooe, Balsor		Walker, James	
Pretty, Christopher	2	Wetzell, Christopher	2
Pyles, Joshua		White, Alexander	2
Pyles, William	½	Wilkes, Isaac	
Richardson, Joseph	1¼	Windle, Samuel	
Reynolds, John		Wolfe, Lewis	
Riley, Martin	½	Woolwine, Philip	1-3
Rupsomer, Eve		Wood, Thomas	
Rutter, John M.	4	Zane, Isaac	5

RECAPITULATION FOR 1783, FREDERICK COUNTY

White tithables	1263	tax	10 shillings
Slaves	2280	tax	10 shillings
Horses	4555	tax	2 shillings
Studs	21	tax	2 shillings
Cattle	8435	tax	3 pence
Wheels (carriages)	38	tax	6 shillings
Licenses	15	tax	5 pounds
Total tax	2439 pounds, 6 shillings, 9 pence ($8131.12)		

C

CIVIL OFFICERS

CLERKS OF FREDERICK

James Wood	1743-1759
Archibald Wager	1759-1762
James Keith	1762-1824
Thomas A. Tidball	1824-1856
Allen S. Tidball, appointee	1856
Thomas A. T. Riely	1856-1858

274 THE STORY OF WINCHESTER IN VIRGINIA

R. E. Seevers, appointee 1858
James P. Riely 1858-1859
J. C. Riely 1859-1865
C. W. Gibbens, military appointee ....
C. M. Gibbens 1870
J. M. Sherrard 1870-1873
James P. Riely Jr. 1873-1887
Thomas K. Cartmell 1887-

JUSTICES, 1779-1852

Baker, Samuel	1808	Gilkeson, John	1824
Baker, James	1817	Gold, Daniel	1824
Baker, Samuel, Jr.	1819	Gore, Joshua	1799
Baker, Robert L.	1836	Gray, Joseph G.	1836
Baker, Jacob	1843	Hall, James B.	1831
Ball, John S.	1808	Hays, John	1825
Baldwin, Robert T.	1824	Heironomus, Jacob	1811
Baldwin, Cornelius E.	1824	Heiskell, John	1824
Barton, Richard W.	1831	Hite, Cornelius B.	1840
Berkeley, Robert	1811	Hite, Isaac F.	1843
Berry, Joseph	1824	Hite, Walker M.	1843
Bell, John	1813	Jolliffe, John	1801
Blake, Joseph	1799	Jones, William S.	1819
Blakemore, George	1798	Kackley, Jonathan	1824
Blakemore, George N.	1824	Lockhart, Jonah	1831
Brent, Charles Jr.	1811	Long, Joseph	1847
Brookings, James B.	1836	Lovett, Daniel	1843
Bruce, John	1847	Lynn, William	1811
Buck, Thomas	1783	Lynn, George	1811
Burgess, James H.	1847	McCoole, Lewis	1808
Burwell, Nathaniel	1825	McCormick, Dawson	1825
Carson, Beatty	1813	McGuire, Edward	1802
Carson, Simon	1819	Magill, John S.	1840
Castleman, William	1804	Marshall, James M.	1804
Clark, Charles E.	1831	Marshall, Robert M.	1831
Collins, Daniel	1843	Meade, David	1816
Cooke, William	1804	Miller, Abraham	1831
Cox, Samuel	1847	Miller, John W.	1836
Cramer, Thomas	1824	Mason, Seth	1836
Davidson, Edward J.	1838	Mason, James W.	1847
Davis, Baalis	1815	Neill, Joseph	1840
Davisson, John S.	1831	Newman, John	1815
Drew, Dolphin	1811	Norris, George H.	1817
Gamble, Joseph	1813	O'Rear, Moses	1801
Gardner, Samuel	1824	Page, William B.	1815
Gardner, Nash L.	1831	Parkins, Alfred	1847
Gibson, James	1831	Phifer, Elijah	1836

Appendix

Pugh, John W. 1824
Pyfer, John W. 1847
Reed, George 1819
Richards, John 1831
Richards, Henry W. 1836
Riely, James P. 1843
Rosenburg, William 1847
Rowland, William J. 1847
Russell, Moses 1802
Rust, John 1831
Senseny, Jacob 1836
Smith, John 1779
Smith, Charles 1798
Smith, Edward 1804
Smith, Treadwell 1816
Smith, Frederick 1819
Smith, E. J. 1824
Smith, Philip 1831
Smith, William 1847
Snickers, William 1811

Snyder, Richard M. 1836
Steel, Mager 1847
Stephenson, William 1819
Stribling, Francis 1824
Stribling, Taliaferro 1831
Taylor, Griffin 1808
Taylor, Mandley 1811
Taylor, Bushrod 1811
Tidball, Joseph 1804
Tilden, John B. 1799
Vance, Robert 1808
Vanmeter, William 1808
Ware, James 1809
White, Isaac 1783
White, John 1819
Whiting, Francis B. 1831
Wiggenton, James B. 1817
Wood, William 1825
Wright, George 1847

MAYORS AND RECORDERS

1804—Lewis Wolf
1805—Charles Magill
1806—Lewis Wolf
1807—Charles Brent
1808—Beatty Carson
1809—Charles Brent
1810—Beatty Carson
1811—Joseph Gamble
1843—James P. Riely
1843-47—George W. Seevers
1847—J. H. Sherrard
1865—Robert Y. Conrad
1868—George W. Ginn
1870—L. N. Huck
1872—J. B. T. Reed
1876—John C. Williams
1888-88—William M. Atkinson

Joseph Gamble—Recorder
Lewis Wolf—Recorder
Charles Magill—Recorder
Beatty Carson—Recorder
Charles Brent—Recorder
Beatty Carson—Recorder
Charles Brent—Recorder
Beatty Carson—Recorder
Lemuel Brent—Recorder

Joseph H. Sherrard—Recorder

Richard L. Gray—Recorder

SUPERVISORS

Anthony M. Kline (Chairman) 1870-1886
James W. Stephenson 1870-1882
Josiah Rinker 1870-1878
A. Wade Muse 1870
James A. Russell 1872

Jacob W. Richard 1874-1880
M. M. Adams 1879-1896
Martin Wisecarver 1879-1881
E. R. Thatcher 1881-1891
A. W. Dunlap 1881-1884
Charles E. Clevenger 1882-1884
John M. Silver 1884-1886
James K. McCann (Chairman) 1887-1897
Joseph A. Miller (Chairman) 1887-1892
Martin Wisecarver 1891-1897
William M. Dinges 1892-1897
R. Bruce Muse 1884-1893
James T. McIlwee 1897-1901
John W. Parish 1901-1904
H. P. Whitacre 1896-1908
James Cather 1897-1898
Clark Cather 1897-1908
James T. McIlwee 1904-1907
B. N. Lockhart 1908-

D

A list of men serving in the French and Indian war and adjudged by Mr. Cartmell to belong to the Lower Valley. The names were collected from those to whom some form of pension was subsequently paid. Where two names are identical a star is set down. It is not certain from the lists that two individuals were intended. All were privates, except when there is mention to the contrary.

Alfort, Thomas
Allen, John—Ensign
Allen, Thomas
Bageant, John
Bailey, Nathaniel
Bailey, Peter
Barr, James
Beatty, Henry
Beckman, John
Bell, George
Bennett, George
Bewtoole, Gasper
Black, George
Blackburn, Andrew
Blackburn, Benjamin
Blackburn, William
Blakeman, George
Braithwaite, William

Brook, Humphrey
Buckner, Philip P.
Buckus, Robert
Burkem, Solomon
Bush, Dennis
Camp, James
Capper, John
Campbell, John
Campbell, Owen
Carroll, Joseph
Cave, Reuben
Champain, John—Sergeant
Colbert, John
Colston, Charles
Conaly, Thomas
Cook, John
Combs, Josiah
Cooper, John

Appendix

Cooper, Leonard
Cox, Samuel
Crawford, Thomas
Cross, William
Degell, Edward
Dickson, John
Duckworth, John
Dunlevy, Anthony
Edwards, Peter
Ewings, John
Faucett, Joseph
Fiell, William
Fleming, Joseph
Foolam, Bang
Foster, James
Fulhone, Benjamin
Ghink, Will Elimus—doctor
Gooseberry, Robert
Gordon, Gilbert
Greenway, Joseph
Grigson, James
Grim, John
Haley, Daniel
Hall, William
Hamilton, James
Hampton, John
Haney, John
Harbinson, Matthew
Hardin, John *—Lieut.
Hardin, Mark
Haven, Edward
Hawkins, Richard
Hefferlin, John
Hensell, George
Horden, John—Ensign
Hudson, John
Hugh, James
Hughes, James
Hughes, William
Humble, Michael
Huston, James *
Jack, James
Jackson, Jesse
Jacobs, William
James, David
Jenkins, Edward
Job, Moses

Johnson, Daniel
Johnson, Stephen
Johnston, Daniel
Johnston, Hugh
Jones, James
Jones, John
Jones, Levi
Kenney, Patrick
Keyser, Andrew
Kiger, John
Kingore, William
Knipe, Henry
Kramer, Conrad
Laman, John
Lauck, Peter
Legat, James
Lender, Lawrence
Linsey, Edward
Linsey, Isaac *
Linsey, Thomas
Littleton, Charles—Sergeant
Littleton, Solomon
Lockard, William
Lonas, George *
Lucas, Basil
Lucas, Edward
Lyon, Joseph
McCormack, Francis
McCrimas, Francis
McDonald, A.
McDowell, Joseph—Ensign
M'Gill, John
McGuire, Andrew
McIntire, Nicholas
McKenney, Henry
McMullen, Alexander
Magill, John
Maginis, Francis
Marshall, James M.
Martin, Edward
Mason, Samuel
Mathews, William
Mauk, Daniel
Mauk, Henry
Mauk, Rendy
Mauk, Richard
Meamick, James

Mergee, Edward
Merger, Jacob
Miller, Daniel
Miller, John
Miller, William
Money,, Brian
Monroe, William
Morris, James
Morris, John
Murray, Richard
Murphy, Richard
Odle, Jeremiah
Odle, Jonathan
Oliver, James
Parke, John
Parrall, Hugh
Pearis, Robert
Perry, Holoway
Perry, Moses
Petanger, Peter
Philips, William
Pierce, Joseph
Piper, John
Pittman, Andrew
Polson, John
Price, Thomas
Prickett, Jacob
Regan, John
Rice, George
Riely, James
Robinson, Thomas
Ruddall, Archibald—Lieut.
Sampson, Joseph
Sargeant, Jeremiah
Schultz, John
Seifert, George
Selser, Henry—Sergeant
Shade, Jacob
Shirley, Jarvis
Shirley, Walter
Smith, John—Colonel
Southard, Stephen

Speak, Thomas *—Captain, Lieut., En.
Sperry, Jacob
Springer, Josiah
Stearman, Richard
Stephenson, Hugh
Stephenson, John *
Stephenson, William
Stradler, Stephen
Stewart, Robert
Stubbs, Samuel
Suthard, Samuel
Sweet, Benjamin
Tate, Magnus—Ensign
Taylor, John
Tharp, Thomas
Thomas, Isaac
Thompson, James
Thruston, James
Timmons, Edward
Treson, James *—Sergeant, Ensign
Tummens, Edward (same as Timmons?)
Turner, Anthony
Vance, Andrew
Vance, John *
Vance, Samuel
Van Landingham, George
Vanmeter, Henry
Vanmeter, Joseph
Wallbroke, Joseph
White, Isaac
White, Robert
White, William
Williams, David
Williams, Remembrance
Wilson, William
Wingfield, Owen
Wright, George *—Sergeant
Young, John

APPENDIX 279

FRENCH AND INDIAN WAR

List of soldiers from Frederick County and Winchester as shown by Act of General Assembly of Virginia, September 1758—32d George II, Hening's Statutes, Vol. 7, page 215.

(NOTE: This does not purport to be a complete list of soldiers. It does not include those serving in the regular military organizations, but only the militia.)

Archibald Ruddall, lieutenant; Henry Sesler, sergeant; John Jones; Jeremiah Odle; Moses Job; Reudy Mank; George Bennet; Jonathan Odle; James Thruston; Patrick M'Kenney; Richard Mank; Henry Mank; Daniel Mank; Henry M'Kenney; Nathaniel Bailey; Peter Bailey; William Cross; Richard Murphy; Thomas Speak, ensign; Charles Littleton, sergeant; Daniel Johnston; Stephen Suthard; Edward Linsey; Josiah Springer; Jacob Pricket; Stephen Stradler; Charles Colson; John Hampton; Samuel Mason; Peter Petanger; Francis M'Cormick; Thomas Alfort; Richard Stearman; Thomas Linsey; Robert Pearis; Thomas Speake, lieutenant; John Horden, ensign; William Matthew; John Stephenson; John Vance; James Meamack; James Morris; William Hall; William Miller; Benjamin Foolam; William Locard; Thomas Linsey; Levi Jones; Edward Martin; Josiah Springer; Mark Hardin; Solomon Burkem; Samuel Stubbs; Gilbert Gorden; George Bell; Charles Colson; James Grigson; George Rice; John Miller; William Jacobs; Joshua Ewings; Thomas Conaly; Isaac Lindsey; David James; Edward Tummens; Owen Wingfield; Walter Shirley; Robert Goosberry; Jarvis Shirley; John Parke; Isaac Thomas; James Jack; Hugh Johnson; James Jones; Francis Maginis; Joseph Lyon; Joseph M'Dowell, lieutenant; John Allen, ensign; James Ireson, sergeant; Thomas Allen; Andrew Blackburn; William Stephenson; John M'Gill; Benjamin Blackburn; Isaac White; Matthew Harbison; William Blackburn; Bryan Money; James Hughes; Joseph Fleming; William White; John Young; Joseph Taucett; John Capper; David Williams; Leonard Cooper; Joseph Carroll; John Cook; William Wilson; Samuel Vance; Andrew Vance; James Huston; William Hughes; John Cooper; Thomas Speak, captain; John Hardin, lieutenant; Magnus Tate, ensign; Charles Littleton, sergeant; John Champain, sergeant; Daniel Johnson; Stephen Suthard; James Lindsey; Thomas Lindsey; Jacob Pricket; Thomas Price; Robert Stewart; Stephen Johnson; Isaac Lindsey; John Regan; Edward Timons; John Hampton; John Colston; Solomon Litleton; Thomas Robinson; Edward Degell; Francis M'Crimar; Gasper Bewtoole; Hugh Stephenson; Edward Haven; John Hudson; Benjamin Fullom; John Vance; John Stephenson; Josiah Combs; James Morris; John Laman; James Legat; John Dickson; Holaway Perry; Joseph Pierce; Henry Vanmeter; Lawrence Lendar; Edward Mergee; Joseph Vanmeter; Jacob Mergee; Remembrance Williams; Joseph Polson; William Fiell; Nicholas M'Intire; Edward Lucas; Robert Buckus; Benjamin Sweet; John Taylor; Anthony Turner; John Allen, lieutenant; James Iresen, ensign; George Wright, sergeant; William Hughs; Bryan Money; John Magill; James Hugh; James Huston; John Cooper; James Camp; Richard Hankins; John Cook; Andrew Vance; Samuel Vance; John Duckworth; Joseph Greenway; Joseph Wattbroke; Anthony Dunlevy; William Wilson; John Vance; Will Elimus Ghink Doctor; Jesse Jackson.

E

The "Index of Revolutionary Soldiers," by W. T. R. Saffell includes the men serving in the Eleventh and Fifteenth regiments under General Daniel Morgan in 1777-1778. But to make sure of the names belonging only to this locality, it would be necessary to quote thirteen pages of the said book.

In 1776 Captain Berry raised a company for the Eighth regiment. About the same time Captain Charles Thruston joined the army in New Jersey. In 1777 the company of Captain Helmes was three months in service. In 1778 the company of Captain Gilkerson guarded prisoners. Next year the company of Captain Joseph Ball was in service three months. In 1781 the companies of Captains Joseph Gregory and Josiah Swearingen were sent against the Indians, the latter being stationed at Fort McIntosh on the Muskingum. In the latter half of the same year the companies of Captain Joseph Looney and Captain Bell were at the siege of Yorktown. Several other companies were also in the Yorktown campaign and guarded prisoners to Winchester.

For the above facts we are indebted to "Virginia Militia in the Revolutionary War," by J. T. McAllister. From the same source is derived the following list of militia officers who qualified in Frederick in the years 1776-1780. (Lt. is lieutenant, En. is ensign, Cp. captain.)

Abernathy, William—Lt.
Bobb, Peter—Cp.
Baldwin, Thomas—Cp.
Barnett, George—En.
Barrow, John—En.
Bell, George—Lt. and Cp.
Berry, Francis—Cp.
Branson, Amos—En.
Brinker, Henry—En.
Brown, James—Lt.
Burk, James—En.
Bush, Vance—Lt.
Byerly, Robert—En.
Cockley, Jacob—Cp.

Calmes, Marquis—Lt. Col.
Calvert, Samuel—Lt.
Camp, John—Lt.
Carter, Joseph—Cp.
Catlett, John—Cp.
Catlett, Henry—Lt.
Cochran, James—En.
Combes, Benjamin—Lt.
Crim, Jacob—Lt.
Daniel, Hugh—En.
Denny, Samuel—En.
Denny, Robert—Lt.
Dobbins, Robert—En.
Dorsey, Joshua—Lt.

Eastin, Johnston—En.
Elkins, Benjamin—Lt.
Evans, William—Lt.
Frost, William—Cp.
Gilham, Peter—Lt.
Gilkerson, Samuel—Cp.
Hampton, Thomas—En.
Hancher, William—En.
Harrell, John—En.
Heaton, James—Lt.
Helphingston, Philip—Lt.
Hill, John—Lt.
Hisewanger, John—Maj. vice R. White
Hiskill, Adam—Cp.
Hiskill, Peter—En.
Horseley, Richard—En.
Kemp, John—En.
Kindrick, Abraham—Cp.
Kendrick, Christly—Lt.
Kennedy, David—Col., vice J. Smith
Larrick, John—Cp.
Lawrence, James—Lt.
Lindsay, Abraham—Lt.

McCormick, Francis—Lt.
Mercer, Aaron—Cp.
Myers, Jacob—Cp.
O'Brien, John—En.
Pyles, Joshua—Lt.
Redman, Jeremiah—Lt.
Rice, John—Cp.
Rinherbo, Casper—Cp., vice R. White
Simerall, James—Lt.
Smith, John—Co. Lt., resigned 1777
Smith, Samuel—Lt.
Stribling, William—Lt.
Taylor, Richard—En.
Taylor, William—Cp.
Vance, William—En.
White, Robert—Lt. Col., vice M. Calmes
Wilson, Hugh—En.
Wolfe, Henry—En.
Wolfe, John—En.
Wood, James—Co. Lt., resigned 1777

* * * * * *

REVOLUTIONARY WAR

Soldiers from Winchester and Frederick County who served in the Revolutionary War, taken from list published by the Secretary of War in 1835, which includes only those entitled to pensions or bounty land warrants and then living.

James Beckham; John Bageant; Wm. Braithwaite; Dennis Bush; Samuel Cox; Thomas Crawford; Daniel Haley; James Hamilton; John Haney; John Harris; John Hefferlin; John Kiger; Wm. Kingore; A. McDonald; Alexander McMullin; Daniel Miller; Richard Murray; James Oliver; Moses Perry; George Seifert; Jeremiah Sargeant; James Thompson; George Van. Landengham; George Wright; James Barr; Henry Beatty; George Black; George Blakeman; Humphrey Brook; Philip P. Buckner; John Campbell; John Colbert; Peter Edwards; James Foster; John Grim; George Hensell; Michael Humble; Henry Knipe; Conrad Kramer; Peter Lauck; George Lonas; John Schultz; George Lonas; Basil Lucas; James M. Marshall; William Monroe; Hugh Parrall; William Philips; John Piper; Andrew Pittman; James Riely; Jacob Shade; John Smith; Colonel of Va. State Line; Jacob Sperry; Andrew McGuire; Robert White; Owen Campbell; Reuben Cave; Richard Jenkins; Andrew Keyser; Joseph Sampson; Thomas Tharp.

282   THE STORY OF WINCHESTER IN VIRGINIA

Soldiers serving under General George Rogers Clarke in 1778. The company from Frederick was commanded by Captain Joseph Bowman. Some of the names may belong to the Fauquier company of Captain Leonard Helm. Mr. Cartmell, who gathered the names, does not differentiate the names belonging to the two companies.

Bender, John
Bender, Lewis
Bender, Robert
Bentley, John
Berry, William (1)
Berry, William (2)
Bowman, Christian
Bowman, Isaac—Lieut.
Brazer, Peter
Breeden, John—Ensign
Breeden, Richard
Bulger, Edward
Bush, John
Cartmell, Nathan
Cartmell, Thomas
Conn, John
Coontz, Christopher
Detering, Jacob
Doran, Patrick
Dust, Daniel—Sergeant
Eskridge, William—Lieut.
Funk, Henry
Haller, Francis
Henry, Nathaniel—Lieut.
Hite, George
Honaker, Frederick
Honaker, Henry
Isaacs, John
James, Abraham
Keller, Abram.—Lieut.
Keller, Isaac—Sergeant
King, George
Lee, Zebeniah
Long, Philip
McBride, Isaac
McClanihan, Robert
McIntire, Alexander
Master, Barney
Miller, Abraham
Miller, George
Murrey, Edward
Myers, William

Perry, Thomas
Peters, John
Rubey, William—Sergeant
Setser, John
Setser, John
Shepard, George
Shepard, Peter
Simpson, Joseph
Slack, William
Sowers, Frederick
Speers, Jacob—Sergeant
Strode, Samuel—Sergeant
Swearingen, Van
Vance, Thomas H.
Vanmeter, Isaac
Walters, Barnaby
White, Robert

SUPPLEMENTARY

Soldiers serving in the Northwest in 1781 under Captains Benjamin Biggs and Uriah Springer.

Bailey, William
Barr, William
Bean, John
Carter, Richard
Clark, David
Conn, John
Conrad, Jacob
Crawford, Robert
Daugherty, John
Kairnes, Michael
Lockhart, John
Lockhart, Joseph
Morgan, Charles
Morrison, John
Osburn, Samuel
Rhodes, Jacob
Rinker, Jacob
Smith, James

APPENDIX

F

SOLDIERS OF 1812

Names followed, respectively, by 1, 2, and 3, refer to the companies of Captains Thomas Roberts, William Morris, and Michael Coyle. The first was Cavalry Company Number Four of the First Regiment. The second was an artillery and the third an infantry command. Names starred are those of emergency men.

Allen, John—2
Ashby, Jonas—1
Aulick, Frederick—3
Austin, Thomas—2
Baker, Jacob—1
Ball, William—1
Barnes, William—2
Barr, James—2
Beatty, Lewis—1
Beckwith, Francis—2
Beckwith, Richard—1
Bennett, James—1
Booker, Levi—2
Bowers, Peter—1
Bowers, Philip—2
Rowley, John—1
Brill, ——— —3
Brown, Daniel—3
Burwell, Nicholas—1
Bush, Andrew—1
Campbell, James—1
Campbell, William—1
Carter, John—1
Cather, David—2
Clark, John C.—1
Cochrane Louthan—2
Conrad, Charles—1
Cooley, John—2
Copenhaver, Jacob—3
Copenhaver, Michael—3
Coyle, John—3
Crawford, Zachariah *
Crebs, Henry—3
Dalby, William—2
Davidson, Robert—2
Day, John—2
Denny, John—1

Everly, John—1
Everly, John—2
Farmer, John—2
Foster, John—1
Foster, Thomas—2
Fulkerson, Roger—2
Gibbs, Richard—2
Glaize, Henry *
Grant, Stewart—1
Gray, Daniel—2
Haas, John—2
Hansberry, Presley—1
Heeser, John—2
Heinrick, George—2
Heister, Solomon—1
Herdsman, Samuel—2
Hester, S.—3
Hillman, Simeon *
Hoff, Philip—1
Hoffman, John—2
Hoffnagle, John—2
Holliday, Alexander—1
Holliday, William C.—1
Hutchison, William—2
Hutchinson, Sandy—1
Jack, Robert—1
Jenkins, John—3
Jenkins, Stephen—3
Jenkins, William—3
Johnson, John—2
Jones, Richard—2
Jones, Richard *
Joyce, Asa—2
Kane, William—1
Keeler, John—2
Kiger, Daniel—2
Kiger, George W.—2

Klyfustine, John—2
Kremer, Joseph—2
Kurtz, Isaac—1
Lafferty, Thomas—2
Lauck, Isaac—1
Lauck, Isaac—2
Lauck, Jacob—3
Long, Robert—3
McCann, James—2
Macfee, William—2
Magson, John M.—1
Magson, John—3
Meredith, James—1
Mesmer, Jacob—3
Miller, John—1
Miller, John—2
Miller, John W.—1
Morris, John—2
Newman, Alexander—1
Owen, Simeon
Parkins, Nathan—2
Perry, Nicholas *
Poe, John—2
Price, John—1

Reed, Joshua—1
Regan, Jackson *
Regan, Nathaniel *
Schreck, George—2
Schultz, John—2
Scrivener, Benjamin—3
Shaw, Craven—2
Sherer, Philip—1
Sloat, John—1
Sloat, Henry—3
Spengler, Solomon—1
Streit, Augustus—1
Streit, William—2
Swallum, John—1
Thatcher, Evan *
Throckmorton, William—3
Touchstone, Simpson *
Vance, James—1
Van Horn, William—2
Welsh, James *
White, James—1
Winn, Elisha—2
Young, Henry—2
Young, William—2

G

CIVIL WAR

Soldiers of Winchester and Frederick County serving in the Confederate Army in the Civil War of 1861-1865. This list has been compiled from The Muster Roll in the office of the Clerk of the Circuit Court of Frederick County, Virginia, and from the Roll of The Turner Ashby Camp of Confederate Veterans and the original roll of Company K, 5th Virginia Infantry, the last two rolls being now in the possession of Captain George W. Kurtz of Winchester.

This list includes some soldiers not from Winchester and Frederick County, who served in organizations organized largely of personnel from Winchester and Frederick County. No doubt there are some soldiers from Winchester and Frederick County whose names do not appear in the list.

Soldiers from Winchester were chiefly in the following commands:
Continental Morgan Guards, or Co. K, 5th Va., Infantry, Stonewall Brigade. Marion Rifles, or Co. A, 5th Va., Infantry, Stonewall Brigade. Winchester Rifles, or Co. F, 2nd Va., Infantry, Stonewall Brigade. The Boomerangs, or Co. H, 13th Va., Infantry, Elzey's Brigade. Company A, 1st Va., Cavalry. Newtown Artillery, or Cutshaw's Battery. Com-

APPENDIX 285

pany D, 33rd Va., Infantry. Company C, 12th Va., Cavalry; Company A, 39th Va., Bat. Cavalry, scouts, guides and couriers, attached to Headquarters and known as General R. E. Lee's Bodyguard. Company K, 23rd Va., Cavalry. Company H, 11th Va. Cavalry. Company F, 18th Va. Cavalry, Imboden's Brigade. Company E, 11th Va., Cavalry, Laurel Brigade. Company B, 11th Va. Cavalry, Laurel Brigade. Chew's Battery, Stuart's Horse Artillery, Rockbridge Battery.

COMPANY "B" 11th VIRGINIA CAVALRY
Laurel Brigade

Cartmell, M. B., Capt.
Cartmell, Thomas K., Capt. of Secret Service
Larrick, George B.
Orrick, Johnson
Baker, Jas. R.
Bragonier, D. H.

COMPANY E, 11th VIRGINIA CAVALRY
Laurel Brigade

(The personnel of this Company was largely from Shenandoah County)

OFFICERS
Hess, J. T., Capt.
Hooff, J. L., Capt.
McGuire, H. H., Capt.
Hottel, G. W., 1st Lieut.
Hockman, Wm., 2nd Lieut.
Spiker, G. W., 2nd Lieut.
Burke, R. W., 3rd Lieut.

PRIVATES
Baker, Daniel
Baker, G. W.
Baker, Nicholas
Baker, Henry
Borden, D. M.
Borden, Perry
Borden, Joseph
Bly, Mason
Bly, Richard
Brown, James
Brent, J. W.
Beard, J. E.
Bruce, Buck
Barrenger, Joe
Booth, Corden L.
Booth, John
Boyer, Benton
Boyer, J. A.
Bell, Polk
Beall, John
Bowman, J. K.
Crabill, L. C.
Crabill, O. H.
Crabill, David
Crabill, Hal
Crabill, Jacob
Crabill, Ben
Coffman, Walter
Collins, Carson
Chase, ——
Dodd, R. D.
Dewar, J. J.
Dickenson, James
DeHaven, Martin
Everly, Jacob
Everly, Isaac
Effinger, W. E.
Funkhouser, Amos
Feely, W. A.
Feely, Silas
Feely, John
Fauver, Noah
Green, Zach
Green, James

Grove, Sam M.
Glaize, G. W.
Hottel, W. F.
Hockman, J. W.
Hammond, Lawrence
Hamman, John
Huffman, A. J.
Hinkins, G. A.
Hinkins, Jacob
Hodge, John
Heflin, James
Hess, L. Daw
Hyde, D. B.
Harrison, Howard
Holmes, H. W.
Holmes, James
Hieronomus, Hutch
Holler, Jno. G.
Holler, G. H.
Holler, Jno. A.
Hoover, Wm.
James, Sam
Killener, James
Karnes, Ephraim
Lutholt, Robert
Luttrell, Archibald
Lynn, G. B.
Lynn, James
Luke, Wm.
Lee, Sam.
Lee, G. W.
Miller, W. F.
Miller, Wm.
Miller, Jacob F.
McClency, R. P.
McCloud, James
Mort, Jerry
Maphis, James
Pangle, Abraham
Pangle, Wm.
Pangle, Joe
Pingley, D. M.
Pogue, J. T.
Rutherford, J. A.
Reedy, Abe

Ryan, John
Ridenour, Alfred
Senseney, Edward
Stover, David
Smith, James
Scroggins, J. E.
Sonner, J. H.
Sonner, J. W.
Showalter, Thorn
Shambaugh, Cline
Shambaugh, James
Seavers, G. W.
Swishers, J. H.
Shotts, Marcus
Shaffer, Theodore
Snyder, Henry
Snyder, John
Stickley, D. H.
Stickley, Wm.
Stickley, Ben.
Stickley, G. W.
Stickley, Dan.
Stickley, Jos. H.
Stickley, P. D.
Stickley, D. E.
Stickley, Josiah
Stickley, John
Stickley, Walter
Omps, James
Viers, Chas.
Veach, Jacob
Whittington, Gersham
Whittington, Joseph
Wright, Milton
Wright, Ben
Warner, Philip
Welch, Sam
Welch, Joseph
Watson, Samuel
Watson, Jacob
Watson, Benj.
Winegoard, John
Winegoard, Joseph
Windle, Wm.
Williams, Jno. J.

APPENDIX 287

COMPANY "H" 11th VIRGINIA CAVALRY
Laurel Brigade

OFFICERS

Pierce, A. M., Capt.
Sherrard, Joseph H., 1st Lieut.

PRIVATES

Ashwood, Joseph
Crosen, Ran
Cooper, R. M.
Clark, James
Dinkle, Peter
Eskridge, Heck
Fauver, Sam
Fauver, John
Frye, Joseph P.
Frye, B. F.
Huff, John
Himmelright, James
Himmelright, Joseph M.
Keiffer, James
Lickliter, Daniel
Lineburg, Martin
Marker, Amos E.
Orndorff, Ananias
Orndorff, Phineas
Orndorff, Setz
Orndorff, Amos
Orndorff, Lemuel
Shell, Samuel
Smith, Sandy
Smith, D. H.
Whetzel, James
White, Ira
Wilson, Martin

COMPANY "C" 12th VIRGINIA CAVALRY
Laurel Brigade

OFFICERS

John H. Ford, Capt.
Wm. H. Myers, 1st Lieut.
Jos. R. Wood, 2nd Lieut.
Rich'd. M. Sydnor, 3rd Lieut.
R. S. D. Heironimus, Ord. Sergt.

PRIVATES

Adams, John D.
Ashwood, Thomas
Ashwood, Eli
Brumback, Jacob
Brumback, Dallas
Baker, Hugh W.
Beall, Henry D.
Bell, Joseph
Bell, John
Bell, Henry
Bowers, Frank
Bennett, Peter
Bayliss, Milton H.
Chrisman, Jacob
Colston, John T.
Chenowith, George
Copenhaver, Chas.
Carter, Joseph
Daugherty, William
Diffenderfer, Benj.
Everhart, Jackson
Eddy, Thomas N.
Frye, Jesse
Frye, Marshall
Fugitt, George
Flowers, Franklin
Fenwick, William
Fenwick, Nathan
Glaize, Henry W.
Groves, Joshua
Grim, Charles
Huntsberry, Henry C.
Huntsberry, Jacob A.
Hillyard, Geo. W.
Hillyard, Jacob
Hiett, Joseph F.
Hunter, Geo. W.
Herbert, Wm. H.
Harris, Sutton
Jackson, T. J.

Jenkins, John
Jones, Charles
Kreemer, William
Kefer, Fred
Lepperd, Bid
McDonald, Marshall E.
McDonald, Jas. H.
McDonald, Samuel N.
Miller, Dudley L.
Miller, Robert W.
McDonald, James
McDonald, Joseph
Meade, James
Marker, John
Pitman, Archibald H.
Pitman, Joseph
Pitman, John L.
Perry, Joseph
Pifer, Calvin
Patterson, Newton
Patterson, Henry
Pitzer, Charles
Pitzer, Alexander

Pitzer, Martin
Rudolph, Joseph
Rudolph, Nashville D.
Reed, Edward
Shull, Briscoe C.
Schenck, Henry C.
Snapp, Simon
Snapp, Sydnor
Stump, J. Calvin
Sydnor, Fauntleroy
Sydnor, Cyrus
Striker, Robert I.
Sperry, William L.
Strode, David
Shepherd, Newton
Shrout, Lewis
Shireley, John W.
Tanquary, Henry
White, John
Wright, Robert
Wisecarver, Amos
Wisecarver, Isaac

COMPANY "A" 39th BATTALION
Virginia Cavalry

Scouts, Guides, Couriers, attached to Headquarters and forming General R. E. Lee's bodyguard.

OFFICERS
Augustus P. Pifer, Capt.
Frank Lupton, 2nd Lieut.
R. M. Cartmell, 3rd Lieut.
John R. Lupton, 2nd Sergt.
William Ward, 3rd Sergt.
C. H. Forsyth, 4th Sergt.
J. Frank Lupton, 3rd Corp.

PRIVATES
Arnold, John W.
Baker, Jacob E.
Baker, John R.
Brill, Henry
Brown, Walter
Booker, Wesley
Campbell, Bean C.
Campbell, Robert M.
Carter, Frank
Carter, Pitman
Cooper, Jackson
Denny, James W.
Frye, Philip
Fidler, James
Grim, James
Grim, John
Harper, Granville H.
Harmer, John R.
Harper, George W.
Hardesty, Kirk
Hite, Marion C.
Hodgson, Abner W.
Houck, Charles W.
Fidler, George

APPENDIX 289

Huntsberry, Jacob A.
Kauffman, John
Kern, Hamilton
Lupton, John M.
Lupton, Joseph M.
Lupton, John C.
Lupton, Joshua
Lupton, Thomas G.
Miller, Albert
Miller, Albert C.

Milhorn, Joseph
Pifer, A. P.
Renner, Alexander
Sloat, A. T.
Sloat, C. D.
Sloat, T. E.
Taylor, George
Walter, Frank G.
Whetzel, J. M.
White, Mordecai

COMPANY "F" 18th VIRGINIA CAVALRY
Imboden's Brigade

OFFICERS

R. Bruce Muse, Capt.
Joseph Seibert, 1st Lieut.
John Good, 2nd Lieut.
Lafayette Lafollette, 3rd Lieut.
Beverley Lockhart, Ord. Sergt.
Arsker Bywaters, 1st Corp.
Robert Chamberlain, 2nd Corp.
Thomas Morrison, 3rd Corp.

PRIVATES

Anderson, D. H.
Anderson, Zebulon
Anderson, Bruce
Anderson, Alfred
Arnold, Filberry
Arnold, Harvey
Arnold, Lemuel
Anderson, Snowden
Braithwaite, John
Cline, Strother
Cline, Snowden
Crim, William
DeHaven, Andrew
DeHaven, James
Duffy, John
Evans, Robert
Fletcher, Jacob
Giffin, Joseph
Giffin, Edward
Giffin, David
Griffin, James
Garrett, Samuel

Johnson, James
Johnson, Sabe
Johnson, John
Johnson, Richard
Johnson, Lemuel
Kern, Washington
Kern, Robert
Kern, Benjamin
Kelso, John
Luttrell, Robert
Luttrell, Joseph
Lafollette, Caney
Loy, Charles
Loy, John
Larrick, Benjamin
Martin, Pope
Mounts, Joseph
McIntyre, Lige
McKee, Wood
McCoy, John
Mills, ——
Nixon, John
Nixon, William
Oliver, Joseph
Popkins, Addison
Payne, Richard
Pool, John
Pugh, V. S.
Pugh, George
Pugh, Francis
Reid, Dorsey
Reid, Frank
Reid, David

Rogers, Hamilton
Smith, William
Siler, John
Stickley, Benjamin
Shermon, Isaiah
Strother, French
Spade, Lemuel

Stottler, John
Triplett, William
Ward, Evan
West, Frank
White, Frank
White, Frank

COMPANY "K" 23rd VIRGINIA CAVALRY

OFFICERS
Jack Adams, Capt.
Edward Cushour, 1st Lieut.
George F. Glaize, 2nd Lieut.
Wm. Chapman, Ord. Sergt.

PRIVATES
Chapman, John B.
Barr, Oscar
Kurtz, Robert
Jones, William R.
Jones, William
Hollis, Charles W.
Brown, J. Robert
Bowles, Charles
Smith, Henry
Grim, George W.
Grim, Chas. H.
Renner, Amos
Keligan, James
McDonald, Lycurgus
Neville, Richard
Lewis, John K.

Hanshaw, Marion
Roland, James
Grim, Charles
Barr, William
Forney, Samuel
Coe, James
Bowles, Wilson
Holingsworth, Clark
Haymaker, George
West, James
Jefferson, Thomas
Parker, James
Willis, George
Willis, Bushrod
Logan, Charles
Hupp, Isaac
Grim, Theophilis
Perry, John
Gearley, Mart.
Daring, John
Daring, Newton
Wall, William W.

COMPANY F, 2nd VIRGINIA INFANTRY
Stonewall Brigade

OFFICERS
Clark, Wm. L., Captain
Burgess, Jas. B., Captain
Corbin, Frank, 1st Lieut.
Barton, W. Strother, Lieut.
Harris, Chas. S., 4th Lieut.
Burgess, E. O., Sergeant
Fletcher, Jno. J., 2nd Sergeant
Kinsey, Sam'l., 3rd Sergeant
Glaize, Isaac W., 1st Corporal

Nulton, Jos. A., Lieut.
Bell, Chas. E., Sergeant

PRIVATES
Amick, William
Addison, J. Hite
Aulick, Chas. E.
Baldwin, C. H. (Doctor)
Baldwin, Jno. H.
Barton, W. Strother

APPENDIX

Barton, R. T.
Barley, Adam
Barton, Wm.
Barton, R. T.
Barton, Randolph
Beemer, John W.
Bell, Chas. E.
Burke, Wm.
Carnigan, Chas.
Clark, William
Crim, Jas. W.
Crim, Jno. B.
Dandridge, P. P.
Dean, Wm.
Dinkle, Peter
Dinkle, Enos
Glenn, Wm.
Grim, St. George T.
Hamilton, D. H.
Hines, James W.
Hines, John
Jenkins, John
Kidd, Thos.
Koontz, Jas. R.
Lambden, Geo. W.

Mason, Jas. M.
Mason, Jno. A.
Mitchell, Chas.
Milborn, Joseph
Monroe, J. Marshall
Munsey, Robert
McCarty, Timothy
McCarty, Joseph
McCord, James A.
McGuire, Edward
Milton, Jos. A.
Pettitt, Allen
Powell, Lloyd
Prevail, Layton
Sherrard, Jos. H.
Simpson, Wm. H.
Singleton, Obediah
Singleton, Caldwell
Spaid, Wm.
Smith, Robert G.
Steele, Stephen M.
Winters, Harry
Wollingham, Geo.
Young, Wm.

CHEW'S BATTERY, STUART'S HORSE ARTILLERY, CAVALRY CORPS

(The following are the men from Winchester who were in this battery)

Boyd, Philip W.
Bowley, Devereau
Burgess, Beall
Brady, George
Brady, Lewis
Conrad, Charles
Conrad, Frank E.
Deahl, Henry
Holliday, B. T.
Kohlhousen, Luther

Marstella, Wm.
Powell, Raleigh
McGuire, Wm. P.
McVicar, Chas. W.
Reed, Edward
Powell, P. P.
Stewart, George
Williams, T. Clayton
Williams, Jno. J.

COMPANY K, 5th REGIMENT
Stonewall Brigade

OFFICERS
John Avis, Captain till June 9, 1862

George W. Kurtz, Captain after said date
John R. Mesmer, First Lieutenant

J. A. Ewing, Second Lieutenant
Meredith Forney, Second Lieutenant
George W. Gordon, Orderly Sergeant
William H. Fleet, First Sergeant
Elias Marsh, Second Sergeant
George A. Connor, Third Sergeant
Joseph B. Shiner, Fourth Sergeant
James Hiner, First Corporal
W. E. Marsh, Second Corporal
W. H. Brown, Third Corporal
J. H. Grove, Fourth Corporal
Bush, Chas. Lieutenant

PRIVATES

Ambrouse, Uriah
Albin, Jas. A.
Avis, Joseph L.
Baggett, Samuel
Barr, William B.
Barton, William
Bauserman, James C.
Benshoff, John
Berry, John A.
Batt, Moses
Biggs, Nicholas L.
Bumpas, Joseph J.
Bowman, Robert
Carpenter, John
Carper, George
Carper, Jacob
Charlton, James J.
Clem, Noah
Clem, Solomon
Curtain, Daniel
Cain, Chas.
Cain, Jas. H.
Charlton, Jas. J.
Carpenter, John
Clink, Robert
Cloud, John
Cloud, Uriah
Coffman, Jacob
Diffenderfer, John G.
Cooley, George

Eagle, George W.
Eavy, Daniel
Fariss, John
Fleet, Jas. L.
Fleet, Wm. H.
Floyd, John H.
Fitch, Charles W.
Fugett, George
Fuller, John W.
Forney, Meredith
Grandstaff, George W.
Guy, James H.
Green, Benj. F.
Golliday, Geo. W.
Grove, Jas. H.
Gordon, Geo. W.
Hamilton, James W.
Hiner, Jas.
Holmes, Jos.
Haymaker, Charles
Henry, William
Hisey, Robert F.
Hodgson, Luther
Hoover, William H.
Hottle, Joseph
Jackson, William A.
Jones, Wm. H.
Johnson, Jno. W.
Johnson, Benj. N.
Jenkins, Benjamin
Johnson, Erasmus
Kaski, Daniel
Keenan, James W.
Koski, Samuel
Kerchasky, Joseph
Kibbler, Noah
Kiger, Cornelius
Lepline, Peter
Limerick, Philip
Latham, Wm.
Lloyd, Jno. H.
Linn, George B.
Lotts, Philip
Lucas, R. B.
McCord, Charles P.
McCord, George, Jr.
McCoy, James

APPENDIX 293

Magill, Thos.
McElhone, Dennis
Maphis, Sam'l
McCown, Jas. L.
March, George W.
March, James M.
Martin, Joseph
Mizer, John S.
Moreland, William
Nolen, John
Neagley, Robt. M.
O'Neal, Bernard
Palmer, William
Palmer, William T.
Palmer, Ed. G.
Parker, Archibald
Parker, Charles C.
Pennybaker, John W.
Reed, William H.
Robinson, Jos.
Rhodes, John J.
Riffles, Jacob
Ripetoe, Dewitt
Ritter, P. L.
Ritter, Carter
Ritter, Jos.
Ritter, Henry
Rudy, David
Schmucker, Jacob L.
Seabright, William
Shaftmaker, William
Shelly, Thomas H.

Shierley, Peter
Shipe, Isaac N.
Skinner, John W.
Slagle, John W.
Smith, Edward R.
Smootz, Isaac
Samsell, David
Snapp, Levi
Sprought, James W.
Swartz, August
Swartz, William F.
Shipe, Levi
Stewart, Chas.
Shiner, J. W.
Swartz, Isaac
Swartz, John L.
Swartzel, George H.
Swartzell, John W.
Saum, Jacob
Sprouse, Andrew J.
Thompson, James
Trier, Ford
Wahl, Theodore
Wilson, David
Wood, John M.
Woods, John S.
Yago, Jacob
Young, Charles A.
Young, Edward
Zea, Martin
Zago, Jacob

COMPANY A, 5th INFANTRY
Stonewall Brigade

OFFICERS

Lewis J. Fletcher, Captain
M. S. Brown, Captain
A. S. Markell, Lieutenant
J. W. Jones, Lieutenant
J. W. O. Funk, Lieutenant
W. W. Faulkner, Lieutenant
H. K. Pritchard, Lieutenant
P. L. Kurtz, Orderly Sergeant
George W. Grim, 2nd Sergeant
Joseph H. Lyder, 3d Sergeant
William L. Evans, 4th Sergeant
Isaac H. Faulkner, 5th Sergeant
H. B. Striker, 1st Corporal
William H. Wood, 2d Corporal
J. Henry Jennings, 3d Corporal
C. D. Shiner, 4th Corporal
Washington Grim, Color Sergeant

PRIVATES

Allen, Thomas
Anderson, John C.

Baggs, C. C.
Baker, Charles W.
Barr, Cornelius
Barr, John W.
Barr, Oscar
Barr, Hugh
Bell, J. Vance
Brown, C. H.
Calvert, William H.
Carper, James
Castleman, E. P.
Chamberlain, John
Clanahan, William
Coffelt, ——
Cooley, James B.
Corbin, John
Dall, D.
Dawes, John J.
Deshoney, John W.
Diffenderfer, W. H.
Duncan, James
Evans, David
Evy, D.
Faulkner, Isaac H.
Faulkner, James F.
Foster, Thomas
Fugitt, Jeremiah
Funk, Stover
Gillock, Reuben
Gillock, William
Gochenour, Philip
Gochenour, William
Grim, Cornelius
Grim, James W.
Haines, C. E.
Hamilton, James W.
Hamilton, Robert H.
Harding, William H.
Harris, John
Harris, William A.
Henry, Richard
Henry, Franklin
Henry, Kaywood
Hovermale, William
Hovermale, Nathan
Hilliard, Jacob
Hoover, Harrison

Hopewell, William
Hopewood, Peter
Huffman, Edward
Hottle, Peter
Jenkins, John H.
Jennings, J. Henry
Jobe, R. M.
Johnston, Noble T.
Johnston, Samuel
Jones, Jeremiah
Jones, John R.
Kaufman, B. F.
Kirby, John
Kline, John H.
Kurtz, Robert J.
Langley, Leo M.
Langley, Philip
Long, Andrew
Lyder, Charles A.
Lyder, John L.
Lynn, Joseph
McClelland, J. C. D.
McCord, C. P.
McCray, Joseph
Miller, ——
Moneymaker, Eli
Newcome, William
Newton, Charles A.
Noakes, George H.
Ober, Jacob
Palmer, Leo
Palmer, ——
Parker, George D.
Parker, R. M.
Prince, William H.
Purcell, T. V.
Riddle, A. A.
Rodgers, ——
Ross, ——
Schmucker, William
Schultz, J. William
Seabright, John H.
Sharp, James
Showalter, Jacob
Spurr, John O.
Spurr, Andrew L.
Starr, William H.

Stickley, E. E.
Stipe, John H.
Strickler, Daniel
Strickler, Joseph
Stricker, James
Taylor, George W.
Taylor, William H.
Thompson, Charles E.
Warner, J. T.
Way, Willoughby
Welch, Michael
West, James
Wierman, William
Wood, Robert A.
Young, William H.

COMPANY H, 13th INFANTRY—STONEWALL BRIGADE

OFFICERS

Lewis, N. Husk, Captain
William H. Sherer, Captain
William G. Conway
  1st Lieutenant
Lewis N. Huck, 2d Lieutenant
Robert B. Streit, 3d Lieutenant
J. Peter Miller, 1st Sergeant
J. W. F. Legg, 2d Sergeant
William H. Harrison,
  3d Sergeant
Samuel D. Buck, 4th Sergeant
H. Clay Krebs, 1st Corporal
C. H. Baker, 2d Corporal
Bell, John N., 3d Corporal
Wolfe, G. Miller, 4th Corporal

PRIVATES

Baker, George M.
Bayley, Marcus M.
Bowles, Henry C.
Brannon, William W.
Campbell, L. Frank
Carter, J. Pitt
Carter, James H.
Carter, J. Wesley
Chandler, B. R.
Copenhaver, C. J.
Coyle, Joseph
Duke, George
Eller, John
Farnsworth, J. W.
Farnsworth, L. B.
Fifer, John C.
Franks, James M.
Goodrum, W.
Hampton, William H.
Harrison, Isaac S.
Haymaker, James M.
Hieronimus, H. C.
Holliday, Edward S.
Krebs, H. C.
Lamar, John T.
Legg, Edward K.
Logan, L. D.
Lupton, J. Frank
McDaniel, George W.
Mason, James M.
Mattingly, William E.
Musselman, Jno. E.
Maxwell, R. A.
Ogden, Thomas H.
Palmer, Kennedy
Patterson, James
Pitzer, Elias M.
Ritenour, George H.
Russell, F. Stanley
Russell, Jas. B.
Scanlin, R. T.
Seevers, Charles W.
Sherer, Charles E.
Sherer, George E.
Smith, F. A.
Smith, John W.
Smoke, John W.
Van Buskirk, P. C.
Welch, E. P.
Welch, James H.
Brannon, Levi Gray

COMPANY D, 33d INFANTRY (MOUNTAIN RANGERS)

OFFICERS
F. W. M. Holliday, Captain
H. A. Herrell, 1st Lieutenant and Captain
R. Bruce Muse, 2d Lieutenant; became 1st Lieutenant, 1862
F. J. Dunlap, Orderly Sergeant; later 2d Lieutenant
J. B. McGuffin, Lieutenant, 1862
Joshua Wotring, 3d Lieutenant
John H. Wotring, Lieutenant, 1862
R. S. Payne, 2d Sergeant
W. S. Boak, 3d Sergeant
James M. Lockhart, 4th Sergeant

PRIVATES
Anderson, G. N.
Anderson, M. S.
Burton, Isaac
Booker, William F.
Bowen, William
Boyce, David
Boyce, George
Boyce, Henry
Braithwaite, Thornton
Braithwaite, David
Brill, Harrison
Capper, Jonathan
Coe, James
Crabill, George
Dispanett, Joseph
Evans, Robert
Frankhouser, Henry
Gardner, Joseph F.
Good, John D.
Hall, James F.
Himmelright, Thomas
Hockmiller, John
Hook, Edward
Hoyle, A. J.
Johnson, David
Johnson, John E.
Jolly, Elias
Kemp, Jacob
Kerns, Benjamin F.
Kerns, Francis D.
Lawyer, James
Lawyer, John
Lewis, W. O.
Lockhart, Algernon
Lockhart, B. N.
Lockhart, James F.
Lockhart, W. H.
Luttrell, Richard
Luttrell, Robert
McAtee, John
McGuffin, J. B.
McKee, Samuel
McKeever, Tilbury
McCoy, Wm.
Marple, Henry
Marple, Joseph
Marple, Joshua
Marple, Perry
Marple, Washington
Mason, J. M.
Mason, Bingley
Mason, William
Mason, Martin
Mason, Thomas D.
Miller, Alfred
Miller, A. T.
Miller, Daniel F.
Miller, Jacob
Omps, Benjamin
Omps, James
Orndorff, Querry
Orndorff, John
Payne, A. J.
Pennington, James F.
Plumb, A. Vance
Plumb, John
Puffenberger, John
Seibert, James
Simmons, Charles
Smith, W. R.
Snapp, James
Spaid, John W.
Strosnider, Henry

APPENDIX 297

Strosnider, James
Strother, George
Strother, Henry
Triplett, Daniel
Triplett, Nathan
Vance, Henry
Vance, James

White, Elisha
White, Henry
Wotring, Benjamin
Wotring, Francis
Wotring, John
Wotring, Joshua
Wright, Henry

CUTSHAW'S BATTERY
Newtown Artillery

OFFICERS

W. E. Cutshaw, Captain
C. M. Barton, 1st Lieutenant
B. B. Brinker, 2d Lieutenant
Jacob Marks, Sergeant
David Barton

PRIVATES

Allemong, Joseph
Anderson, James
Barrow, A. Jackson
Beeler, James
Bradford, W. S.
Cadwallader, John
Campbell, William
Carrifcough, George
Chipley, Richard
Clemm, Michael
Clevenger, James
Clevenger, John
Cobourn, Franklin
Cooley, Joseph
Debar, Isaac
Dellinger, George W.
Dellinger, James
Dinges, John
Edmondson, Strother
Edmondson, J. Washington
Ewing, Samuel
Finley, Solomon
Frazier, James
Grim, Joseph
Hite, Thomas T.
Hoffman, James W.
Hoffman, Albert
Hoosa, Robert

Jones, John
Jones, William J.
Keeler, Elisha
Keeler, George
Kerns, David
Keyser, Charles
Keyser, Joseph
Kline, D. W.
Kline, S. A.
Kline, S. B.
Kline, W. S.
Lauck, Henry
Lefever, Thomas
McCarty, Andrew
McCarty, John
McCutcheon, William
Miller, Jacob
Miller, William J.
Newcomer, Kepler
O'Connor, Patt
Ogden, Thomas A.
O'Neil, John
Orndorff, Jackson
Pifer, W. E.
Poulton, George
Reed, Joseph
Reed, William
Rhodes, John
Ridenhouer, Amos
Ridenhouer, Hampton
Ridings, Fred
Ridings, Thomas
Ridings, Geo.
Rogers, Charles
Senseny, Anthony
Shryock, James

Simmons, Charles
Simmons, John
Smith, James
Sperry, Cornelius
Sperry, John
Stoff, Albert W.
Taylor, George

Wilkenson, I. M.
Willey, Frederick
Willey, Jacob
Willey, J. W.
Willey, Lawson
Williams, George A.
White, Samuel

COMPANY A, 1st CAVALRY

OFFICERS

James H. Drake, Captain
John M. Lock, Captain
Thomas W. Trussell, Captain
Robert H. Long, Lieutenant
James S. Larrick, Lieutenant
D. W. Rosenberger, Lieutenant
Robert W. Crawford, Lieutenant
Holmes Conrad, Sergeant
Randolph Pifer, Sergeant
William Shippey, Sergeant
C. D. Bucher, Sergeant
John A. Ewing, Sergeant
Peter W. Renner, Sergeant
Henry A. Dinges, Corporal
George Carver, Corporal
William A. Bush, Corporal
John Walter, Corporal
John M. Wise, Corporal
Edward Williams, Corporal

PRIVATES

Beam, A. J.
Beaty, John W.
Beaty, Thomas K.
Bowley, B. F.
Brown, John
Cadwallader, J. M.
Cole, John
Canter, James H.
Chipley, William D.
Cock, H. C.
Cross, John W.
Cross, Samuel W.
Dinges, David
Donaldson, Frank
Dinges, Henry

Drake, Gershier
Funkhouser, Daniel
Funkhouser, Josiah
Funkhouser, William H.
Grimes, Harry
Guard, Amos
Hamilton, ——
Harrison, Benjamin
Hartman, J. L.
Hanger, John
Hanger, William
Hildebrand, G.
Hagan, F. T.
Holmes, Henry W.
Hottle, M. H.
Hailman, J. L.
Irving, Jos.
Jones, M. W.
Kelley, John
Keyser, James C.
Kline, Michael
Landstreet, Edward
Light, James
Long, William
Lock, Jacob
McComb, Andrew
McLeod, Robert T.
Massie, John B.
Massie, Robert
Massie, Thomas W.
Milburn, William
Miller, Robert W.
Montgomery, ——
Newman, Alexander R.
Nightingale, A. J.
Nolen, Charles
Owens, Edward

APPENDIX 299

Parkins, Milton
Phillips, Charles W.
Pitman, Joseph L.
Renner, Addison
Rittenour, George H.
Rittenour, Moffett
Ritter, Jacob B.
Rogers, James
Shryock, James
Smith, B. F.
Smith, Zed
Snapp, Jacob
Steele, M. B.
Stickley, David
Stout, James
Teaford, David
Tharpe, Isaac
Thomas, Reuben
Tucker, ——
Trenary, John W.
Walter, Edward
Walter, Enoch
Walter, Jacob
Walter, John
Walters, Henry
Weaver, Charles
Welch, Jacob
Wise, William
Young, A. H.

SOLDIERS IN VARIOUS COMMANDS

Albin, M. H., Co. A 11 Va. Cav.
Arnold, Geo. H., Co. F 12 Va. Cav.
Argenbright, B. T., Co. G 33 Va. Inf.
Barton, Bolling W., Lt. Irish Bn. 2 Corps.
Barton, Randolph, Capt., Stonewall Brig.
Baker, Albert, Ord. Dept.
Barton, R. T., Rockbridge Battery
Boyd, E. Holmes, Rockbridge Battery
Bragonier, D. H., Co. C 11 Va. Cav.
Baker, M. R., Co. A 12 Va. Cav.
Bowers, Malcomb, Co. F 7 Va. Cav.
Basove, J. W., Co. B 62 Va. Inf.
Boggs, Edmund N., Co. E 25 Va. Inf.
Burkhart, R. C., Co. B 1 Va. Cav.
Bowers, Wm., Co. B 7 Va. Cav.
Barton, J. Randolph, Stonewall Brig.
Baylor, E. W., Co. C 1 La. Artillery
Bryarly, Robt. P., Co. B 1 Va. Cav.
Barr, Jas. W., Co. C 1st Md. Cav.
Barr, M. L. Co. I 2nd Va. Inf.
Beall, Henry D., Co. B 12 Va. Cav.
Bruce, J. D., Lt. Col. 47 Va. Inf.
Boyd, Jno. E., Co. B 1 Va. Cav.
Byrd, Wm.
Baylis, J. W., Co. B 7 Va. Inf.
Brown, C. H.
Barr, Jas. W., Co. C 1 Md. Cav.
Conrad, Holmes, Maj., 1 Va. Cav.
Carpenter, Newton, Co. B 7 Va. Cav.
Chamblin, Thom., Co. H 1 Va. Cav.
Clarke, Chas. H., Co. D 1 Md.
Crebs, John H., Co. D 23 Va. Cav.
Chipley, R. S., Carpenters Battery
Colston, W. B., 2 Va. Inf.
Cherry, E. D., Surgeon 1 Ga. Inf.
Cookus, Jno. N., Co. I 13 Va. Inf.
Coffman, Geo. A., Co. C 7 Va. Cav.
Dorsey, U. L., Co. D 1 Md. Cav.
Dovel, H. C., Co. D 7 Va. Cav.
Davis, Wm. A., Surgeon
DeHaven, C. W., Mosby's Command 43 Bat.
Dulany, R. H., Col. 6 Va. Cav.
Forsythe, Chas. H., Co. A 39 Va.
Faulkner, Jas. F., Co. E 43 Va. Cav.
Faulkner, W. W., Co. E 43 Va. Cav.
Ferguson, Alfred, Co. I 12 Va. Cav.

Frankland, Walter E., Co. F 43 Va. Cav.
Gibson, Bruce, Capt., Co. A 5 Va.
Glaize, John, Q. M., 2 Corp.
Grubb, J. F., 2 Va. Inf.
Gore, Norval W., Co. A 11 Va. Cav.
Gray, Richard L.,Co. C 31 Va. Inf.
Grubbs, Philip, Co. C 2 Va. Inf.
Herbert, L. M., Co. E 2 Va. Inf.
Heflin, Wm., Co. A 43 Va. Cav.
Hodgson, John R., Co. A 11 Va.
Harness, W. H., Col. 14 Va. Cav.
Hunter, R. W., Maj. Gordon's Div. Adgt.
Holliday, F. W. M., Lt. Col., 33 Va. Inf.
Higgins, Owen, Co. D 12 Va.
Hollis, E. G., Lt. Crenshaw's Battery
Hobson, John F., Co. L 5 Va. Inf.
Hollis, Wm. B.
Henkle, Casper C., Surgeon
Hyde, J. P., Chaplain 10 Va. Inf.
Hagan, F. T., Co. A 1 Va. Cav.
Jefferson, Meade, Co. D 1 Va. Cav.
Jackson, Lafayette, Co. A 11 Va. Cav.
Jones, Beverley R., Rockbridge Battery
Knight, Benjamin, Secret Service
Kline, Daniel, Carpenter's Battery
Kreemer, Jas. P., Quartermaster
Lockhart, B. N., Co. E 23 Va. Cav.
Lupton, T. N., Commissary
Langley, J. L., Wise Artillery
Lannis, J. H., Co. A 2 Md. Cav.
Lewis, R. H., Co. D 6 Va. Cav.
Lemly, J. H., 48 Va. Inf.
Moore, L. T., Col., 5 Va. Inf.
Marple, Joshua, 33 Va. Inf. Co. D
Miller, Samuel, Co. K 33 Va. Inf.
Manning, C. J., Co. B 12 Va. Cav.
Murray, J. Ogden, Co. K 7 Va. Cav.

McCarty, James, Co. F 12 Va. Cav.
McCormick, Geo. W., Co. D 7 Va. Cav.
McDonald, B. F., Co. K 13 Va. Inf.
Noland, J. H., Med. D.
Neville, P. G., Co. E 7 Va. Cav.
Nipe, Geo. R., Co. G 12 Va. Cav.
Orndorff, Tilbury, Co. I 18 Va. Cav.
Payne, Martin, Co. B 1 Va. Cav.
Payne, O. F., Co. B 1 Va. Cav.
Powell, Wm. H., 33 Va. Inf., Co. A
Pence, Wm. A., Co. K 7 Va. Cav.
Page, C. R., Gen. Pendleton's Staff Co. 14 Va. Inf.
Pitman, A. H., Co. C 12 Va. Cav.
Pendleton, Mason, Co. E 43 Va. Cav.
Russell, Isaac W., Field Hosp. 2 Corp.
Rust, J. R., Co. I 7 Va. Cav.
Rouss, Milton, Co. B 12 Va. Cav.
Rouss, Charles Broadway, Co. B 12 Va. Cav.
Robinson, R. S., Co. K 7 Va. Cav.
Rutherford, John B., Co. F 52 Va. Inf.
Ray, John, 2 Va. Inf. Co. B
Ritter, Wm., Co. A 11 Va.
Rohr, F. J., 12 Va. Cav.
Reardon, P. H., Co. E 43 Va.
Reedy, I N., Co. B 7 Va.
Rothgeb, A. B., Dixie Artillery
Stephenson, John, Co. I 15 Va.
Smith, Robert, Co. F 12 Va.
Swimley, S. J., Co. D 12 Va.
Sencendiver, J. M., Co. B 1 Va. Inf.
Smith, B. F.
Snead, W. W., Crenshaw's Battery
Timberlake, G. A., Co. G 2 Va. Inf.
Timberlake, Thos. W., Co. B 12 Va. Cav.

APPENDIX 301

Timberlake, Harry, Co. B 12 Va. Cav.
Trenary, R. E., Co. L 5 Va. Inf.
Trenary, J. B., Co. A 1 Va. Cav.
Thorp, Jas. R., Co. H 18 Va. Cav.
Taylor, Geo. W., 43 Va. Cav.
Vermillion, W. H., Co. C 1 Md. Cav.
Vance, Jas. H., Co. F 7 Va. Cav.
Wierman, Wm. L, Co. F 10 Va. Inf.
Ward, Geo., W. A. A. G. Gen. Carson's Staff
Wall, W. W., Co. G 23 Va. Cav.
Wall, Asa., Surgeon
Wilkinson, I. M., Carpenters Battery
Woodward, L. E., Co. E 43 Va.
Yeakley, William, 31 Va. Inf.

H

SOLDIERS OF THE WORLD WAR

(A)

Men in the selective service from Winchester and Frederick. The figures at the right are the draft numbers.

WHITE

Adams, Clarence L.	1056
Adams, Marvin L.	1178
Adams, Morvil W.	1242
Adams, William C.	464
Affleck, Charles E.	1315
Affleck, Fred	
Albin, Milton J.	
Albin, Stonewall J.	
Allamong, Carson H.	76
Allamong, Harry E.	
Allamong, Isaac F.	
Allamong, Walter C.	
Ambrose, Charles F.	425
Ambrose, Elmer G.	1271
Anderson, Charles C.	
Anderson, Charles R.	
Anderson, Clifton W.	674
Anderson, Curtis G.	343
Anderson, Edgar	140
Anderson, Fred S.	
Anderson, Guy S.	107
Anderson, John W.	836
Anderson, John H.	
Anderson, Marion H.	1353
Anderson, Robert L.	1278
Anderson, Stewart	1439
Anderson, Waldo M.	
Anderson, Wesley	1202
Andrews, George L.	1059
Argenbright, Lloyd M.	521
Armel, Benjamin H.	106
Armel, John W.	1100
Armel, Wilton R.	1340
Armentrout, Lawson W.	564
Arthur, Joseph W.	2133
Arthur, William H.	448
Ash, John	385
Ash, John H.	
Ashby, Louis	
Ashley, Foster F.	470
Ashton, Roy L.	29
Ashwood, Charles M.	1329
Athey, Charles C.	1259
Athey, John H.	953
Avery, Thomas J.	954
Bailey, Earl S.	567
Bailey, Ora L.	795
Baker, Alonzo E.	1103
Baker, Goodwin G.	89
Baker, James G.	248
Baker, Lewis M.	755
Baker, William W.	671

Baker, W. Alexander	
Barris, George E.	456
Barton, Joseph M., Jr.	943
Barton, Lewis N.	1075
Barton, Robert T.	995
Barton, Thomas C.	1215
Beale, Ira R.	401
Beaver, Thomas D.	130
Beck, Albert E.	1086
Beck, Frank F.	783
Beck, Walter E.	201
Benner, Hunter J.	119
Beverley, William	
Beverley, William A.	1468
Bohrer, Cecil A.	113
Bohrer, Eldon L.	613
Bolner, Milford J.	
Boone, Arthur	
Boone, Marshall W.	
Bowers, Robert W.	1048
Bowers, Thomas W.	514
Bowley, Devereux L.	
Bowman, John G.	286
Bowman, Philip C.	940
Bowman, William F.	
Boyce, Baylis M.	132
Boyce, Branson	43
Boyce, Crowell R.	
Boyce, George C.	
Boyce, John C.	689
Boyd, Ernest E.	186
Boyd, Robert S.	370
Boyer, Howard L.	1166
Boyles, Henry C.	
Braithwaite, Fred	753
Braithwaite, Lester E.	48
Branner, George L.	153
Breckenridge, William B.	290
Brill, Charles E.	1052
Brill, Elijah	1458
Brill, Robert L.	183
Brill, William B.	96
Brill, William E.	175
Bromley, Paul L.	
Brooks, Oliver B.	923
Brown, Charles D.	568
Brown, Charles E.	46
Brown, David L.	763
Brown, H———	880
Brown, John I., Jr.	127
Brown, Lee A.	1994
Brown, Leslie M.	107
Brown, Ralph S.	
Brown, William H.	697
Browne, Bowyer	
Browne, Horace C.	
Brownley, Paul L.	
Bruce, Willis M.	
Bryant, Harry R.	
Burkhart, Newton H.	173
Burner, Walter H.	413
Butler, Charles T.	395
Butler, Elmer	45
Butler, Harry W.	109
Butler, Henry R.	1045
Butler, Robert B.	879
Byrd, Richard E.	
Byrd, Thomas B.	789
Cadwallader, William M.	893
Cafferty, Peter J.	1163
Cain, Ralph E.	2180
Campbell, Charles S. H.	1325
Campbell, James W.	728
Cammer, Claude R.	
Capper, Henry W.	1170
Carbaugh, Charles F.	1384
Carbaugh, George A.	1313
Carbaugh, James P.	63
Carpenter, Edward C.	466
Carpenter, Lou G.	131
Carpenter, Robert A.	
Carpenter, Robert C.	
Carpenter, Russell S.	1198
Carper, Eaton C.	704
Carper, James M.	550
Carper, Philip H.	387
Carr, J. W.	
Carson, Annie L.	
Cather, Dr. David	
Cather, David C.	
Cather, Lohring R.	1282
Cather, Thomas R.	722
Catlett, Lucas W.	638
Cave, Samuel L.	

Chapman, A. P. ....
Chapman, Ewell 792
Choucleris, James 668
Clark, Charles F. 1460
Clark, Hugh E. ....
Clark, Norman L. 20
Clark, Dr. T. A. ....
Clark, William H. 86
Clemens, Hannibal C. 593
Clemens, Henry 832
Clevenger, Grover H. 168
Clevenger, Lohr J. 1152
Cline, Carl P. 471
Cline, Harry G. 621
Clowser, Clarence W. 573
Clowser, Earl J. 59
Coble, Alexander L. ......
Cochran, Charles E. 904
Cochran, John C. 1273
Cochran, Martin L. 209
Compton, Olga M. ....
Conrad, Henry W. 655
Connor, Lloyd N. 444
Connor, Morris E. 1183
Conrad, Bryan ....
Conrad, George B. ....
Conrad, Robert Y. ....
Cooley, James R. 1244
Cooper, Edward M. 748
Cooper, Eugene B. 1061
Cooper, Henry H. 32
Cooper, Hunter N. 450
Cooper, Julian C. 1133
Cooper, Leslie 332
Cooper, Lohring J. 504
Cooper, Vernon W. 1128
Cooper, Wayne ....
Copeland, Edward D. 1144
Copeland, William 484
Copenhaver, Harry 850
Copenhaver, Marcus L. ..
Corbin, Abraham M. 1154
Cornwell, William J. 58
Costello, John W. 66
Cresswell, Evan C. 844
Crouse, Edward ....
Curl, Albert F. ....

Curl, Charles R. ....
Curl, James W. ....
Curtis, Albert E. ....
Dailey, James L. 1136
Darlington, Charles E. ... 203
Darlington, Harold M. ... 825
Day, Helen ....
DeHaven, Ashby S. 1342
DeHaven, Hugh G. 1101
DeHaven, Hunter A. 758
DeHaven, Julian D. 459
DeHaven, Roy F. 1155
DeHaven, Ursel 1165
DeHaven, William M. 31
Derflinger, Benjamin A. .. 905
Dick, Lee O. 282
Dick, Troy 358
Didier, Angelica F. ......
Dix, Isaac B. 1222
Dix, Samuel R. 269
Dodson, Bergil L. 1189
Dorsey, Raymond W. 1058
Drake, Edgar E. 411
Drummond, Kirby J. 204
Dunn, William W. 74
Dutton, Dr. Benjamin B... 1388
Eagle, David H. ....
Eaton, Roy C. 1272
Ebersole, Paul E. 101
Edwards, Harold R. 16
Elliott, John W. 353
Emmart, Harmon B. 725
Emmart, Wade H. 424
Evans, Elmer F. 1250
Evans, Howard R. 843
Fansler, Arthur W. ......
Fansler, Frank ....
Fansler, George E. 815
Fansler, Harry ....
Fansler, Paul ....
Fansler, Ralph S. 22
Farmer, Roy C. 121
Farmer, William F. 1000
Fauver, Silas E. 285
Fawcett, Elvara E. 24
Fawcett, Louis G. 119
Fiddler, Ernest C. 119

Field, Arthur M.	1091	Grim, William E.	
Fisher, James H.		Grim, William H.	
Fleet, Joseph L.	138	Grove, Acquilla C.	333
Fletcher, Clarence L.	582	Grove, Bernard	
Fletcher, Dora C.	211	Grove, Charles W.	658
Fletcher, Russell L.	104	Grove, Claude M.	1335
Fletcher, Thurman C.	839	Grove, Raymond	
Follin, Craven J.	81	Gruber, Charles W.	1356
Ford, Benjamin P.	52	Grubbs, Clarence C.	253
Franks, Joseph M.	55	Grubbs, Kinsel B.	279
Fries, Arthur R.	72	Guthridge, William E.	240
Frye, William F.	1050	Haddox, George C.	
Funk, Edward	154	Haines, Edwin M.	210
Gardner, Garland A.	100	Haines, Marvin D.	924
Gaylord, Paul C.	669	Haines, Nelson A.	974
Gazes, James	103	Haiser, Robert	
Giles, Samuel N.	148	Hamilton, Charles D.	723
Gilkerson, Charles L.	91	Hardy, Charles C.	159
Ginn, John O.	497	Harloe, Charles B.	696
Glenn, Charles L.	91	Harloe, Curtis G.	1275
Golliday, John B.	710	Harloe, William E., Jr.	490
Golliday, John F. H.	249	Harmer, Harry	1135
Good, James W.	889	Harrison, Katharine Y.	
Good, Oliver C.	717	Harrison, Matthew	208
Good, William J. B.	81	Hart, James W.	1300
Gordon, Robert	156	Hartford, Samuel R.	1037
Gore, Norval P.	25	Harvey, Andrew	295
Goss, Edward C.		Hatcher, Julian S.	
Goss, William E.		Hatcher, Richard F.	
Gough, Hubert N.	986	Hawkins, Linden O.	19
Gray, Allen B.	884	Hawkins, Harry E.	
Gray, Frank P.	87	Hawkins, Stanford G.	729
Greenwalt, Cyrus M.	1088	Headley, John W.	169
Greenwalt, Daniel B.	68	Heishman, Percy B.	838
Griffith, Richard E.	88	Henkel, Alfred S.	727
Grim, Andrew C.	288	Henretty, Raymond	1242
Grim, Claude M.		Henry, Ellsworth A.	274
Grim, Clifford D.	1072	Henry, Edward L.	
Grim, Ford A.	553	Henry, James	1322
Grim, George B.	1220	Henry, Theodore	
Grim, George H.		Henry, Wilmer C.	334
Grim, Harry G.	1266	Hensell, Nelson C.	31
Grim, Howard L.	189	Herbaugh, Luther C.	791
Grim, James W.	897	Hewitt, Charles L.	
Grim, Manily C.	112	Hewitt, Wilber E.	2020
Grim, Oliver F.	930	Hibbard, Charles B.	117
Grim, Strother W.	400	Hicks, Elmer T.	1236

Hicks, Harry W.	71	Kelchner, Justin N.	
Hicks, Stella		Kendall, Benjamin	
Hicks, Wickham B.	581	Kendall, Maynard L.	439
High, Edward S. J.	639	Kennedy, Philip E.	
Hillyard, Ashby H.	152	Kenney, Frederick S.	127
Hillyard, Harrison L.	182	Kern, Edward W.	1097
Hillyard, Roy		Kern, Hunter W.	
Hillyard, William H.	1270	Kern, Lohr E.	39
Himelright, Earl	570	Kern, Ramey B.	1173
Hiner, George W.	1428	Kern, Roy P.	625
Hite, Alfred H.	706	Karns, Homer C.	112
Hite, Earl E.	80	Karns, Hunter	53
Hodgson, Isaac S.	51	Karns, Ward W.	507
Hodgson, Milton	1363	Kidwell, John N.	742
Holler, Lee C.	12	Kidwell, Leslie	
Holliday, Carson K.	336	Kidwell, Robert E.	739
Holliday, Owen C.	899	Kline, Everett D.	1489
Hook, Charles L.	65	Kline, John F.	220
Hook, Clagett F.	105	Kline, Roger A.	94
Hook, Russell E.	33	Kline, Samuel R.	549
Hoover, George M.		Knapp, Martin J.	787
Hott, James W.		Knight, Benjamin M.	1555
Hottle, Julian L.	1736	Kremer, Dallas M.	
Hottle, Kiley G.	813	Kremer, John R.	48
Hottle, William H.	1475	Kremer, Paul	
Hovermale, Earl	129	Kromer, Carl P.	820
Howe, John		Lacy, J. H., Jr.	
Hudson, Willie E.	1184	Lacy, Sedden C.	
Hughes, John H.		Lamp, James R.	1102
Hummer, Charles E.	803	Lamp, Jerry R.	108
Hutzler, George S.	1430	Lanham, Clyde B.	
Hyssong, William L.		Lantz, Howard M.	1209
Jackson, Taylor F.	1020	Larrick, Earl M.	989
Jenkins, Robert R.	56	Larrick, Eugene G.	1029
Jenkins, William E.	26	Larrick, Jonah L.	
Jolliffe, Lawrence V. H.	15	Larrick, Lou M.	394
Johnson, Benjamin L.		Larrick, Robert B.	
Johnson, Harry J.	73	Larrick, Roy S.	60
Johnson, Haywood S.	733	Larrick, William E.	1251
Jones, Clayton W.		Lauck, Herbert S.	1458
Jones, Robert L.		Legg, Theodore H.	
Jones, Robert S.		Lemley, Fred M.	1176
Kater, Joseph A.	820	Lemley, Gervis E.	1455
Keating, William B.	39	Lemley, Maurice P.	936
Keckley, Clarence	87	Lenol, William	
Keith, William Sr.	10	Lewis, Earl S.	
Kelchner, Justie C.	1083	Lewis, Henry N.	1110

Lewis, Hugh M.	778	Marsh, Harold C.	461
Lewis, Leslie C.	16	Marshall, Peyton J.	133
Lichliter, Dudley C.	53	Mason, Albert M.	1199
Light, Ernest H.	861	Mason, Ralph E.	1151
Lineburg, Hesler	1597	Massey, Carl F.	752
Lineburg, John E.	1067	Mattison, Raymond L.	137
Lineburg, Lohring R.	1225	Mauck, Clyde B.	554
Lineburg, Willie B.	396	Mauzy, Frederick	1413
Lockhart, Clarence D.	580	Mavelis, William	103
Lonas, Edgar	122	Metz, William R.	95
Lonas, Edward R.	275	Milburn, Janney	355
Lonas, Elmer E.	414	Miller, E. C.	
Long, Raymond L.	1479	Miller, Harrison M.	1348
Long, Reuben L.	167	Miller, Ivanhoe	650
Lowery, George W.	937	Miller, Percy D.	164
Lowery, Luther C.	1014	Miller, Theodore R.	
Lowery, Luther W.	1426	Miller, Weeden A.	546
Loy, William S.	1395	Mills, Frederick D.	630
Lupton, Edmund C.	764	Mills, George R.	1233
Lupton, Harry M.	693	Mills, John H.	994
Lupton, James R.	185	Moling, John H., Jr.	623
Luttrell, Smith	562	Moore, Benjamin F.	882
Lynch, Anna E.		Moore, Harden C.	290
Lynch, Harry H.	1150	Moreland, Thomas R.	
Lyon, Gilbert L.	58	Morrison, Clinton R.	246
McAboy, Harry J.	116	Morrison, Hetra (?)	
McCann, Harry L.	2014	Mowery, Frank I.	141
McCarty, George L.	1346	Mumaw, Arthur M.	569
McCarty, Robert L.	1474	Murman, John H.	202
McCauley, Clayton W.	1065	Murman, Maurice M.	264
McCauley, Harry C.	63	Myers, Allen H.	631
McCauley, Herbert H.	251	Nagley, Elisha P.	273
McCauley, Walter G.	77	Nail, Frederick S.	515
McClure, Floyd		Nesmith, Lohring L.	1447
McFadden, Annie E.		Newcome, Harry C.	1448
McFadden, John R.		Newell, Ward M.	
McFadden, Patrick J.	75	Newlin, James B.	50
McFadden, Samuel D.	1093	Newlin, Joseph	
McFarland, Carter C.	772	Newlin, Miller	599
McFarland, Lucius		Noonan, James E.	8
McFarland, Stewart C.	707	Noonan, Mahlon	266
McKee, William D.	840	Novick, Abram J.	8
McKeever, Ernest W.	1290	Nulton, Louis M.	
Manuel, Thomas H.	410	Oates, Caudy W.	1206
Maphis, John A.	909	O'Connell, Nadiel F.	734
Maphis, J. Luther		O'Leary, Daniel C.	701
Marple, Charles A.	196	O'Leary, Joseph C.	180

Appendix

Omps, Emmett 1309
O'Rear, G. Miller 694
Orndorff, Alfred L. 1265
Orndorff, Briscoe B. 1287
Orndorff, Charles H. 855
Orndorff, Ernest C. 1307
Orndorff, Gordon D. 1285
Orndorff, Harry C. 178
Orndorff, Homer B. 715
Orndorff, Jacob D. 835
Orndorff, Jacob W. 1445
Orndorff, Joseph H. 242
Orndorff, Robert C. 226
Orndorff, Romanus 236
Owens, Roy L. 34
Page, William N. ....
Pangle, Isaac N. 856
Pangle, Leslie L. 856
Patrick, Harry G. ....
Patton, Albert R. 373
Patton, Leslie E. 122
Payne, Cecil ....
Payne, Manily C. 1464
Pearson, John W. ....
Peery, Wilford W. 174
Perry, Christopher C. 111
Perry, Howard F. 912
Perry, Jesse M. 469
Perry, Thomas L. 62
Perry, William C. 852
Pettigrew, — ....
Pickeral, Harly ....
Pickeral, Howard E. 337
Pierce, Hugh D. ....
Pierce, Paul P. ....
Pifer, Clark S. 749
Pingley, Clayton E. 368
Pingley, Francis W. ......
Pingley, Holmes L. 18
Pingley, William B. 768
Pitzer, Henry B. 13
Place, Joseph 1025
Plank, Purcell D. 983
Pollard, Ralph ....
Pope, Richard H. 996
Price, Ernest 1360
Price, Harry J. 1194

Price, William R. 32
Printz, Isaac C. 69
Puffinberger, Lorenzo 1196
Puffinberger, Roy 997
Puffinberger, Thurman L. . 187
Racey, John W. 1441
Racey, Madison M. 150
Randall, Harry S. 47
Reardon, David M. ......
Reardon, Harry L. 158
Reed, James L. 141
Rees, John W. 1299
Rees, Samuel E. 72
Reid, Joseph W. ....
Reid, Sanford H. 1366
Reilly, Theodore K. 1177
Reynolds, Carroll A. 67
Reynolds, Lloyd E. 1095
Rhodes, David S. 641
Rice, Louis K. 168
Richards, Boyd R. 907
Richards, Nelson F. ......
Richards, Roy W. ....
Richards, William P. 999
Ridgeway, Grover R. 1243
Rinker, Clayton L. 316
Rinker, Roy R. 1235
Rinker, Walter N. 934
Ritter, Arthur N. 313
Ritter, Floyd V. 89
Ritter, John 47
Ritter, Roy H. 981
Ritter, Walter N. 228
Robinson, Charles A. 934
Robinson, Elmer L. 1359
Robinson, Harry D. 131
Roe, Joseph H. 67
Rogers, William E. 1259
Rothgeb, Dale D. 592
Rosenberger, Holmes 603
Rosenberger, John H. 303
Rosenberger, Lloyd M. ... 1425
Rosenberger, Raymond L. . 1122
Rosenberger, Ralph R. ... 284
Roszel, Brantz M. ....
Roszel, George B. ....
Ruebush, Edgar W. 155

Rush, Scott L.	673	Snapp, Ralph B.	
Russell, Barthlew F.	527	Snapp, Robert	
Russell, Lee F.		Snyder, Benton	
Ryan, Claude H.		Snyder, Edwin	
Ryan, Glenn N.	408	Snyder, Elwood	
Ryan, Robert R.	116	Snyder, John E.	162
Sager, Arthur C.	359	Snyder, William B.	759
Sanger, Arthur C.		Solenberger, Howard M.	245
Schenk, R. E.		Solenberger, Hugh S.	721
Schindel, Frederick H.	1440	Sonner, Earl K.	944
Schmidt, Carl F.		Spillman, Carl C.	
Schlack, Grover H.	1003	Spillman, Paul C.	
Schuler, Herbert D.	1337	Spillman, Douglas D.	
Scrivener, Garner F.	960	Spillman, Holmes	477
Scruggs, Robert L.	805	Spillman, Paul C.	
Semeples, John P.	428	Sprint, Frank H.	513
Sencindiver, Turner E.	1304	Sprint, Thomas H.	421
Shade, Walter M.	1345	Stalling, George F.	1167
Shanholtz, Harmon L.	462	Steel, Willie	30
Sherman, John C.	1239	Steele, Carson R.	1434
Sherrard, Samuel D.	1386	Stephenson, Henry N.	
Shorts, Arthur F.	642	Stewart, Richard C.	270
Shrum, Guy L.	28	Stickley, William D.	53
Shryock, Paul F.	1227	Stimmel, James H.	990
Shryock, Wilmer F.	271	Stine, Albert W.	1062
Shull, Ernest C.	339	Stine, Wilmer H.	543
Shuller, Fred G.	1125	Stotler, Harry W.	542
Sibert, Tressel	81	Stottler, Grenville M.	1461
Sine, Paul M.	1246	Stottler, Jerome L.	54
Singhaas, Lindon A.	11	Strosnider, Ernest S. E.	1284
Sirbaugh, Howard P.	324	Strother, Joseph H.	526
Sisk, Lewis	125	Stuart, John A.	1373
Slonaker, Daily R.	1077	Sullivan, Bernard M.	126
Sloop, Carroll V.	873	Swartz, George H.	
Smith, David F.	1371	Swartz, Howard C.	44
Smith, Lewis W.	617	Taylor, George C.	898
Smith, Robert W.		Taylor, Houston W.	46
Smith, William D.		Taylor, James H.	75
Smith, William D., Jr.	1054	Taylor, William A.	788
Smoke, John W.	388	Tevalt, Arthur G.	1214
Snapp, Carroll L.	1219	Tevalt, Clarence E.	88
Snapp, Joseph A.	1314	Thurston, Thomas L.	804
Snapp, Leslie M.		Trenary, Charles E.	64
Snapp, Loring C.	36	Trenary, Marshall B.	239
Snapp, Louis E.		Triplett, Arlie H.	962
Snapp, Maynard L. C.	1258	Vance, Andrew R.	555
Snapp, Newton E.	545	Vance, Ollie F.	1321

APPENDIX 309

Vance, Walter	83
Vance, William	1324
Vance, William	1394
Vincent, Wade L.	737
Wallace, Isaac N.	512
Ward, Frank	
Ware, Kelly S.	1053
Weaver, Dewitt T.	95
Weems, Courtney W.	295
Weems, Donald L.	627
Weems, Eugene V. H.	1092
Wheat, Francis	
Whitacre, Basil G.	458
Whitacre, Hiram P.	78
Whitacre, Isaac M.	1021
Whitacre, James R.	502
White, Amos M.	1238
White, Loring A.	456
Whitlock, Charles	18
Wiggenton, Charles A.	808
Wiggenton, John C.	695
Wiley, Robert A.	14
Willey, Clark R.	628
Willey, Edgar O.	752
Willey, Theodore R.	647
Willey, Thomas M.	1098
Williams, Esther S.	969
Williams, Lloyd H.	69
Williams, John C.	533
Williams, Patrick H.	692
Williams, Thomas A.	1129
Williams, William C.	440
Willis, Charles H.	
Willis, William C.	
Wilson, William O.	6
Wingfield, Walter G.	350
Wise, Norman K.	1552
Wisecarver, Carson	883
Wisecarver, Maurice F.	684
Wood, Stuart F. B.	
Woodford, John H.	509
Worsley, Harry F.	896
Wright, Gilbert P.	492
Yeakle, John W.	871
Yeakle, Randolph	1179
Yeakley, George T.	876
Young, Charles A.	92
Yost, Edwin C.	118

(B)

COLORED

Addison, Samuel	1241
Alexander, Charles	82
Allen, Roy G.	1431
Arnstead, Frank	267
Arnstead, Randolph	230
Arnstead, Thomas	
Ball, Allen	1454
Ball, Cosby	78
Ball, Horace	1267
Bank, Edward R.	52
Bannister, John L.	810
Bannister, Samuel E.	403
Brown, Robert	520
Brocks, Charles E.	1391
Brocks, Harold A.	735
Burns, Charles H.	800
Burns, Harrison H.	777
Carter, Samuel	45
Cook, John H.	160
Cooper, Lewis M.	506
Crumbell, Joseph	1419
Curry, George W.	278
Dixon, Townsend V.	1132
Dixon, William	708
Ellis, William	1186
Fairley, Robert E.	97
Festus, John G.	992
Fisher, Lloyd P.	863
Fletcher, Charles	205
Green, Harry W.	979
Green, William	100
Harsey, Andrew	
Hubbard, David P.	
Jackson, Christopher	1041
Jackson, Frank B.	38
Jacklyn, Harry	1197

James, Peter 1498
Jefferson, Robert L. 1080
Johnson, Solomon 49
Jones, Theodore E. 1482
Lavender, Herbert B. 1171
Lee, Otho H. 94
Leftridge, Daniel M. 1345
Long, Beverley 227
Long, George D. 292
Mason, Howard 528
Mason, Jesse 170
Mayberry, Roy 1477
Mitchell, Harvey A. ......
Montgomery, Edward 26
Morris, John H. 68
Myers, Roy 594
Nelson, Clifton A. 445
Newman, McKinley 33
Newman, Milton 1127

Nickens, Ambrose S. 171
Nickens, Charles E. 841
Pearson, John W. 1162
Peterson, Charles 895
Robinson, Herod A. 70
Robinson, Randolph R. ... 157
Scott, Charles 1317
Scott, Nelson 1293
Scott, Robert 257
Shorts, Felix G. 892
Stephenson, Aquilla ......
Strange, Charles E. 315
Thomas, Charles M. 407
Thomas, Houston W. 46
Thomas, James H. 75
Thomas, William A. 788
Trenary, Charles E. 64
Trenary, Marshall B. 239
Triplett, Arlie H. 962

(C)

The following is a list of the men who did not wait to be called into service in 1917, but volunteered beforehand. Many of the names will be found also in List A. Others were not subject to the draft, yet they volunteered.

Allemong, Isaac F.
Anderson, Charles R.
Anderson, Waldo M.
Armentrout, Lawson W.
Bailey, Ora R.
Baker, Goodwin G.
Baker, William A.
Baker, William W.
Barton, Robert T.
Barton, Joseph M.
Barton, Lewis N.
Barton, Thomas C.
Barrie, George O.
Beverley, William
Beverley, William A.
Boyce, Crowell R.
Boyles, Henry C.
Brown, Charles D.
Brown, Leslie M.
Brown, William H.

Browne, Bowyer B.
Browne, Horace C.
Breckenridge, William
Brubaker, Charles W.
Butler, Robert R.
Byrd, Thomas B.
Cammer, Claude R.
Carpenter, Robert C.
Carson, Ann L.
Cather, David C.
Cather, Thomas R.
Cave, Samuel L.
Chapman, Arnold P.
Clark, Hugh E.
Clowser, Earl J.
Coble, Alexander L.
Conrad, Bryan
Conrad, Robert Y.
Cooper, Eugene B.
Cresswell, Evan C.

APPENDIX

Curl, James W.
Darlington, Harold M.
Didier, Angelica B.
Dutton, Benjamin B.
Field, Arthur M.
Ford, Benjamin P.
Glenn, Charles L.
Golliday, John B.
Goss, Edward C.
Grim, Claude M.
Grim, Clifford D.
Griffith, Richard E.
Grubb, Kinzel B.
Haines, Edwin McG.
Haines, Marvin D.
Haiser, Robert
Hardy, Charles C.
Harloe, Charles B.
Harrison, Catharine
Harrison, Matthew
Hart, James W.
Hatcher, Julian S.
Hatcher, Richard F.
Henkel, Alfred S.
Hicks, Stella V.
Hicks, Wickham B.
Hillyard, Ashby H.
Hiner, George W.
Hoover, George M.
Hott, James W.
Hyssong, William L.
Johnson, Benjamin L.
Keating, William B.
Kennedy, Philip E.
Kremer, Daller M.
Lacy, Seddon C.
Lewis, Earl S.
Lewis, Henry N.
Lowery, George W.
Lynch, Anna E.
McFadden, Anna E.
McFadden, John R.
McFadden, Patrick J.
McFadden, Samuel D.
Marshall, Peyton J.

Massey, Carl F.
Mattison, Raymond L.
Mills, Frederick D.
Mills, John H.
Moling, John H., Jr.
Nall, Frederick S.
Noonan, James E.
Noonan, Mahlon
Novick, Abram J.
Nulton, Louis McC.
O'Connell, Daniel F.
O'Leary, Daniel C.
Page, William N.
Pierce, Hugh D.
Plank, Persell D. McK.
Reardon, Harry L.
Reid, Joseph W.
Richards, Boyd R.
Richards, Nelson F.
Robinson, Charles A.
Robinson, Harry D.
Roe, Joseph H.
Rosenberger, Holmes G.
Rosenberger, John H.
Rosenberger, Ralph R.
Roszel, Brantz M.
Roszel, George B.
Russell, Lee P.
Schlack, Grover H.
Slonaker, Dailey R.
Shryock, Wilmer F.
Smith, Robert W.
Snapp, Leslie McI.
Snapp, Louis E.
Snyder, John E.
Solenberger, Howard M.
Spillman, Douglas D.
Sprint, Frank H.
Sprint, Thomas B.
Stephenson, Henry N.
Sullivan, Bernard M.
Weems, Courtney W.
Williams, Philip
Willis, William C.
Wood, Stuart F. B.

(D)

ROSTER OF COMPANY I

K means "killed in action;" w'd means "wounded in action."

Captain
Conrad, Robert Y.—k. Oct. 8

First Lieutenants
Dinges, Harold R.—promoted
Grim, George H.—promoted

Second Lieutenants
Barrett, George C.—w'd Oct. 15
Bachelor, Wallace W.
Douglass, Harold A., D. S.
Greckman, Adam—w'd Oct. 15
Norfleet, Eric—w'd Oct. 15
Trout, Fred C.—w'd Oct. 8
Wood, Harold F.

First Sergeant
Smith, Robert W.—w'd Oct. 8

Supply Sergeant
Jones, Marvin D.

Mess Sergeant
Hoover, Benjamin P.

Sergeants
Bolner, Milford J.—k. Oct. 15
Boyce, Crowell C., D. S.
Brewer, Joseph H.
Coleman, Robert L.—w'd Oct. 8
Frye, Jesse—w'd Oct. 15
Funk, Edward
Hinton, Frank—k. Oct. 15
Johnson, Robert C., D. S.
Pierce, Richard M.
Snapp, Louis—w'd Oct. 15
Sullivan, Edwin L., D. S.
Webber, George W.

Corporals
Allemong, Harry E.—w'd Oct. 15
Allemong, Isaac F.—gassed Oct. 11

Arnold, Thomas O.
Ash, John—w'd Oct. 8
Boone, Arthur
Boyce, George C.—w'd Oct. 8
Clatterbuck, Willis
Crichton, John W.—w'd Oct. 13
Curtis, Albert M.—w'd Oct. 8
Curtis, Orin L.
Goss, William E.—w'd Oct. 8
Grimes, Richard T.—w'd Oct. 15
Grimm, Howard E.—w'd Oct. 15
Hoover, George M.
Jenkins, Arthur
Johnson, Edward S.—w'd Oct. 8
Joynes, William M.
Kelly, Anie C.
Kelly, James C.—w'd Oct. 8 and 15
Kidwell, Leslie E.—w'd
Kleinhaus, Howard P.—company clerk
Legg, Theodore
McDaniels, Eugene—w'd Oct. 8
McFarland, Charles E.—gassed Oct. 8
McFarland, Samuel
Payne, Cecil M.
Payne, Manley C.
Pierce, Paul—w'd Oct. 15
Reid, Joseph
Rider, Winson
Snapp, Robert M.
Terrell, William G.
Wood, Stuart T. B.

Cooks
Boyce, John C.
Fox, William F.
Henry, Theodore
Taylor, Milbourn C.

Mechanics

Beahm, Carroll R.—w'd Oct. 15
Chappell, Robert R.—w'd Oct. 15
Cox, Welby C.—gassed Oct. 18
Feltner, Emil K.—w'd Oct. 15

Buglers

Morrison, Hilra
Timmons, Alvin G.

Privates

Aaron, John C.
Ahrberg, Robert F.
Airheart, Earl D.—k. Oct. 24
Albin, Stonewall J.
Apple, Edward T.
Aragona, Joseph
Balgovyen, Herman
Bell, Levi P.—w'd Aug. 31
Berry, James R.—w'd Oct. 15
Blane, Silvane
Boone, Marshall
Breeden, Lonnie R.—w'd Oct. 15
Brill, Worth
Brown, Boyd I.—w'd Oct. 8
Brunson, James R.
Burton, Clyde H.—w'd Aug. 31
Butler, John—w'd Oct. 15
Capps, Vernon L.
Carroll, William I.
Chandler, William E.
Chappell, Albert B.
Chappell, John H.
Chosak, Reuben—w'd Oct. 8
Clatterbuck, Linwood
Clayton, Irving B.
Coone, Peter
Cook, George D.—w'd Oct. 15
Crockett, Robert C.
Crowley, John S.—w'd Oct. 8
Dale, Henry R.
Daniels, Thomas M.—w'd Oct. 8
Derflinger, Clarence—k. Oct. 15
DeMagis, Richard—w'd Oct. 15
DeSpirito, Salvatore—w'd Oct. 8
DeVesconcelles, Jose T.—w'd Oct. 8

Dodson, Rumsey—w'd Oct. 15
Donald, Charles E.
Donague, John
Eagle, David H.—gassed Oct. 8
Edmonds, Lloyd—w'd Oct. 8
Ellis, Ernest M.
Feinman, Samuel
Ferris, Clyde E.
Ferry, Talmadge H.—w'd Oct. 15
Findley, Charles M.—w'd, died Oct. 15
Ford, Florida Jr.
Fowler, Wade H.—w'd Oct. 14
Fuller, Robert W.—w'd Oct. 8
Fragapone, Carmelo—w'd Sept. 5
Geary, James
Gomick, Benjamin
Gondall, Kenneth B.
Gray, Clifford—k. Oct. 15
Gray, James H.
Greckman, Adam J.—k. Oct. 15
Haines, Robert
Harden, Homer B.
Harlsey, William B.—w'd Oct. 8
Harrington, Parker—w'd Oct. 15
Harris, Irvin M.—w'd Oct. 15
Harrison, George
Harrison, Joseph A.—w'd Oct. 8
Hart, James
Heil, Louis
Henbuer, Hags
Higgenbotham, Earl—gassed Oct. 10
Hitchcock, Walter—k. Oct. 12
Hoffman, Ashby H.—w'd Oct. 15
Holdsworth, Herbert
Hooten, Leroy
Hopkins, Maxwell—w'd Oct. 8
Horton, Cecil M.
Hoyden, Francis C.—w'd Oct. 15
Hughes, John W.—w'd Oct. 24
Hutchins, Charles
Hutchinson, Cornelius
Imbeci, Antonio—w'd Oct. 15
Ingram, Isaac—w'd Oct. 15
Jackson, Howard—k. Oct. 15

James, David C.
Jenkins, Robert L.—w'd Oct. 15
Jewell, Clarence
Kerns, Ramey B.
Kirkley, Willis—w'd Oct. 15
Kramer, George
Kremer, Dallas M.
Kupfahl, Walter E.—k. Oct. 15
Lafferty, Robert L.—k. Oct. 8
Layton, Frank
Levenburg, Abraham
Limosaro, Luigi
Lord, Linwood J.—w'd Oct. 15
Love, John F.—w'd Oct. 8
Lucas, Floyd—k. Oct. 15
Luttrell, Eldridge—w'd Oct. 15
McCollough, Riley
McDonough, Edward J.
McGillicuddy, James P.—w'd Oct. 15
McKeen, Michael A.
McTague, James
Mallory, Martin P.
Mattox, William
Meyers, Albert F.
Miller, Frank
Moore, John J.
Moore, Y. C.—gassed Oct. 8
Nutter, Noah
Myers, John A.—gassed Oct. 8
Oden, Clarence
Pack, Lester A.
Pack, Roscoe C.—k. Oct. 15
Papadakis, John A.
Patridge, James B.—gassed Oct. 8
Peacher, Clarence
Peffer, Clarence—w'd Oct. 8
Perrone, Lorenzo
Pierre, Hugh
Phaife, John
Pommerville, Leslie—w'd Oct. 15
Prophet, James—w'd Oct. 8
Ragsdale, John L.
Randall, Alpheus

Reid, James H.
Richardson, Joseph G.—w'd Oct. 8
Ricks, James B.
Riggis, Angelo
Rogers, Roy L.—w'd Oct. 15
Ronzetti, Gabriele—gassed Oct. 8
Russell, Lee F.
Sawitz, Isaac
Scruggs, Robert—gassed Oct. 18
See, Herman
Shank, Raymond S.—k. Oct. 15
Sherman, Jacob—w'd Oct. 15
Shiley, Frank P.
Skinner, George S.
Smith, James—w'd Oct. 13
Smith, William H.—w'd Oct. 8
Snyder, William I.—w'd Oct. 15
Solicalis, Louis
Stewart, Rodney C.
Stickles, Robert
Southerland, Edgar—k. Oct. 15
Sutherland, Henry
Sutton, Henry H.
Taylor, James W.
Thornhill, John R.—w'd Oct. 8
Tinsley, Thomas S.
Tyus, Samuel C.—w'd Oct. 15
Van Nassar, Henry W.—gassed Oct. 12
Verscheuren, Rens
Vinciprova, Edward—w'd Oct. 15
Walker, William L.—gassed Oct. 8
Weakley, Lee G.
Webb, Clyde H.
Weber, Henry J.—w'd Oct. 15
Werner, William H.—w'd Oct. 8
Wilbourn, James—k. Oct. 8
Wilson, Thomas H.—w'd Oct. 8
Wilson, Robert P.—k. Oct. 15
Woodward, Carl W.
Yowell, Jackson F.

GENERAL INDEX

For names of persons see "Index of Names."

Abraham's Run	24
Acts Relating to Winchester	202, 204
Angerona	234
Annals, Newspaper	115, 127
Appearance of Winchester and Environs, 1865	193, 194
Apprentices	117, 118, 120, 126
Approach of War	146, 147
Attorneys, List of	198
Authors, Local	228
Banks	113
Banks, General, in Shenandoah	153, 155
Baptists	215
Blue Ridge	22, 23
Book Binderies	223
Boomerangs	190
Braddock Expedition	63, 64
Braddock's Sash	64
Broaddus College	237
Building Materials	52
Burnaby's Visit, 1760	85
Business Houses, 1824	114
Call of the Water	229, 230
Camps in 1812	121, 122
Cannonball House	158
Carter's Farm, Battle of	161
Castiglioni's Visit	111
Catholic Church	215
Cedar Creek, Battle of	171-176
Centinel, Virginia	223
Church Organizations	216
City Hall	138
Clark Expedition	88
Climate	24, 25, 119
Coaches of 1810	119
Coins, Values of	54, 55
Colonials as Soldiers	82
Colonies in 1724	18, 19
Constellation	223
County Government, Colonial	16
Courthouse	135
Courthouse Lot	134

316   THE STORY OF WINCHESTER IN VIRGINIA

Court Proceedings, 1743-1756 53
Devastation of Shenandoah 169, 170
Ducking Stool 136
Dunbar Female Institute 237
Dunmore War 85, 86
Duquesne, Capture of 79
Dutch Mess 88
Diary of W. S. Tyler 191, 192
Early at Winchester, 1864 159
Early in Maryland 159
Early in Lower Valley, 1863 160
Early Lot Owners 158
Early Opinions on Schools 49
Early Settlement 231
Early Settlement, Composition of 38-40
Early's Advance after Cedar Creek 39
Early's Army, Strength of 176
Early's Retreat through Middle Valley 162, 163
Early's Return after Cedar Creek 169
Early's Valley Campaign, Results 170
Eastern and Western Districts 176, 177
Economics, War-Time 35, 36
Education, Colonial 188
Efforts for Free Schools 17
Election of 1860 239
Elks, Order of 145
Episcopal Church 220
Episcopal Female Institute 205-207
Established Church 237
Europe in 1724 .... 20, 21
Evening Item 224
Evening Star 224
Executions 127
Exiles from Pennsylvania 90, 91
Explorations of 1671 37
Fairs 50, 111
Falling Waters, Battle of 150
Fairfax and Hite Controversy 30, 31
Fairfax Hall 237
Fairfax Line 29
Fairfax Stone 29
Federal Sympathizers 187, 188
Federals and Townspeople 192
Fire Companies 109-111
Fire Department 138
First Fairfax Addition 47, 48
First Houses in Winchester 40

GENERAL INDEX 317

First Land Purchase	39
First Regiment	90
Fisher's Hill, Battle of	168, 169
Fithian's Visit, 1775	86, 87
Flour Sent to Boston	86
Fort Collyer	181
Fort Frederick	74
Fort Loudoun	73, 77, 119
Fort Loudoun Seminary	237
Fourth of July, 1841	125
Fraternities, Sundry	220
Frederick, Contraction of	102
Frederick, Organization of	36
Free Schools Organized	240
French, Controversy with	62
French Explorations	37
Friends, Society of	43, 207, 208
Gas Works	109
Geary at Winchester	157
George Washington Hotel	109
German Language Schools	234
Golden Buck	107
Gordon's Visit, 1755	84
Greenway Court	29
Hampshire County Organized	62
Harper's Ferry, Confederate Occupation of	149, 150
Healthfulness	26
Hillman Tollgate	191
Historic Associations	27
Hotel Jack	109
Hotels	104-109
Illegitimacy	54
Incorporation of Winchester	59
Indian Road	40, 41
Indians, Relations with	61
In-Lots and Out-Lots	48
Jackson at Winchester	152
Jackson's Retreat	156, 157
Jail	135
John Brown Raid	143
John Kerr School	240
Journal, Winchester	225
Kernstown, First Battle of	154, 183
Kernstown, Second Battle of	160
Lancastrian School	235
Later Enlargements of Winchester	49
Law Courts	196, 197

Law School 238
Leader, Winchester 225
Lee, Surrender of 192
Legislators 200-202
Local Book Publications 227-229
Louis Philippe 107
Lower Shenandoah Valley 22
Lutheran Church 210-212
Magill School 237
Manassas Gap Railroad 130
Markers in Courthouse Square 139, 140
Market House 136, 137, 204
Martinsburg and Potomac Railroad 131
Masonic Order 218-220
Medical College 144, 238
Methodist Episcopal Church 213, 215
Methodist Episcopal Church, South 214
Military Events, 1861 .... 150, 151
Military Events, 1864 .... 163, 164
Military Transfers of Winchester, Number of 193
Milroy's Defeat 158
Milroy's Fort 185
Moorefield, Engagement at 161
Moravian Visit 52
Morgan's Rifle Company 87
Mosby's Surrender 178
Negro Refugees 184
Negroes and Slavery 145
New Virginia 35
Night on the Battlefield 190, 191
North Carolina Soldiers 184
Northern Neck 28
Northern Neck, Sale of Fairfax Interests 32
Northern Women Prisoners 186
Occupation by Banks 182, 183
Occupation by Milroy 185-187
Odd Fellows 220
Office of County Clerk 136
Old Churchyard 140
Opequon, Battle of 164-168
Opequon Creek 24
Orange County 36
Paper Money 188
Petitions to Legislature 96-101
Pillories 136
Place-Names 26, 41
Postoffices, Colonial 17

General Index

Potomac Advertiser 221
Potomac River 23
Potomoke Settlement 37, 38
Presbyterian Church 209
Prisoner for Debt 92
Proposed Division of Virginia in 1816 113
Quakers and War 75
Quitrents 31, 32, 46
Railroad Beginnings 128
Red Bud Run 24
Red Lion Hotel 106, 120
Red Men, Order of 220
Roads and Pikes 103, 104
Romney Expedition 152, 153
Ruined Stone Church 211, 212
Salt in the War 189
Scenic Setting of Winchester 26
School Enrollments 240
Schools, Miscellaneous 238
Schoolhouse of 1748 231
Second Fairfax Addition 49
Sentinel, Winchester 225
Shawnee Village 35, 40, 62
Sheep Hill 48
Shenandoah as a Wilderness 34
Shenandoah Valley Academy 233, 234
Shepherdstown, Battle of 158
Sheridan and Early 161, 162
Sheridan in Command 161
Sheridan's Advance, 1865 .... 177, 178
Sheridan's Army, Strength of 162
Sheridan's Ride 173, 174
Sigel's Advance 159
Smuggling, War-Time 189
Soils 23
Soldiers, Behavior of 187
Solomon's Temple 138
Spies 188
Spotswood's Tour 37
Spottsylvania County 36
Springs 24
Stage Lines 104
Star Fort 157
Storms 25
Strategic Importance of Winchester 147-149
Streets 102, 103, 140
Schools of 1840 236

Taverns 51, 52
Taylor House 105, 112
Teachers, Early 231, 232
Temperance Societies 126, 217
Textbooks 236, 240
Thanksgiving, 1815 122
Theatrical Societies 124
Times in 1759-1783 84
Tom's Brook, Battle of 170
Tory Insurrection 88
Town Site a Forest 43
United Brethren Church 215
Valley Female College 237
Valley Female Institute 236
Values, Colonial 55, 59
Virginia Chronicle 221
Virginia in 1724 13-15
Visits by Indians 119
Wagon Yard 138
War Prisoners of Revolution 88-90
War Times in Winchester, 1864 .... 190, 191, 194
Washington: a Parallel 80-82
Washington and Dagworthy 67
Washington and Ohio Railroad 131-133
Washington as Frontier Commander 65
Washington, Burning of City 121
Washington's Election 79, 80
Washington's Letters from Winchester 65-77
Washington's Regiment 65
Whipping Post 136
White in Winchester 157, 185
Winchester Academy 232
Winchester Advertiser 221
Winchester, England 41
Winchester and Potomac Railroad 129,130
Winchester and Strasburg Railroad 130
Winchester and Western Railroad 133
Winchester as a Camp 180, 181
Winchester as a Hospital 189
Winchester, Choice of as County Seat 46
Winchester Female Academy 235
Winchester First Battle of 156, 183, 184
Winchester in 1753 111
Winchester in 1777 85
Winchester in 1796 112
Winchester in 1810 112
Winchester in 1833 112

Winchester in 1840	112
Winchester Inn	109
Winchester News	224
Winchester Newspapers	225, 226
Winchester Republican	224
Winchester Times	224
Winchester Virginian	224
Winchester Topography	22, 41
Woodmen of the World	220
Wood's Addition	49
Wood's Bond	44
Wood's Town Site	44, 47
World of 1724, The	20
Year of Stress, A	190
Young Men's Christian Association	217

INDEX OF NAMES

In this index are the names found on pages 17-265 inclusive. With a few minor exceptions, the appendices consist quite wholly of lists of names arranged in alphabetic order. For the said reason they are not repeated in this place. But the supplementary names in Appendix A, are to be found in this index.

Adam, Ludwig 211
Adams, J. Q. 126
Affleck, Thomas 91
Albert, Simon 266
Albrith, Michael 211
Aldridge, John 269
Alfridge, Frederick 108, 266
Alexander, Morgan 218
Alexander, W. A. 198
Allen, Thomas 123, 124
Altrick, Christopher 210
Amherst, Lord 103
Amick, P. L. 106
Anderson, Jacob 266
Anderson, James 209
Anderson, Robert 88
Anderson, Gen. R. H. 162
Arbogast, Benjamin 237
Armstrong, Maxwell 198
Armstrong, William 97
Arnett, W. W. 198
Arnold, Edgar 228
Asbury, Francis 213
Ash, James 198
Ashby, John 206
Ashby, Robert 79
Ashby, Richard 180
Ashby, Turner 150, 180
Ashby, T. A. 144
Atkinson, W. M. 197, 198
Aulick, Frederick 106, 114
Averill, Gen. 166
Avirett, J. B. 228, 237
Avis, John 144
Aydelotte, B. 120
Aydelotte, Joshua 120
Babcock, William 270

Balch, L. P. W. 198
Baldwin, J. C. 120
Baldwin, Dr. 186
Baker, E. S. 201
Baker, George 266
Baker, Henry 118, 211, 232
Baker, Henry F. 123
Baker, H. S. 217
Baker, H. W. 113
Baker, J. and G. 123
Baker, Jacob 113, 266
Baker, John .. 99, 198, 266, 271
Baker, Jonas 101
Baker, Joseph 215, 235, 266
Baker, Joshua 268
Baker, R. L. 201
Baker, Wm. A. 120
Baker, W. W. 97
Ball, Samuel 270
Balmain, Alexander 140, 206, 207, 232
Balthasar, P. 211
Banks, Gen. N. P. 105, 153
Barley, (Simpson and Barley) 123
Barnes, C. 198
Barnhart, George 123
Bartgis, ——— 221
Barton, David W. 194, 198
Barton, Randolph 198
Barton, Robert T. ....
.... 198, 200, 201, 228
Barton, Richard W. 201
Barton, Strother 151
Battle, Gen. 163
Baum, Leonard 119
Baum, W. M. 212
Baylor, F. C. 228

Beall, H. D. 224
Beatty, Capt. Henry 122
Becker, Heinrich 210
Beeler, Joseph 219
Beierlin, Kathrina 38
Bell, Capt. David 65
Bell, J. N. 236
Bell, John N. 123
Bell, William 122
Bell, —— 118
Berger, Immanuel 210
Berkeley, Lord 28
Berry, Benjamin 118
Berry, Henry 198
Bethel, William 79
Beveridge, A. J. 103, 197
Billings, Cornelia 237
Billings, Mary 237
Billings, Silas 237
Blincoe, Simpson 198
Bliss, Oliver 198
Boehm, Henry 217
Bogan, John 271
Boley, Newton 126
Borden, Joseph 79
Boscawen, Admiral 102
Bostin, Martin 49
Botts, Lawson 198
Bowen, James 201
Bowen, J. R. 216
Bowen, Richard 223
Bowers, G. S. 212
Bowley (Dorsey and Bowley) 123
Bowling, Jeremiah 120
Bowman, Capt. Joseph 88
Bowyer, J. C. 224
Boyce, N. L. 198
Boyce, Richard 261
Boyd, Belle 188
Boyd, Elisha 198
Boyd, E. H. 198
Boyd, Holmes, Jr. 198
Boyd, Hunter 228
Boyd, L. McC. 228
Boyer, Godlove 270
Boyle, John 266
Brackenson, Edward 118

Braddock, Gen. E. 63
Bradford, William 238
Brady, —— 105
Bragonier, D. H. 198, 208
Brannon and Forney 123
Brannon, Robert 108
Bratten, Jesse 49
Braun, Jacob 210
Braxton, Capt. 166
Braxton, Charles 201
Brent, Charles L. 198
Brent, George W. 198
Brent, Henry M. 129
Brent, William 127
Brian, Bryant 96
Brinker,, Henry 49, 79, 208
Briscoe, John 78
Brock, Samuel 127
Brockenbrough, William 197
Bronough, Capt. Wm. 65
Brooke, Walter 198
Brooker, William 206
Brown, Elijah 91
Brown, John 129, 143, 198
Bruce, Mrs. A. 93
Bruce, E. C. 228
Bruce, George 49
Bruce, John 129, 232
Bryarly, James 106
Bryce, J. G. 201
Buck, Charles 206
Burgess, John H. 123
Burgess, Owen 151
Burkhart, Christian 270
Burkhart, Henry 270
Burnaby, Andrew 44, 85
Burns, James 79
Burns, Robert 232
Burrass, —— 76
Burwell, Nathaniel 116
Bush, Andrew 106
Bush, David 208
Bush, Henry 106, 118
Bush, Mathias 267
Bush, Philip .. 89, 91, 96, 105, 107
.... 118, 208, 210, 232
Bush, —— 49

Bushnell, Benjamin 114
Bushnell, Richard 114
Butler, Adam 268
Butler, Mrs. 64
Byrd, Harry F. 201
Byrd, Richard E. ....
  131, 146, 198, 201, 202, 224,
  225, 233, 239
Byrd, William 13, 31, 79, 198
Byrne, Henry 198

Caither, Elijah 198
Caldwell, —— 49, 235
Caldwell, James 223
Caldwell, Joseph 198
Calmes, Marquis 44, 49, 58
Calmes, William 79
Calvey, John 79
Campbell, Andrew 44, 200
Campbell, B. C. 198
Campbell, Robert 120
Campbell, Thomas 114
Campbell, Thomas B. 123
Campbell, William 114, 219
Cantwell, Thomas 118
Carey, Matthew 227
Carlile, John S. 197
Carlile, Jonathan D. 197
Carlyle, John 49
Carlyle, J. D. 198
Carr, Dabney 197
Carson, Beatty 113
Carson, James M. ....
  .... 124, 198, 200, 201
Carson, Joseph S. 197, 198
Carter, Joseph 61
Carter, Robert 39
Cartmell, —— 51
Cartmell, M. B. 129
Cartmell, T. K. 228
Cass, Lewis 235
Castiglioni, Count 111
Castleman, Ludovick 49
Castleman, William, Jr. 201
Cather, James 201
Cather, T. Russell 200
Cather, W. S. 228

Catlett, James 127
Chandler, Goldsmith 114
Chapline, William 54
Chester, Thomas 23, 44
Chew, Larkin 39
Chilton, William 198
Chipley, James 198
Chisler, John 267
Christie, William 227
Christopher, L. M. 118
Clark and Windle 123
Clark, John 98
Clark, John C. 120
Clark, William L. ....
  .... 144, 151, 197, 198, 228, 232
Clark, (Goldsborough and
  Clark) 224
Clay, Henry 105
Clifford, Sir Thomas 103
Clinter, William 269
Clough Henry 271
Coburn, J. R. 236
Cochrane, James 198
Cochran, William 49, 79
Cochs, William 49
Colbert, John 100
Coleman, Peter 267
Colston, Raleigh 32
Colston, R. 232
Colt, Capt. Thomas 65
Conrad, Daniel 238, 267
Conrad, D. H. 198
Conrad, Frederick ....
  .... 96, 116, 208, 232
Conrad, Frederick, Jr. 267
Conrad, F. W. 212
Conrad, Heriot 99, 203
Conrad, Holmes .. 197, 198, 201
Conrad, John 97
Conrad, P. 198
Conrad, Robert Y. ....
  .. 146, 194, 197, 198, 200, 239
Conway, Gen. 81
Cook, E. E. 198
Cook, Giles 198
Cooke, John E...81, 107, 191, 194
Cooke, John R. 198

Index to Names

Cooley, —— 232
Cooper, Hamilton 118
Cooper, John R. 129
Cooper, N. 97
Copenhaver, Andrew J. 127
Corday, Edward 79
Cornwallis, Lord 89
Cox, Gen. J. D.. 163
Coyle, Capt. Michael 122
Coyle, (Lauck and Coyle) .. 120
Craig, Thomas 218
Craig, John 209
Croft, George 271
Craigen, Robert 49
Crane, —— 127
Crane, A. M. 225
Crawford, Valentine 79
Crawford, William 79
Cromley, James 205
Crockwell, John 219
Crockwell, John, Jr. 267
Crook, Gen. 160
Cross, J. L. 234
Crossley, Mary 53
Crum, Christian 215
Crum, Henry 215
Culpeper, Lord Alex. 28
Culpeper, Catharine 29
Culpeper, Thomas 28
Cunningham, James 269
Curl, James 98
Curtis, John 269
Curtis, Robert 270
Custer, Gen. G. A. 163, 171
Custis, Martha 79

Dagworthy, Capt. 67
Daingerfield, Henry 198
Dame, N. P. 207
Dandridge, Bettie 64
Dandridge, E. P. 198, 201
Danner, —— 126
Darke, Gen. 90
Davenport, Frances E. 26
Davenport, John, Jr. 98
Davidson, William 124
Davis, C. A. 214

Davis, Jefferson 186
Davis, P. S. 208
Davis, Samuel H. 100, 224
Davison, Richardson 120
Davisson, J. S. 201
Deegin, E. S. 117
Denny, J. W. 198
Denny, W. R. 214
Deitrick, David 210
Delaplain, Joe 270
Dinwiddie, Gov. Robert ....
 .... 62, 70, 73, 81
Dixon, John 198
Dobie, Samuel, Jr. 218, 219
Donaldson, John 118
Doring, Eberhard 210
Dorsey and Bowley 123
Dorsey, F. 214
Dosh, T. W. 212
Dougherty, —— 198
Dougherty, Patrick 268
Douglass, Adam 268
Douglass, Isaac R. 197
Douglass, Robert 208
Dowdall, James 96
Dowdall, John 268
Dowdall, J. G. 218
Dowdall, Samuel 97
Dowden, J. G. 232
Doyle, Edward 53
Drinker, Henry 91
Dunbar, Col. 63, 65
Dunmore, Lord 85, 86
Duryea, Gen. 174

Earle, Samuel 49, 200
Early, Gen. Jubal ....
 .... 158, 159, 160, 161, 177
Echols, Gen. John 177
Eddy, Charles 91
Edmondson, A. M. 108
Edmondson, Thomas ....
 .... 49, 96, 118, 202, 232
Edmonson, Samuel 268
Edwards, Jonathan 209
Edwards, William R. 214
Eichelberger, Lewis ... 212, 224

Elking, —— von 89
Elmer, C. D. 234
Embury, Philip 213
Emory, Gen. 162
Enders, James 123
Essek, A. 212
Eskridge, George 201
Evans, A. H. 236
Evans, Gen. 163
Evans, Joseph 120
Evans, Randolph 101
Evans, (Fitch and Evans) .. 126
Evard, —— 114
Everly, John 266
Ewell, Gen. R. S. 155

Fairfax, Denny 32
Fairfax, Col. G. W. ...66, 70, 200
Fairfax, Thomas, Lord ....
  27, 29, 46, 47, 58, 65, 102,
  109, 134, 139
Fairfax, William 29
Fauntleroy, T. T. 198, 201
Fauntleroy, T. T., Jr. 201
Faulkner, C. J. 198
Feif, James 49
Ferguson, Gen. 166
Fern, Fanny 221
Filzel, J. M. 208
Fisher, J. W. 217
Fisher, Miers 91
Fisher, Thomas 91
Fitch and Evans 126
Fithian, —— 55, 86, 209
Fitzsimmons, Michael 114
Fitzsimmons, Nicholas 120
Flood, Mary 54
Forney, (Brannon and
  Forney) 123
Forney, F. W. 110
Foster, Jonathan 223
Foster, —— 227
Fowke, —— 198
Franckel, Stephen 210
Franklin, Benjamin 64
Frazier, Lake J. 200
Fremont, Gen. J. C. ... 155, 156

Fridley, Henry 108
Foster, —— 227
Friendley, Andreas 210
Fritley, Andrew 49
Frye, Christopher 98, 213
Frye, George 213
Frye, Michael 213
Funk, J. H. S. 144
Funsten, O. R. 200
Furlong, Henry 214
Furman, A. T. 198

Gallaher, J. S. 200, 224
Galston, Samuel 209
Gates, Gen. Horatio.. 81, 90, 93
Geary, Gen. 157
Gerard, Lord Charles 103
Germain, Lord 103
Gibbons, J. I. 214
Gibson, Alexander 114
Gibson, James 201
Gilbert, D. M. 212
Gilkeson, John 129
Gilpin, Thomas 91
Ginn and Stackhouse 123
Ginn, Charles L. 198
Gist, —— 67
Given, Francis 267
Glack, Michael 210
Glaize, Isaac 151
Glover, Lewis 198
Glover, Thomas 267
Godwin, Gen. 163
Goertner, N. W. 212
Gold, Daniel 113
Gold, Thomas D. 201
Goldsborough and Clark ... 224
Goodwin, Gen. 167
Goodwin, R. A. 207
Gordon, —— 206
Gordon, Lord Adam 64
Gordon, Gen. J. B. 162, 170
Gordon, T. H. 225
Graham, James R. ....
  .... 37, 182, 192, 210, 228
Granbury, Bishop 214
Grant, Gen. U. S. 160

Index to Names 327

Gray, Richard 97, 118
Gray, Robert .. 113, 120, 118, 267
Graves, George B. 114
Green, John L. 198
Greenfield, John 49
Gresby, Nimrod 269
Grey, —— 198
Griggs, Thomas 198
Grim, C. H. 110
Grim, George 88
Grim, John 88
Grim, L. T. F. 108
Grimes, Gen. 163
Grimes, Charles 270
Grimshaw, Thomas W. 125
Gressett, William 270
Grover, Gen. 166
Guest, Job 214
Guillon, M. 238

Haas, Amos 268
Haas, Frederick 118
Haas, John 268
Haggerty, John 213
Hall, William 118
Halleck, Gen. H. W. 186
Hambert, Godfrey 49
Hamilton, James 233
Hamilton, William 214
Hancock, Gen. W. S. 178
Harbeson, (Kinzing and Harbeson) 118
Hardesty, George 118
Hare, Joseph 26
Harr, William 106
Harmon, Jacob 268
Harrison, B. W. 198
Harrison, John 114, 123
Harrison, Matthew 60
Harrison, Thomas W. ......
 .... 197, 198, 200, 224
Harrow, John 49
Hart, John B. 126
Hartings, Samuel 267
Hartman, Daniel 113
Hasfeldt, John 120
Hauge, Jonas 267

Hawkins, Ephraim 99, 203
Haycock, W. 118
Hayes, Gen. R. B. 171, 193
Haymaker, Adam 268
Haymaker, John 268
Haynes, Charles 96
Heard, Maj. James E. 94
Heath, Henry 51, 54, 79, 105, 108
Hefferman, William 127
Heintz, Christopher 210
Heiskell, Henry 88
Heiskell, John 129, 223
Heizel, Donald 210
Helphinstine, Peter .. 88, 210, 218
Helm, Thomas 79, 267
Helms, Meredith 44, 79
Henderson, R. H. ....
Hendricks, (Newbrough and Hendricks) 120
Heneckel, Christopher 210
Hening and Barhart 120
Henry, G. R. 224
Henry, Patrick 87
Henry, Robert 221
Henry, William 269
Heterick, Robert 232
Hibbard, E. A. 108
Hill, John 58
Hill, William 122, 210
Hillman, Charlotte 191
Hironymus, Pendleton 105
Hite, John 49, 112
Hite, M. 123
Hite, Yost 30, 36, 37, 43, 46
Hobson, William 151
Hoff, John 98
Hoff, Lewis 113
Hoff, Philip 120
Hoff and Morris 120
Hoge, George 44
Hoge, John 209
Hoge, J. B. 198
Hoge, William, Jr. 51
Holliday, Dr. 186
Holliday, F. W. M. 198, 228
Holliday, James 96, 97
Holliday, W. 97

Holliday, William .. 96, 118, 268
Holliday, William D. 123
Hollingsworth, Joseph 117
Hollingsworth, Isaac 113
Hollingsworth, Lydia 43
Hollingsworth S. and D. 120
Hollis, —— 225
Hollis, Thomas 270
Holmes, David 198, 268
Holmes, Hugh 198, 201
Holmes, Joseph ... 118, 201, 232
Holtzel, Charles 268
Hoover, Philip 106
Hope, —— 49
Hopkins, John 198
Howard, John 38, 49
Hopton, Lord 28
Hotchkiss, Major Jed 170
Hott, Jacob F. 215
Howe, G. W. 215
Howell, —— 219
Howling, Adam 266
Hubard, J. R. 207
Huck, Lewis N. 198
Huff, Lewis 98, 211
Humphreys, John 218
Hunt, John 91
Hunter, Adam 79
Hunter, Andrew 198
Hunter, Gen. David 122, 159
Hunter, E. P. 198
Hunter, Moses T. 198
Hunter, R. W. 198, 201
Huntsberry, W. E. 110
Huntington, C. P. 132
Hupp and Martin 123
Hyde, J. P. 237

Imboden, Gen. John 162, 166
Inman, Robert 270
Innes, Col. 70, 81

Jackson, James E. 206
Jackson, Gen. T. J. ....
  .... 149, 151, 152, 162
Jefferson, Thomas 55
Jenkins, J. W. 198

Jervis, Charles 91
Jolliffe, Amos 117
Jolliffe, Meredith 146
Jolliffe, Joseph N. 145
Jolliffe, William 45
Johnson, Col. B. T. 183
Johnson, Gen. Edward ......
  .... 155, 158, 162
Johnson, William 233
Johnston, Gen. J. E. 150, 151, 163
Johnston, Samuel 114
Johnson, W. R. 198
Jones, Abner 268
Jones, Gabriel .. 53, 198, 200, 206
Jones, John 49
Jones, J. H. 231
Jones, Owen 91
Jones, Peter 13
Jones, William 120
Jordan, Branch 262
Jordan, E. C. 202
Jordan, Hugh 118
Julian, Isaac 66

Kahn, Jacob 118
Kain, Bishop 215
Kaine, John 96
Kaufman, M. R. 201
Kean, William 270
Kehoe, Peter 118
Keiser, J. R. 212
Keith, James 53
Kellogg, M. K. 191
Kelly, A. A. 212
Kelly, Michael 53
Kemper, Charles E. 38
Kenly, Col. 155
Kennedy, Andrew 198
Kennedy, David 218
Kent, R. W. 120
Kepler, Samuel 214
Kercheval, Samuel .34, 85, 86, 112
Kercheval, Samuel, Jr. 198
Kern, Asbury 199
Kern, Harry R. 200
Kerr, John 125, 240
Kershaw, Gen. 162

Index to Names

Kiger, George 211
Kiger, Jacob 120
Kiger, James 106
Kimball, Gen. 154
Kimmelmyer, F. 120
Kincaid, William 96
King, Alexander 268
King, Elizabeth 54
King, Joseph 53
King, William 117
Kinzing and Harbeson 118
Kirchner, J. C. 211
Kirk, Felix 231
Kitching, Col. 172
Kilpatrick, Abner 236
Klauprecht, —— 49
Knapp, James 53
Koppenhaber, Jacob 210
Krauth, Charles 228
Krauth, C. P., Jr. 212
Krebs, William 214
Kremer, Conrad 108, 211
Kurtz, Adam 88
Kurtz, Adam, Jr. 120
Kurtz, George 88
Kurtz, George W. 40, 144
Kurtz, Peter 106
Kurtz, P. L. 224

Lacy, Horace 198
Lafayette, Gen. 122
Lambert, Christopher 210
Lamon, Ward 228
Lamont, —— 236
Lancaster, Joseph 235
Larrick, Herbert S. 200
La Rochefoucauld 112
Laubinger, George 210
Lauck and Coyle 120
Lauck, Peter 88, 106, 211
Lauck, Simon 88
Lauck, William 199
Leapold, G. A. 208
Lederer, John 37
Lee, Daniel 113, 197, 199
Lee, Edmund I. 199
Lee, Gen. Fitzhugh 166, 167

Lee, Gen. Henry 122
Lee, Gen. R. E. 206
Lee, R. H. 199, 206
Legrand, Nash 209
Leicester, Earl of 103
Lemar, —— 232
Lemley, J. 210
Lemmon, Robert 205
Lemon, James 49, 79
Lentz, Johannes 211
Lewis, Maj. Andrew 65, 85
Lewis, Col. 64
Lewis, Capt. Joshua 65
Lewis, John 218
Lindsay, John 105, 206
Lindsay, Samuel 218
Lingan, —— 122
Linn, Daniel 105
Little, Daniel 105
Little, James 120
Lodge, Matthew 199
Logan, Lloyd 123
Lomax, Gen. L. L. 161
Long, N. S. 123
Loudoun, Lord 70, 77, 102
Love, Dr. 108
Louis, Philippe 107
Lovell, J. T. 200
Lovett, Jonathan 201
Low, Hugh 144
Lowry, William 118
Lucas, William 199
Ludi, Anton 211
Lupton, John M. 123
Lupton, S. L. 201
Lynch, Harry 199
Lynch, M. M. 199, 200

McAlister, James 97, 116
McAlister, John 97, 116
McBride, —— 219
McCann, J. K. 202
McCann, William 199
McCausland, Gen. John 160, 176
McCloun, Thomas 49
McClure, John 98
McCormick, John 79

McCormick, J. T. 200
McCormick, Marshall 200
McCormick, Province 199
McCoughtry, James 123
McCrory, J. C. 105
McCune, J. G. 201
McDaniel, George 190
McDonald, A. 118
McDonald, Alexander 49
McDonald, Col. Angus .. 86, 218
McDonald, Col. A. W... 150, 199
McFee, William 114
McGarey, Edward 268
McGill, Archibald 201
McGill, Charles 200
McGlennan, Thomas 123
McGuire, Edward ....
  49, 96, 105, 215, 218, 132, 268
McGuire, Mrs. Edward 120
McGuire, D. H. 199
McGuire, H. H. 228, 238
McGuire, William 201
McGuire, W. P. 228
McIntosh, Gen. 164
McIntosh, Joseph 123
McKee, William 79
McKim, Randolph 175
McKinley, Major William 193, 219
McKenney, John 271
McLeod, J. B. 201
McMachen, Samuel 199
McMachen, William 44
McPharlane, John 199
McReynolds, Gen. 157
McSherry, William 105
McVicar, Kate 187, 229
Mackey, Catharine 116
Mackey, Dr. 119
Mackey, John 113
Mackey, Martha 116
Mackey, Robert 232
Macon, Mrs. 182
Magill, —— 235
Magill, Ann 237
Magill, Archibald .. 97, 113, 199
Magill, Charles 199
Magill, C. T. 199

Magill, Eva 237
Magill, John S. 199, 201
Magill, M. T. 228, 237
Mann, John 216
Manning, Gen. 174
Mantor, E. B. 199
Marshall, Charles 199
Marshall, James 32, 146
Marshall, James M. 199
Marshall, John .. 32, 35, 134, 196
Marshall, Thomas 199
Martin, (Hupp and Martin) 123
Martin, J. S. 214
Martin, Philip 32
Martin, Col. T. B. ....
  .... 49, 65, 80, 200, 206
Marvin, J. W. 236
Mason, James M. ....
  .... 183, 197, 199, 228
Mason, John T. 199
Mason, Samuel 231
Massie, Joseph 120
Massie, Josiah 106
Mathews, Alexander 79
Maund, John J. 199
May, —— 218
May, Samuel 96, 232
May, Samuel, Jr. 269
Meade, N. B. 200, 224, 225
Meade, William 206
Mealey, Andrew 51
Medlicott, James 127
Mehrlin, Thomas 49
Meldrum, —— 206
Mercer, George 49, 65, 200
Mercer, John 65
Meredith, James 114
Meredith, W. C. 207
Merritt, Gen. 163, 171
Michel, Louis 37
Michler, Peter 268
Miller, A. J. 208
Miller, Barbara 101
Miller, Daniel 101, 117, 118
Miller, D. J. 201
Miller, Godfrey 113
Miller, John 113, 118, 214

Index to Names

Miller, Joseph A. 202
Miller, L. A. 201
Miller, L. G. M. 212
Miller, William 123
Milroy, Gen. 155, 185
Minor, C. L. C. 228
Mitchell, Charles 151
Monmouth, Duke of 103
Montgomery, John 209
Moore, Gen. 171
Moore, Henry 79
Moore, L. T. 199
Moore, Ryley 79
Moore, S. J. C. 199
More, Thomas 270
Morgan, Betsy 94
Morgan, Gen. Daniel ....
  85, 87, 88, 89, 90, 93, 108, 117
Morgan, Morgan 40, 44
Morgan, Willoughby 122
Morgan, Nancy 94
Moriarty, Jeremiah 238
Morris, (Hoff and Morris) .. 120
Morris, William 113, 122
Morrow, Lucinda 236
Morrow, Robert 270
Morrow, Thomas 267
Morse, Jedediah 112
Morton, Sir William 28
Mosby, Col. J. S. 178
Muhlenberg, Gen. J. P. 88
Murphy, Humphrey 269
Murphy, John 118
Murray, G. 199
Murray, Patrick 96
Murray, John 269
Myer, Mrs. 106
Naylor, William 199
Neill, Lewis 44, 49, 206
Nelson, Charles F. 202
Nelson, C. M. 199
Nelson, Philip 119
Nelson, R. B. 207
Neville, Pressley 94
Newcomer, Christian 215
Newbrough and Hendricks .. 120
Newlin, Joseph B. 200

Newport, John 45
Newsam, George 115
Nicholas, George 199
Nicholls, Mrs. Selim 235
Norton, Daniel 116
Norton, G. F. 224, 225
Norton, John 270
Norton, J. H. 232
Nooler, Marcus 268
Nulton, Joseph 216
Nurse, Gabriel 268
O'Gullion, Duncan 51
Omps, R. L. 202
O'Neal and O'Laughlin 118
O'Neal, Charles 232
Opie, H. L. 200
Otto, Tobias 49, 211
Overacre, Thomas 270
Overfield, M. 123
Owens, Richard 213
Owram, Thomas 97, 117
Page, J. E. 199
Page, Mann 201
Page, Matthew 201
Page, Robert 113, 199, 201
Page, Robert, Jr. 199
Page, William B. 200, 201
Painter, F. V. .N. 229
Palb, Merder 49
Parker, Richard 144, 197, 199
Parker, Richard E. 197
Parker, Col. Thomas 121
Parkins, —— 49
Parkins, Elisha 79
Parkins, Isaac 200
Patchett, Reuben 79
Patterson, Gen. 150, 181
Patton, Col. 166, 167
Payne, Gen. 171
Peachy, William 65
Peans, Robert 79
Pegram, Gen. 163
Pemberton, Israel 91
Pemberton, James 91
Pemberton, John 91
Pendleton, Edmund 106
Penn, William 39, 61

Pennington, Edward	91
Perez, Don M.	238
Perkins, Capt.	151
Perkins, Isaac	49, 205
Perry and Huston	118
Perry, Thomas	79
Peter the Great	21
Peyton, John	74
Peyton, John L.	35
Phelps, Mary	145
Phillips, William	114
Pifer, John W.	145
Pike, Thomas	91
Pilcher, James	49
Pitt, William	78
Pleasant, Samuel	91
Pope, Gen. John	157
Porteus, James	199
Postgate, Thomas	45
Potter, Charles	120
Potter, William	79
Powell, Alfred H.	100, 126, 129, 182, 199, 200
Powell, C. L.	199
Powell, Lloyd	151
Powell, Humphrey	199
Powers, Edward	116
Price, Michael	107
Prince, Peter	106
Princelear, Nicholas	79
Printz, Peter	224
Pritchard, H. K.	224
Quaker, John	269
Quinn, James	214
Quinton, J. W.	207
Ramseur, Gen. S. D.	161, 191
Randolph, J. J.	199, 236
Rayworth, ——	232
Rea, Samuel	123
Reardon, James P.	200
Reck, Abraham	212
Read, T. B.	173
Reed, George	98, 214
Reed, J. B. T.	193
Reed, Michael W.	123
Reed, Robert W.	123
Reed, Samuel	199
Reese, Lewis	271
Reger, Michael	211
Reynolds, John	96
Rhodes and Smith	123
Rice, Warren	200
Richards, Benjamin	106
Richards, James M.	123
Richardson, William	116, 118
Ricketts, Gen.	166
Ridings, Mrs. J. W.	192
Ridley, James	116, 127
Riely, J. P.	199
Ringer, Heinrich	87
Riordan, Richard	118
Ritchie, Thomas	147
Roberts, James	120
Roberts, Mary	54
Roberts, Thomas	120, 122, 124
Riley, Michael	270
Robinson, E. W.	201
Robinson, John	71, 77, 78
Robinson, R. A.	234
Robinson, W. J.	199
Robinson, (Sherrard and Robinson)	224
Rodes, Gen	162, 167
Roots, George	92, 199
Roseberry, Lord	42
Ross, ——	207
Ross, John	43
Rosser, Gen.	169
Roszell, B. M.	234
Rouss, C. B.	110, 138, 141
Rumsay, James	116
Runner, George	271
Russell, ——	102
Russell, David	120
Russell, E. E.	106
Russell, Gen.	166
Russell, Matilda B.	190
Russell, Robert	219
Russell, William	39, 79
Russell, W. G.	225
Rutherford, Mary	60
Rutherford, Robert	79, 200
Rutherford, Thomas	44, 53
Rutherford, William	268

Index to Names

Ryan, Natty 122
Ryland, —— 215
St. Albans, Earl of 28
Salling, John 49
Samuels, —— 199
Sargeant, —— 64
Schmidt, Thomas 211
Schrack, Nicholas 211
Schultz, John 88, 122
Schumacker, Christian 211
Scott, Dr. 117, 121
Scott, John 197
Seabrook, W. L. 212
Seaman, John D. 123
Searle, Mrs. 123
Sebastian, —— 206
Seivers, R. E. 199
Senseny, Dr. 215
Senseny, G. E. 224
Senseny, Jacob 123
Sexton, Joseph 199
Seymour, —— 199
Shepherd, G. C. 237
Sherer, Jacob 114
Sheridan, Gen. P. H. ... 161, 176
Sherman, William 123
Sherrard and Robinson 224
Sherrard, Joseph H. ....
.... 129, 197, 199, 223
Sherrard, Robert 97
Shields, Gen. James ... 153, 154
Shields, J. H. 199
Shirley, Gov. William .. 67, 68
Shreve, Benjamin 96
Shumate, T. 199
Sigel, Gen. Frantz 159
Sigmond, H. J. 210
Silver, J. M. 202
Simmons, Robert 123
Simpson and Barley 123
Sinclair, Adjutant 174
Singleton, James 201
Singleton, W. G. 199
Sink, Nicholas 267
Sittler, Isaac 232
Slater, Edward 115
Slaughter, Thomas 68

Sloat, J. I. 224, 225
Smith, A. C. 199, 200, 232
Smith, A. M. 233, 234, 240
Smith, David 271
Smith, E. 117
Smith, Edward 96, 113, 214
Smith, Edward J. 113
Smith, Isaac 127
Smith, John 74,
113, 118, 177, 200, 201, 214, 232
Smith, John B. 199
Smith, J. B. D. 126, 201
Smith, J. F. 212
Smith, John G. 123
Smith, J. P. 238
Smith, M. 123
Smith, Maria 231
Smith, S. F. 236
Smith, William 91
Smith, William D. ....
.... 91, 200, 201, 207
Snapp, George 88
Snicker, Moses 23
Snickers, Beverly 199
Sniggars, Edward 79
Snodgrass, J. L. 199
Sommerville and Poland 120
Sower, Jacob 51
Sowers, Jacob 208
Sparks, Jared 80
Spear, Thomas 233
Sperry, Peter 49, 88
Sperry, Mrs. 40
Spickert, Julius 211
Spiddle, Martin 217
Spotswood, Alexander 37
Sprecker, Andrew 271
Spurr, William H. 127
Stackhouse, (Ginn and Stackhouse) 123
Stanwix, Col. 71, 78
Star, William 271
Steck, John M. 200, 202
Steele, Robert 124
Stephen, Gen. Adam 65, 88
Stephens, Daniel 49
Stephens, Lewis 49

Stevenson, Edward	79
Stephenson, W. R.	199
Steward, John	49
Stewart, John	53
Stewart, Robert	65
Stickley, E. E.	199
Stine, Isaac	181
Stork, G.	212
Straith, J. H.	238
Strawbridge, Robert	213
Streit, Christian	211, 212, 234
Stribling, Taliaferro	79
Strother, Gen. D. H.	113, 184
Strother, James	127
Strother, Joseph	199
Stuart, John	51
Stuart, Gen. J. E. B.	150, 151
Summers, George W.	149
Summerville, John	270
Swan, Thomas	199
Swartz, M. W.	229
Swearingen, Levi	79
Swearingen, Thomas	79, 80, 200, 205
Sweet, Albert	238
Swift, Jonathan	118
Sydnor, R. M.	201
Taffs, Joseph	267
Tapscott, ——	199
Tarleton, Col. B.	89, 90, 93
Tate, Magnus	79, 268
Tate, William	199
Tavenner, Frank	201
Tavenner, F. S.	201
Tavenner, J. V.	202
Taylor, Bushrod	105, 238
Taylor, Edmund	219
Taylor, James B.	123
Taylor, Jesse, Jr.	97
Taylor, Gen. Richard	183
Taylor, Gen. Zachary	64
Terry, Gen.	163
Thoburn, Gen.	171
Thomas, Joseph	229
Thomas, Daniel	199
Thomas, Mrs.	123
Thomas, S. W.	200
Thompson, John A.	199
Thornton, George F.	125
Thorpe, ——	235
Throckmorton and Holliday.	120
Throckmorton, Warner	199
Thruston, ——	206
Thruston, Buckner	199
Thruston, C. M.	200, 201
Tidball, ——	124
Tidball, Alexander S.	129, 199
Tidball, E. M.	201
Tidball, John	268
Tidball, Joseph	118
Tidball, Josiah	199
Tipping, Mrs.	123
Torbert, Gen.	162
Togno, Dr.	236
Trautvein, Jacob	211
Trevelyan, Otto	78
True, Jacob	269
Tucker, H. St. G.	122, 197, 199, 200, 228, 232, 238
Tucker, John R.	199, 228
Turner, Robert	199
Twigg, M.	117
Tygert, ——	124
Tyler, W. S.	191
Upt, Henry	269
Vallandigham, C. L.	145
Vance, Alexander	79
Vance, David	44
Vanfossen, J. C.	240
Van Horn, William	106
Vanmeter, Isaac	30
Vanmeter, John	21
Vaughan, Gen.	162
Vernon, William W.	120
Waddington, Thomas	79
Waite, Obed	125, 199, 233
Wales, J. S.	238
Walker, Cornelius	206
Walker, Elijah	106
Walker, John	269
Wall, John	120
Wall, John F.	201
Wall, William T.	123
Walls, J. W.	238

INDEX TO NAMES 335

Walters, John 108, 268
Walton, Carroll 199
Walton, M. 199
Ward, George W... 199, 200, 201
Ward, George W., Jr. 199
Ward, Henry P. 123
Ward, J. F. 224
Ward, R. M. 199, 201, 224
Waring, Michael 211
Washington, George ....
27, 49, 51, 62, 64, 65, 81, 82, 99
102, 108, 118, 200, 219
Washington, Lawrence .. 80, 82
Washington, Lawrence A. ..
.... 83, 93, 119
Waters, —— 76
Waters, William 213
Watrous, C. L. 199
Watson, Solomon 127
Waughdy, Henry 54
Waughdy, Mary 54
Webster, Daniel 105
Weitreit, —— 49
Welch, James 266
Weld, Isaac 112
Wells, Morgan 199
Wells, —— 116
Wendell, Samuel 211
West, Hugh 79, 80, 200
Wetsell, Christopher 49, 211
Wharton, Gen. 166
Wharton, Thomas 91
Wheat, J. C. 237
Whipple, John 267
White, Alexander 60, 91, 199, 201
White, Gen. 157, 185
White, John 44
White, N. S. 199
White, Richard 118
White, Robert 197, 199, 201
White, R. B. 197
Whiting, Francis 199
Whiting, Frank B. 199
Whiting, N. S. 199
Whitacre, Nimrod 201
Whittaker, James P. 199
Wickham, Gen. W. C. 168

Wilcox, Henry 221
Wilkenson, Gen. James 105
Wilkes, Commodore 183
Willcocks, Henry 271
Willert, Joseph 268
Williams, Frederick 123
Williams, G. W. 208
Williams, Isaac H. 199
Williams, Jared 201
Williams, J. H. 199, 201
Williams, J. J. 199
Williams, Margaret A. 26
Williams, Philip 199, 200
Williams, P. B. 201
Williams, R. Gray 200
Williamson, —— 199
Willis, E. J. 237
Willis, H. H. 110
Willis, Nathaniel 221
Willis, N. P. 221
Wills, Robert 118
Wilmarth, W. 236
Wilson, Gen. 163
Wilson, L. 123
Wilson, Norval 214
Wilson, P. R. 191
Wilt, Peter 51
Windle, (Clark and Windle) 123
Wise, Henry A. 127
Wolf, Lewis..96, 97, 199, 200, 232
Wolf, Mary 54
Wolfe, C. T. 107, 108, 227
Wolfe, Gen. James 103
Wood, Abraham 37
Wood, A. R. 201
Wood, Elizabeth 60
Wood, James ....
38, 41, 44, 46, 47, 49, 53, 56,
57, 58, 59, 79, 85, 89, 90, 109,
134, 136, 139, 140, 200, 201,
222, 231, 268
Wood, James, Jr. 60, 92
Wood, John 60
Wood, Mary 60
Wood, Robert 60, 83, 232
Wood, William 201, 239
Woodbury, Capt. 192

Woodcock, S.	201	Xaupy, J.	238
Woods, Thomas	49	Yancey, C. A.	199
Worthington, Robert, Jr.	79	Yocum, Solomon	266
Worthington, William	268	York, Gen.	163, 167
Wright, Gen. H. G.	160	York, Sidney P.	213, 236
Wright, John	98	Young, John	120
Wright, Matthew	97	Young, Lewis	120
Wright, Richard	213	Young, William	151
Wright, Uriel	199	Zane, Isaac	90, 200, 201
Wyatt, Sir Dudley	28	Zane, Sarah	111

www.ingramcontent.com/pod-product-compliance
Lightning Source LLC
Chambersburg PA
CBHW060941230426
43665CB00015B/2021